*Pathways
to Multicultural
Counseling Competence:
A Developmental Journey*

Pathways
to Multicultural
Counseling Competence:
A Developmental Journey

Bea Wehrly
Western Illinois University

Brooks/Cole Publishing Company
I(T)P™An International Thomson Publishing Company

Pacific Grove • Albany • Bonn • Boston • Cincinnati • Detroit • London • Madrid
Melbourne • Mexico City • New York • Paris • San Francisco • Singapore • Tokyo • Toronto • Washington

 A CLAIREMONT BOOK

Sponsoring Editor: *Claire Verduin*
Marketing Team: *Nancy Kernal, Margaret Parks*
Editorial Associate: *Patsy Vienneau*
Production Editor: *Nancy L. Shammas*
Manuscript Editor: *Barbara Kimmel*
Permissions Editor: *May Clark*

Interior and Cover Design: *Terri Wright*
Art Coordinator: *Kathy Joneson*
Indexer: *James Minkin*
Typesetting: *Weimer Graphics*
Cover Printing: *Phoenix Color Corporation, Inc.*
Printing and Binding: *Quebecor/Fairfield*

For more information, contact:

BROOKS/COLE PUBLISHING COMPANY
511 Forest Lodge Road
Pacific Grove, CA 93950
USA

International Thomson Publishing Europe
Berkshire House 168-173
High Holborn
London WC1V 7AA
England

Thomas Nelson Australia
102 Dodds Street
South Melbourne, 3205
Victoria, Australia

Nelson Canada
1120 Birchmount Road
Scarborough, Ontario
Canada M1K 5G4

International Thomson Editores
Campos Eliseos 385, Piso 7
Col. Polanco
11560 México D. F. México

International Thomson Publishing GmbH
Königswinterer Strasse 418
53227 Bonn
Germany

International Thomson Publishing Asia
221 Henderson Road
#05-10 Henderson Building
Singapore 0315

International Thomson Publishing Japan
Hirakawacho Kyowa Building, 3F
2-2-1 Hirakawacho
Chiyoda-ku, Tokyo 102
Japan

Printed in the United States of America

10 9 8 7 6 5 4 3 2 1

Library of Congress Cataloging-in-Publication Data

Wehrly, Bea, [date]
    Pathways to multicultural counseling competence : a developmental
journey / Bea Wehrly.
        p.   cm.
    Includes bibliographical references and index.
    ISBN 0-534-33849-6
    1. Cross-cultural counseling.   2. Counselors.   I. Title.
BF637.C6W39   1995
158′.3—dc20

92-12691
CIP

Dedicated to my grandchildren:
Andrew, Anna Lee, Chastity, Joel, Leah, Pete, and Samuel.
May you be enriched by the diversity of our multicultural world.

CONTENTS

CHAPTER 3   *Developmental Models for Multicultural Counselor Preparation*   43

CHAPTER 4   *Ethnic Identity Development over the Life Span*   65

CHAPTER 5   *Multicultural Counseling on the International Scene*   79

PREFACE

In less than two decades, the field of counseling psychology has been enriched by many scholarly books that address the topic of cross-cultural and multicultural counseling. These manuscripts present a variety of perspectives on topics and content needed by counselors working in our contemporary culturally pluralistic world.

Scholars in multicultural counseling now recognize that the process of becoming competent in multicultural counseling is a lifelong endeavor that includes both *cognitive* and *affective* components. The professional literature has given considerably less attention to describing the affective process of attaining multicultural counseling competence than to the cognitive content of the field.

The goal of *Pathways to Multicultural Counseling Competence: A Developmental Journey* is to remove some of the mystique of the process of multicultural counseling by delineating both the cognitive and affective processes that accompany the development of multicultural counseling competence. The book builds on and operationalizes the work of many scholars who have written books and journal articles in cross-cultural and multicultural counseling.

In addition to giving an overview of cognitive content needed by counselors, this book outlines a developmental model for the process of gaining multicultural counseling competence. *Pathways to Multicultural Counseling Competence: A Developmental Journey* is written for counselor educators, for counselors in training, and for counselors in the field who are interested in expanding their knowledge and awareness of the impact of culture and diversity on the counseling process.

Part I, "Multicultural Counselor Preparation: Pathways to the Present," delineates basic aspects of multicultural counseling, gives the history of and rationale for the field, and reviews models for multicultural counselor preparation.

Chapter 1 addresses the concept that culture has an inescapable impact on the counseling process. The chapter reviews the changing terminology in the field, gives attention to many ways in which culture can impact counseling, discusses the cultural context as a critical factor, and calls attention to ways in which the Euro-Western, White, middle-class, male basis of much of traditional counseling has served to maintain a negative sociopolitical environment for people of color. This chapter also introduces readers to the impact of discrimination, oppression, and racism on both the perpetrator and the recipient.

Because I believe there is much truth in the old adage that those who do not know history are destined to repeat it, Chapter 2 is devoted to a thorough overview of the history of cross-cultural and multicultural counseling. Readers are introduced to the work of pioneer social scientists who laid the foundations for broadening the cultural base of counseling at the midpoint of the 20th century. Readers will also see that it took the dramatic impact of the Civil Rights movement of the 1960s and 1970s to begin to bring about significant changes in the monocultural, Euro-Western, mainstream, White, middle-class, male counseling psychology base. The ongoing struggles by many professionals to continue to move the counseling profession toward theories and practices that are appropriate for the needs of a diverse population are detailed in this chapter. Chapter 2 also provides a rationale for special training for cross-cultural and multicultural counseling.

Chapters 3 and 4 give an overview of current models for multicultural preparation and emphasize the importance of work by a variety of theorists and researchers on racial and ethnic identity development. Research on racial identity and ethnic identity development began more than two decades ago, but it is only in the last decade that this research has gained widespread recognition for application to the counseling process.

Chapter 3 describes developmental models for multicultural counselor preparation as well as generic and culture-specific models for racial identity development. Chapter 4 is unique in that it describes life-span ethnic identity development (through childhood, adolescence, and adulthood) and the implications of this work on racial and ethnic identity development for counselors and for counseling. Chapters 3 and 4 provide much of the cognitive base for the stage model of multicultural counselor development described in Chapters 7 through 11 of this book.

The content of Chapter 5 is a "first" for books on multicultural counseling. This chapter introduces readers to work being done in other countries to prepare counselors for their respective culturally pluralistic populations. This content comes from (1) questionnaire responses received from counselors and counselor educators in 22 countries on 5 continents, (2) cross-cultural professional exchanges at international conferences and symposiums, and (3) the professional literature.

I have had the privilege of participating in several international counseling conferences and have had the opportunity to lead six counselor study groups to Europe, the South Pacific, and Asia. These experiences have helped me recognize that other countries are also working to deliver culturally sensitive counseling services to their culturally diverse populations. My work as an editorial reviewer and, more recently, as one of the editors of the *International Journal for the Advancement of Counselling* has also helped me to recognize and respect counseling services in other countries. Co-editing the April, 1983, special issue on "International Guidance and Counseling" of *The Personnel and Guidance Journal* was another world-view expanding experience (Wehrly & Deen, 1983).

Part II, "Multicultural Counselor Preparation: Pathways from the Present to the Future," delineates the five-stage developmental model for multicultural counselor preparation. The model is operationalized through inclusion of detailed descriptions of the cognitive content and the affective elements of each of the five stages.

Chapter 6 gives the background for the five-stage developmental model outlined in Chapters 7 through 11. In Chapter 6 I also list the goals for each of the five stages of the developmental model, delineate the assumptions that undergird the model, and state the limitations of the five-stage model.

In Chapters 7 through 11, each chapter is devoted to describing one of the five stages of multicultural counselor preparation proposed. Each of these chapters describes student characteristics; dicusses process guidelines for creating a climate for student growth in beliefs and attitudes, knowledge, and skills; states goals for each developmental stage; and outlines appropriate learning environments and experiences for achieving these goals. Each chapter builds on the goals attained from previous chapters. Chapters 7, 8, and 9 outline content suggested for a course in multicultural counseling. Chapters 10 and 11 describe multicultural counselor development during the Counseling Practicum and the Counseling Internship.

Chapter 7, "Multicultural Counselor Preparation: Stage One" gives special attention to initiating the process of multicultural counselor training. Here, the emphasis is on making the process less threatening by concentrating mainly on cognitive content and exercises. For example, students are introduced to the cultural milieus of persons of color through use of ethnic novels. Other cognitive exercises are suggested to help heighten awareness of the impact culture has on all people.

Chapter 7 also includes exercises and suggestions for readings to help students understand the limitations of the monocultural, middle-class, White male, and Western European base of traditional counseling theories and techniques. Attention is called to the challenges of cross-cultural communication as an initial step in learning multicultural counseling skills.

Stage Two of multicultural counselor preparation is outlined in Chapter 8. Emphasis is on studying the values of one's ethnic and racial heritage, both to learn the strengths of this heritage and to recognize cultural values that may need to change if one is to be an effective cross-cultural counselor. Through this in-depth self-study of one's own ethnicity, students realize the impact of generations of ethnic cultural values. Chapter 8 also includes guidelines for initiating the study of the cultural values, the historical backgrounds, and the sociopolitical environments of different people of color groups in the United States. Student-participation exercises bring attention to the prevalence and the dangers of stereotyping. This chapter also offers suggestions for continuing the process of multicultural counseling skill development.

Chapter 9 addresses the ongoing process of multicultural counselor development in Stage Three. This chapter includes a variety of participatory exercises to assist the students' growth in beliefs and attitudes, knowledge, and skills. Nine vignettes are included for students to apply concepts from the racial and ethnic identity development models described earlier in Chapters 3 and 4. Students are also challenged to assess their own stages of racial and ethnic identity development. An additional development task of Stage Three is for students to learn about contemporary racism and to examine their own personal involvement in racist behaviors.

Counseling skills for Stage Three build on those developed in Stages One and Two. At Stage Three, the sensitive process of cross-cultural relationship building is examined and practiced as a critical element of multicultural counselor skill development. Students are also challenged to look at the "big picture" of cross-cultural counseling to understand the many dimensions included.

Chapter 10, Stage Four, discusses the process of multicultural counseling development during the counseling practicum. The text of this chapter is one of the first publications in the field to pull together information on the roles of the counseling practicum student and the counseling practicum supervisor in developing multicultural competence. Among the four goals presented and discussed is one that outlines counseling interventions for cross-cultural counseling with people of color *as well as* with White people. Students are challenged to assess their clients' racial and ethnic identity development and to apply stage appropriate interventions. Reference is made to Appendix E and Appendix F, which list sample multicultural items for evaluation of the practicum student and the supervisor.

The content of Chapter 11, Stage Five, which addresses roles and challenges faced by counseling internship students and their supervisors, is also one of a very few publications related to multicultural counselor development during the counseling internship. One of the important goals of this stage is for the counseling student and supervisor to work together to help the student experience a variety of appropriate multicultural counseling roles. Atkinson, Thompson, and Grant's 1993 eight counselor roles (adviser, advocate, facilitator of indigenous support systems, facilitator of indigenous healing systems, consultant, change agent, counselor, and psychotherapist) are discussed through integration of concepts from many sources.

Chapter 11 also emphasizes the importance of a variety of opportunities and the climate for learning at the internship site. This chapter explores the counseling intern's need for support and encouragement to enable ongoing multicultural counseling professional development. Reference is made to Appendixes G and H, which list sample multicultural items for evaluating the internship student, the site, and the supervisor.

Chapter 12, "The Possible Futures," addresses the unfinished business and the incomplete status of multicultural counselor preparation. This chapter outlines how continuing professional organization leadership can improve multicultural education and training. Professionals are challenged to continue to expand the work both on multicultural counseling theories and on the research and development of models of multicultural counseling and multicultural counselor preparation. Readers are challenged to continue work toward the goal of making multiculturalism the fourth force in counseling.

HOW TO USE THIS BOOK

This book is distinctive in that Part II places heavy emphasis on describing the *process* of attaining multicultural counseling competence. Because of the amount of detail given to the process, some descriptions of cognitive content are more limited. If students are to gain the full benefit of this book, they will need to have access to many of the sources cited (but not explained in detail) in the book. Librarians can be very helpful in assembling many of these publications and placing them on reserve for students.

ACKNOWLEDGMENTS

Several of the original concepts for this developmental model of multicultural counselor preparation were included in my November, 1991, *Counseling and Human Development* publication, "Preparing Multicultural Counselors." They are included here with the permission of the Love Publishing Company. My special thanks to Dr. Stanley Love and his associates for their help on the original manuscript.

I am grateful for the support from a Western Illinois University Foundation summer stipend that enabled me to devote all my time to this writing endeavor during the summer of 1993. I also wish to acknowledge that I have learned a great deal from the hundreds of people with whom I have interacted in the years since I began teaching Counseling/Helping in a Multicultural Society at Western Illinois University in 1986, giving inservices in multicultural counseling and in diversity development, and attending professional development seminars related to multicultural counseling.

I wish to acknowledge with gratitude the assistance of these counselors and counselor educators from beyond the U.S. borders who furnished information for Chapter 5. Without their help, this chapter could not have been written. Contributors are listed in alphabetic order by country: *Australia,* Peg LeVine, Stuart Millard, and Karen Simpson; *Canada,* William Borgen, Frank Dumont, William Hague, Ishu Ishiyama, Walt Pawlovich, Sharon Robertson, and Marvin Westwood; *Finland,* Antti Tapaninen; *France,* Jean Guichard; *Germany,* Kurt Heller and Lothar Martin; *Greece,* Kassandra Zanni-Teliopoulos; *India,* Gerda Unnithan; *Ireland,* James Chamberlain; *Israel,* Moshe Israelashvili; *Lithuania,* Gintautas Valickas; *Malaysia,* Abdul Halim Othman; *Mexico,* Ricardo Blanco-Beledo; *New Zealand,* Gary Hermansson; *The Netherlands,* Nathan Deen; *Nigeria,* Olaniyi Bojuwoye and Samuel E. Okon; *The Philippines,* Vicentita M. Cervera and Lily Rosqueta-Rosales; *South Africa,* Tahir Salie; *Spain,* Maria Luisa Rodriguez Moreno; *Taiwan,* Sue Jiang; *Thailand,* Pramot Khapklomsong, Saree Pratomthong, and Pol Sangsawang; *United Arab Emirates,* Abdalla M. Soliman; *United Kingdom,* Colin Lago and Brian Thorne.

To my good friend and colleague of more than two decades, Josephine Johnson, I give special credit for reading the complete manuscript twice and offering many helpful suggestions. Thanks, also, to the following colleagues at Western Illinois University who have read and provided feedback on various chapters of this book: Robert Collier, Robert Caruso, Keren Humphrey, and William McFarland. Graduate assistants Paula Wise, Valinda Beesley, and Kate Murphy and our secretary, Rebecca Day, deserve much credit for assisting with the tedious task of checking citations and references.

My special appreciation goes to Joseph Ponterotto and to Jean Phinney for meeting with me to share ideas and to clarify my questions early in the process of preparing this book. Working in this field has been, and will be, an exciting lifelong endeavor!

To my husband, Jim, I extend a very special thank you for all his help on the logistics of converting computer disks and helping with numerous other computer-related tasks. Most of all, I wish to extend my appreciation to Jim for the support that he has given me for more than four decades as a nontraditional wife, mother, grandmother, and career woman.

Prepublication reviews have been an invaluable aid in assisting me to clarify and organize my thoughts. The following reviewers provided this assistance and have my sincere appreciation: Joseph Ponterotto, Fordham University at Lincoln Center; Ronnie Priest, The University of Memphis; Marvin Westwood, University of British Columbia; and Jesse Brinson, University of Nevada, Las Vegas.

Thanks, also, to the splendid assistance and support of the staff at Brooks/Cole. Claire Verduin's encouragement throughout the lengthy process of developing the original proposal and writing the book was unfailing. Others who have also been "pillars of support" at Brooks/Cole have been Gay Bond, Patsy Vienneau, Carline Haga, Nancy Shammas, May Clark, Roy Neuhaus, Adrienne Carter, and Barbara Smallwood. My thanks also go to Barbara Kimmel, my copy editor. They have helped me over, through, and around the many hurdles of this prodigious task!

Bea Wehrly

Part One

Multicultural Counselor Preparation: Pathways to the Present

CHAPTER 1

Culture and Its Inescapable Impact on Counseling

A White high school counselor working with African American students wonders why her empathic responses to the students' descriptions of their problems seem to fall on deaf ears. An elementary school counselor working with newly arrived Central American immigrant families is surprised to see how formal they are in their interactions. After a college counselor encourages a female Asian American client to move out of her parents' home, the young woman does not return for counseling. A community agency counselor working with a Native American client is bewildered when the young man requests to bring friends along for his counseling sessions. In each of these instances, culture has impacted the behavior of the client.

Ivey (1993) states, "I now believe that all helping practice is based on a set of cultural assumptions" (p. 225). In each of the four preceding cases, the counselor may be hindered by making assumptions about the client from a Western, Euro-American, middle-class perspective. These counselors' ineffectiveness may be caused by assumptions such as these: (1) people will respond to empathy and be willing to self-disclose; (2) it is best to interact with other people from an informal and egalitarian relationship; (3) young people of college age should be independent and willing to live on their own or with their peers; (4) we work with the individual who has the problem, not with friends of that individual.

It is increasingly obvious that culture has a critical and inescapable influence on the behavior of all people (Axelson, 1993). To be effective, the counselor needs to understand the role of culture in his or her own life as well as in the life of the counselee.

Hoare (1991) delineates the powerful role that culture plays in shaping one's identity; she states that "identity is constructed from within the person and culture in which it is forged" (p. 70). After reviewing the work of scholars in psychology and human development, Hoare points out that individuals can never completely escape the reality of their own culturally influenced identity and be totally objective in understanding the cultural reality of another person's identity. With culture playing such a powerful role in identity development, counselors are wise to understand the impact of culture on all people.

The purpose of Chapter 1 is to help the reader develop a broader understanding of the inescapable impact that culture has on the counseling process. Attention is directed to some of the many ways that both the counselor and the counselee are influenced by culture. The delimiting and negative influences of traditional counseling for people who do not share Euro-Western, White, middle-class, or male values is also introduced.

CULTURE AND RACE AS CRITICAL ELEMENTS OF CULTURAL DIVERSITY

When counselors first began to recognize the impact of culture on the counseling process, *cross-cultural counseling* was the term of choice to indicate that the counselor was working with a client from a different cultural heritage. As the term *culture* came to denote not only differences in ethnic cultural heritage but also differences such as age, socioeconomic status, lifestyle preferences, sex roles, and so on, the term *multicultural counseling* became common. Now *cultural diversity* and *cultural pluralism* are commonly used to indicate a society with many racial and cultural roots and variations. To address all these differences, some training programs are now known as *diversity training*.

In *Workforce America*, Loden and Rosener (1991) include race, ethnicity, gender, age, sexual/affectional orientation, and physical abilities and qualities as primary dimensions of diversity. These authors also propose that work background, income, marital status, military experience, religious beliefs, geographic location, parental status, and education are secondary dimensions of diversity. Again, the multiplicity of diversity dimensions is evident.

As noted earlier, the term *culture* has undergone a variety of definitions in recent history. My definition of culture is a traditional one and is adapted from a definition by Jualyne Dodson (personal communication, February 23, 1985) and from Herskovits' 1956 description of culture. I view culture as a dynamic construct that includes the values, beliefs, and behaviors of a people who have lived together in a particular geographic area for at least three or four generations. I agree with Johnson (1990b), who emphasizes that cultural patterns "are specific to particular times and places" (p. 44). To me, identifications such as age, lifestyle, socioeconomic status, gender identification, and so on are aspects of diversity that also impact the uniqueness of each individual. To recognize each individual's uniqueness, counselors must be prepared to address all aspects of a client's diversity.

Das and Littrell (1989) address the importance of understanding the difference between "culture as a *construct* and culture as it is manifested in the lives of people" (p. 9). In their view, culture as a construct includes modal practices of a group's way of life that are held in common. Culture as it is manifested in the lives of people will show many individual differences, with no individual exemplifying all the group's modal practices.

An ethnic culture or ethnic group is "a group set apart from others because of its national origin or distinctive cultural patterns" (Schaefer, 1990, p. 27). Each of us is socialized into an ethnic culture (or ethnic cultures if our parents are of differing ethnic heritages). This occurs whether we are raised by our natural parent(s) or by someone else. It is in this ethnic culture (or cultures) of socialization that we take on ethnic group values, beliefs, and behaviors.

Each of us is also born into (or socialized into) a family with one or more racial heritages. People of color are much more conscious of having a racial heritage than are White people (Helms, 1992). The term *race* has been used to differentiate people and groups in ambiguous ways. Schaefer (1990) states, "Probably the only thing about race that is clear is that we are confused about the origins and proper use of the term" (p. 12). *Race* or *racial* are terms that are sometimes used to refer to biological or physical differences. Pinderhughes (1989) calls attention to the fact that "Over time, race has acquired a social meaning in which these biological differences, via the mechanism of stereotyping, have become markers for status assignment within the social system" (p. 71). For some people of color, especially people with visibly different skin color, racial heritage may have a dominant influence on their lives.

Both racial identity and ethnic cultural identity, known as *ethnicity*, are core elements in the many aspects of diversity. It is important for counselors to recognize the powerful roles that ethnicity and race play in their own lives as well as in the lives of the people with whom they work. Each of us is born with a racial heritage, and each of us is socialized into an ethnic heritage. This socialization has a subtle but very pervasive influence on our lives.

Many aspects of diversity other than ethnicity and race make each of us unique. Some of these dimensions are shown in Figure 1.1. The importance of each of these components will vary from individual to individual, but two core elements will remain constant: the individual's racial heritage and the individual's ethnicity.

■ Nomenclature of ethnic groups

An additional challenge in studying multiculturalism is keeping current on the names ethnic groups prefer for identification. Over the years these preferences have changed, as illustrated in Exhibit 1.1 (Waugh, 1991). This changing terminology is very evident in historical documents in the field. For example, most documents of the 1960s and 1970s referred to Black Americans, but now the term *African American* is used more frequently. Although there is still a lack of

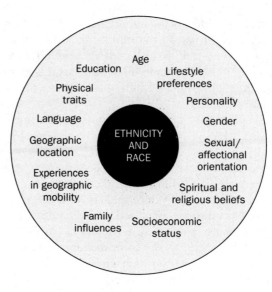

FIGURE 1.1
Ethnicity and Race: The
Core of Diversity

Age
Education
Lifestyle preferences
Physical traits
Personality
Language
ETHNICITY AND RACE
Gender
Geographic location
Sexual/ affectional orientation
Experiences in geographic mobility
Spiritual and religious beliefs
Family influences
Socioeconomic status

uniformity in the use of names for identification of various groups, counselors should strive to keep abreast of current trends.

THE ROLE OF CULTURE IN COUNSELING

Johnson (1990b) states that the role or function of culture in counseling is to provide the counselor with a framework "to better comprehend the systems of relationships involved in multicultural counseling than they have in the past" (p. 45). Sue and Zane (1987) state that counselors' inability to offer culturally appropriate treatment is the single most important reason ethnic minorities are inadequately served at mental health centers. These authors point out that "The role of cultural knowledge is to alert therapists to possible problems in credibility" (Sue & Zane, 1987, p. 41).

Culture and the terminology used to describe culture may be studied from a multitude of perspectives. In discussing culture, it is difficult to examine its many aspects as separate entities because they are not mutually exclusive categories. An additional challenge is to avoid the danger of stereotyping. Readers need to be aware that no single individual will manifest all the characteristics of the values and behaviors of a particular cultural category (Das & Littrell, 1989).

The remainder of this chapter will introduce readers to some of the basic aspects of culture that are significant in expanding a knowledge base for multicultural counseling competence.

EXHIBIT 1.1

FACTS ABOUT GROUP NAMES

People of color: Refers to everyone who isn't white. Has replaced Third World as term of preference.

White: Most commonly used term, a non-ethnic racial designation that has replaced Caucasian as preferred term.

Anglo: Refers only to those of English ancestry and is considered offensive by some, like the Irish, when used as an all-inclusive alternative for "white."

European American: An emerging term favored by some as a preferred alternative to white, Anglo and Caucasian, because it refers more broadly to the continent of origin and is culture-based rather than color- or race-based.

African American: Ramona H. Edelin, president of the National Urban Coalition, proposed it during an African American Summit in New Orleans in April, 1989. The Rev. Jesse Jackson's subsequent endorsement probably did more to popularize the term than anything else. Since adopted by major newspapers and prominent political leaders, such as Mayor David Dinkins of New York.

Negro: Still used by some blacks, especially in the South. The U.S. Census Bureau cited this reason for keeping it as a race category, with black, on the 1990 Census Form.

Black: Came into vogue during the black power movement of the late 1960s. Considered of great symbolic importance by many because it represented a casting-off of terminology—Negro—imposed by others. Used interchangeably with African American.

Hispanic: A term grouping all people of Spanish-speaking descent. UC-Berkeley scholar Margarita Melville says its first official sanction came with the 1968 presidential proclamation of National Hispanic Week. An ethnic advisory committee of the U.S. Census Bureau formed to recommend terminology in the 1970s recommended it as more inclusive than other terms, and it first appeared on the 1980 census form.

Latino/Latina: Generally preferred over Hispanic by Spanish-speaking people of the United States, especially in California because it emphasizes their Latin American origins, while Hispanic is seen by some as an officially imposed term connoting Spanish origins.

Chicano: A Southwestern term for working-class Mexican Americans that some consider pejorative. It gained wide political and popular favor among Mexican American activists during the 1960s Chicano civil rights movement. Still used as a term reflecting pride in the working-class roots of the Mexican American people.

Oriental: The East. Still used in many parts of the world, including Hawaii, to refer to people from Asia, or "the Orient." In disfavor among Asian Americans in many parts of the United States for reflecting an antiquated British perspective of the world.

Asian American: A now widely accepted term in the United States, especially in California, for people of Asian ancestry. Current usage is "Asian and Pacific Islanders" to include people from the Pacific Islands. Use of the term grew out of the Asian American Political Alliance that was formed by student activists on the UC-Berkeley campus in 1967 prior to the ethnic studies strike.

(continued)

EXHIBIT 1.1 *(continued)*

Native American/American Indian/Indian: All three are used to refer to indigenous peoples. Individuals often refer to themselves by tribal heritage. Native American may be in wider usage than the other two terms. The census uses Indian.

Source: From sidebar accompanying "Ethnic Groups Change Names with the Times: Activists Discard Old Appellations in Ongoing Search for Self-Identity," by D. Waugh, *San Francisco Examiner (EX)*, September 2, 1991, Fourth Edition, NEWS Section, p. A6. Copyright 1991 San Francisco Examiner Inc. Reprinted by permission.

CULTURE AS A SILENT PARTNER

As noted earlier in this chapter, culture pervades all our lives but rarely do we become consciously aware of its impact on our daily activities (Herskovits, 1956). Culture shapes and determines the assumptions that, although largely unspoken, undergird our daily behavior. Because culture has such a pervasive influence, the counselor with a working knowledge of cultural values and assumptions can capitalize on cultural awareness. This awareness can be a powerful silent partner in the helping process.

■ *Impact on the thinking/cognitive processes*

Culture has an impact not only on what we think but also on the way we think (Kaplan, 1989). Figure 1.2 illustrates Kaplan's schema for the development of thought patterns in various languages.

Linear thinking as practiced by most English-speaking people who have been influenced by Western values is not used by everyone. Kaplan (1989) discusses how the languages of cultures influence the way people think and write. He states that neither logic nor rhetoric are universal, and he discusses how logic and rhetoric evolve out of the languages of the cultures in which they are used. "The English language and its related thought patterns have evolved out of the Anglo-European cultural pattern . . . [which] descended from the philosophers of ancient Greece and [was] shaped subsequently by Roman, medieval European, and later Western thinkers" (Kaplan, 1989, p. 208). He notes that the English thought patterns are different from other languages' thought patterns.

Kaplan (1989) discusses how the Arabic language and most Semitic languages employ a complex series of parallel constructions in developing a paragraph. The King James version of the Old Testament is an example of this use of parallel constructions. Kaplan also discusses the development of thought in other cultures of the world. Oriental (Kaplan's term) thought is marked by indirection: looking at

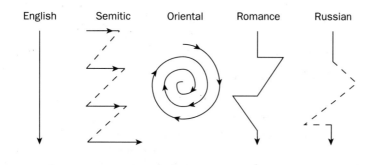

English   Semitic   Oriental   Romance   Russian

FIGURE 1.2

Cultural Influences on Patterns of Thought

SOURCE: From "Cultural Thought Patterns in Inter-Cultural Education," by R. B. Kaplan. In J. S. Wurzel (Ed.), *Toward Multiculturalism: Readings in Multicultural Education,* pp. 207–221. Copyright © 1989 Intercultural Press, Inc. Reprinted by permission.

the topic from a variety of views, discussing the subject in terms of what it is not, but never addressing the topic directly.

Triandis (1985) notes that clients from minority backgrounds often use associative information processing, which works well in communicating with people who have shared the same background. In associative information processing, people use all clues (verbal and nonverbal), plus the context in which communication is taking place, to understand and interpret a message. This type of thinking has also served as a survival mechanism for people who have been oppressed. Triandis cautions that the minority client who relies on associative information processing may have difficulty communicating with a therapist who uses an abstractive-pragmatic style. The abstractive-pragmatic style of communication relies almost entirely on the spoken word and focuses on verbalization directly related to the topic under discussion.

The following is an example of an associative-information-processing college student client interacting with an abstractive-pragmatic counselor early in a first counseling session. The counselor has greeted the client by name, defined counseling for the client, and launched directly into an attempt to get the client to tell why he has come for counseling. The client is feeling very awkward and uneasy, as it is his first time seeing a counselor, and the counseling center surroundings are completely unfamiliar to him.

> *Counselor:* (looks directly at the client): You seem to be having some difficulty telling me exactly how you see your problem and why you came to the counseling center.
>
> *Client:* (looks away from the counselor after noticing that the counselor seemed to move his chair away when the client had attempted to pull his chair closer to the counselor; the client has also noted that the counselor has made no attempt to personalize the relationship): Well, my problem isn't that serious, I probably don't really need to see a counselor. I think I can talk some more to my family about this and get the problem solved.

Counselor: If you're worried about my telling someone else what you share with me here, please remember that I will keep what we talk about in counseling confidential.

Client: Well, my family really didn't want me to come to see you in the first place.

Counselor: (shows disdain when he realizes client is so dependent on his family): Since you are in college now, perhaps you would like to try working on solving your problems by yourself. We are here to help students with any problems they bring to us.

Client: (notes the look of disapproval on the counselor's face and pulls back in his chair): I'll call my family, and we'll work this out.

Counselor: How about coming back to talk with me after you call your family?

Client: I don't know . . . (long pause) maybe.

In this example, the abstractive-pragmatic counselor has relied totally on the words spoken by the associative-information-processing client, has failed to respond to the client's nonverbal cues, and has been unaware of his own nonverbal behavior. The counselor has failed to understand the client's feelings of discomfort and has made no attempt to personalize the situation to help the client feel more comfortable. As the counselor continues to encourage the client to talk about his problem, the client begins to minimize the importance of his problem, and the counselor shows no understanding that the client's culture may not condone counseling as a method for solving problems. Instead, the counselor interprets the client's talk about getting help from his family as a sign of the client's immaturity or enmeshment with his family. The counselor seems oblivious to his own negative nonverbal reactions to the client.

After reviewing research on the impact of ethnicity on cognitive and motivational styles, Banks (1988) and Rotheram and Phinney (1987b) state that African American and Mexican American students are more field sensitive, or field dependent, in their learning styles than are mainstream White students. Field sensitive people, as compared to field independent people, are more sensitive to social cues, are more gregarious, and prefer to interact socially in a physically close environment. Field dependent people appear to have a high group orientation. Rotheram and Phinney (1987b) also note that in interacting with others, children who are more field dependent will be more sensitive and attentive to the feelings and expectations of the people around them.

The field sensitive client as described by Ramirez in 1991 (cited in Axelson, 1993) will probably learn deductively, may show interest in personalizing the relationship with the therapist, and may find social rewards from the therapist as important to progress. Other authors have come to similar conclusions. Sue and Sue (1990) emphasize the importance of counselor self-disclosure in the cross-cultural relationship as an important component of building trust. Sue and Zane (1987) also seem to be talking about the need to personalize the relationship in cross-cultural counseling when they discuss the benefits of gift giving by the therapist. Some examples of gifts that clients might receive from counselors are relief from anxiety and depression, the realization that they are normal, and the acquisition of new skills (Sue & Zane, 1987).

■ Impact on belief systems

Closely related to the cultural impact on the thought process is the cultural impact on the beliefs the individual holds related to the following: the supernatural; the existence or nonexistence of a supreme being (or beings); the importance of religious or spiritual practices, such as worshipping a supreme being (or beings); beliefs about life after death; and the number and ways in which life's rituals are accomplished (Cohen, 1991). From a variety of ethnic novels, we learn that culture can influence such things as a Northern Nigerian tribe's beliefs in the power of witches and in the solace of laughter (Bowen, 1954), a Southwest American Chicano family's faith in the healing power of the curandera (Anaya, 1972), a Native American youth's perception of spirituality and reverence for nature as guiding forces (Herbert, 1984), and a first-generation Chinese American female's socialization into a world of ghosts (Kingston, 1976).

Belief systems related to religion and spirituality play vital roles in the lives of many people of color. Western-trained therapists may downplay or ignore the importance of these belief systems because minimal attention is given to the importance of religion or spirituality in most U.S. counselor training programs (Kelly, 1992). Axelson (1993) delineates the importance of key beliefs of the world's major religions as shown in Table 1.1. Counselor knowledge of, and respect for, these differing belief systems can be of invaluable assistance in developing a working relationship between counselor and client.

■ Impact on the definitions and influence of family or kin

The group of people who are considered family or kin may vary from a small nuclear family to an extended unit in which many people are considered family members (Kinzie, 1978). Those acculturated in mainstream Western society are probably influenced mainly by the small nuclear family that places a high value on individualism.

Those influenced by nonmainstream Western cultures may see family or kin as an extended unit that does not necessarily limit itself to "blood" relatives. The nonmainstream client who talks about her "auntie" may be speaking of a female who is an important part of the extended family but not necessarily a blood relative. When working with people in an extended family network, the counselor may need to work with the extended family as a system. Capitalizing on the strengths of the

TABLE 1.1 ■ KEY POINTS OF THE WORLD'S MAJOR RELIGIONS OR BELIEF FORMS

Source of Power or Force (Deity)	*Historical Sacred Texts or Source of Beliefs*	*Key Beliefs or Ethical Life Philosophy*
Christianity God, a unity in tripersonality: Father, Son, Holy Ghost	Bible Teachings of Jesus through the Apostles and the Church Fathers	God's love for all creatures is a basic belief. Salvation (saving from sin or resurrection from death) is gained by those who have faith and show humility toward God. Brotherly love is emphasized in acts of charity, kindness, and forgiveness. Jesus' teachings insist on justice and mercy toward all people.
Islam[a] Allah (the only God)	Koran (the words of God delivered to Mohammed by the angel Gabriel) Hadith (commentaries by Mohammed) Five Pillars of Islam (religious conduct) Islam was built on Christianity and Judaism	God is just and merciful; humans are limited and sinful. God rewards the good and punishes the sinful. Mohammed, through the Koran, guides and teaches people truth. Peace is gained through submission to Allah. The sinless go to Paradise and the evil go to Hell. A "good" Muslim obeys the Five Pillars of Islam: 1. Confess faith daily. 2. Pray five times a day. 3. Give charitable donations. 4. Fast and observe sexual abstinence during the ninth month of the Islamic calendar. 5. Visit Mecca at least once during a lifetime if possible.
Hinduism Brahma (the Infinite Being and Creator that pervades all reality) Other gods: Vishnu (preserver) Siva (destroyer) Krishna (love)	Vedas (doctrine and commentaries)	All people are assigned to castes (permanent hereditary orders, each having different privileges in the society; each was created from different parts of Brahma): 1. *Brahmans*: created from Brahma's face; includes priests and intellectuals. 2. *Kshatriyas*: created from Brahma's arms; includes rulers and soldiers. 3. *Vaisyas*: created from Brahma's thighs; includes farmers, skilled workers, and merchants. 4. *Sudras*: created from Brahma's feet; includes those who serve the other three castes (servants, laborers, peasants).

TABLE 1.1 *(continued)*

Source of Power or Force (Deity)	Historical Sacred Texts or Source of Beliefs	Key Beliefs or Ethical Life Philosophy
		5. *Untouchables*: the outcasts, those not included in the other castes. They fill the most menial occupations (street sweepers, latrine cleaners, scavengers). Mahatma Gandhi desired to change their identities to *Harijans*, or "Children of God."
Buddhism[b] Buddha Individual responsibility and logical or intuitive thinking	Tripitaka (scripture) Middle Path (way of life) Eightfold Plan (guides for life) Sutras (Buddhist commentaries) Sangha (monastic or ideal living)	Buddhism attempts to deal with problems of human existence such as suffering and death. Life is misery, unhappiness, and suffering with no ultimate reality in the world or behind it. An endless cycle of existence (birth and rebirth) continues because of personal desires and attachments to the unreal self. Understanding the cause of all human suffering and misery as due to desire, and the ultimate transcendence of all desires, leads to nirvana ("blowing-out"), a state of happiness, peace, and love. The "middle path" of life avoids the personal extremes of self-denial and self-indulgence. Visions can be gained through personal meditation and contemplation; good deeds and compassion also facilitate the process toward nirvana, or enlightenment. The end of suffering is in the extinction of desire and emotion, and ultimately the unreal self. Present behavior is a result of past deeds; overcoming attachment to personal desires and worldly things leads to nirvana.
Confucianism No doctrine of a god or gods or life after death Individual responsibility and logical and intuitive thinking	Five Classics (Confucian thought) Analects (conversations and sayings of Confucius)	Considered a philosophy or a system of ethics for living, rather than a religion that teaches how people should act toward one another. People are born "good." Moral character is stressed through sincerity in personal and public behavior. Respect is shown for parents and figures of authority. Improvement is gained through self-responsibility, introspection, and compassion for others.

(continued)

TABLE 1.1 *(continued)*

Source of Power or Force (Deity)	Historical Sacred Texts or Source of Beliefs	Key Beliefs or Ethical Life Philosophy
		Early phases of Confucianism dealt with the problems of living by looking to the past exemplary society. Later phases of Confucianism stress personal enlightenment through meditation, introspection, and study.
Shintoism Gods of nature, ancestor worship, national heroes	Tradition and custom ("the way of the gods") Beliefs were influenced by Confucianism and Buddhism	Reverence for ancestors and traditional Japanese way of life are emphasized. Loyalty to places and locations where one lives or works and purity and balance in physical and mental life are major motivators of personal conduct.
Taoism All the forces in nature	Tao-te-Ching ("The Way and the Power")	Quiet and happy harmony with nature is the key belief. Peace and contentment are found in the personal behaviors of optimism, passivity, humility, and internal calmness. Humility is an especially valued virtue. Conformity to the rhythm of nature and the universe leads to a simple, natural, and ideal life.
Judaism God	Hebrew Bible (Old Testament) Torah (first five books of Hebrew Bible) Talmud (commentaries on the Torah)	Judaists have a special relationship with God; obeying God's law through ethical behavior and ritual obedience earns the mercy and justice of God. God is worshiped through love, not out of fear. Personal satisfaction is gained through love of learning. Heartfelt good deeds without concern about rewards are stressed. Justice for all and morality in living are major goals in life. Coexistence with enemies is sought. Belief-practices range from orthodox-conservative to ultraliberal. The distinction depends on the level of adherence to codes of daily living and the amount of Hebrew spoken in services.

TABLE 1.1 *(continued)*

Source of Power or Force (Deity)	Historical Sacred Texts or Source of Beliefs	Key Beliefs or Ethical Life Philosophy
Tribal Beliefs[c] Animism: Souls, or spirits, embodied in all beings and everything in nature (trees, rivers, mountains) Polytheism: Many gods, in the basic powers of nature (sun, moon, earth, water)	Passed on through ceremonies, rituals, myths, and legends. Oral history, rather than written literature, is the common medium.	All living things are related. Respect for powers of nature and pleasing the spirits are fundamental beliefs in order to meet basic and practical needs for food, fertility, health, and interpersonal relationships and individual development. Harmonious living is comprehension and respect of natural forces.

Summary of Other Belief Forms

Atheism: the belief that no God exists, as "God" is defined in any current existing culture or society.

Agnosticism: the belief that whether there is a God and a spiritual world or any ultimate reality is unknown and probably unknowable.

Scientism: the belief that values and guidance for living come from scientific knowledge, principles, and practices; systematic study and analysis of life, rather than superstition, lead to true understanding and practice of life.

Maoism: the faith that is centered in the leadership of the Communist Party and all the people. The major belief goal is to move away from individual personal desires and ambitions toward viewing and serving each other and all people as a whole.

---

[a]Islam has two major sects: (1) *Sunni* (orthodox): traditional and simple practices are followed; human will is determined by outside forces; (2) *Shiite*: practices are rapturous and trancelike; human beings have free will.
[b]Buddhist subsects include (1) *Lamaism* (Tibet): Buddhism is blended with spirit worship; (2) *Mantrayana* ("sacred recitation") (Himalayan area, Mongolia, Japan): intimate relationship with a *guru* and reciting secret *mantras* are emphasized; the belief in sexual symbolism and demons is also practiced; (3) *Zen* (Japan, China): self-reliance and awareness through intuitive understanding are stressed; *Satori* ("enlightenment") may come from sudden insight or through self-discipline, meditation, and instruction.
[c]Although the need for self-sufficiency with a spiritual foundation is a major goal of Native North American identity, Christianity and other nonnative beliefs have influenced or been incorporated in aspects of some Native American tribes. The Creeks, for example, handled new experiences by the process of gradual assimilation: "They absorbed many folk-tales from the European settlers into their mythology, and many from the negro slaves from West Africa. The Creeks in turn had a considerable influence on the Trickster Spirit, personified as the Rabbit, on to the cycle of Ashanti stories about Anansi, the Trickster. In Jamaica Anansi suffers a spelling change and is often called Nancy, but in the south-eastern United States he took over the name of his Creek Indian archetype and has since charmed the world as Brer Rabbit" (Burland, 1965, p. 110).
SOURCE: From *Counseling and Development in a Multicultural Society*, Second Edition, by J. A. Axelson. Copyright © 1993 Brooks/Cole Publishing Company.

extended family as a support network can be invaluable to the counselor (Hines & Boyd-Franklin, 1982).

■ Impact on the definitions of self

The concept of the self as an individual separate from family and nature is common in mainstream Western, individualistic societies. This definition of self assumes that "I" am a separate individual and that "I" am responsible for myself. The individual is viewed as dominant over nature and in control of personal achievements or failures. This interpretation often leads to a very fluid concept of self in which the self is as the self does. Most of traditional Western psychotherapy is built on these assumptions.

In many cultures of the world, and particularly in Native American and Asian cultures, self is not seen as a separate entity from the group or from nature (Attneave, 1969, 1982; Shon & Davis, 1982). Self is often viewed as part of the larger family or group. Hoare (1991) reviews the work of the Western-trained Indian psychoanalyst Sudhir Kakar and states, "In dramatic contrast with the individualistic Western image of a sharply defined, autonomous, and ego-oriented self, the Asian is harmoniously part of flowing nature, spirit world, community, and traditions" (p. 49). Hoare emphasizes that the Western world's notion of the self as autonomous is only one of many cultural ways of defining self.

■ Impact on decision making and attitudes toward action

Westernized, individualistic, middle-class cultures place much emphasis on planning and doing. Life is viewed as largely controlled by the individual, predictable with a reasonable degree of accuracy, and as something that needs planning. As noted in the previous section, the individual assumes both the responsibility and the credit for the results of his or her decisions and behavior. The sense of self is highly influenced by personal achievements as well as by personal failures. Hence, there is often an ongoing feeling of urgency to work toward accomplishing "something."

Some non-Westernized cultures place more emphasis on "being" than on "doing." Life is to be accepted; the individual is to flow with the tide of life rather than to control it. The individual is viewed as a part of nature or subjugated to nature. In non-Westernized cultures, a person's status is often ascribed on the basis of the particular culture's belief systems about ascription. The status of the family into which one is born and one's age and sex may be dominant ascriptive factors. Because status is ascribed rather than achieved, there is no sense of urgency "to do" or "to become." An individual simply is and learns to live as a part of the cosmos.

Combining culture definitions of family and self with cultural perspectives on the importance of "being" or "doing" can lead to different forms of decision making for the individual acculturated outside the Euro-Western, individualistic societies. Decisions may be made in a collectivist manner, a consensual collateral manner, or through a process in which the kinship network rather than the individual is central to the decision-making process (Attneave, 1969, 1982; Bernal, 1982; Cohen, 1991; Falicov, 1982; Garcia-Preto, 1982; Hines & Boyd-Franklin, 1982; Shon & Davis, 1982). The international student couple who call home to request that parents or grandparents help in naming their baby exemplify collectivist or consensual collateral decision making. An example of a kinship decision-making network may be the African American college student who goes home regularly to help solve family problems.

It is of vital importance that the counselor recognize that non-Western mainstream individuals may engage in different types of decision making, as traditional counselor training might cause the counselor to label such individuals as enmeshed with their families. In addition, Western-trained therapists may expect their clients to get actively involved in planning and doing. The non-Western client who resists being active may be viewed as passive or disinterested in planning and doing.

■ *Impact on time orientation*

Cultures vary greatly in the emphasis placed on the past, present, and future. The Western-trained therapist with a White, middle-class orientation will probably be heavily influenced by a future time orientation. As such, this therapist may expect clients to get involved in future goal setting. This may be in conflict with the past and present time orientation of an Asian American or a Hispanic client, and with the present time orientation of an African American or a Native American client (Sue & Sue, 1990).

■ *Impact on verbal behavior*

How, when, where, and why we use language are all conditioned by the culture (or cultures) in which we are interacting. Some ethnic cultural groups such as the Irish are noted for verbal eloquence. Verbal expression of feelings is also culturally conditioned. The British, for example, are noted for "keeping a stiff upper lip and muddling through" rather than openly expressing negative feelings. Native Americans use silence—nonuse of verbal behavior—as an important part of communication.

Even within a language such as English, there are many dialects that are impacted by ethnic culture. Kochman (1981) has helped us understand the many nuances within Black (Kochman's term) English—not only the way words are pronounced but also the importance of the context as a determinant of when and how one speaks. (More about the importance of context will be included in a later section of this chapter.)

■ *Impact on nonverbal behavior*

"But I always show affection to my first graders through patting their head or ruffling their hair!" said one of the teachers with whom I was working to help recently arrived Southeast Asian refugee children in the mid-1980s. It was very hard for this teacher to understand that touching the head might be interpreted by her two new Cambodian first graders as a sign of disrespect. Cheek (1976) points out that Black Americans (Cheek's term) also may be insulted by White people ruffling their hair.

The enigma of how to interpret nonverbal behavior is one that challenges anyone in cross-cultural communication. Kinzie (1978) underscores the critical importance of the affective messages conveyed by nonverbal communication. Not only do our gestures and facial responses send messages, but the distance we stand from people when speaking and other use of space communicate our nonverbal cultural conditioning. As Falicov (1982) notes, "An office that has a couch that comfortably seats three Mexican American family members, accommodates only two Anglo-American family members" (p. 153).

It is especially difficult to discuss verbal and nonverbal behavior as separate entities. In interpreting communication, it is important to understand both verbal and nonverbal cues within the context of the culture. In some cultures, such as those of Japan or Malaysia, the word "no" is seldom spoken. "One needs to understand that a 'maybe' means 'no' " (Triandis, 1985, p. 25). Members of these cultures also know the nonverbal cues that indicate "no" even though the word is not spoken.

THE CULTURAL CONTEXT AS A CRITICAL FACTOR

Bateson (1979) helped us see that "nothing has meaning except it be seen as in some context" (p. 15); context brings meanings to words and actions, and context is the pattern that connects. Cultures provide the context that brings meaning to the rituals of life (Cohen, 1991). Culture is "a process that specifies the *contexts* of human behavior" (Johnson, 1990b, p. 43). The counselor must understand the context in which clients' behaviors occur to have the insight and understanding needed to work cross-culturally. Behaviors that tend to shock therapists may be totally appropriate when understood in the cultural context (Triandis, 1985). The following discussion addresses some of the many variations of context that may have powerful influences on people.

■ *The individual within the context of the cultural group*

Even though an individual operates within the context of a cultural group, it is important to recognize that each individual will interpret and act out the culture in a slightly different way. Johnson (1990b) cautions counselors to recognize that each individual shares the context of the group in a unique way and that this is never identical with the context of the group.

Das and Littrell (1989) acknowledge that we are all products of our cultural heritages. They emphasize that we cannot predict the behavior of an individual on the basis of that person's cultural background because so many factors within each culture mediate the culture's influence on the individual. Das and Littrell also remind us that many people of color are socialized to live not only in their own culture but also in the White culture. Negotiating more than one culture on a regular basis influences when and how cultural behaviors will be exhibited.

■ Emic versus etic perspectives

The emic perspective is the view from within a culture, and the etic perspective is the view from outside a group. In cross-cultural counseling, the counselor's view is from an etic perspective. Counselors working with someone from a different cultural background need to learn, as much as possible, the client's emic perspective of her or his culture.

Hoare (1991) encourages counselors to learn the symbols and messages of their clients' cultures, to recognize that clients are the experts on their own cultures, and to work to transpose themselves into the unique worlds of clients. This may involve reading and studying about the client's culture, listening carefully to what the client has to say, and asking many culturally sensitive questions to understand the client's emic view. Hoare calls this process *contextual identification*.

■ The generational context

A young Mexican American male transferring from an urban community college to a four-year university more than 200 miles from the family's home told how his mother cried all the way on the trip to take him to college. Finally, an older sister begged her mother to stop crying and to realize that Manuel was not dying and that he would be coming home. It was obvious that the mother had a very different perspective on her son's going away to college; she may have perceived this act as one in which she was shirking her parental responsibility (Quevodo-Garcia, 1987).

Amy Tan's story of four Chinese mothers and their daughters, *The Joy Luck Club* (1989), includes numerous descriptions of generational differences between the mothers who emigrated from China to the United States and their daughters who were born and raised in the United States. A counselor working with any of the individuals in the Mexican American family described previously or with any of the Chinese women in Tan's novel would need to be cognizant of possible generational differences and be trained in helping clients with generational conflicts.

■ Collectivist versus individualistic cultures

Collectivist cultures give attention to *who* a person is; individualistic cultures give more attention to what a person *does* (Triandis, 1985). In-groups are the people who are trusted and with whom members of the culture will collaborate, and they are part of both collectivist and individualistic cultures.

In collectivist cultures, in-group members with authority are expected to do the right thing. Many behaviors are influenced by these in-groups, and considerable attention is given to the norms and rules of the in-group (Triandis, 1985). Collectivist cultures often limit the variation within the in-groups. Age, sex, language, religion, tribe, race, or status can differentiate people in collectivist cultures. In collectivist cultures, individuals often have an ascribed status that is determined by factors such as age or sex (Sue & Zane, 1987).

Individualistic cultures give considerably more latitude to people's behavior. Each in-group influences only a few behaviors, and, because norms and rules of the in-group are limited in number, personal enjoyment is often more important than norms and rules (Triandis, 1985). People may join or leave in-groups for the sake of increasing their personal enjoyment. Considerable variation may be found in the behaviors of people in individualistic cultures. Status is attained on the basis of what a person does rather than who that person is; it is achieved rather than ascribed (Sue & Zane, 1987).

Triandis (1985) states that most Western cultures are individualistic, citing the United States, Britain, Canada, and Australia as examples. He notes that there is still a considerable degree of collectivism in the cultures of Southern Europe. Triandis also notes that those people in collectivist cultures who are strongly influenced by Western cultures and who are educated and urban are more likely to have adopted some behaviors of people in individualistic cultures. Sue and Zane (1987) point out that status may also be achieved in contemporary Asian cultures.

■ *The sociopolitical context*

In the 1982 American Psychological Association position paper on cross-counselor counseling competencies, Sue, Bernier, Durran, Feinberg, Pedersen, Smith, and Vasquez-Nuttall emphasized that the study of minority group cultures alone was insufficient for counselors. Sue et al. also called for the study of the sociopolitical history of oppression, racism, and discrimination that minorities have experienced. This statement emphasized the critical importance of the context in which people of minority cultures interact with the oppressive and racist aspects of the prevailing sociopolitical system. Some years before the 1982 APA position paper, Cheek (1976) wrote about the impact of the sociopolitical context on the behavior of Black Americans (Cheek's term).

One of the major themes of Sue and Sue's 1990 book *Counseling the Culturally Different* is that cross-cultural counselors must be fully aware of the broader sociopolitical environment of minority people in the United States. They underscore the critical and devastating impact of racism and oppression on the culturally different.

The sociopolitical context influences whom people believe they can trust and the degree to which individuals believe they can predict their environment (Triandis, 1985). When people struggle to survive on a day-to-day basis for prolonged periods, they will not view the environment as predictable, and they may find it difficult to trust outsiders. The White, middle-class therapist from a highly predictable environment may bring an entirely different world view to the counseling situation and may find it very difficult to understand clients who seem to lack trust or who seem to be disinterested in planning for the future.

The individual's sense of self is impacted by the sociopolitical context in which the person is raised. Because of the oppressive environment in which some people of color grow from childhood to adulthood, a strong sense of self as a member of a particular minority group may not exist. In some Japanese-American families where parents considered themselves White, children felt cheated of their cultural heritage and suffered from a lack of self-esteem. Gehrie (1979) believes that many people pay an extremely high price in giving up their cultural identity to try to appear as White middle-class Americans.

Steele (1988, 1990) describes the oppressive sociopolitical environment in which Black Americans (Steele's term) have lived and are still living in the United States. Steele posits that decades of this oppressive environment have led to a situation where many Black Americans feel overwhelmed and victimized. Steele issues a clarion call for Black Americans to rise above this victim status in which they allow themselves to be trapped and challenges White Americans to look beyond color for the real content of the character of all individuals.

The sociopolitical influence of the post–Civil War era on White Americans living in the South is vividly described both in Lillian Smith's *Killers of the Dream* (1961) and in the autobiography of Virginia Foster Durr, *Outside the Magic Circle*, edited by H. F. Barnard (1985). These autobiographical memoirs describe their rigid behavioral boundaries and the compartmentalization of their lives that enabled White southerners to justify segregation of Black people (their term) following the Civil War. These women's stories span nearly a century, beginning in the late 1800s, and recount what happened to White women—as well as to White men—who had the courage to stand up for the cause of desegregation and civil rights for all people. It appears that many of the values that permitted Jim Crowism to exist were adopted not only by White southerners but by many White people outside of the South.

PSYCHOTHERAPY'S ROLE IN MAINTAINING CULTURAL BIASES

Sue and Sue (1990) describe how traditional counseling practices based on the Western world's majority value system have collaborated in supporting the oppression of people of color and have led to much neglect of the minority population's needs. Some of the ways in which traditional Western world, middle-class, White male psychotherapy has participated in these oppressive efforts are (1) the use of mainstream definitions of normal and abnormal behavior, (2) "foot dragging" in efforts to broaden counselor education programs to include preparation for work with culturally diverse populations, (3) deficits and inadequacies in social science research models, and (4) inadequate literature related to minority ethnic cultural groups in the United States.

Hoare (1991) emphasizes that the dominant Euro-Western values of mainstream U.S. society that have influenced psychotherapy are those of White, middle-class men. Ivey (1993) also stresses that traditional psychotherapy has developed from a male European and Euro-American stance and that we have much to learn from the beliefs and values of women and people of color.

SUMMARY

In her 1985 book *The Aquarian Conspiracy*, Marilyn Ferguson underscored the inescapable impact of culture on all people when she said:

> The bonds of culture are often invisible, and its walls are glass. We may think we are free. *We cannot leave the trap until we know we are in it.* (p. 105)

This chapter discussed culture and race as inescapable forces impacting all people. The growing realization that the United States is a nation of diverse ethnic and racial groups is affecting the ways counselors interact with clients and implement their roles. Several aspects of culture influence everyone's daily activities, behaviors, and belief systems. Similarly, people's cultural context has profound effects on their behaviors and self-concepts. It has become clear that the Euro-Western, White male, middle-class counseling profession has collaborated in maintaining the negative sociopolitical context for many people of color.

CHAPTER 2

History of and Rationale for Multicultural Counselor Preparation

Counseling as a profession first emerged to meet the needs of people in Westernized societies. In traditional societies, problem-solving help comes from family members, religious leaders, and/or indigenous healers. Counseling came into existence when the prime agents of socialization approved of going to someone outside of the family, church, or indigenous healers for assistance.

Chapter 2 provides an in-depth review of the history of cross-cultural and multicultural counseling. This chapter also discusses the rationale for special training to engage in cross-cultural or multicultural counseling.

THE EARLY YEARS: A MONOCULTURAL FOCUS

In the United States, the origins of the helping services known as guidance and counseling are often traced to several sources: the early vocational counseling ideas of Frank Parsons, the school counseling efforts of people like Jesse B. Davis, developments in testing and assessment, and the mental health and child study movements. Aubrey (1977) stated that "Guidance arose in the dawning 20th century as one of several movements answering the upheaval and turmoil created by the 19th century Industrial Revolution" (p. 288); and Super (1983) reminded us that guidance started "when industrialization and democratization opened up options to youths who had not had them before" (p. 511). A host of historical, political, economic, and social conditions interacted to bring about the need for these specialized services. From its beginnings in the United States, counseling as a response to society's needs has sometimes been used as a vehicle for sociopolitical purposes or to maintain the status quo (Herr, 1979; Ponterotto & Casas, 1991; Sue, 1981, 1993; Sue, Arredondo, & McDavis, 1992a, 1992b; Sue & Sue, 1990).

■ *Early influences on guidance and counseling*

The early helping services were mainly guidance oriented. It was not until the 1940s that the guidance thrust began to subside and to be replaced by counseling as a central focus (Aubrey, 1977; Herr, 1979). Counseling's roots have often been traced to the beginnings of psychology in Europe in the late 19th century. The early history of counseling in the United States reflects the Euro-American or Western emphasis on individualistic psychology. Atkinson, Morten, and Sue (1989), Copeland (1983), Herr (1979), and Sue (1981) are among authors who have traced the roots of counseling to the founding principles of the U.S. Declaration of Independence. The men who signed this important document had roots in western Europe and brought with them the values of their ethnic origins, as well as strong needs for independence and freedom from tyranny.

It is paradoxical that, as more immigrants flocked from Europe to the mainland of North America, the founding principles of the Declaration of Independence and the Bill of Rights seem to have been interpreted as the rights of the White ethnic majority only. The rights of Native Americans, slaves brought from Africa, and any nonmainstream group emigrating to this land were viewed and interpreted from a very different normative stance. The White immigrants who had come to the North American continent to lead a better life and to escape tyranny and injustice often looked the other way when tyranny and injustice were meted out to the non-White population in their midst.

■ *From the melting pot to assimilation*

For a time, it was thought that the United States would become a melting pot of all the cultures brought by the immigrants and an idealized blended national culture would emerge. As more and more immigrants came to the United States in the late 19th and early 20th centuries, the White European men in power became concerned about the different values and behaviors brought by immigrants, and so the norm was changed from the melting pot to that of assimilation. Cultural assimilation, as practiced in the United States, is the expectation by the people in power that all immigrants and all people outside the dominant group will give up their ethnic and cultural values and will adopt the values and norms of the dominant society—the White, male Euro-Americans.

In spite of the fact that the United States has been (and is) a nation of immigrants whose value systems differ, a major theme of Euro-American individualistic psychology seems to have been that of assimilation. In principle, the "melting pot" notion of creating one idealized national culture prevailed until well past the midpoint of the 20th century. But in practice, many immigrants retained their cultural values in the ethnic enclaves in which they settled.

Writers in the field of counseling psychology have been slow to recognize the impact of culture on the counseling process and the need to broaden the theoretical base of counseling beyond that of Western, individualistic psychology. One might assume that the majority of early counseling professionals "bought into" the melting pot and assimilation concepts and believed that we, as a people, were monocultural.

THE SHIFT TOWARD A CROSS-CULTURAL FOCUS

Professionals from the social sciences began to call attention to the need to consider cultural values in counseling in the middle of the 20th century. Unfortunately, the historical literature often fails to acknowledge the contributions of these early theorists to the field of cross-cultural or multicultural counseling.

Contributions of early anthropologists.   There has been limited recognition of the contributions of the early 20th century anthropologists, such as Clyde and Florence Kluckhohn and Edward T. Hall, to the field of multicultural counseling. On the basis of a comparative study of values in five cultures, C. Kluckhohn and others (1951) presented a lengthy treatise on values and value orientation. In this essay, the authors repeatedly discussed the influence of culture on values and stated that "values are clearly . . . cultural products" (p. 398). In 1961, F. Kluckhohn and F. Strodtbeck summarized values influenced by culture under the following five categories.

1. How people view human nature (bad, good, or bad and good)
2. The relation of people to nature (in control of, subjugated to, or with respect for living in harmony with)
3. The temporal or time orientation of the cultural group (past, present, future, or a combination of these perspectives)
4. What people believe about human activity (doing, being or being-in becoming)
5. The relational orientation of people to other people (lineal, collateral, or individualistic)

Adaptations of the Kluckhohn and Strodtbeck framework have been used by many involved in cross-cultural training. (More discussion of the application of the Kluckhohn and Strodtbeck schema to cross-cultural/multicultural counseling is included in Chapter 7, "Multicultural Counselor Preparation: Stage One," Goal 5, of this book.) Hall (1959), detailed the impact of culture on all aspects of our nonverbal behavior in his book *The Silent Language*.

Contributions of Maslow and Kelly.   Shortly after the mid-20th century, other authors began to recognize the impact of culture on values and to question the monocultural theoretical foundations of the counseling and guidance movement. In 1954, Abraham Maslow referred to the complex impact of culture on personality in his classic book *Motivation and Personality*. Maslow (1954) stated "that in general the paths by which the main goals in life are achieved are often determined by the nature of the particular culture" (p. 45). He emphasized the unity of basic needs from culture to culture, but stressed that the paths to achieve need fulfillment are determined by culture and may vary greatly, depending on the norms of the culture.

George Kelly devoted a considerable amount of discussion to the impact of culture on personality in his two-volume work *The Psychology of Personal Constructs*. Kelly (1955) encouraged clinicians to be aware of cultural variations among clients and outlined procedures for assessing the client's culturally influenced constructs, but he cautioned therapists that "a client who is to be genuinely understood should never be confined to the stereotype of his culture" (p. 833). Kelly further admonished clinicians to view the cultural approach as only a "preliminary step in understanding of his client, the first in a series of approximations which bring the client into sharp focus in a complex matrix of basic psychological dimensions" (pp. 833–834).

Contributions of Abel, Patterson, and Wrenn.   After discussing how cultural patterns affect the psychotherapeutic process from a psychodynamic perspective, Theodora Abel (1956) made three recommendations for therapists who were preparing to work with patients of different cultures. First, she recommended that therapists have some formal training in cultural anthropology. Second, Abel recommended that therapists learn more about their own cultural backgrounds through writing their own cultural autobiographies and discussing these with cultural anthropologists. Her third recommendation was for therapists "to do some research or at least give some thought to the role cultural regularities play in the therapeutic process and when interpretations of cultural patterns are indicated" (pp. 738–739).

In a 1958 publication discussing the place of values in counseling and psychotherapy, C. H. Patterson recognized that the "therapist's own values cannot be kept out of the therapeutic relationship" (p. 216), that the counselor can never be completely neutral. Patterson alluded to the impact of culture on deciding what is normal or abnormal behavior in a given society. However, his statement that "The goal of psychotherapy might be thought of as the development of responsible independence" (Patterson, 1958, p. 218) reflects the prevailing Western, individualistic psychological paradigm of that era.

In 1962, C. Gilbert Wrenn urged counselors to broaden their perspectives on reality when he wrote about the "culturally encapsulated" counselor. Wrenn described how "we protect ourselves from the disturbing reality of change by surrounding ourselves with a cocoon of *pretended* reality—a reality which is based upon the past and the known, upon seeing that which is as though it would always be" (p. 445). Wrenn saw counselors "as subject as any to cocoon maintenance and reality evasion" (p. 446). Casas, in a 1984 historical review, credits Wrenn's paper as one of the first efforts by a psychologist to respond to the needs of racial/ethnic minorities. Wrenn's call for counselors to expand their realities came at a time when the United States had launched into the space age and when the Civil Rights movement was gaining momentum.

The deficit emphasis of the Great Society era.   The 1950s and 1960s saw the beginnings of recognition of cultural pluralism in our country. However, much of the writing of that era described the culturally different as "culturally disadvantaged" or "culturally deprived" and seemed to imply deficits among those whose cultures were different (Calia, 1966; Deutsch, 1966; Riessman, 1962; Sue, Arredondo, & McDavis, 1992a, 1992b; Warren, 1966).

Many of the Great Society programs of the 1960s tried to add to or correct the deficiencies or inferior characteristics of those whose cultures were different. Socioeconomic differences and class differences were not separated from cultural differences. People continued to ignore the ugly impact prejudice and racism had and there was still little recognition of the worth and importance of values of all cultures. The ethnocentric viewpoint of the dominant society prevailed.

THE IMPACT OF THE CIVIL RIGHTS MOVEMENT

The early efforts for civil rights in the United States in the 1950s and 1960s were led by African Americans and joined by other human rights advocates. "The new wave of discontent and emphasis on racial pride and cultural identity in the early 1960s served as the impetus for other powerless and disenfranchised groups . . . to demand relevant services" (Copeland, 1983, p. 11). The Civil Rights movement also awakened "mental health professionals to the possibility that cultural issues that had been ignored in society in general had also been ignored in the counseling process" (Helms, 1985, p. 239).

Vontress' early contributions to cross-cultural counseling.   Clemmont E. Vontress (1966a, 1966b, 1967, 1970, 1971a, 1971b), a counselor educator at George Washington University, has a long and prolific record of speaking and publishing on several aspects of cross-cultural counseling. Vontress' early writings addressed factors that influence the counseling relationship when the cultures of the counselor and the client differ. He was also a pioneer in helping White counselors understand the special challenges of working with Black clients.

Attneave's Network Therapy.   In the late 1960s and early 1970s, Carolyn Attneave pioneered combining clinical interventions with the existing social network of an American Indian tribe to implement Network Therapy at an urban community guidance service. Attneave, a clinically trained American Indian therapist, gives a detailed description of her use of network clan therapy using "Indian modes of relationship and communication rather than clinical techniques alone" (Attneave, 1969, p. 196). In reflecting on the contributions of Attneave, Ivey (1993) states that "Attneave's constructions represent our field's best chance for a contextually oriented counseling and therapy" (p. 226).

Arbuckle's and Pine's challenges to the status quo.   Two articles addressing the challenges of counselor work with minority people were published in the early 1970s in *Counseling and Values* (Arbuckle, 1972; Pine, 1972). Pine (1972) confronted counselors with the negative perceptions that minority people had of both the counseling profession and counselors and described how cultural differences, barriers, and value conflicts between counselors and clients could act to make counseling totally ineffective.

Both authors discussed the challenges and responsibilities faced by counselors working with members of minority groups and emphasized the importance of counselors' being aware of their own values. Arbuckle (1972) stated that "counselors do carry their values into the counseling relationship and these *are* values which may well make the counselor a dangerous, rather than an effective, person" (p. 242). Arbuckle also emphasized that all counselors, whether from majority or minority groups, must reach a level of self-identity that allows a total acceptance of differences in human beings and the ability to help people work toward accepting differences in values and ways of life. Pine (1972) called for "the counseling process to be reexamined and, if necessary, redefined and restructured" (p. 37), and emphasized that "to be culturally different does not mean culturally deficient, culturally disadvantaged, culturally deprived" (p. 39).

Torrey's argument against an ethnocentric perspective.   Torrey (1972a, 1972b) challenged the ethnocentric view of Western psychotherapists in his publications on the similarities between Western psychotherapists and doctor-healers around the world. Torrey described four components for curing patients that he believed are the same regardless of the culture. With all four, however, he carefully noted the impact of culture on each of these universals.

Torrey's first area of commonality is the need to choose the appropriate name for the illness or problem; but it is imperative that the therapist share the same cultural world view as the client if the naming is to be effective. The second universal component is that of the personal qualities of the helper; but optimal qualities for a therapist in one culture would not necessarily be the same for therapists in other cultures. Patients' expectations make up the third universal; however, each culture will impact the expectations brought by the helpee. Special techniques of therapy are the fourth universal described by Torrey. Some cultures favor one technique, whereas other cultures choose other techniques. Torrey underscored the fact that "There is no technique used in Western therapy that is not also found in other cultures. . . . There are techniques, however, used in other cultures that are rarely used by Western psychotherapists" (Torrey, 1972a, p. 56). Ponterotto and Benesch (1988) subsequently applied Torrey's universals to cross-cultural counseling. (See Chapter 7, "Multicultural Counselor Preparation: Stage One," Goal 2.)

Harper's emphasis on understanding the Black experience.   In 1973, Harper delineated aspects of the history, sociology, economics, and psychology of Black Americans (Harper's term) that counselors need to know to work effectively with that cultural group. Harper (1973) stated that "the general social sciences tend to limit or omit examining the black American experience . . . [or to] examine black experiences from a negative perspective as related to white middle class Protestant norms" (p. 109). Harper (1973) also cautioned that one should not assume that all Black counselors and Black counselor educators are aware of the "dynamics of the social sciences of blacks . . . [and that they] are effective in interpersonalizing with black counselees just because they are black" (p. 116).

Stewart's comparison of values across cultures.   During the same era, Stewart (1972) published *American Cultural Patterns: A Cross-Cultural Perspective*. In Part III, "American Assumptions and Values," Stewart outlined a framework for looking at the values of any culture and comparing these values with the mainstream U.S. culture. Stewart placed the components of culture under four headings: "form of activity, form of relation to others, perception of the world, and perception of self" (Stewart, 1972, p. 31). Stewart credited Florence Kluckhohn with providing many of the theoretical concepts for his framework for viewing culture, and a revised edition of *American Cultural Patterns* was published in 1991 (Stewart & Bennett, 1991). Stewart and Kluckhohn's work is discussed further in Chapter 7.

Cheek's focus on the Black experience.   Cheek (1976) was also concerned about the Black (Cheek's term) viewpoint. He warned of the inadequacy of traditional psychological theories for understanding the Black experience and was particularly concerned about the wholesale application of White assertiveness training to Black people. Cheek outlined the background needed for working with Black individuals and presented a Black perspective on assertive guidelines. Ivey (1993) credits Cheek as being the first cognitive-behaviorist because of his ability to integrate cognitive and cultural issues with assertiveness.

Beauvais' and Draguns' recognition of the impact of culture.   In 1977, Beauvais described the history of difficulties of attracting Navajo people into any of the health care professions and recognized "how value laden psychotherapy really is" (p. 82). As a participant researcher, Beauvais saw that a traditional medicine man was able to help a severely depressed student whom Beauvais had been unable to help. His call for flexibility and openness mirrors that of Wrenn in 1962.

Draguns (1977) reviewed the 20th century research on mental health and culture. Although he recognized the existence of cultural differences in psychopathology, he cautioned against "drawing implications from information gathered so far and bringing them to bear upon the practical concerns of service and treatment"

(p. 65). Draguns also noted the dearth of research on the "cultural shaping of abnormal behavior in children" (p. 66).

OTHER INFLUENCES ON MULTICULTURAL COUNSELING

Other major contributors to the field of multicultural counseling began to speak and write for the national audience in the mid- and late 1970s. Paul Pedersen, Darrell Wing Sue, and Allen Ivey were among counselor educators who built on the work of many earlier cross-cultural counseling advocates. Pedersen and Sue in particular were early publishers in the field (Pedersen, Lonner, & Draguns, 1976; Sue, 1981).

Pedersen's early contributions. Pedersen (1977, 1978) developed and researched his triad model for cross-cultural counselor training while at the University of Minnesota. He then moved to the East-West Center at the University of Hawaii for four years where he directed a National Institute of Mental Health training grant for developing interculturally skilled counselors. The application of Pedersen's model to multicultural counselors' training is described in Chapter 9, Goal 3.

D. W. Sue's groundwork. D. W. Sue engaged in early research on the impact of culture on counseling, taught at California State University, and gave leadership to cross-cultural counseling while he served as editor of the *Personnel and Guidance Journal* in the 1970s. Sue was one of the first in the field to research and publish on the concept of world views (Sue, 1978a, 1978b). The application of Sue's concepts of world views to multicultural counseling is introduced in Chapter 7, Goal 5, and is presented schematically in Figure 7.1.

Ivey's early contributions. Another early proponent of the need for cultural expertise by those in the helping professions was Allen Ivey. In 1977, Ivey described how helpers can use The Ivey Taxonomy of the Effective Individual (p. 298) in a culturally sensitive way to assist helpees to become culturally competent. Ivey (1977) underscored the fact that "The cultural-environmental-contextual focus is perhaps the most complex of all and people have the most difficulty working in this area" (p. 300).

GROWTH TOWARD A MULTICULTURAL APPROACH

The growth in cultural awareness, development in basic cross-cultural disciplines, and major efforts by culturally different groups to gain equality of opportunity and status continued to build throughout the 1970s (Draguns, 1981). The wall of assimilation began to crack with the movement toward recognition of and appreciation for cultural differences. An ever-widening circle of counseling professionals responded to the need for recognition of the impact of culture on counseling.

By the mid-1970s and early 1980s, recognition of the importance of culture on counseling led to publication of additional books on cross-cultural counseling (for example, Atkinson, Morten, & Sue, 1979; Marsella & Pedersen, 1981; McGoldrick, Pearce, & Giordano, 1982; Pedersen, Draguns, Lonner, & Trimble, 1981; Vacc & Wittmer, 1980; Walz & Benjamin, 1978). The fact that some of these books are now in second or third revisions and that many other authors have joined the ranks of multicultural book publishers indicates the growing interest in the field.

During the same period, a number of professional journals gave increasing attention to the impact of culture on counseling. Many new journals appeared: for example, the *Journal of Non-White-Concerns in Personnel and Guidance* (which became the *Journal of Multicultural Counseling and Development* on July 1, 1985); the *Hispanic Journal of Behavioral Sciences*; *The Journal of Black Psychology*; and the *International Journal for the Advancement of Counselling*. Other established journals devoted special sections or entire issues to cultural pluralism and counseling: for example, the *Personnel and Guidance Journal* (now the *Journal of Counseling and Development*); *The Counseling Psychologist*; *Psychotherapy*; and the *AMHCA Journal*.

In 1983, I had the privilege of serving with Nathan Deen (of the Netherlands) as guest co-editor of *The Personnel and Guidance Journal*'s special issue on "International Guidance and Counseling." In our editorial, we recommended "that cultural pluralism no longer be neglected or considered irrelevant but be addressed in counselor education" (Wehrly & Deen, 1983, p. 452).

In increasing numbers, manuscripts appeared addressing the inadequacies of the Euro-American counseling theories and techniques to meet the needs of the culturally different, the underuse of counseling facilities by minority people, and ways to rectify the situation. And a surge in convention programming, professional symposiums, and journal articles on multicultural counseling topics occurred in the mid- and late 1980s. J. D. Lee (1984) summarized what many people were saying: "As counselors cross cultures, it is imperative that they realize that our theories, techniques, and the profession itself are cultural phenomena reflecting our culture's history, beliefs, and values" (p. 596).

■ *Debate on the need for multicultural counseling training*

In spite of the wealth of support for multicultural counseling, the movement was not without criticism. In 1987, *Counselor Education and Supervision* included a series of five articles on the need for special training for multicultural counseling. Lloyd (1987a) authored the stimulus paper and questioned whether multicultural counseling belonged in a counselor education program, stating that "An approach to multicultural counseling that emphasizes differences between groups and attempts to teach simplistic views of cultural traits, characteristics, and beliefs does not seem to be the type of instruction that should be part of teacher education or counselor education" (pp. 166–177).

Ivey (1987) responded by discussing how his microcounseling concepts have evolved from being culturally blind to recognizing cultural intentionality as the core of effective helping. Ivey stated that "counselors' first step toward understanding the unique human being before them is awareness of multicultural context" (p. 170).

Hood and Arceneaux (1987) agreed that Lloyd's stimulus paper served a purpose in pointing to the dangers of ignoring differences within each culture, but they argued that multicultural counseling courses allow students "to replace the false stereotypes with accurate concepts and information . . . [and] to modify their views about their own traditions, customs, and philosophies based on exposure to those of others" (p. 174).

Parker (1987) questioned Lloyd's awareness of developments in multicultural counselor training. He encouraged counselors to be flexible in their approach to culturally different clients and emphasized the need "to affirm both likenesses and differences in our approaches to multicultural counseling" (p. 180). In the last article in the series, Lloyd (1987b) closed with responses to his reactors.

Two years later, Das and Littrell (1989) focused on three issues related to the 1987 forum generated by Lloyd's stimulus paper and recommended that students "understand both conceptually and experientially the fundamental concept of *culture* . . . recognize the strong set of western assumptions that permeate counseling theories and techniques . . . [and] recognize that traditional communication and counseling skills may need modification, depending on the counseling context" (pp. 13–14).

■ *The missing "woman factor" in multicultural counseling*

Arredondo, Psalti, and Cella (1993) discuss how the "woman factor" is missing in much of the early work in multicultural counseling. This omission has led to stereotyped perspectives that often portray a deficient picture of women. These authors challenge researchers and writers to "gather additional information from a cross-section of women representing different cultural groups, ages, sexual orientations, and social classes . . . [and to] look at all women as individual cultural beings who live in culture-based contexts that oppress women because they are women" (Arredondo et al., 1993, p. 7). New and more inclusive interdisciplinary models of multicultural counseling that include the woman factor in multicultural counseling are needed.

■ *"Multiculturalism as a Fourth Force in Counseling"*

In 1991, P. B. Pedersen edited a 250-page special issue of the *Journal of Counseling and Development* (September/October, 1991) that focused on "Multiculturalism as a Fourth Force in Counseling." Fifty authors contributed to the twenty-five manuscripts in the four parts of this special issue. (Perspectives from many of these manuscripts are included in this book.) In his concluding comments to this lengthy collection of articles, Pedersen made the following five recommendations for change.

1. Counselors must become aware of the assumptions they have learned from their own cultural heritages and recognize that culturally learned assumptions may be different but are not "wrong" or "irrational."
2. Counseling theories need to be studied and complemented to make them appropriate for use with culturally different populations.
3. Multicultural perspectives need to be incorporated into counselor education and training.
4. Cultural differences must be acknowledged in research so that research findings will accurately represent research participants' different cultural perspectives.
5. Skills, strategies, and techniques of counseling will need to be translated to be culturally appropriate for the many different populations to be served in counseling. Pedersen (1991) warned that "Until and unless the multicultural perspective can be understood as not only generic to all counseling but also increasing the accuracy of counseling, culture will remain an exotic concept" (p. 250).

■ Recent trends in multicultural counseling

Casas and San Miguel (1993) recognize that there has been an increase in the number of journal articles addressing cross-cultural issues over the past decade; however, they point out that this increase does "not reflect a substantive and consistent representation of such articles from one issue to the next" (p. 234). Much of the increase has been in the form of special journal issues focusing on cross-cultural and multicultural counseling. Casas and San Miguel also call for more recognition of qualitative research results in professional journals.

Textbooks on counseling theories and techniques have begun to recognize the impact of "Multiculturalism as a Fourth Force." In discussing each counseling theory, Corey's 1991 text includes sections on "Contributions to multicultural counseling" and "Limitations for multicultural counseling." Similarly, the impact of culture on the counseling process is recognized throughout Ivey's developmental counseling and therapy paradigm (Ivey, 1991). Ivey (1991) states that "Multicultural awareness is the frontier of counseling and therapy training" (p. 208), and the title of Ivey, Ivey, and Simek-Morgans' 1993 book, *Counseling and Psychotherapy: A Multicultural Perspective*, reflects how the multicultural focus has taken "center stage" in Ivey's estimation.

At the 1983 APA convention in Anaheim, papers and course syllabi content were the subject of a two-hour round table discussion on the limitations of psychology as a monocultural science. This round table was sponsored by the APA Education and Training Board and the Committee on International Relations in

Psychology. Subsequently, the *American Psychologist* published a special issue from this round table. In their introductory section to this special issue, Kennedy, Scheirer, and Rogers (1984) urged U.S. psychologists to "reach out toward a more truly international science, one fully sensitive to the powerful, multiform variable of culture" (p. 996).

An APA 1990 convention symposium titled "The White American Researcher in Multicultural Counseling: Significance and Challenges" was organized by Joseph Ponterotto. The symposium examined the history of involvement by White researchers in cross-cultural research and looked at how ethnic-minority researchers feel about this involvement by White researchers. Mio and Iwamasa summarized highlights of and reactions to the speakers at this symposium in a "Major Contribution" manuscript in the April, 1993 issue of *The Counseling Psychologist*. In concluding their article, Mio and Iwamasa (1993) list four lessons to be learned from the symposium:

1. Parham's discussion of the resentment that White researchers are evoking among many minority researchers should be taken as a given but should not be a stopping point.
2. White researchers can use the discomfort they felt while attending this symposium to understand how it feels to be an oppressed minority.
3. Minority researchers need to recognize the good intentions of White researchers who are attempting to be part of the solution.
4. Both minority and majority researchers may "have a moral imperative to try harder to find common ground to publish together" (p. 209).

Participants in this APA symposium wrote retrospectively on their participation as reaction papers to Mio and Iwamasas' manuscript (Atkinson, 1993; Casas & San Miguel, 1993; Helms, 1993; Ivey, 1993; Parham, 1993; Pedersen, 1993; Ponterotto, 1993; and Sue, 1993). Many of their contributions are discussed as they relate to several of the issues addressed in this book.

THE IMPACT OF DEMOGRAPHIC REPORTS

Demographic reports of the changing U.S. population characteristics of the 1970s and 1980s supported the call to revise counselor preparation programs. Among the many attention-getting statistics of Hodgkinson's 1985 report "All One System: Demographics of Education, Kindergarten through Graduate School" was the statement "by around the year 2000, America will be a nation in which one of every THREE of us will be non-white" (p. 7). Perhaps the demographic statistics that received the most attention were those related to the projected cultural background of the workforce of the first two decades of the 21st century, when the baby boomers will retire. Many people in the United States are now concerned about the adequacy of education and helping services for people of all cultural and ethnic backgrounds. They now recognize past and present inadequacies of the nation's educational system in serving non-White students and the fact that in the early 21st century a non-White population will make up a majority of the U.S. workforce paying into retirement systems. In 1991, Hodgkinson updated his 1985 report on the basis of the 1990 census and issued an even more urgent call for changes in the educational system.

The increase in people of color populations is evident in Table 2.1. In the 10-year period between the two census enumerations, all people of color groups increased at a faster rate than the White population, which showed an increase of only 6.01%. Particularly notable are several Asian or Pacific islander groups, which increased more than 100%, and the Hispanic groups, which showed an average increase of 53% between 1980 and 1990.

ETHICAL AND TRAINING STANDARDS AND ISSUES

In the early 1980s, national professional groups began to recognize the need to address ethical and training standards and issues. A number of subcommittees devoted attention to drafting standards for cross-cultural counselor training. Professional organizations approved several of these efforts and published the suggested standards in their journals.

As a result of deep concern over the inadequacies of preparation of counseling psychologists for cross-cultural therapy, the Education and Training Committee of Division 17 of the American Psychological Association (APA) presented a position paper, "Cross-Cultural Counseling Competencies," to the APA Division of Counseling Psychology Executive Committee in September, 1980, at Montreal, Canada. Two years later, this position paper was published in *The Counseling Psychologist* (Sue et al., 1982). After presenting a section on rationale for the competencies, the paper describes characteristics of culturally skilled counseling psychologists under the headings of beliefs/attitudes, knowledges, and skills. Casas (1984) gives an overview of the many years of work by APA subgroups that preceded this APA position paper.

Casas (1984) credits the American Personnel and Guidance Association (APGA) for its early efforts in addressing the needs of racial/ethnic minorities through establishing the Human Rights Committee in 1965, initiating a division for Non-White Concerns in 1972, and recognizing the need for special training for the uniqueness of non-Whites in 1977. Several committees within this national professional group have developed position papers on training for multicultural competence.

For clarification, note that the American Personnel and Guidance Association (APGA) has undergone two name changes since this group's early efforts to

TABLE 2.1 ■ UNITED STATES ETHNIC CENSUS, 1980 AND 1990

	Number (1000)		Percent Distribution		Change 1980–90 Number (1000)	Percent
	1980	1990	1980	1990		
All Persons	226,546	248,709	100.00	100.00	22,163	9.78
Male	110,048	121,239	48.58	48.75	11,191	10.17
Female	116,498	127,470	51.42	51.25	10,972	9.42
Race						
White	188,372	199,686	83.15	80.29	11,314	6.01
Black	26,495	29,986	11.70	12.06	3,491	13.18
American Indian, Eskimo, Aleut	1,420	1,959	0.63	0.79	539	37.96
American Indian	1,364	1,878	0.60	0.76	514	37.68
Eskimo	42	57	0.02	0.02	15	35.71
Aleut	14	24	0.01	0.01	10	71.43
Asian or Pacific Islander	3,502	7,274	1.55	2.92	3,772	107.71
Chinese	806	1,645	0.36	0.66	839	104.09
Filipino	775	1,407	0.34	0.57	632	81.55
Japanese	701	848	0.31	0.34	147	20.97
Asian Indian	362	815	0.16	0.33	453	125.14
Korean	355	799	0.16	0.32	444	125.07
Vietnamese	262	615	0.12	0.25	353	134.73
Hawaiian	167	211	0.07	0.08	44	26.35
Samoan	42	63	0.02	0.03	21	50.00
Guamanian	32	49	0.01	0.02	17	53.13
Other Asian/ Pacific Islander	N/A	822	N/A	0.33	N/A	N/A
Other Race	6,758	9,805	2.98	3.94	3,047	45.09
TOTAL	226,547	248,710	100.00	100.00	22,163	9.78
Hispanic Origins*						
Hispanic Origin	14,609	22,354	6.45	8.99	7,745	53.02
Mexican	8,740	13,496	3.86	5.43	4,756	54.42
Puerto Rican	2,014	2,728	0.89	1.10	714	35.45
Cuban	803	1,044	0.35	0.42	241	30.01
Other Hispanic	3,051	5,086	1.35	2.04	2,035	66.70
Not of Hispanic Origin	211,937	226,356	93.55	91.01	14,419	6.80

*Persons of Hispanic origin may be of any race.
Note: Slight differences in some totals due to rounding.
Source: From U.S. Bureau of the Census, 1992, *Statistical Abstract of the United States. The National Data Book*, 112th Edition, p. 17, Washington, D.C.

address needs of culturally different clients, and the APGA division addressing concerns of people of color has had one name change. The American Personnel and Guidance Association (APGA) became the American Association for Counseling and Development (AACD) on July 1, 1983. The American Association for Counseling and Development became the American Counseling Association (ACA) on July 1, 1992. On July 1, 1985, the divisional name of the Association for Non-White Concerns in Personnel and Guidance became the Association for Multicultural Counseling and Development.

After a review of studies of the representation of racial/ethnic minorities in applied psychology and in programs of graduate study, Casas (1985) concluded that, although professional organizations have put forth efforts at policymaking levels, "much has yet to be done to improve the general status of racial- and ethnic-minority persons relative to training and subsequently to make racial- and ethnic-minority counseling a substantive reality" (p. 271). He attributed this lack of success to the profession's failure to act on good intentions, and he outlined changes needed in accreditation, licensing, and certification. In an earlier publication, Casas (1984) presented a detailed critique of the status of racial/ethnic minority groups in counseling psychology, and he presented 16 recommendations for policy, training, and research.

In 1985, S. Sue, Akutsu, and Higashi discussed training issues in conducting therapy with ethnic-minority group clients in light of the importance of match, or fit, of treatment intervention with the client's background. These authors outlined implications for training under the categories of "Knowledge of Culture and Status, Actual Experience, and Innovative Strategies."

After participating in a panel on multicultural counseling at the national convention of the American Association for Counseling and Development (AACD), D. W. Sue (1985) summarized the following important themes:

1. The critical importance of counselor self-awareness of his/her standards, values, and assumptions
2. The need for counselors to be knowledgeable of sociopolitical factors operating in their clients' worlds
3. The critical importance of being able to understand the world view of each client
4. The need for counselors to know that they may inadvertently discriminate if they treat all clients alike

Ibrahim and Arredondo also (1986) presented proposed ethical standards for cross-cultural counselor preparation, counseling practice, assessment, and research. A component of their proposal that was infrequently mentioned in previous literature was an emphasis on the need for counseling students to learn to examine how their own culture has influenced their professional philosophies and behavior and to become aware of their own "cultural baggage."

Ponterotto and Casas identified and surveyed leading cross-cultural counselor training programs in the United States in 1987. As a result of this study, these authors suggested that content for multicultural training follow the guidelines of the APA 1982 Education and Training Committee of Division 17 position paper (Sue, et al., 1982) and suggestions outlined by S. Sue et al. (1985). In addition, Ponterotto and Casas (1987) made strong recommendations for "the counseling profession to take a firm stand on the systematic implementation of required multicultural competencies by all programs" (p. 433). Their recommendations were to develop a clear definition of multicultural competence, to incorporate this definition into accrediting board standards, to modify ethical guidelines of APA and AACD to include factors agreed upon in the definition, to change certification and licensing laws to include multicultural training, and for AACD and APA to initiate ways to "develop multicultural sensitivity and competence in all counselor training programs" (Ponterotto & Casas, 1987, p. 434).

A committee of the Association for Multicultural Counseling and Development (AMCD) of ACA also developed a position paper on multicultural counseling competencies in the early 1990s. After approval by the AMCD board, this position paper on multicultural counseling competencies was published in both the *Journal of Counseling and Development* (Sue, Arredondo, & McDavis, 1992a) and the *Journal of Multicultural Counseling and Development* (Sue, Arredondo, & McDavis, 1992b). (See Appendix A.)

The most recently revised guidelines of the Council for Accreditation of Counseling and Related Educational Programs (CACREP) were finalized in October 1992, published in January 1993, and went into effect January 1994. They include more emphasis on multicultural and diversity study than previous editions. Program objectives must "reflect current knowledge and positions from lay and professional groups concerning counseling and human development needs of a pluralistic society" (CACREP, 1993, p. 48).

Guidelines to include multicultural and diversity components are included under four of the eight common core areas: Area 2, Social and Cultural Foundations; Area 3, Helping Relationships; Area 5, Career and Lifestyle Development; and Area 6, Appraisal. Under Clinical Instruction, students in practicum and internship experiences are required to counsel clients who are "representative of the ethnic, lifestyle, and demographic diversity of their community" (CACREP, 1993, p. 55).

A statement under Section IV, Faculty and Staff, requires that an accredited counselor education program include evidence of an attempt to recruit and retain faculty members representative of the diversity in society. Section V, Organization and Administration, Standard J, requires that programs provide documentation that "A policy to recruit students representing a multicultural and diverse society has been developed and is implemented by program faculty" (CACREP, 1993, p. 59). The guidelines for specific program accreditation for Community Counseling, Gerontological, Marriage and Family Counseling/Therapy, Mental Health Counseling, and School Counseling programs also mention the need for sociocultural and diversity training.

A number of professionals have expressed concerns about lags in updating counselor training to include more emphasis on multicultural issues. Casas and

San Miguel (1993) explained why training programs have been slow to include multicultural competencies. One reason is that mandates from APA and ACA are not really mandates but rather strong recommendations and guiding principles. Another reason is that these guiding principles have lacked specificity and are, therefore, difficult to implement. The Sue, Arredondo, and McDavis 1992 position paper on multicultural counseling competencies and standards is more specific than previous guidelines in detailing these competencies.

Another reason for the lag is the time it takes to revise accreditation guidelines for agencies like CACREP. The 1994 CACREP standards were finalized in October, 1992, and first published in January, 1993. The 1994 guidelines state that a comprehensive and systematic review of the guidelines will be conducted every seven years.

Procedures for requesting the CACREP board to consider new standards or to clarify existing standards during the period between the normal 7-year revision are detailed under "Standards Revisions: Policies and Procedures" (CACREP, 1993, pp. 20–21). The 1993 guidelines state that the CACREP board will consider recommendations "which are of such a nature as to clarify existing Standards statements or, by which delaying implementation, will negatively affect the preparation of counselors and other personnel specialists" (p. 20). It is obvious that much advance work and years of lead time are needed to bring about changes in accreditation guidelines.

INTRODUCTION OF RACIAL AND ETHNIC IDENTITY THEORIES

An important movement that has increased in prominence in the 1980s and the 1990s is the work on models and theories of racial and ethnic identity development. This work came as a result of the realization that there were variables in the counseling dyad that were not being measured and that two of these variables were the racial identity development of the counselee and that of the counselor. Early attention focused on the racial identity development of minority people in counseling. A few years later, concepts on theories of White racial identity development were published. These and other models of ethnic and racial identity development are discussed in Chapters 3 and 4.

PRESENT AND FUTURE CHALLENGES

Although much work has been done to improve multicultural counselor preparation, there are several issues that need more attention.

Misapplication of the Western, monocultural viewpoint. One issue related to multicultural counseling that has received minimal attention in the literature is that of the inappropriateness of the Western monocultural focus of counselor education for students whose cultural origins are different from the White majority U.S. population. As a response to demographic changes in society and studies showing that many non-White clients may prefer non-White counselors, counselor preparation programs have begun to recruit non-White students from both inside and outside the United States. At the same time, however, U.S. counselor educators (the majority of whom are White) have been slow to broaden their programs or do the necessary self-study to accommodate the needs of non-White graduate students in their midst.

In 1982, Gutierrez discussed the challenges faced by minority counselor-education students as "relationships with other counseling students, counselor educators, agency supervisors, and the clients themselves" (p. 220) and made recommendations to ameliorate these problems. It seems paradoxical that so little direct attention has been given to this issue in the professional literature.

Others who are ill-served by the cultural exclusiveness of counseling are the international students who come to study counseling in the West. Writing as a counseling professional at King Saul University in Riyadh, Saudi Arabia, and as a product of Western counselor education, Saleh (1989) deplored the inappropriateness of Western, monocultural counselor education programs for international students. He described how many recently trained students return home, take positions as trainers of counselors in their own countries, and "unwittingly become transporters of a Western connotation of counseling which, untempered, may ill-fit the needs of their clients" (p. 6). Saleh called for counseling to disengage from its Western exclusiveness and to broaden theories, approaches, and training models to be useful in a world that is in great need of the counseling profession. Among the many other authors who have questioned exporting or transplanting U.S. guidance and counseling practices to other settings and who have emphasized the need to base counseling orientations on the values of the culture are Ivey (1977), Pratomthong and Baker (1983), Stewart (1983), Super (1983), and Wohl (1982).

Racial/ethnic minority counseling research. There are still many problems related to racial/ethnic minority counseling research. The 1990 APA symposium discussed earlier in this chapter focused on many of these research issues. Ponterotto and Casas' 1991 *Handbook of Racial/Ethnic Minority Counseling Research* is a definitive source on topics related to racial/ethnic minority counseling research.

The Association for Assessment in Counseling (a division of the American Counseling Association) published a monograph, *Multicultural Assessment Standards: A Compilation for Counselors* (Prediger, 1993), as a significant step in resolving some issues related to racial/ethnic minority counseling research. The September 17–18, 1993, ninth Buros-Nebraska Symposium on Measurement and Testing focused on multicultural assessment.

Other challenges.   Although the amount of research and writing on the topic of the impact of culture and ethnicity on the helping interview has expanded greatly in the past two decades, the number of counselor education programs with specializations in cross-cultural or multicultural counseling is still limited (Ponter-otto & Casas, 1987). Courses in multicultural counseling became increasingly popular in counselor education programs in the decade of the 1980s and the early 1990s. In the Hollis and Wantz (1990) edition of *Counselor Preparation, 1990-1992: Programs, Personnel, Trends,* which reported on a survey of 560 counselor education programs in the United States, the multicultural counseling course ranked first in popularity of courses added, with 59 programs adding a course in multicultural counseling in 1989–90 and 17 more programs anticipating addition of the course in 1990-91. In the 1986 edition of the same book, the multicultural counseling course ranked fifth in popularity of new courses.

Hills and Strozier (1992) reported on a 1988–89 survey of APA-approved counseling psychology programs to determine "the extent to which multicultural issues were addressed in coursework, practica, and research" (p. 43). They also gathered information on the extent to which faculty were involved in multicultural teaching, supervision, professional development, and research; pressures felt to expand multicultural curricula and research; and the numbers of students of color accepted into these programs.

Given an 80% return rate, Hills and Strozier (1992) reported that 43 of the programs included at least one multicultural course; 31 programs included multi-cultural units in other courses; 29 programs had a requirement for a multicultural counseling course; and 22 programs could create a subspecialty in multicultural counseling. Junior faculty were the most involved in all areas of multicultural training. However, the involvement of senior faculty seemed to be important in demonstrating the commitment of the department to multicultural counseling. The availability of a subspecialty in multicultural counseling was reported in 45% of the programs and was "directly related to the research activity of full professors, and secondarily to the teaching activity of the adjunct faculty" (Hills & Strozier, 1992, p. 48).

A major challenge that has not changed much since the early 1980s is that of attracting people of color into graduate programs (Ponterotto & Casas, 1991) and hiring them to teach in counselor training programs (Atkinson, 1993; Ponterotto & Casas, 1991). Kohout, Wicherski, and Cooney's 1989–90 survey of APA graduate departments of psychology (1992) revealed that 92% of the full-time faculty in clinical, counseling, and school psychology programs were White. People of color professionals on these faculties were represented as follows: Black, 5%; Hispanic, 2%; Asian American, 1%; and Native American, less than 1%. The results of the Kohout et al. (1992) survey of APA graduate departments of psychology are similar to those of Hills and Strozier (1992), who found that 11% of the faculty members in the APA-approved counseling psychology programs were non-White, with the percentage of non-White faculty increasing as rank decreased.

The June, 1993, membership in the Association for Counselor Educators and Supervisors (ACES) division of the American Counseling Association shows a slightly more encouraging demographic distribution among this group: African American, 5.4%; Hispanic/Latino, 1.6%; Asian American, 1.3%; Native American, 0.9%; other 2.5%; and Caucasian, 88.3%. People in the group identifying self as "other" may be people of mixed race who are beginning to self-identify this way (as many did in the 1990 national census). Brinson and Kottler (1993) addressed the problem of attracting and retaining minority faculty in counselor education and offered guidelines for cross-cultural mentoring of faculty of color.

Multicultural counseling has reached an exciting moment in its history. Research on racial and ethnic identity development for all people has provided insight into important components of multicultural counseling and has laid the groundwork for additional research. The integration of information from stage models of racial and ethnic identity development and from developmental models of counselor supervision (Loganbill, Hardy, & Delworth, 1982; Stoltenberg, 1981) holds much promise for the improvement of multicultural preparation (Ponterotto, 1988).

SUMMARY

This chapter traced historical developments that brought about recognition of the need for special training for cross-cultural and multicultural counseling and detailed how the counseling profession has responded. Although several psychologists and counselors began to recognize the impact of culture on therapy soon after the midpoint of the 20th century, their messages were not recognized by the majority of people in counseling psychology. Counseling continued to be a monocultural science and reflected the values of Euro-Western, mainstream, White, middle-class males.

It was not until the Civil Rights movement of the 1960s and early 1970s that counseling psychologists began to respond to calls to broaden the profession's theoretical base. Progress to change counselor education and counseling and to research new models has been made. However, there is much unfinished business related to changing counseling theories and practices and to broadening the base of counselor education and counseling psychology programs to meet the needs of all people in our increasingly culturally pluralistic and diverse society.

CHAPTER 3

Developmental Models for Multicultural Counselor Preparation

C urrently, there is a plethora of printed, audio, and video information on ways and means to improve the preparation of multicultural counselors. The recent proliferation of literature on the subject makes it difficult to put this overabundance of concepts into a meaningful format for readers. From one perspective, it seems as if the multicultural advocates are "taking off in all directions."

The purpose of Chapter 3 is to give an overview of both the general and the race-specific literature for conceptualizing multicultural issues in counselor preparation. Models of racial identity development for non-White as well as for White people are also presented to help readers acquire a broad realization of the vast differences among people of the same racial heritage.

As we saw in Chapter 2, many professionals in the field have expressed the need for specific guidelines for multicultural counselor preparation. In 1987, Ponterotto and Casas offered these suggestions for giving a clearer focus to multicultural counselor preparation: clear definitions of terms; more specificity in the guidelines for multicultural counselor preparation used by accrediting, certification, and licensing boards; and more help from both AACD (now ACA) and APA to integrate multicultural components in counselor preparation. In 1993, Casas and San Miguel stated that specificity is needed to turn the current guiding principles into mandates so that the profession does not continue to "underestimate or downplay the need for all counselors to receive cross-cultural training" (p. 235). Given the current state of affairs, it seems that the old adage, "If you don't know where you are going, how will you know when you get there?" is applicable.

The Association for Multicultural Counseling and Development (AMCD) 1991 position paper, "Multicultural Counseling Competencies and Standards: A Call to the Profession" (Sue, Arredondo, & McDavis, 1992a, 1992b); see (Appendix A), gives more specificity to earlier guidelines. The authors of this paper provide a clear rationale for immediate implementation of their listing of cross-cultural competencies and standards. Competencies related to training counselors in beliefs and attitudes, knowledge, and skills are delineated for three major areas: "Counselor Awareness of Own Assumptions, Values, and Biases . . . Understanding the World View of the Culturally Different Client . . . [and] Developing Appropriate Intervention Strategies and Techniques" (Sue, Arredondo, & McDavis, 1992a, pp. 482–483).

CONCEPTUALIZING ISSUES FOR MULTICULTURAL COUNSELOR PREPARATION

Several authors have outlined paradigms for improving counselor training for our contemporary culturally pluralistic society: in 1977, McDavis and Parker described the process of developing and implementing a course in counseling ethnic minorities at the University of Florida; Arredondo-Dowd and Gonsalves (1980) reviewed important components of their bilingual, bicultural counselor preparation program at Boston University; and Copeland (1982) discussed advantages and disadvantages of four basic models for including multicultural content—the separate course model, the area of concentration model, the interdisciplinary model, and the integration model.

Ibrahim (1984) presented an existential/psychological approach "for understanding people within the context of universal existential categories" (p. 166) that subsumed both an emic (insider's) and etic (outsider's) approach. Ibrahim outlined the existential philosophical base of her paradigm and explained how the value emphases and value-orientation research of Clyde Kluckhohn et al. (1951) and Florence Kluckhohn and Strodtbeck (1961) provided the bridge for both understanding individuals' unique world views and as a means of comparing these views within and across cultures.

In a point/counterpoint pair of articles, Fukuyama (1990) argued for a universal, or transcultural, approach to multicultural counseling, stating that a universal approach provides "a broad and inclusive perspective for understanding the influences of culture in counseling" (1990, p. 7). Locke (1990) took the stand for a more focused approach, as Locke believes that " a broad interpretation of multicultural counseling allows, even encourages, students to avoid a focus on themselves and the group(s) they are likely to encounter" (p. 22). Locke (1991) described his own paradigm of cross-cultural counseling as encompassing self-awareness, global influences, dominant culture, subculture, and research theory and curriculum.

■ Integration of current theories

Other authors have argued for approaches that integrate concepts from current theories of counseling and from philosophy to meet the needs of the multicultural populations with which they work. Arciniega and Newlon (Arciniega & Newlon, 1981; Newlon & Arciniega, 1983) presented a theoretical rationale for applying principles of Adlerian psychology to cross-cultural family counseling. Vontress (1985, 1988) discussed applying concepts from existential philosophy in the process of cross-cultural counseling; Harper and Stone (1986) posited adapting multimodal counseling concepts for multicultural counseling; and Ponterotto (1987) described the use of Lazarus's multimodal approach as a framework for counseling Mexican Americans.

■ *Indigenous models*

In 1987, Das reviewed folk, mystical, and medical traditions of the Buddhist, Hindu, and Islamic religions in the traditional societies of India, China, and Japan, and he described how the world views of people in most Eastern societies are shaped by these religions. "Religious traditions define the ideals of what is considered a good life, and prescribe the rules and regulations by which people must live their daily lives if they want to attain the good life" (Das, 1987, p. 25). Das reviewed scientific investigations of how the practices used in indigenous mystical and medical traditions work. He noted that modified forms of meditation and other healing practices have been introduced in Western societies and successfully used along with Western therapy to reduce stress.

In two related articles, Ishiyama (1987; 1990) discusses applications of Japanese Morita therapy philosophy and techniques with Western clients. Morita therapy challenges assumptions that negative feelings must be removed before necessary helpful action can occur. Ishiyama's 1987 paper focuses on the cross-cultural application of Morita therapy with clients who suffer social anxiety; his 1990 manuscript delineates the cross-cultural application of Morita therapy to helping clients learn to deal with attitudinal blocks to action. Ishiyama describes the basic Moritist stance as a difficult one and one that challenges counselors to examine their own attitudes and helping strategies. Some of the issues he addressed are: "Selective acceptance of emotion . . . Feeling-controlling strategy . . . Not allowing feelings to change spontaneously . . . [and] Counselor avoidance of confronting clients" (1990, p. 569).

Le Vine (1991, 1993) outlines the application of Morita-based therapeutic interventions in outpatient therapy with Australian women who struggle with bulimia, and compares Morita-based therapy with Rational Emotive therapy. In her 1993 manuscript, Le Vine recounted her application of Morita-based therapy in five sessions with a 27-year-old woman who met the DSM-III-R (American Psychiatric Association, 1987) criteria for bulimia nervosa. As a result of her experiences, Le Vine believes that Morita-based therapy is appropriate for use across cultures in treating bulimia nervosa.

Nwachuku and Ivey (1991) outline a three-step process of developing culture-specific counseling models that draw on and adapt indigenous models of helping. Nwachuku, an African from the Igbo culture, based this model on naturalistic research with people of his own culture. The first step of the Nwachuku and Ivey model comprises two parts. In Step 1(a), an individual or group from the culture examines the values of the culture (including the existing indigenous helping processes). In Step 1(b) theories and strategies of counseling that will be congruent with these values are outlined. Step 2 involves developing training materials that cultural outsiders can use to learn culturally sensitive skills and strategies for use with cultural insiders. In Step 3, the theory is tested. Nwachuku and Ivey's model was developed for use with people of the African Igbo culture, and so it incorporated many Afrocentric values. In summarizing the model, the authors state, "Perhaps the most important contribution of this method is that it starts with the client's cultural population with a minimum of preconceptions rather than with existing cultural encapsulated counseling theory" (Nwachuku & Ivey, 1991, p. 111).

■ Cubical models

Cubical models provide a three-dimensional perspective for viewing the process of multicultural counseling, which may help the learner understand the possible complexities of the process. McFadden (1986) developed a stylistic approach for counseling minorities. He presented the dimensions of his approach in a cubical model that placed the following three dimensions on a hierarchical plane: cultural/historical dimensions (ethnic/racial isolation, dynamic of oppression, and value system); psychosocial dimensions (ethnic/racial identity, psychological security, and self-inspection); and scientific/ideological dimensions (ethnic/racial relations, logical behavioral chains, and individual goals).

Atkinson, Thompson, and Grant (1993) also present a cubical paradigm for helping service work with racial/ethnic minorities. Their three-dimensional model for selecting counselor roles envisions three continua for conceptualizing counselor roles and strategies: locus of problem etiology, degree or level of acculturation, and goal(s) of helping. Atkinson, Thompson, and Grant (1993) discuss eight possible counselor roles that may be appropriate, depending on how the three continua intersect on their cubical model. The eight possible roles are adviser, advocate, facilitator of indigenous support systems, facilitator of indigenous healing systems, consultant, change agent, counselor, and psychotherapist. The authors recognize that some of these are unconventional or nontraditional roles for counselors, and they discuss specific guidelines and circumstances under which the roles would be appropriate. The application of the Atkinson, Thompson, and Grant model is discussed in Chapter 11, "Multicultural Counselor Preparation: Stage Five," Goal 2, of this book.

Cheatham, Ivey, Ivey, and Simek-Morgan (1993) developed the multicultural cube, shown in Figure 3.1, as a paradigm for understanding concerns that a client, family, or group of any ethnicity or culture may bring to counseling. Along the horizontal axis are multicultural issues such as language, gender, ethnicity, and so on. The vertical dimension shows five possibilities for locus of the issues brought by clients. The third dimension is the levels of awareness of multicultural issues, using Bailey Jackson's levels of cultural identity. Different levels of racial or ethnic identity development named by other authors could be substituted for the levels on

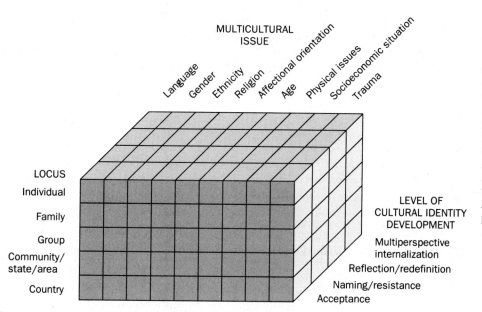

MULTICULTURAL
ISSUE

Language Gender Ethnicity Religion Affectional orientation Age Physical issues Socioeconomic situation Trauma

LOCUS

Individual

Family

Group

Community/
state/area

Country

LEVEL OF
CULTURAL IDENTITY
DEVELOPMENT

Multiperspective
internalization

Reflection/redefinition

Naming/resistance

Acceptance

FIGURE 3.1

The Multicultural Cube

SOURCE: From "Multicultural Counseling and Therapy: Changing the Foundations of the Field," by H.E. Cheatham, A.E. Ivey, M. B. Ivey, and L. Simek-Morgan. In Allen E. Ivey, Mary Bradford Ivey, and Lynn Simek-Morgan, *Counseling and Psychotherapy: A Multicultural Perspective,* Third Edition, pp. 99–123. Copyright © 1993 by Allyn and Bacon. Reprinted by permission.

the third dimension. Cheatham et al. state that "Each of these multicultural dimensions may be vitally important in establishing a working interview and treatment plan . . . [and may require] a multifaceted treatment approach" (1993, p. 105). They also emphasize that the importance of the various dimensions may change over time.

EARLY DEVELOPMENTAL MODELS

Recently, authors in the field have presented models for putting the myriad concepts related to multicultural counselor preparation together into a sequential and developmental format. To begin, the APA position paper on cross-cultural counseling competencies (Sue et al., 1982) provided basic developmental concepts related to beliefs and attitudes, knowledge, and skills.

Carney and Kahn's developmental model. Carney and Kahn (1984) were among the first to present a developmental model based on the APA position paper (Sue et al., 1982). Carney and Kahn gave a rationale for the model, detailed five stages of training development, and described trainee characteristics and appropriate learning environments. A table summarizing the original Carney and Kahn model can be found in Chapter 6, "Introduction to a Developmental Model of Multicultural Counselor Preparation."

Gibbs's developmental model for White/Black relationships. After presenting an overview and discussion of the reasons many Black clients terminate early in work with White counselors (Gibbs's terms), Gibbs (1985) outlined a five-stage developmental "Model of Interpersonal Orientation to Treatment" (p. 188) for cross-cultural work with Black clients. Gibbs describes five evaluation microstages that Black clients go through in developing a relationship with a counselor of a different race: appraisal, investigation, involvement, commitment, and engagement. Parallel with each of these five microstages are five appropriate counselor behavior responses: personal authenticity, egalitarianism, identification, acceptance, and performance. This developmental microanalysis of the early stages of Black/White, counselor/client interaction provides critical insight for cross-cultural work. Application of the Gibbs' developmental model is described in Chapter 9, "Multicultural Counselor Preparation: Stage Three," Goal 3, of this book.

■ *Christensen's developmental model for cross-cultural awareness*

Christensen (1989) delineated another five-stage model for cross-cultural awareness that includes descriptions of similarities and differences for both majority and minority individuals for each of the following stages: (1) unawareness, (2) beginning awareness, (3) conscious awareness, (4) consolidated awareness, and (5) transcendent awareness. Christensen also described transitional periods between each of the successive stages and examined implications for both counselor education and research.

■ *Counselor self-awareness*

The importance of counselor self-awareness has been stressed in training programs since the beginnings of counselor education. Counselor self-awareness is generally considered a developmental aspect of counselor training. A major component of counselor self-awareness that received little attention until the 1980s is the racial identity development of the counselor.

Sabnani et al. (1991) consider the Carney and Kahn (1984) model a significant development in the field but one that fails to address the central issue of "the counselor's own racial-identity development to the overall training process" (p. 77). These authors (Sabnani et al., 1991) credit research "on the salience of both the client's *and* counselor's racial-identity development to the cross-cultural encounter . . . [as the] single most significant advancement" (p. 77) in the field. They recommend that counselors become cognizant of their own levels of racial identity development as well as the levels of racial identity development of their counselees.

The detailed, 1991 Sabnani et al. model is included in Appendix B of this book, and concepts from the model are included in the five chapters of this book that describe the stages of multicultural preparation. The remainder of this chapter is devoted to an introduction to and an overview of racial and ethnic identity development models.

OVERVIEW OF RACIAL AND ETHNIC
IDENTITY DEVELOPMENT MODELS

A White counselor who has worked hard to understand her own prejudices is feeling discouraged and is blaming herself because one of her African American clients does not seem to want to work with her. Some members of a community in which a university is located do not see the value of the campus cultural centers for the African American, Hispanic/Latino(a), Asian American, and Native American students. Members of a local Native American group find it difficult to understand why a White counselor seems so intensely interested in them and wants to get involved in all their Native American community activities.

In each of the three situations described, knowledge of racial and ethnic identity development as it applies to all parties involved could be helpful. Knowing the behavioral characteristics of the various stages of racial and ethnic identity development can lead to a breadth of understanding of the behavior of self and others in interpersonal relationships.

Racial and ethnic identity development models share some features in common, whether they describe minority, majority, or both minority and majority racial and ethnic identity development (Atkinson, Morten, & Sue, 1979, 1983, 1989, 1993; Christensen, 1989; Helms, 1984, 1985, 1990; Kim, 1981; Parham & Helms, 1981; Phinney, 1989, 1993; Ponterotto, 1988; Ruiz, 1990; Smith, 1991). The racial and ethnic identity development models are cognitive models that describe three to six stages and/or phases that individuals may experience as they move from a lack of awareness of their own racial or ethnic identity to a sense of fulfillment (Helms, 1984; Phinney, 1993; Smith, 1991). In the stages between lack of awareness and fulfillment, some individuals may experience strong feelings both for and against their own racial group as well as other cultural groups.

Racial and ethnic identity models include descriptions of stages of reference group identity, not personal identity. As noted by Atkinson, Morten, and Sue (1993) not every person will necessarily go through all the stages of racial or ethnic identity development.

Empirical research to test the validity of constructs in some of the various racial and ethnic identity models is still in its infancy; but these constructs shed light on levels of readiness for counselors in training to accept and internalize the learning necessary for multicultural counselor development (Sabnani et al., 1991). Ethnic and racial identity development models also provide clues for therapist interventions with clients at the various levels of racial or ethnic consciousness (Helms, 1984, 1990; Phinney, Lochner, & Murphy, 1990).

Although a complete overview of the research and development of racial and ethnic identity development models is beyond the scope of this book, a considerable amount of detail on the development and current status of these models is included for two reasons. First, this information hopefully will help readers recognize their own stages of racial and ethnic identity development. Second, this content should help readers learn to recognize the within-group developmental differences of people of any racial or ethnic group. Understanding the effects of differences in racial or ethnic identity development of both helper and helpee can be crucial information for counselors and can help improve cross-cultural counseling competencies.

Allen Ivey (personal communication, July 17, 1993) points to the similarity that racial and ethnic identity development models have with other life-change developmental models. He sees clear parallels between stages of racial or ethnic identity development and the stages in models of recovery from grief and other life-change models. Ivey believes it is important to look for crossovers with other theories when examining the racial and ethnic identity models. Similarly, readers of this text are encouraged to look for similarities among these models and other models of change rather than getting bogged down in a morass of details on each theory. (Exercises to practice application of information from racial identity development models are included in Chapter 9, "Multicultural Counselor Preparation: Stage Three," Goal 1, of this book.)

The early racial identity development models described the developmental process for people of color. This was congruent with the early cross-cultural counseling efforts that concentrated on the White counselor learning how to work cross-culturally with minority clients. It took several years, and help from counselors of color, for White counselors to realize that they also needed to study their own racial and ethnic development.

This section begins with an overview of one of the early generic minority identity development models with which many counselors are familiar. The chapter then moves on to describe culture-specific racial identity development models for African Americans, Asian Americans, Chicano/Latino Americans, and White Americans. Ethnic identity development models are reviewed in Chapter 4.

■ *Atkinson, Morten, and Sue's Minority Identity Development Model*

The Minority Identity Development Model (MID) of Atkinson, Morten, and Sue (1979, 1983, 1989, 1993) has received much publicity in the cross-cultural counseling literature. The first edition of this model (Atkinson et al., 1979) was based on the authors' knowledge of five early minority identity models and on their own clinical observations. For some counselors, the MID was the first racial or ethnic identity development model to which they were introduced.

The 1993 Minority Identity Development Model is presented as "a schema to help counselors understand minority client attitudes and behaviors within existing personality theories" (Atkinson, Morten, & Sue, 1993, p. 28). Five levels of development included in the schema are: conformity, dissonance, resistance and immersion, introspection, and synergetic (working together) articulation. For each of the five stages, the authors present four corresponding attitudes that summarize the behavior of the minority individual toward self, others of the same minority, others of a different minority, and people of the dominant group (see Table 3.1).

Atkinson, Morten, and Sue (1993) caution that the developmental process outlined is not intended to be perceived as irreversible. They believe that not all

TABLE 3.1 ■ *SUMMARY OF MINORITY IDENTITY DEVELOPMENT MODEL*

Stages of Minority Development Model	*Attitude toward Self*	*Attitude toward Others of the Same Minority*	*Attitude toward Others of Different Minority*	*Attitude toward Dominant Group*
Stage 1 Conformity	Self-depreciating	Group-depreciating	Discriminatory	Group-appreciating
Stage 2 Dissonance	Conflict between self-depreciating and appreciating	Conflict between group-depreciating and group-appreciating	Conflict between dominant-held views of minority hierarchy and feelings of shared experience	Conflict between group-appreciating and group-depreciating
Stage 3 Resistance and immersion	Self-appreciating	Group-appreciating	Conflict between feelings of empathy for other minority experiences and feelings of culturocentrism	Group-depreciating
Stage 4 Introspection	Concern with basis of self-appreciation	Concern with nature of unequivocal appreciation	Concern with ethnocentric basis for judging others	Concern with the basis of group depreciation
Stage 5 Synergetic articulation and awareness	Self-appreciating	Group-appreciating	Group-appreciating	Selective appreciation

SOURCE: From Donald R. Atkinson, Morten, & Sue. *Counseling American Minorities,* 4th edition. Copyright © 1993 Wm. C. Brown Communications, Inc., Dubuque, Iowa. All Rights Reserved. Reprinted by permission.

minority people go through the entire range of stages in their lifetime. Some people of color are born and raised in a family functioning at Level Five and appear to never experience a Level One existence. Others that are born in a home functioning at Level Five may move to Level One in their struggle to build their own minority identity.

The authors also note that they did not intend to outline a process with the more valued attitudes at the higher stages of development; the schema is presented to reflect what they have observed in three decades of work with minority clients.

Developmental Models for Multicultural Counselor Preparation ■ 51

The authors also discuss implications of this model for counseling, and recognize the need for empirical testing of their model. The first step in testing would be to produce an instrument to measure the development of minority identity across different minority groups.

Sue and Sue (1990) broadened the scope of application of the MID and renamed it the Racial/Cultural Identity Development Model (R/CID). Sue and Sue also adapt the model for use with White identity development.

■ The Cross model of Black identity development

The Cross model is one of the earliest models of racial identity development, and it served as a paradigm for many other theories, including Atkinson, Morten, and Sue's generic minority identity development model. In 1971, William Cross published his model of "The Negro-to-Black Conversion Experience: Toward a Psychology of Black Liberation" in the *Black World* journal. This model was built on experiences of the civil rights and Black militancy movements and described the process of self-actualization for Afro-American adults under conditions of oppression. (Note: in this discussion, Cross's terms are used.) Cross (1971) sought "to construct a model depicting the various stages persons traverse in becoming Black oriented" (p. 14); his five stages were (1) pre-encounter, (2) encounter, (3) immersion/emersion, (4) internalization, and (5) internalization/commitment. Cross's 1971 model became known as the *nigrescence* theory, the theory of "becoming Black." In the more than two decades since Cross's model was published, it has been researched and cited with great frequency.

Since 1971, Cross has addressed and expanded on various aspects of his original model in response to the considerable body of research and review of his model (for example, Cross, 1978, 1987, 1989, 1991; Cross, Parham, & Helms, 1991; Helms, 1990; Parham, 1989). In 1989, Cross recognized that nigrescence has been a theme throughout Black history and has reflected the experiences of both individuals and groups in social movements. In the 1991 revision, Cross describes nigrescence as a *resocializing* experience that "seeks to transform a preexisting identity (a non-Afrocentric identity) into one that is Afrocentric" (p. 190). The following is an overview of the five stages of the resocialization experience delineated in Cross's 1991 model.

Stage 1: Pre-encounter. Individuals in the *pre-encounter* stage hold attitudes that range on a continuum from attitudes in which race holds low salience in their lives to attitudes that are race neutral to attitudes that are anti-Black. For some Black people at this level, other aspects of their lives are more important than being Black. A different attitude that may be found in the pre-encounter Black individual is that of viewing race as a problem, a stigma, or a hassle that must be dealt with now and then. For some Blacks in this stage, being Black is viewed negatively; other Blacks are loathed, and the person feels anti-Black and alienated from other Blacks. Some anti-Blacks will hold positive stereotypes of White people. The anti-Black component of Cross's 1971 model received a great deal of publicity, and much subsequent research focused on a search for anti-Black attitudes.

Cross summarizes his 1991 revision of the pre-encounter stage: "Pre-encounter persons place priority on organizations and causes that have low race salience and/or little nationalistic import, while Blacks who are deeper in nigrescence stress high race salience activities and organizations" (p. 197).

Cross's 1991 description of pre-encounter Black people also discusses how Blacks have been miseducated in the home, school, and community. They have developed a Western Eurocentric cultural and historic perspective that results in a distorted and inhibited perception of Black history and Black culture. In addition, Cross discussed how success, not oppression, can sometimes lead Black people to embrace pre-encounter attitudes in contemporary society. Being in the pre-encounter stage, however, opens the individual to the possibility of an identity conversion experience.

Stage 2: Encounter. The pre-encounter identity is usually shaped by the individual's early socialization process; as such, it provides a secure anchor for the individual. Because the first level of identity is well entrenched, Cross believes that to move that person into the second stage takes some event that catches the person off guard and shakes the individual's feeling of a secure identity. Cross refers to the death of Martin Luther King, Jr., as an event that served as a catalyst for some 1960s pre-encounter individuals. Current pre-encounter Black individuals who have grown up in a mostly White environment may experience such a catalytic event when they leave home to go away to college. Lower socioeconomic Blacks may have such an awakening in their first experience with the law or imprisonment. Sometimes a series of small events will collectively instigate an encounter.

Cross mentions two steps in the encounter: (1) experiencing the encounter, and (2) personalizing the experience because of its powerful impact. The experience need not be a negative one; it can also be the positive result of learning about Black history and the contributions of Black scholars and artists.

The person's initial reaction to the encounter experience is usually one of alarm or confusion and may even lead to depression; it can be painful to discover that one's frame of reference is not functional, not Afrocentric enough. Surface manifestations may be few, as the turmoil is usually inside the individual. Intense feelings of guilt, anger, anxiety, or a combination may be experienced. The person will feel outraged at having "bought into" a lie and will feel a strong determination to become the right kind of Black person. Cross (1991) states that these strong feelings "combine to form a psychic energy that flings the person into a frantic, determined, obsessive, extremely motivated search for Black identity" (p. 201). When this happens, the pre-encounter person is dying and the Afrocentric individual is being born.

Stage 3: Immersion/emersion. Cross (1991) describes this stage of nigrescence as "the most sensational aspect of Black identity development, for it represents the vortex of psychological nigrescence" (p. 202). On entering the third stage, the individual is more aware of the identity he or she wants to destroy than of the identity he or she wants to embrace. Feelings of rage against White people and White culture are common. The first phase of Stage 3 is that of *immersion*; individuals frantically immerse themselves in everything Black and take on as many visible signs of Afrocentric behavior as possible, from dress to hairstyle to changing names to an intense interest in learning about "Mother Africa." It is common for people in this stage to be concerned about whether they are Black enough; Cross calls this the "Blacker than thou" syndrome.

The second phase of Stage 3 is that of *emersion*, in which there is "an emergence from the emotionality and dead-end, either/or, racist, and oversimplified ideologies of the immersion experience" (Cross, 1991, p. 207). It is a leveling-off period. The ways individuals experience the emersion phase may be very different, but there will be a realization that the initial experiences of Blackness during the immersion phase were superficial and lacked substance, texture, and complexity. The person moves on to a search for more serious ways to understand and be committed to Black identity.

Stage 4: Internalization.   During the *internalization* phase, the individual incorporates Black identity so that it becomes a natural part of everyday existence. Cross states that the extreme emotions of the third phase give way to a calm inner feeling of satisfaction and connectedness with one's Blackness. Nigrescence does not change basic personality structures; rather, the leveling of emotions during internalization allows core personality factors to be reestablished.

Nigrescence results in higher salience being given to Blackness in one's reference group identity. When the individual reaches the internalization stage, the person is free to experiment with different levels of identity with Blackness because the person is thoroughly grounded in Black identity. Some individuals become bicultural and work through the realities of Blackness "as well the enigmatic, paradoxical, advantageous, and supportive aspects of one's 'American-ness' " (Cross, 1991, p. 213). Other individuals are able to continue this broadening of identity and embrace a multicultural perspective.

Stage 5: Internalization/commitment.   According to Cross, the main difference between the fourth and fifth stages is the sustained commitment to Black identity evident in the *internalization commitment* stage. Cross recognizes that some Blacks develop a Black identity but do not maintain a long-term interest in Black affairs. The sustained commitment to the Black identity is the earmark of the internalization commitment stage.

■ *The follow-up work of Parham and Helms*

To study Black (Parham and Helms' term) students' racial identity attitudes and their preferences for Black or White counselors, Parham and Helms (1981) developed and researched a Black Racial Identity Attitude Scale (RIAS-B). This scale was based on Cross's 1971 model of Negro to Black racial identity development, but Parham and Helms combined Stages 4 and 5 into one stage called internalization. The RIAS-B was the first scale to measure racial identity development.

In summarizing research on the validation of the RIAS-B, Parham and Helms (1981, p. 255) state, "In general, the results of the study support the idea that possession of certain racial identity attitudes influences Black people's acceptance of Black and White counselors." The authors emphasize that the study supported the existence of intragroup differences in racial identity among Black people that can account for differences in Black clients' feelings about a counselor's race. Results of the research have important implications for appropriate counselor interventions by either Black or White counselors.

Helms (1984) presented a Black and White model of racial identity development in which she described attitudes toward Blackness and Whiteness for these four stages: (1) pre-encounter, (2) encounter, (3) immersion/emersion, and (4) internalization. Helms also described how these stages of racial consciousness might influence the behavior clients present in counseling as well as the behavior counselors exhibit. She then suggested four types of counseling relationships that might occur, depending on the racial consciousness level of both counselor and client, and proposed interventions for clients, as well as for counselor trainees, appropriate to their levels of racial consciousness.

In 1990, Helms edited *Black and White Racial Identity: Theory, Research, and Practice,* which contains a section on "Practical Applications of Racial Identity Theory." Some of these practical applications will be included in later chapters in this book.

Parham (1989) presented a model in which individuals who reached nigrescence at an earlier point in life may recycle through the same stages as they wrestle with new encounters that challenge their Blackness. This addition to Cross's basic theory of nigrescence lends support to the concept that racial identity development models are *not* linear in nature.

Since the early-1980s work of Parham and Helms on models of racial identity development, the professional literature has been replete with manuscripts reporting research on these models and discussing issues related to this type of research (see Akbar, 1989; Carter, 1990; Carter & Helms, 1992; Cross, 1989; Ford, Harris, & Schuerger, 1993; Helms, 1985, 1989; Nobles, 1989; Parham, 1989; Parham & Helms, 1985; Ponterotto, 1988, 1989; Ponterotto & Casas, 1991; Pope-Davis & Ottavi, 1992; Sabnani & Ponterotto, 1992; Taub & McEwen, 1992; Tokar & Swanson, 1991).

■ *The Kim model of Asian American racial identity development*

In 1981, Kim conducted an exploratory study of the process that Asian Americans in a White-dominated society experience in attempting to resolve identity conflicts. Kim used qualitative research methods involving unstructured, focused, individual interviews of ten sansei (third generation) Japanese women. After analyzing the retrospective information from these in-depth interviews, Kim posited five distinct progressive and sequential stages experienced in Asian American identity development: (1) ethnic awareness, (2) White identification, (3) awakening to social political consciousness, (4) redirection to Asian American consciousness, and (5) incorporation.

The first stage, *ethnic awareness*, begins when the child is about 3 or 4 years old. Interactions with family members help the child form a beginning awareness of her or his ethnic origins. Kim found that at this age the children had either positive or neutral attitudes about their ethnicity. "At this stage, greater exposure to Japanese ethnicity is related to a positive self-concept and more clear ego identity while less exposure is related to a neutral self-concept and confused ego identity as Japanese Americans" (Kim, 1981, p. 124).

For most subjects, the ethnic awareness stage lasted until the children entered school. At that time, the children's social environment became less hospitable as they began to have more contact with the White society "and concomitant exposure to racial prejudices of other people" (Kim, 1981, p. 125). When this occurred, they moved into the *White identification* stage. For the women in Kim's study, moving into the formal educational structure included memories of being on the receiving end of prejudicial behavior that reflected negatively on their feelings about themselves.

As the Asian American children had more contact with White people and became the targets of racist behaviors, they began to realize they were different from others. Many of these young girls began to believe that it was their fault that they were different; this period was remembered as a painful time and a time in which self-concepts suffered greatly.

A method of coping with these negative times was for the young Asian American females to identify with the White society, to attempt to take on the values of White people, and to alienate themselves from the Asian American culture. During adolescence, energies often went toward academic activities and leadership roles rather than toward dating. "Most subjects compensated . . . by becoming involved in formal, organizational roles and responsibilities within the school as class presidents, class officers, club leaders, editors of year books, etc." (Kim, 1981, p. 132).

The degree of identification with the White society varied from those who identified actively to those who identified passively. The young women who saw themselves as White took on behaviors of their White peers and did not want to be viewed as Asian. Those who identified this actively with the White culture were more likely to have come from families that were not very involved in Japanese cultural activities; they often repressed negative feelings and experiences. Conversely, the young women who identified only passively with White society were more likely to have come from families that were more involved in Japanese cultural activities.

In the *awakening to social political consciousness* stage, the women adopted new perspectives about who they were in the larger society. They were deeply influenced by the civil rights and women's movements of the 1960s and 1970s. Significant events such as moving to an area with politically conscious Asian

Americans often precipitated movement into this stage. Although there was variation among the women's level of political involvement, the important factor seemed to be learning "about the plights of oppressed people wherever there was an opportunity" (Kim, 1981, p. 141).

This awakening to social political consciousness led to abandoning identification with the White society and sometimes led to feelings of alienation from the White society. Energies were directed toward social and political movements where the women found meaningful support systems. Self-concepts began to be more positive as the women identified with being oppressed, being a minority, and feeling a connectedness with other minority people.

In the *redirection to Asian-American consciousness* stage, the women became increasingly comfortable with their Asian American heritage. Early in this stage, they often felt strong desires to immerse themselves in Asian culture and activities. This immersion sometimes led to strong feelings of anger toward White society when the young women realized that the negative experiences of their youth had been the result of White racism. Over time, they were able to work through these strong negative feelings and see themselves and other Asian Americans from a new perspective. They were now able to feel pride in being Asian American.

In the fifth and final stage, *incorporation*, the Asian American women in Kim's study came to a clear and positive perspective on who they were. They were comfortable with their identity as Asian Americans and they were able to respect people of other racial heritages. They no longer felt the need to identify either with or against White people. Kim (1981) states that "The hallmark of this stage is the Asian American identity blending in with the rest of the individual's identities" (p. 152).

Kim found that in all cases where conflicts in identity development were resolved, the women emerged with positive Asian American racial identities. Several factors acted as catalysts to resolution of identity conflicts and enabled the sansei women to move to the next stage: obtaining both political and ethnic information, having the support of individuals and groups, and being involved with other Asian Americans (or people of other minorities) in social political movements.

■ The Ruiz model of Chicano/Latino identity development

Ruiz reviewed existing models of identity development and saw the need to develop a culture-specific model for people of Chicano/Latino identity. He presented a five-stage Chicano/Latino ethnic identity model that addressed the negative consequences of the dominant society's insistence on assimilation (Ruiz, 1990). His model was formulated from case histories of counseling sessions with people of this population. The five stages of the Ruiz model are (1) causal, (2) cognitive, (3) consequence, (4) working through, and (5) successful resolution.

In Stage 1, *causal*, the person is experiencing an ethnic identity conflict brought on by conflicting messages about the Chicano/Latino ethnicity from the environment. Affirmation of the ethnic identity is lacking.

Stage 2, *cognitive*, is permeated by three erroneous beliefs about the Chicano/Latino heritage: (1) identification with this heritage will lead to poverty and prejudice, (2) assimilation to the majority culture is the only way to escape poverty and prejudice, and (3) assimilation is the only possible path to success.

In Stage 3, *consequence*, "the fragmentation of ethnic identity becomes more evident" (Ruiz, 1990, p. 35). The client feels even more hurt and embarrassed about anything related to her or his heritage (accent, name, where one lives, skin color, cultural customs, and so on). This can result in feeling estranged with an almost total lack of identification with the Chicano/Latino heritage.

Stage 4, *working through*, begins with the psychological distress of being unable to cope with the ethnic conflict and the realization that one cannot go on pretending to identify with an alien cultural heritage. At this point, the client is ready to receive culturally sensitive counseling to resolve this deep distress.

By Stage 5, *successful resolution*, the client has found greater acceptance of her or his culture and ethnicity. The individual has gained a sense of self-esteem and pride in ethnicity, and this ethnicity is seen as a pathway to success.

Ruiz's model includes counselor interventions for each of the five stages to help the Chicano/Latino individual regain pride in his or her ethnic and cultural identity. Ruiz's model could be useful to Chicano/Latino students in counselor education programs to help them understand their own racial identity development as well as to provide suggestions for working with Chicano/Latino clients.

■ *Models of White racial identity development*

Katz and Ivey (1977) were among the first to call attention to the need for White racial awareness in racism awareness training. They recognized that White people rarely identified themselves as having a racial identity.

The concept of White racial identity was introduced in the discussion of the work of Parham and Helms. Helms (1990) reviewed the development of models of White racial identity that "have focused on defining racism" (p. 50), pointing out that the early models seemed to assume racism was damaging only to the victims of this oppression. Little or no consideration was given to the effect of racism on the perpetrators.

As the work on racial identity development progressed, some researchers became aware of the need to apply the models to both counselor and counselee, as Helms and Parham had done in much of their work. Because many of the counselors were (and still are) White, they recognized the need for more work on White models of racial identity development. Ponterotto and Pedersen (1993) describe White racial identity development as the process by which White people in the United States acknowledge White identity and accept "the social implications of their racial group membership—power, privilege, and responsibility for change" (p. 63). The section that follows gives more details on the Helms' White racial identity development model and introduces two additional models of White racial identity development.

Hardiman's model of White racial identity development.   Hardiman developed a generic, five-stage model of White social identity development based on sex-role identity and racial identity development theories. From this generic model, she moved to the work on her White racial identity development model (1982). As the basis for her White identity development theory, Hardiman researched six biographies and autobiographies of White, antiracist activists. From perusal of these life stories, she posited five stages of White identity development: (1) lack of social consciousness, (2) acceptance, (3) resistance, (4) redefinition, and (5) internalization.

Hardiman's theory differs from most of the other racial identity theories in that the first stage, *lack of social consciousness*, covers the period of birth to about age 4 or 5. In the first stage, the individual is not aware of racial differences and racism. In the second stage, *acceptance*, people accept the beliefs of adults around them regarding the privileged position of Whites and institutionalized racism. Because Whites are the people in power, the assumptions undergirding the acceptance stage are rarely discussed; there is an unconscious identification with Whiteness. Acceptance may last for many years or even a lifetime.

Most White people experience painful emotions in entering the third stage, *resistance*, because this involves rejection of the White supremacy beliefs and a rejection of Whiteness. The fourth stage, *redefinition*, involves search for a White identity that transcends racism. Upon transitioning to stage five, *internalization*, White individuals integrate the new White identity into all aspects of their consciousness and behavior.

Helms' model of White racial identity development.   As noted in a previous section, Helms (1984) developed a Black and White model of racial identity development. It is important to remember that Helms' model describes the behavior of White people in interaction with Black people (Helms' terms). Helms encouraged empirical research of her model and has made refinements on the basis of this research. Helms' 1990 model of White racial identity development conceptualizes two phases: Phase 1, *Abandonment of Racism*; and Phase 2, *Defining a Nonracist White Identity*. Each of the two phases includes three stages, giving the model a total of six levels.

In Phase 1a, *contact*, the White person has become aware through direct contact that Black people exist. However, interaction is limited, and the White person will often claim that he or she is colorblind—that racial differences are not important. If the White person continues to interact with Black people, it will be impossible to remain oblivious to the racist acts that abound. Becoming conscious of these experiences can propel the person into Phase 1b, *disintegration*. At this point, White people acknowledge their White identity as well as the racial realities of the world in which they live; this results in a conflicted acknowledgment of Whiteness and feelings of guilt and anxiety. Helms states that White people in such a state of cognitive dissonance can respond in one of three ways: (1) remove themselves from environments in which cross-racial interactions occur, (2) attempt to change the racist attitudes of other Whites, or (3) seek support—from either Blacks or Whites—that racism either is not the White person's fault or does not exist. Regardless of the methods of attempting to resolve the cognitive dissonance, the White person will experience pressure to conform to the standards of the White group. The desire to be accepted by others who are White will be very strong and will move the person into Phase 1c, *reintegration*.

In the reintegration stage, the White person accepts White superiority and Black inferiority and rationalizes this racist attitude. The White person will feel fear of and anger toward Black people. Helms believes that it is fairly easy for White people to remain or fixate at the reintegration stage in the contemporary, White-dominated U.S. society. A traumatic event may be needed to move the person into the second phase, *defining a nonracist White identity*.

The first stage of the second phase (2a) of Helms' White racial identity theory (and the fourth stage of the overall theory) is labeled the *pseudo-independent* stage. In this phase, the White person begins to redefine what it means to be White. Individuals begin to acknowledge White responsibility for racism and look to see how they have perpetuated racism. Helms states that this stage is largely one of intellectualization and curiosity, and the individual may still engage in acts that unknowingly support racism (such as encouraging Blacks to become more White). At this pseudo-independent stage, the White person will not feel entirely comfortable with the new White identity and may find him- or herself in a rather marginal position related to both Blacks and Whites. The continued search for a positive White identity will thrust the person into the next stage (2b), *immersion/emersion*.

In the immersion/emersion stage, the White individual struggles to define a positive White racial identity to adopt. The individual undergoes a process of reeducation through activities such as reading biographies or autobiographies of other White people who have made such a journey, or by participating in White consciousness-raising groups. The goal of the person is now to change White people, not Black people. Both cognitive restructuring and emotional change may take place during this stage. Successful resolution of the stage will probably require emotional catharsis of feelings that have previously been denied. Release of these feelings will result in a positive identification with being White and "provide the fuel by which the person can truly begin to tackle racism and oppression in its various forms" (Helms, 1990, p. 62).

The sixth, and final, stage (2c) of Helms' White racial identity development model is that of *autonomy*. In this stage, the individual is no longer threatened by the concept of race and abandons rigid world views. The autonomous individual actively seeks ways to learn about other cultural groups and internalizes a healthy White identity. The person is able to relate to all forms of oppression and seeks to act to eliminate them. Helms points out that going through these phases of reference group identity with Black people does not change personal identity aspects. The person's personality characteristics will not be much different from the individual's personality before experiencing the White racial identity search.

Ponterotto's White racial consciousness development model. Ponterotto (1988) outlined a four-stage model for racial consciousness development among

White counselor education students, based mainly on his work in a counseling program that was 94% White. This model differs from the White and Black models of Hardiman and Helms in that it extended to White interactions with people of all minority groups. Ponterotto's model was built on theoretical concepts of Helms' 1984 model combined with experiences with hundreds of White counselor education students involved in the study of multicultural counseling in Nebraska and New York. The four stages posited by Ponterotto are pre-exposure, exposure, zealot/defensive, and integration.

Students in the *pre-exposure* stage are naive about many aspects of multicultural counseling. They have given little thought to themselves as having a racial identity or to the privileges of being White. Their notions about racism are usually outdated and they have little or no comprehension of the subtle racism of modern times.

Students enter the *exposure* stage when they are required to consider multicultural issues; for many students, this begins when they take a course in multicultural counseling. They are confronted with the realities of continuing racism in the United States, and they begin to learn about individual, group, and institutional racism. Students find the new and accurate information enlightening but also feel anger and guilt that the counseling profession has perpetuated institutional and cultural racism by centering on White, middle-class values. Students also recognize how their own behavior is subtly racist. The strong feelings they experience propel them into the third stage.

In the *zealot/defensive* stage, Ponterotto sees students responding in one of two ways to the strong feelings experienced in the previous stage. One choice is to become very zealous about multicultural topics and to study them intensively. Ponterotto notes that this zealous behavior serves as an outlet for the guilt experienced in the previous stage. The other choice is to retreat from multicultural issues and attempt to be only passive recipients of information. Some students retreat because they take the criticism of the White system very personally. Students who wish to complete the course cannot stay in the retreat alternative, however; to complete the class, they are required to deal with and process their feelings in some manner.

As the strong dichotomous feelings of the zealot/defensive stage subside, students move into the last stage, *integration*. Students who have chosen either the zealot or retreat behavior in the previous stage now show more balanced behavior related to multicultural content and work. "Students now accept the realities of modern racism, they acknowledge their own subtle (and at times not so subtle) racism, and they feel a sense of empowerment about eliminating racism in themselves and in society" (Ponterotto & Pedersen, 1993, p. 75). At this stage, students often show a renewed interest in looking at both their racial and ethnic roots, in expanding their interest in learning about other cultural groups, and in beginning work to lessen other kinds of oppression.

Similarities of White racial identity development models. There are a number of similarities in the descriptions of the stages of the three White racial identity development models just reviewed:

1. Entering with a very naive perspective on racial identity and racism awareness
2. Moving to a stage of realization that being White is a privileged position
3. Vacillating between the comfort of the "old" White identity and gaining the courage to move to a wider perspective of White identity
4. Responding to feelings of guilt and anxiety as well as experiencing considerable cognitive dissonance by plunging forward or by retreating
5. Finally finding a "new" and broader White identity with which one can live

In 1991, Sabnani, Ponterotto, and Borodovsky integrated concepts from all three models into an inclusive White racial identity development model that consists of five stages: (1) pre-exposure/precontact, (2) conflict, (3) prominority/antiracism, (4) retreat into White culture, and (5) redefinition and integration. Appendix B lists Sabnani et al.'s (1991) cross-cultural counseling training goals and tasks in the areas of beliefs and attitudes, knowledge, and skills for each of these five stages.

LIMITATIONS OF RACIAL IDENTITY DEVELOPMENT MODELS

Authors of all the models reviewed in this chapter have expressed the need for research to test their models or the need for replication of research already conducted. At present, many of these models are a collection of theoretical concepts from clinical or academic observations with little support from empirical research. The Cross model with the follow-up work by Parham, Helms, and others seems to have been the most researched.

A different limitation of current models of minority and racial identity development theory has been voiced by individuals studying the identity development of people with more than one racial heritage (Kerwin, Ponterotto, Jackson, & Harris, 1993; Poston, 1990; Reynolds & Pope, 1991; Root, 1990, 1992). Current theories of minority or racial identity development are seen as inappropriate descriptions for the development of a positive biracial or multiracial identity.

SUMMARY

This chapter highlighted several models for training counselors for multicultural competence. Special attention was given to models of minority and racial identity development because of the increasing awareness of individual differences in racial identity among people of the same racial group. It is important for the counselor to recognize these developmental aspects of both client and counselor.

More information on the impact of the racial identity of both counselor and counselee is presented in the chapters on the stages of counselor development of multicultural competence. The next chapter gives an overview of ethnic identity development throughout the life span, from childhood through adulthood.

CHAPTER 4

Ethnic Identity Development over the Life Span

This chapter reports on work done by theorists who have delineated models of ethnic identity development and on some of the research on these ethnic identity development models. Most authors and researchers of ethnic or racial identity development theories have focused on the stages or phases the adult experiences in developing a racial identity. Much less attention has been given to how the child and the adolescent develop an ethnic or racial identity and how this might influence these components of adult identity. Phinney and Rotheram's 1987 book *Children's Ethnic Socialization* is one of the few recent publications that addresses the ethnic development of the child; Jean Phinney (1993) continued on to develop and research a theory of ethnic identity development in adolescents.

Some theorists prefer the term *ethnic identity development* to *racial identity development*. Elsie Smith (1991) considers the term *ethnic identity* to be broader and more inclusive than *racial identity* and that is the term used in this chapter.

Because adults do not arrive "ready-made," this chapter on ethnic identity development begins with a discussion of children's ethnic socialization; this is followed by a discussion of the ethnic identity development of adolescents. Much of the information on children's ethnic development is drawn from Phinney and Rotheram's 1987 book; the information about adolescents draws heavily from Phinney and associates' more recent work. A brief discussion of adult ethnic identity and an overview of Elsie Smith's theory of ethnic identity development conclude this chapter.

THE CHILD'S DEVELOPMENT OF AN ETHNIC IDENTITY

The child's development of an ethnic identity is a complex process that includes many overlapping or interactive components: "ethnic awareness, . . . ethnic self-identification, . . . ethnic attitudes, . . . and ethnic behaviors" (Rotheram & Phinney, 1987a, p. 13). The child's level of cognitive development is a critical factor to consider in exploring and understanding children's thinking about ethnic/racial awareness, identity, attitudes, and behavior. Factors that influence how children respond to questions about their racial identity are "their dependence on concrete information, their tendency to categorize on that basis, and their inability to consider information from multiple perspectives" (Ramsey, 1987, p. 72).

Young children in the preoperational level of development operate in a world of absolutes and overgeneralizations in order to handle the vast amount of complex information on race they receive from their environment (Ramsey, 1987). Information that contradicts these overgeneralizations is often suppressed or assimilated to fit into prior knowledge. The centration block that accompanies the early stage of cognitive thinking makes problem solving more difficult because the child is unable to focus on more than one aspect, or attribute, of a problem at one time (Thompson & Rudolph, 1992). Because of their inability to focus on more than one attribute at a time, young children are not always able to perceive individual differences. Ramsey (1987) notes differences in the thinking processes of children and adults when she says "a distinction must be made between adults who willfully assume that 'they're all alike' and children who can only process one attribute at a time" (p. 68).

Katz (1987) also underscores the need to consider cognitive developmental aspects in studying children's development of racial awareness, attitudes, and self-identification: "Children's tendency to overgeneralize, their inability to deal with contradictory information, and their greater receptivity to global and affect-laden statements may make them particularly prone to prejudicial thinking" (p. 95). Why some children grow out of this type of thinking, whereas others do not is not yet known.

■ *Ethnic awareness*

Hardiman (1982) refers to the beginnings of ethnic awareness for White children in her 1982 model of White identity development; Kim (1981) described how the Japanese American children in her study became aware that they were ethnically different when they entered school (see Chapter 3). *Ethnic awareness* is a developmental process in which the child grows increasingly more competent in describing the characteristics or attributes of his or her own ethnic heritage. The beginnings of ethnic awareness appear to emerge as the child develops the mental capacity to perceive such things as skin color, language, or customs. Ethnic awareness is present before the child is able to self-identify as a member of an ethnic group (Rotheram & Phinney, 1987a).

Ramsey (1987) notes that by the age of 3, both Black and White children can identify and classify people as Black or White (Ramsey's terms) and that these classification skills increase between the ages of 3 and 5. Children in the preoperational level of development seem to classify along visible traits; but when asked to explain their categorizations, they do not always mention these visible factors. This may also indicate that they do not yet fully understand the concept of race. Ramsey speculates that their nonverbal categorization may be ahead of their verbal reasoning capacity. Rotheram and Phinney (1987a) emphasize that, although ethnic awareness is a cognitive aspect of one's ethnic identity, it is highly influenced by affective and evaluative aspects.

■ *Ethnic self-identification*

Ethnic self-identification occurs when the child is able to use an accurate ethnic-group label consistently. The ethnic label chosen should be the same label others would apply to members of that ethnic group. In young children, the development of a healthy ethnic identity often appears to border on ethnocentricity (Akhtar, 1984).

Sometimes young children misidentify themselves. Rotheram and Phinney (1987a) state that "it is not clear whether [minority] children really think they belong to another group, would like to belong to another group, or simply admire the other group because of its higher status in the culture" (p. 18). To achieve ethnic self-identification, the child must be mentally capable of understanding that he or she is both a child and a member of an ethnic group at the same time; so measures for assessing ethnic self-identification need to be looked at carefully from a developmental perspective. Social cognition, which includes affect, is a part of ethnic self-identification (Rotheram & Phinney, 1987a).

Aboud (1987) critiques four features of common procedures for assessing ethnic self-identification: (1) the inappropriateness of using dolls for self-identification; (2) the limitations of appearance as "the appropriate critical attribute to present to children when requesting them to make an ethnic identification" (p. 38); (3) the problems posed by forced-choice techniques; and (4) the low reliability and validity of several identity measures.

Similarly, Vaughan (1987) questioned early research on children's ethnic self-identification and pointed to four possible problems: the cognitive problem of children's knowledge of what they really look like, the affective problem of what they want to look like, the methodological problem of the lack of construct validity of using dolls or pictures to represent people, and the statistical problems in early analyses.

Vaughan (1987) also called attention to results of his research on Pakeha (White) and Maori children in New Zealand between the ages of 4 and 12, showing that self-identification occurred much later for Maori than for Pakeha children. For Maori children, self-identification occurred at 9 to 10 years, and for Pakeha children between 4 and 5 years. Vaughan noted that these findings were comparable to some studies of American Black children, showing that Black children self-identify later than White children. Vaughan then examined results of children's tests for self-identification and concluded that, for young children, the exercise becomes a test with both cognitive and affective elements.

Hopson and Hopson (1990) cast further doubt on the efficacy of using dolls as an assessment tool. They were able to increase Black children's choices of Black dolls through social modeling. This result is an example of the limitations of the use of dolls to assess self-identification.

Cross (1991) traces the history of the misuse of information from Kenneth and Mamie Clark's 1930s doll study of Negro identity (Clarks' term) in children. Cross notes that the Clarks' report of self-hatred came from only 14% of the African American children tested. However, this report of Negro self-hatred received wide publicity; it was used for sociopolitical purposes, and it set the stage for the widespread belief that self-hatred is part of the personality development in African American children. This resulted in "an image of the Negro dominated by feelings of inferiority" (Cross, 1991, p. 37).

■ *Ethnic attitudes*

The feelings children have about their own and other ethnic groups influence their *ethnic attitudes*, which are greatly influenced by the ethnic attitudes of significant people in the child's early socialization process. Ramsey (1987) describes how young children adopt these attitudes and beliefs through the process of assimilation. Whom they see and whom they do not see, as well as the overt and covert reactions of significant others in their environment, can influence children's ethnic attitudes (Ramsey, 1987).

Some children may develop an aversion to dark-skinned people at an early age, and when asked to express friendship choices, children often show a preference for children of their own race; but they cannot give logical reasons for their choices. Katz (1987) reminds us that research does not confirm that all these attitudes come from parents; she suggests that other sources such as peers, siblings, books, and television also may have a powerful impact on children's ethnic and racial attitude development.

Clark, Hocevar, and Dembo (1980) researched aspects of cognitive development in children's explanations, preferences, and attitudes toward skin color. The primary goal of their study "was to investigate the cognitive prerequisites that underlie a child's understanding of the origins of skin color" (Clark et al., 1980, p. 333). Their findings supported their hypotheses that there is a cognitive developmental sequence in children's skin color explanations and that these explanations correlate with other stage-related abilities. Additionally, the research of Clark et al. showed strong evidence that an understanding of physical conservation precedes an understanding of skin color causality.

Clark et al.'s (1980) results of test performance on social identity were less clear and seemed to suggest that an understanding of both skin color causation and social identity may develop concurrently. The study also assessed the degree to which children's attitudes toward skin color have a developmental aspect. Results indicated that the relationship between White skin color preference and age is curvilinear.

An additional finding of the Clark et al. (1980) research was that social desirability may have influenced the children's choices. When the children were working with a White examiner, there were no cognitive developmental decreases in preference for White skin, as there were in work with a Black examiner. Clark et al. suggest that this evidence of social desirability is of special significance, because the child who understands when to give a socially desirable response on a skin-color attitude test exhibits an advanced understanding of the concept of skin color and its social ramifications.

■ *Ethnic behaviors*

Ethnic behaviors develop within the context of the child's socialization process. The way children learn to behave depends on the values and behaviors of the ethnic group or culture in which they are socialized. G. H. Mead's concepts of symbolic interactionism (1934) state that children see specific behaviors and situations as they interact in their culture, begin to interpret and understand the meaning of these behaviors, and develop their own world views and behaviors as they interact with others in their culture. Weinreich (1986) also reminds us that "the earlier identifications of young children in the home, at school and in the wider community have a thoroughgoing impact on the development of their identities" (p. 312). The powerful impact of the values and behaviors of significant others on the child's development of ethnic behaviors is evident.

Children's ethnic behaviors are also influenced by other socializing influences on their lives. The behavior of peers with whom they interact and behaviors modeled on television and in other media can also play important roles in socializing the child's ethnic behaviors. The media's portrayals of people of color in a stereotypical manner have been deplored for decades and can be another influence on the development of ethnic behavior in children. In a sense, peers as well as media characters become significant others in the lives of children.

It is obvious that the process of the development of ethnic awareness, ethnic identity, ethnic attitudes, and ethnic behaviors in children is a complicated one. There is strong evidence of the roles of cognitive development and affective elements in this developmental process. Critiques of existing research on the child's ethnic socialization process support the need for additional research to increase our understanding of the child's development of ethnic awareness, ethnic identity, ethnic attitudes, and ethnic behaviors.

ADOLESCENT ETHNIC IDENTITY DEVELOPMENT

By early adolescence, young people become aware that they have choices in the degree to which they associate with their own and other ethnic groups. Sometimes young people find it difficult to choose one reference group and the lifestyle associated with it and abandon the values, beliefs, and behaviors of their own ethnic heritage.

Some young people cope by learning to live biculturally. Early reports presented negative images of teenagers who tried to live in two cultures and labeled their identity development as marginalized; but recent research on adolescents indicates that living biculturally can be a healthy process (Phinney & Rotheram, 1987b). The biracial children and adolescents in the Kerwin, Ponterotto, Jackson, and Harris (1993) study showed an increased sensitivity to both cultures in which they were growing up; "there was no great sense of perceiving themselves as marginal in two cultures" (p. 228). Cross (1991) also supports biculturalism as a healthy mode of living.

In his early work, Erik Erikson (1950, 1963, 1968) described adolescence as a critical time for developing a stable identity. Rosenthal (1987) credits Erikson with coming "closest to focusing simultaneously on the internal and external worlds of the adolescent" (p. 157) in looking at the intrapsychic, cognitive, and cultural factors that impact identity development in adolescents. A stable ethnic identity provides an ethnic anchor for adolescents during the time in which they are exposed to a plethora of difficult decisions. Teenagers who are unable to develop a healthy ethnic identity may suffer from identity diffusion and lack the sense of history, cultural norms, and cultural behaviors on which to base difficult decisions (Akhtar, 1984).

■ *Erikson's contributions*

Erik Erikson had a major impact on developmental psychology with the theories he presented in *Childhood and Society* (1950, 1963) and *Identity: Youth and Crisis* (1968). In *Childhood and Society*, Erikson presented his "Eight Ages of Man" concepts. "Identity versus Role Confusion," including the attainment of a stable identity, was postulated as the major developmental task of adolescence. "The sense of ego identity, then is the accrued confidence that the inner sameness and continuity prepared in the past are matched by the sameness and continuity of one's meaning for others, as evidenced in the tangible promise of a 'career' " (Erikson, 1963, pp. 261–262). According to Marcia (1966), ego identity and ego diffusion are the polar outcomes of the adolescent identity Erikson described. Erikson (1963) also warned of the cruelty that adolescents may show to those who are different in "skin color or cultural background" (p. 262).

In *Identity: Youth and Crisis* (1968), Erikson devoted an entire chapter to "Race and the Wider Identity," where he discussed the impact of White racism on minority youth. Erikson stressed that the important question related to *identity* is " 'What do I want to make of myself, and what do I have to work with?' " (p. 314). The question is not simply one of who the person believes he or she is. This broader interpretation of identity is important in understanding the full impact of societal racism on minority youth. Erikson believed that adolescents from oppressed and exploited minority groups who were unable to attain the benefits of the majority group would incorporate negative images of themselves from both the majority *and* the minority groups. He predicted that minority youth who were not able to build an identity with the dominant society would also be "upset in sexuality, and most of all unable to apply aggression constructively" (Erikson, 1968, p. 309).

■ *Marcia's extension of Erikson's work*

James Marcia (1966, 1980) built on Erikson's theory of ego identity formation as a developmental task of adolescence, using Erikson's polar concepts of achieved identity and identity diffusion. Marcia also believed that adolescents need to experience a crisis in identity related to issues such as religion, occupation, and politics.

Marcia developed a model of ego identity in which he postulated four identity statuses: identity achievement, foreclosure, identity diffusion, and moratorium. Distinguishing components of each status were the presence or absence of a decision-making period and evidence or nonevidence of a commitment in ideology or occupation (Marcia, 1980). The *achieved identity* status youth has worked through the adolescent identity crisis and has made a commitment to self-chosen ideological beliefs and occupational goals. The youth with a *foreclosed identity* has not yet experienced an identity crisis. This person expresses commitment but appears to base this commitment solely on the influences of significant others in his or her childhood; it is difficult to tell where the external influences end and the young person's own goals begin.

The adolescent in the *identity diffusion* status shows little interest in commitments to ideological or occupational commitments and gives the impression that one choice may be as good as the other. Adolescents experiencing the *moratorium* status are struggling to make commitments and are actively exploring options that may lead to commitments. The moratorium youth may be struggling to find a compromise between what significant others want, what society seems to demand, and what the youth views as her or his capabilities. This youth may seem to be totally preoccupied by what some people call "adolescent activities" (Marcia, 1966).

Ponterotto and Pedersen (1993) reviewed the research on ego identity development and discussed the findings that higher ego identity seems to be correlated with higher levels of psychological functioning. When sexual values are included, the Marcia model appears to be more applicable to females. Commitment seemed to be the major factor, with college females in the achieved or foreclosed identities showing higher levels of psychological functioning. Delworth's recent work (as cited in Ponterotto & Pedersen, 1993) integrated concepts from leading feminist theorists and concluded that, because females focus on the centrality of relationships, they have a need to feel anchored. For females, the achieved and foreclosed identities provide these anchors. In the case of the former identity, it may be the anchor of career, friends, husband or children; in the latter identity, the anchor may be that of passing on the values of her family and heritage. There are no anchors for females in the diffused or moratorium identity statuses.

Ponterotto and Pedersen (1993) as well as Phinney (1993) note that much of the research on adolescent identity development has focused on identity as it relates to gender roles, occupation, religion, or political ideology. Much less research has been devoted to looking at the commitment of adolescents to an ethnic or racial identity.

■ *Phinney's contributions*

As noted earlier, Phinney and her colleagues (Phinney, 1989, 1990, 1992, 1993; Phinney & Alipuria, 1990; Phinney & Chavira, 1992; Phinney, Lochner, & Murphy, 1990; Phinney & Rotheram, 1987a, 1987b; Phinney & Tarver, 1988) have been engaged in extensive work to develop and test a theory of adolescent development of an ethnic identity across ethnic groups. The Phinney (1993) model of adolescent ethnic identity development extends the identity development work of Erikson, is built directly on Marcia's four ego identity statuses, and draws on social identity theory (Tajfel, 1970, 1982) and the work of other social scientists. Ponterotto and Pedersen (1993) credit Phinney and her associates with providing "a secure bridge linking ethnic identity development to more general models of adolescent identity development" (p. 42).

As background for her research, Phinney (1990) reviewed 70 refereed journal articles dealing with ethnic identity beyond childhood and stated, "On the basis of the research reviewed, it appears that self-identification, a sense of belonging, and pride in one's group may be key aspects of ethnic identity that are present in varying degrees, regardless of the group" (p. 507).

Phinney reviewed ethnic identity development models of Cross (1978), Helms (1990), Kim (1981), and Atkinson, Morten, and Sue (1983). She found that these models share Marcia's (1966, 1980) concept that an achieved identity results from experiencing a crisis, moving into a period of exploration, and eventually making a commitment. Although Phinney recognizes the important conceptualizations these models have provided, she notes that most have focused on one ethnic group and have relatively little research to validate them.

Phinney (1993) states that her years of research have aimed at developing and testing an ethnic identity development model that is (1) based on the theoretical work of Erikson (1964, 1968), (2) congruent with the ego-identity status work of Marcia (1966, 1980) as well as with current ethnic identity models, and (3) relevant for use with all ethnic groups. Phinney's work concentrates on the *process* of ethnic identity formation, "the way in which individuals come to understand the implications of their ethnicity and make decisions about its role in their lives, regardless of their ethnic involvement" (Phinney, 1993, p. 64). Phinney (1990) points out how this differs from research that concentrates on the content of ethnic identity—ethnic behaviors and ethnic attitudes.

The research that Phinney and her associates have conducted with groups of American-born high school and college students includes: (1) the interviews of Black (Phinney et al.'s term) and White middle-class eighth graders to determine the extent and exploration of ethnic identities (Phinney & Tarver, 1988); (2) the interviews and assessment of Black, Asian American, Mexican American, and White tenth-graders to determine ethnic identity exploration, to look at ego identity development, and to assess self-concept and psychological adjustment (Phinney, 1989); (3) The survey of Asian American, Black, Hispanic, and White college students to study the extent of exploration of ethnic issues and determine the importance of ethnicity as a reference group identity area (Phinney & Alipuria, 1990); (4) the 3-year follow-up studies of the tenth-graders studied earlier (Phinney & Chavira, 1992); and (5) the research on high school and college students of Asian, Black, Hispanic, White, and Mixed heritage to validate the Multigroup Ethnic Identity Measure (MEIM) (Phinney, 1992).

From results of the research cited above, Phinney (1993) presents the following three-stage model of ethnic identity development in adolescence.

Stage 1: *Unexamined ethnic identity*. At this level, the individual has not engaged in exploration of ethnicity. Two possible subtypes of this stage are a *diffuse* type, in which the person shows no interest in ethnicity, or a *foreclosed* type, in which the person's views on ethnicity are dominated by the opinions of others.

Stage 2: *Ethnic identity search/moratorium*. In this stage, the person is actively involved in trying to understand what ethnicity means to herself or himself.

Stage 3: *Achieved ethnic identity*. The individual at this stage is clear and confident about her or his own ethnicity.

Table 4.1 summarizes these stages and shows how they compare with those of Cross (1978), Kim (1981), Atkinson et al. (1983), and Marcia (1966, 1980). (The first three models were discussed in Chapter 3.)

Phinney reports some findings that are at variance with earlier models of minority ethnic identity development. One difference is that individuals in the first stage do not necessarily either prefer White identity or hold negative attitudes about their own ethnicity. Minority youth might show a foreclosed identity when they have not examined ethnic issues, but this does not necessarily mean that they hold negative views of their own ethnic group or prefer to be White. Phinney believes that parents of color who have provided positive models of ethnic pride may have influenced their offspring's more positive view.

A second finding of Phinney's research that differs from some other stage theorists is that movement into the second stage is not necessarily precipitated by an emotionally intense or disruptive event (or events) as described in the Cross and Kim models. Phinney (1993) states, "Our interview data revealed little evidence of the intense emotion or of the anger toward the majority culture that may occur in this stage" (p. 71). She speculates that these different findings may be the result of recent historic and social change. Another possibility is that the younger age of many subjects in her research might have influenced the degree of emotion shown.

Phinney additionally states that there is strong evidence that the three stages she posits are sequential, although more research is needed to support this assumption. The Multigroup Ethnic Identity Measure "will allow for large-scale

TABLE 4.1 ■ STAGES OF ETHNIC IDENTITY DEVELOPMENT AND EGO IDENTITY STATUSES

Phinney (1989)	*Unexamined Ethnic Identity*		*Ethnic Identity Search (Moratorium)*		*Achieved Ethnic Identity*
	Lack of exploration of ethnicity *Possible subtypes*		Involvement in exploring and seeking to understand meaning of ethnicity for oneself		Clear, confident sense of own ethnicity
	Diffuse: Lack of interest in or concern with ethnicity	Foreclosed: Views of ethnicity based on opinions of others			
Cross (1978)		Pre-encounter	Encounter	Immersion/ Emersion	Internalization
Kim (1981)		White-identified	Awakening to social-political awareness	Redirection to Asian American consciousness	Incorporation
Atkinson et al. (1983)		Conformity: Preference for values of dominant culture	Dissonance: Questioning and challenging old attitudes	Resistance and immersion: Rejection of dominant culture	Synergetic articulation and awareness
Marcia (1966, 1980)	Identity diffusion	Identity foreclosure	(Identity crisis)	Moratorium	Identity achievement

Sᴏᴜʀᴄᴇ: From "A Three-Stage Model of Ethnic Identity Development in Adolescence," by J. S. Phinney. In M. E. Bernal and G. P. Knight (Eds.), *Ethnic Identity: Formation and Transmission Among Hispanics and Other Minorities*. Copyright © 1993 State University of New York Press. Reprinted by permission.

studies to explore important questions about the development of ethnic identity over a range of ages, ethnic groups, and various demographic and contextual variables" (Phinney, 1992, p. 76).

One of the many important findings of the research of Phinney and associates is the significant relation of high scores on ethnic identity to both higher levels of psychological functioning (Phinney, 1989) and higher levels of self-esteem (Phinney, 1992; Phinney & Alipuria, 1990; Phinney & Chavira, 1992) for the minority youth participating. An interesting new finding of the 1992 research was that for 12 White, high school students, who made up a small ethnic minority in their culturally pluralistic high school, a statistically significant correlation was found between ethnic identity and self-esteem. Phinney believes that this new finding has implications for White students who increasingly will find themselves in the minority as the demographics of the United States change. White students' attention to their ethnicity may become an important aspect of building positive self-esteem.

In their chapter "Ethnic Identity Development and Psychological Adjustment in Adolescence," Phinney et al. (1990) present the following implications for counselors who provide therapy with minority adolescents.

1. Encourage minority adolescents to explore their attitudes and feelings toward their own ethnicity.
2. Help minority adolescents to learn about the history of their own ethnic groups within a multicultural society.
3. Lead discussions with minority youth on ways of dealing with two cultures.
4. Help minority youth to understand the negative images of their own ethnic groups and to reevaluate these images.

The authors recognize that helping adolescents of color through this period "may invoke a somewhat disturbing exploration or moratorium period, [but] the process can be expected to lead ultimately to a more secure sense of self and more healthy adjustment" (Phinney et al., 1990, p. 68).

In summarizing results of the longitudinal study of ethnic identity and self-esteem, Phinney and Chavira (1992) conclude that it is still not clear whether self-esteem is a cause or an outcome of developmental variables. They state, however, that the results of the study are consistent with the previous findings that recognize the importance of ethnic identity in minority youth development, and they emphasize the important role of self-concept. Phinney and Chavira recommend giving equal emphasis to promoting ethnic awareness and identity development and self-esteem enhancement for minority youth. They state "High personal self-esteem may then provide the basis for individuals to explore their own cultural background and to develop a secure, positive view of themselves as minority group members" (Phinney & Chavira, 1992, p. 280).

ADULT ETHNIC IDENTITY DEVELOPMENT

By the time the individual reaches adulthood, the person is often presumed to have a mature sense of his or her ethnic identity. The research on racial identity development (cited in Chapter 3) and the research on adolescent ethnic identity development reveals that this is not always the case. The apparent lack of interest in ethnic self-identity for White European Americans is often attributed to the fact that either (1) these have been the people in power in the United States or (2) attributes such as visible skin color do not identify these people. Some people of color also reach adulthood without having developed a firm sense of ethnic identity. The person who has not developed an achieved ethnic identity in adolescence has unfinished work to accomplish in adulthood.

Akhtar (1984) writes about the problems of adults who fail to develop a healthy ethnic identity—those who suffer from ethnic identity diffusion. Akhtar says that, without a strong ethnic anchor, these people manifest a false liberal attitude which, on examination, reveals a contradictory value system or the absence of any inner values. The person suffering from ethnic identity diffusion will be highly vulnerable to external control and lack inner morality. Akhtar's findings suggest that clarifying one's ethnic identity is critical for developing a strong and consistent value system on which to base attitudes and behaviors. With this solid sense of ethnic identity as a strong anchor, the individual behaves consistently in moral decision making.

■ Smith's theory of ethnic identity development

Elsie Smith (1991) proposes a model of ethnic identity development applicable to members of both minority and majority ethnic groups. Her model goes beyond the issue of oppression and focuses on status inequality; oppression is just one result of status inequality. (Smith's 1991 model expands and revises her earlier models: 1985; 1989.) Smith (1991) chose the term *ethnic identity development* over *racial identity development* because she believes *ethnicity* has a broader scope than *race*, and for some people race may not be the most salient factor in identity development.

Smith (1991) presents several important constructs before delineating the eighteen propositions of her theory. First, Smith describes an ethnic group as a group of people "who share a common history and culture, who may be identifiable because they share similar physical features and values and who, through the process of interacting with each other and establishing boundaries with others, identify themselves as a member of that group" (Smith, 1991, p. 181). Smith agrees with Erikson that establishing a cultural identity is an important part of human development. For Smith, ethnic identity development is a critical human need that furnishes people with a sense of history and a sense of belonging.

Smith discusses ethnic groups as reference groups; birth and a long socialization into an ethnic reference group provide individuals with the basic values, beliefs, and behaviors of that group. The degree to which an individual adopts this ethnic identity can vary from little or none to high identification with the ethnic reference group.

The concept of majority/minority status is a very important aspect of Smith's ethnic identity development theory. Majority status is determined by the power the group has, regardless of its size. In the United States, race and ethnicity often determine the power one has. In each multiethnic society, a social distance scale develops that reflects the values and attitudes of the majority group toward the minority group. Smith believes that, in the United States, race has a superordinate status for determining social distance, the permissible range of roles that an individual may assume, and the partners one chooses.

Smith also believes that individuals use the process of *selective permeability* to internalize or reject certain aspects of ethnic contact situations. "Selective permeability is what allows an ethnic contact experience to become or not become an integral part of one's ethnic identity" (Smith, 1991, p. 183).

Smith's model of ethnic identity development posits a lifelong process that begins in childhood and continues throughout adulthood. It is a process of continually drawing boundary lines to decide what groups make up one's inner boundary groups and what groups make up one's outer boundary groups. Smith proposes that individuals who are strongly embedded in their own culture are more "ethnically hardy" and less vulnerable to negative influences in the environment. Smith seems to concur with the concepts of Akhtar presented in the previous section of this chapter.

In pluralistic cultures, majority or minority status influences ethnic identity development, and ethnic identity conflicts between people of majority and minority status are common. As examples, Smith cites the long history of conflicts between Whites and Blacks in the United States, between the Chinese and the Tibetans in China, and between the Sicilians and the Northern Italians in Italy. Smith sees these conflicts as stages that occur in ethnic identity development for members of both majority and minority groups. She proposes the following four phases for individuals manifesting ethnic identity conflicts:

Phase 1: *Preoccupation with Self, or the Preservation of Ethnic Self-Identity.* The individual *has* experienced either a positive or a negative contact with an outside group, which challenges the individual's ethnic equilibrium. In response, the person uses ego defense mechanisms to preserve the ethnic boundaries in existence before the contact.

Phase 2: *Preoccupation with the Ethnic Conflict and with the Salient Ethnic Outer Boundary Group.* After the significant contact with an ethnic group of which one is not a member, the individual will experience strong feelings and may seek refuge in and support from her or his own group. Because of the strong feelings experienced, the salient ethnic contact experience will be registered for the individual in a figure-ground experience.

Phase 3: *Resolution of Conflict.* The individual realizes he or she cannot continue in a heightened emotional state forever and moves toward working out a solution to the conflict. Decisions are made about how to avoid similar future contacts. Smith states that a person of minority status in a pluralistic society typically uses one or more of the following approaches to resolve conflicts: "(a) assimilate, (b) integrate, (c) segregate, (d) accommodate, or (f) become a marginal person" (Smith, 1991, p. 185).

Phase 4: *Integration.* The individual works to integrate the current experience with previous experiences of ethnic contact. Whether the contact has been positive or negative, the individual attempts to integrate and balance the event with the perspectives of previous ethnic contact experiences.

Smith believes that healthy resolution of these conflicts enables the person to move forward and complete ethnic identity formation through a series of similar contacts. Unhealthy resolution of the salient ethnic identity contact leaves the individual in a state of vulnerability and predisposes the person to ethnic identity confusion and diffusion.

The 18 propositions Smith offers combine her perspectives on ethnic identity development as it relates to minority/majority status and mental health. Readers interested in more details on Smith's theory of ethnic identity development are referred to these 18 propositions (Smith, 1991).

SUMMARY

This chapter presented a life-span overview of ethnic identity development. This chapter discussed ethnic identity development of children, adolescents, and adults and reviewed several authors' concepts of children's ethnic identity development. The complexities of researching ethnic identity development in children were also discussed.

Adolescent ethnic identity development was viewed through the work of Erikson, Marcia, and others, including an overview of the research and development of adolescent ethnic identity theory by Phinney. Concepts from Smith's theory of ethnic identity development within the context of majority/minority status concluded the overview of ethnic identity development.

Several authors have stressed the need for development of a healthy sense of ethnic identity and have shown how this is related to overall psychological functioning. Developing a firm sense of one's own ethnic self is also seen as a prerequisite to working with people who are of different ethnic heritages.

CHAPTER 5

Multicultural Counseling on the International Scene

T his chapter is based on the assumption that we can all learn with and from each other. The intent of this chapter is fivefold: (1) to give a brief introduction to counseling in countries beyond the U.S. borders, (2) to help readers realize the worldwide phenomenon of cultural diversity, (3) to indicate the multiplicity of cultures that exist within several other countries of the world, (4) to introduce readers to the ways in which counselors in many nations are responding to cultural pluralism, and (5) to summarize responses to a multicultural questionnaire from counselors in 22 countries on 5 continents. The information presented here is a limited sample from the many counseling programs around the world.

INTRODUCTION TO COUNSELING OUTSIDE THE UNITED STATES

It is all too easy for those of us from the United States to have an ethnocentric view of our counseling practices and to believe that our counseling services are superior to those in other parts of the world. A basic premise of counseling theory and practice is that it *must* be developed to meet the unique needs of individuals within a society (Ivey, 1993; Pratomthong & Baker, 1983; Saleh, 1989; Stewart, 1983). Locke (1992a) underscores these concepts when he states, "We are wrong to consider counseling in the United States superior to any other system of psychological insight in the world. As cultures and conditions vary country to country, so do counseling practices—and so they must" (p. 13).

Helping services exist in all countries of the world, but counseling as a profession is not universally recognized. In the United States, counseling is a relatively young profession, having been in existence for less than half a century on a widespread basis (see Chapter 2 for the history of multicultural counseling in the United States). In many countries, counseling has not yet been accepted as a profession; people turn to other sources for help with problem solving. In other countries, counseling is still very young, perhaps having been in existence only since the 1960s or 1970s.

When traditional counseling was gaining a strong foothold in the United States, many counseling professors and practitioners saw it as an exportable service that could benefit all people of the world. Counseling services that were developed to meet the unique needs of one society, however, do not necessarily meet the needs of a society to which they are exported (Saleh, 1989; Stewart, 1983). Some of the early programs built on concepts borrowed or transplanted from the United States have not been successfully applied elsewhere. It has become quite apparent that we need to build counseling services to meet the unique needs of each society. As Draguns (1981) noted, "psychotherapy defies isolation from its cultural context" (p. 6).

It took many years, many people, and many events to convince U.S. leaders of the profession that counseling is *not* a monocultural profession. It is only recently that there has been widespread recognition that within the United States there are many cultures to which our theories and techniques must be responsive if we are to deliver culturally sensitive services.

The development of counseling services in some countries seems to have been based on the assumption that there is a single, national culture within each country. New Zealand is a notable exception; counselors in New Zealand have recognized the need to deliver culturally sensitive services since counseling was introduced in New Zealand in the mid-1970s (Gary Hermansson, personal communication, July 15, 1993; Webster & Hermansson, 1983). Malaysia is another country where the importance of culturally sensitive services has been recognized since counseling was introduced there in 1965 (Abdul Halim Othman, personal communication, June 12, 1993).

Certain assumptions underlie programs that prepare counselors for multicultural counseling. Perhaps the first assumption is that the nation recognizes the cultural diversity within its borders. Another very important assumption is that the profession of counseling has been legitimized by the prime agents of socialization in the country.

It is also important to recognize that, in some countries of the world, professional psychological services have been accepted before counseling services. There is a very fine line between these two kinds of services, with the literature describing helping services programs not always being clear as to whether counseling as we know it is the service being offered. Australia is an example of a country (and continent) where psychological services preceded counseling services (Khan, 1983).

Counselors in many countries have recognized the need to deliver culturally sensitive services for more than a decade. In July, 1985, the International Round Table for the Advancement of Counselling (IRTAC) held a special consultation,

"Counselling and Ethnic Minorities," at the University of Utrecht, The Netherlands. The conference was organized by Dr. Nathan Deen of the University of Utrecht under the auspices of the Netherlands' Ministry of Education and Science, The Netherlands' National Commission for UNESCO, and the United Nations Centre for Social Development and Humanitarian Affairs International Youth Year. Two hundred fifty participants came from thirty countries on five continents to take part in sharing concepts on counseling ethnic minorities. Papers presented at this conference are included in two issues of the *International Journal for the Advancement of Counselling* (Deen, 1986a; Deen, 1986b).

Additional international recognition of the need for culturally sensitive services is evident in a current worldwide project of The Johns Hopkins University School of Hygiene and Public Health Center for Communication Programs. As part of a project operating in 65 developing countries worldwide, culture- and gender-specific counseling techniques are taught to health care workers in family planning, maternal child health, and AIDS prevention programs. The programs link interpersonal and mass-media communications. The use of culturally sensitive counseling is "at the heart of most of the family planning programs assisted by the Population Communication Services of The Johns Hopkins University" (Kim, 1993).

SOURCES OF INFORMATION FOR CHAPTER 5

To obtain an overview of how counseling as a profession is responding to cultural pluralism in countries outside the United States, I sent a one-page survey questionnaire to colleagues in 27 different countries. (The questionnaire is reprinted in Appendix C.) This short questionnaire requested responses to the following three questions.

1. What kind of culturally diverse populations are counselors called upon to serve in your country?
2. Has this need to serve culturally diverse populations always been part of counselor work in your country, or have recent changes in the populations of your country contributed to the need for cross-cultural/multicultural counseling help?
3. What type of training is now being offered (or is needed) for counselors in your country to deliver culturally sensitive counseling?

Respondents also were encouraged to include descriptive information on their programs. If no special training was provided, they were asked to respond stating so.

The countries selected and the names of the individuals contacted came from my personal mailing list; no claim is made that this list or these responses represent the entire world. I requested information from counseling professionals in these six areas of the world: Africa, Asia, Australia/New Zealand, Europe, the Middle East, and the U.S. border countries, Canada and Mexico. In some countries, requests were sent to more than one professional because I had previous contacts with the individuals there. Thirty-six responses were received from twenty-two countries.

Several who responded sent additional materials, such as information on counselor training programs, copies of manuscripts published in their professional journals, copies of their country's counseling journals, or references to articles published in the *International Journal for the Advancement of Counselling*. Space limitations preclude including all information from all respondents.

The information is organized by regions of the world in alphabetic order: Africa, Asia, Australia/New Zealand, Europe, the Middle East, and the U.S. border countries of North America. Within these regions, information is presented on a country-by-country basis in alphabetic order. All counselors and counselor educators identified as respondents have given permission to be cited and quoted, and, unless otherwise indicated, quoted material is from the questionnaire responses.

CULTURAL DIVERSITY AND COUNSELOR RESPONSES TO CULTURAL DIVERSITY IN AFRICA

Before examining counseling services in Africa, it is important to underscore the role that traditional belief systems play and to reiterate that helping services are legitimized by the prime agents of socialization in a region. Africa is a vast continent, and its people have a centuries-old tradition of using indigenous methods for solving both physical and psychological problems (Ampadu, 1992; Katz, 1982; Lee, Oh, & Mountcastle, 1992; Vontress, 1991; Yusuf, 1990). Many Africans still believe in the power of evil spirits and in the influence ancestors have on their daily lives. These people often turn to healers to intercede with these supernatural forces that they believe cause problems beyond their personal control. Ampadu (1992) also noted that many Africans go to traditional healers and incorporate these beliefs with Christianity.

Methods of healing have changed little from the way healing was practiced by Africans in the distant past (Katz, 1982; Vontress, 1991). In Africa, healing is considered a family or community responsibility (Katz, 1982; Vontress, 1991). When problems cannot be settled within the family, respected healers are consulted. Among the specialists who deliver healing services are herbalists, fetish men, mediums, healers, and sorcerers (Vontress, 1991). Some healing techniques employed are dream interpretation, dances, sacrifices, pharmacotherapy, shock therapy, exorcism, and music as a therapeutic accompaniment (Vontress, 1991). Spiritualism and religion are deeply imbedded in the healing process (Lee et al., 1992). Healing is often considered a divine gift, and healers participate in many years of training as apprentices or trainees to learn the vast body of knowledge needed to carry on the traditions.

During the colonial period, African educators were introduced to vocational guidance through missionaries (Okon, 1983). In the 1960s, 1970s, and early 1980s, some African scholars went abroad to study counseling; most went to either the United Kingdom or the United States. These scholars returned to their African homelands and introduced career counseling to school and university faculties. Unsettled political and economic conditions throughout much of Africa and resistance to accepting new paradigms for problem solving have presented enormous barriers to rapid expansion of counseling services (Yusuf, 1990).

I received responses on the status of multicultural counseling from Nigeria and South Africa. Readers interested in reports from U.S. consultants who have worked in integrating guidance, counseling, and counselor education in Botswana are referred to Navin (1989, 1992) and to Rollin and Witmer (1992).

Nigeria.[1]   Most counselor educators in Nigeria have been trained abroad in either the United Kingdom or the United States of America; on returning to Nigeria, they translate their counselor training to make it culturally appropriate for use with Nigerian clients.

In the master's degree programs at Nigerian universities, counselors are trained for work in the secondary schools. Their role and function there is outlined by guidelines of the 1985 Federal Republic of Nigeria National Policy on Education; it includes helping students with personal development, study skills, and educational and vocational guidance. Although there is a national policy for secondary-school guidance in Nigeria, there is considerable confusion and variance in the way counselors implement their roles because most secondary schools are under the control of the state governments, rather than the national government (Bojuwoye, 1992).

There are many ethnic groups in Nigeria, and students come from a wide variety of socioeconomic backgrounds. This means that Nigerian secondary-school counselors are called on to serve a very culturally diverse population. Bojuwoye states, "Thus in a society like ours the need to design counsellor education programmes to serve culturally diverse populations becomes more apparent. . . . We therefore make conscious effort to sensitise counsellor trainees to these differences." Okon believes that there is "definitely a pressing need to deliver culturally sensitive counseling to meet individual's mental health needs in various ethnic groups." Okon considers the current counselor training inadequate because "it does not provide the counselors in training with the appropriate skills to counsel culturally different clients."

In other publications, Bojuwoye (1992) and Okon (1980, 1983) provide more information on the history and development of guidance and counseling services in Nigeria. Gothard and Bojuwoye (1992) present a comparison of the counselor

---

[1] From Dr. Olaniyi Bojuwoye, Head of the Department of Guidance and Counselling, University of Ilorin, personal communication, June 7, 1993; and from Dr. Samuel E. Okon, Counselor Educator, Department of Education, Ahmadu Bello University, Zaria, personal communication, June 21, 1993.

education program at the University of Reading, United Kingdom, and the University of Ilorin, Nigeria.

Citing research on the impact of urbanism on adolescents in the Yoruba cities of western Nigeria, Makinde (1987) called for counselors to acquire a broad background of information on these young people. This informational background would include: awareness of the physical circumstances in which the adolescent lives, knowledge of the family constellation, parents' attitudes toward the goals and aspirations of the youth, and the socioeconomic level of the family before they moved to the city. The culture-specific counselor training model for use with African-Igbo people referred to in Chapter 3 (Nwachuku & Ivey, 1991) noted the key behaviors, attitudes, and values of this Nigerian tribe.

South Africa.[2]   Race, religion, and class contribute to the cultural diversity of South African populations. Salie notes that recent political changes in South Africa have "necessitated the development of multicultural counselling on a wider scale." At present, there are very few courses being offered to help counselors deliver culturally sensitive counseling, but Salie states that "This is an emerging need and would most certainly require the development of relevant training courses in the future."

For information on the effects of apartheid on the mental health of South Africa's children and the need to train counselors to meet this challenge, see Hickson and Kreigler (1991). Livingstone (1989) also discusses challenges that apartheid presented to counseling in South Africa. It will be important to see how counseling there changes now that a democratically elected government is in power in South Africa.

CULTURAL DIVERSITY AND COUNSELOR RESPONSES TO CULTURAL DIVERSITY IN ASIA

India.[3]   Unnithan reports that India is "a vast country with great cultural diversity and a very heterogeneous society." All major religions are represented; there is a complicated caste system and an "energizing" class system. Students who come from the rural areas and from underprivileged groups, including women, require special attention.

The cultural diversity of the country has been intensified by the physical as well as the social mobility of the population. Counseling services are offered on a very limited basis. Preservice training is part of the M.A. in Psychology and in some B.Ed. courses. A few universities offer an M.A. in Counseling, and there is some

---

[2] From Dr. Tahir Salie, Director, Careers Research and Information Center, Athlone, Cape Town, personal communication, January 20, 1994.

[3] From Gerda Unnithan, Director of the Students Advisory Bureau at the University of Rajasthan, Jaipur, personal communication, June 10, 1993.

in-service training in the school systems in metropolitan cities, but employment is limited for counselors. Unnithan states, "University courses mainly depend on foreign thinkers/theories. Limited work has been done on Indian counseling theories. The need for counseling, and for culturally sensitive counseling, is very great—it is stupendous!" Readers interested in more information on education and the counseling services in the young democracy of India are referred to Unnithan (1986).

Malaysia.[4]   Othman reports that

> Malaysian counselors have always been called upon to serve clients from a variety of ethnic, religious and socio-economic backgrounds. Sensitivity to these diverse populations is a great asset for counselors and other helping professionals.
>
> Counseling is a relatively recent service in this country. No counselors existed in Malaysia prior to 1965. The multiethnic nature of our population will definitely require counselors with a multi-cultural/cross-cultural focus.

At the Counselor Education Program at University Kebangsaan, students take a course on cross-cultural psychology. During their practicum, students are encouraged to gain experiences with a diverse group of clients. Othman adds, "Sensitivity training through the pre-practicum retreat encourages students to look at themselves in the multi-cultural context."

Philippines.[5]   There is much cultural diversity in the population of the Philippines; Filipinos themselves are of mixed ancestry. Other cultural diversity comes from the Singaporeans, Malaysians, Thais, Japanese, Chinese, Europeans, North/South Americans, Indians, and Africans living on the many islands of the Philippines. In some areas of the Philippines, cultural communities still exist. Migrants and evacuees from war and natural disasters have increased cultural diversity.

The great mobility of people and ASEANS (people from countries in the Association of Southeast Asian Nations) coming to study in the universities in the Philippines have resulted in increased cultural diversity on university campuses. Recent changes call for multicultural counseling services and training. Special readings in multicultural counseling, symposia, forums, workshops, and special training in internship are now part of counselor training. Graduate courses leading to master's and doctoral degrees with internship programs in school, community, hospital, and industrial settings are offered at The University of the Philippines, DeLaSalle University, Ateneo de Manila University, and Silliman University.

---

[4] From Dr. Abdul Halim Othman, Department of Psychology, University Kebangsaan Malaysia, personal communication, June 12, 1993.

[5] From Dr. Vicentita H. Cervera, Philippine Council of Non-Government Organizations Against Drug and Substance Abuse, Manila, personal communications, February 2 and June 13, 1993; and Dr. Lily Rosqueta-Rosales, Professor of Educational Psychology and Counselor Education and Dean, College of Education, University of the Philippines, Quezon City, personal communication, July 8, 1993.

Readers may be interested in Rosqueta-Rosales' 1989 book, *Counseling in Perspective—Theory, Process and Skills.*

From experiences in dealing with victims of the many natural disasters that have struck the Philippines in recent years, Cervera recommends training in both multicultural counseling and in crisis intervention. She also sees a need for counselors to learn about indigenous counseling theories and practices for effective work with the aboriginal people of the Philippines.

Taiwan.[6]   There are at least nine tribes of aborigines spread throughout Taiwan. However, most aboriginal people live in the mountainous areas of this island country. The Ami and the Atayal, the largest tribes, reside in eastern Taiwan around Hualien and Taitong. Twenty-two percent of the total population of 350,000 of Hualien are aborigines.

The aboriginal people of Taiwan have gone through centuries of turmoil created by invasions of the Dutch, Japanese, and Han Chinese. Jiang describes the experiences of the aboriginals in Taiwan: "As they have gradually been left behind the main stream of contemporary Taiwan society, aborigines turn to alcohol as one of the coping mechanisms for their miseries and animosities. The number one cause of death in Taiwan aborigines is by accident, sixty percent of which is alcohol-related." Another recent problem is that of child prostitution among the aboriginal people.

Early efforts to help the aboriginal people of Taiwan were made by the Christian Church with educational, occupational, training, and placement programs. Currently, a number of private social welfare associations are working to help the aborginal people, and counseling services are a part of these helping efforts. World Vision of Taiwan, Goodshaper Association, the Catholic Church, and the Tzu Chi Foundation held a national symposium focusing on problems of health and alcoholism among aborigines. The work of these organizations includes career counseling, occupational training and placement, and alcoholism research.

Jiang reports, "Although we have already realized the cultural differences between the aborigines and the mainstream society in Taiwan, the professional training in cross-cultural counseling is still lacking."

Thailand.[7]   In southern Thailand, the Chinese and the Muslims represent the culturally diverse populations served by counselors. The way of life and the religious beliefs of the Muslims, who make up 80% of the population in the 5 southern provinces of Thailand, are very different from the Thais. Language is often a barrier. Sangsawang notes that there is no special training for Thai

---

[6] From Sue Jiang, Counselor, Buddhist TZU-CHI General Hospital, Hualien, personal communication, July 19, 1993.

[7] From Pramot Khapklomsong, counselor at Kohtgew Pittayasan School, Songkhla, personal communication, July 28, 1993; Saree Pratomthong, counselor at Hatyaiwittayalai School, Hatyai, personal communication, June 20, 1993; and Pol Sangsawang, Prince of Songkhla University, Pattani Campus, Pattani, personal communication, August 20, 1993.

counselors to work with the large Muslim population of the southern provinces of Thailand. Khapklomsong states that the special training provided for counselors to deal with cultural diversity is limited to "the good citizenship training and moral counseling by Thai Buddhist monks."

For a description of the history of guidance and counseling in Thailand and challenges faced in expanding these services, see Pratomthong and Baker (1983). In their article describing barriers to the development of counseling in Thailand, Pratomthong and Baker (1983) emphasize that "The specific counseling approach in any culture must harmonize with the broader cultural ethos" (p. 469). In another article, Tainsri and Axelson (1990) report on group sensitivity training in a Thai industrial setting.

CULTURAL DIVERSITY AND COUNSELOR RESPONSES TO CULTURAL DIVERSITY IN AUSTRALIA AND NEW ZEALAND

Australia.[8]   To preface, Australia is unique in that it is a country as well as an island continent. Even though Australia is a large country, the population base is now very urban, with much of the population located in the Southern and Southeastern cities of Australia. Responses were received from three of the states of South and Southeast Australia and are reported by state.

There is a wide variety of culturally diverse populations in Australia. Simpson, from South Australia, lists "migrants from many countries, recent arrivals and long-standing residents, overseas students, refugees, and aboriginal people." Le Vine, from Victoria, lists "first and second generation: Italian, Greek, Turkish, Indonesian, Malaysian; and survivors of torture from El Salvador, Latin America, and Iran."

Millard, from New South Wales, notes that "A major group of clients served by Counsellors in educational settings, such as Universities, Technical and Further Education (TAFE), and private colleges are visiting Private Overseas Students who attend fee-paying programs, including Learning English and mainstream courses." Large numbers of students come from Asia, especially from Hong Kong and Pakistan. TAFE also serves many other culturally diverse populations from dozens of non-English speaking backgrounds that vary in age from 16 to 70. "Predominant groups, for which TAFE NSW has specifically designated Bi-lingual Counsellors are, Chinese, Vietnamese, Spanish Speaking, Arabic, and Greek students" according to Millard, who also states, "Another [relatively small] cultural group is composed of Aboriginal students."

---

[8] From Dr. Peg Le Vine, Counselor Educator, LaTrobe University, Counselling Psychology Program, Bundoora, Victoria, personal communication, June 17, 1993; Stuart Millard, Senior Counsellor at the Northern Sydney Institute, Hornsby College of Technical and Further Education, New South Wales, personal communication, June 23, 1993; and Karen Simpson, Counselor, Flinders University of South Australia, Adelaide, personal communication, June 30, 1993.

In response to the question on the recency of recognition of the need for multicultural counseling, Simpson (South Australia) states that "Post W. W. II changes have significantly increased the need." Le Vine (Victoria) notes that serving culturally diverse populations has always been a part of counselor work in Australia. Millard (New South Wales) states:

> NSW TAFE recognised the need for multicultural counselling by appointing specifically designated Bi-lingual Counsellors in 1986. These Counsellors catered for Spanish, Italian, Chinese, Greek, Vietnamese and Arabic speaking prospective and enrolled students. In the last few years we have not seen the need for designated Greek or Italian Bi-lingual Counsellors, due to population changes in this country. In recent years, Centres for English training of fee-paying private overseas students have required Counselling staff to serve this population. Similarly, in recent years, special counsellors have focused on providing Counselling for Aboriginal students.

There were varied responses to the question on the type of training now being offered (or needed) for counselors to deliver culturally sensitive services. Simpson (South Australia) stated that her impression is "that there are brief sessions in some professional courses (e.g., social work) but that more is needed . . . [and that] training is somewhat ad hoc." Millard noted that his inquiries had not led to "formal academic subjects in culturally sensitive counselling in NSW Universities. However some faculties include some content within other subjects [for example, Social Work at Sydney University]." Much of the training in New South Wales comes from networking with workers and staff in other organizations who have detailed knowledge from living and working in a specific culture. In New South Wales, workshops on relevant multicultural issues are offered from time to time.

Le Vine (South Australia) sent information on the multicultural training within the counselor education program in which she teaches at LaTrobe University. Le Vine listed two classes in her graduate program: a "master level class in Counselling entitled: Multicultural Perspectives in Counselling and Mental Health Practices . . . [and a] master level class in Counselling entitled: Comprehensive Adult, Child and Family Assessment." The first class listed extends over two semesters and covers a broad spectrum of topics related to the impact of culture on world views and mental health practices. The second class, Comprehensive Adult, Child and Family Assessment, is also a weekly 3-hour seminar that covers two semesters and emphasizes "the complex nature of assessment, accounting for: gender, religion, age, sexual orientation, socio-economic status, ethnicity and disability." Students learn to "critically assess the appropriateness of counselling theories and practices" as viable choices to be accepted or rejected in treating a specific problem or population. Le Vine's adaptation of Japanese Morita psychotherapy for use across cultures (Le Vine, 1991, 1993) was discussed in Chapter 3.

Readers interested in the history of counseling and guidance in Australia are referred to Khan (1983). McWhirter (1988) wrote of his experiences as a Fulbright scholar in Australia, including differences between the cultural values and norms of Australia and those of the United States, and discussed ethnic minority issues and counseling psychology in Australia.

New Zealand.[9]   The culturally diverse populations that counselors are called on to serve in New Zealand are Pakeha, Maori, Pacific Islanders, Polynesians, Chinese, Vietnamese, and some Africans. The indigenous people are the Maori, who make up about 10% of the population. The majority population is composed of the Pakeha, the Maori name for White Europeans who formally settled in New Zealand in 1840. In the last 30 years, migration from other Pacific islands and Polynesian countries has increased. The strong migration of Chinese to New Zealand began when gold was discovered in the 1800s. More recently, refugees from Vietnam and some African countries have settled in New Zealand. Another important aspect of cultural diversity noted by Hermansson is the large migration of Maori and Pacific Island people to the urban areas, so counselors in the cities deal with much cultural diversity among their counselees.

As noted earlier in this chapter, in New Zealand, cultural diversity was recognized from the time counselor training was introduced in the 1970s. Initially, counselors in training were largely from the Pakeha population, so there was a special need for cross-cultural training. Over the years, the numbers of Maori and Polynesian counselor trainees has steadily increased. Shorter training programs for cultural diversity have been held in tertiary institutions. There has also been some push for Maori and Polynesian counselor training programs for those communities.

At first, multicultural training concentrated mainly on identifying differences in communication skills. Recently, there have been major efforts to understand the differing world views of people of different cultural heritages. Much emphasis is now on searching for distinctive Maori and Pacific Island counseling styles.

University courses have responded to the needs for multicultural counselor training in a variety of ways. Cultural consultants have frequently been asked to talk about cultural differences in perspectives. A recent conference of the New Zealand Counseling and Guidance Association was held at a Maori Marae (a traditional meeting center) where the keynote speaker was Dr. Mason Durie, a well-known member of the Rangitane and Raukawa Maori tribes and a leading New Zealand psychiatrist. His speech focused on the inappropriateness of most Western counseling theories for Maori people and described three dimensions of Maori culture that are relevant to counseling: *whanaungatanga*, the person's relationship to his or her family; *whakamanawa*, encouragement, showing compassion, and appropriate use of touch; and *mauri*, the individual's self-esteem and ability to experience things in spiritual terms (Durie & Hermansson, 1990).

Brief courses at the Maori Marae have helped sensitize people to Maori cultural values and lifestyle. Everts (1988) describes the value of the 3-day, Marae-based Hui (important cultural events) as a part of training Pakeha counselors for

---

[9] From Dr. Gary Hermansson, Senior Lecturer in Education, Guidance Counselling Programmes, Massey University, Palmerston North, personal communication, July 15, 1993.

cross-cultural interaction. Many attempts have been made to put together bicultural programs that respect both perspectives. In reference to bicultural counseling programs, however, Hermansson states that "A true bicultural (Pakeha/Maori) foundation is unlikely. This would require equity in terms of staffing and resources for minority group members and dual philosophy." He also points out the challenges in maintaining a dual focus and balance.

The Family Centre for counseling in Wellington has gained worldwide fame for its culturally sensitive "Just Therapy" approach, which focuses on cultural differences in gender, socioeconomic conditions, and ethnicity. Waldegrave and Tapping (1990) describe and discuss the social justice and family therapy at that facility.

Readers interested in more details on the history and development of guidance and counseling in New Zealand are referred to Webster and Hermansson (1983). Manthei (1993) describes recent developments and directions in counseling in New Zealand. For more information on cross-cultural counseling in New Zealand, see Ross (1985).

CULTURAL DIVERSITY AND COUNSELOR RESPONSES TO CULTURAL DIVERSITY IN EUROPE

Finland.[10]   Tapaninen notes, "In terms of culture, Finland is a very homogenous country in spite of two official languages, Finnish and Swedish. During the last two decades some minor groups of people have immigrated to Finland from Chile, Vietnam, Somalia, Ethiopia, Russia and Estonia." Over many years "a considerable number of West European and North American people have moved to Finland, mostly for family reasons."

Most immigrants have come in groups, and public authorities have organized their adaptation and transition to life in Finland. "The most urgent topics of counseling and information have been: manners and conditions of living, accommodation and housing, language training, and employment opportunities." Special bilingual counselors with cultural expertise work with the new immigrants at receiving stations. Immigrants from Europe and those who speak English usually use the services of the Ministry of Labour counselors, with the assistance of an interpreter if needed.

Employment and vocational counselors are trained in their basic course to work with foreign people. In the major employment offices, an officer with special training works with foreigners. Tapaninen notes, however, that "we should be better prepared for immigration from other countries." He states that counselors' cross-cultural training is continuously expanded and that they have cooperated closely with Swedish authorities who have more experience with immigration.

---

[10] From Dr. Antti Tapaninen, Chief Inspector, Ministry of Labour, Helsinki, personal communication, June 24, 1993.

France.[11]   France has a very culturally diverse population as a result of immigrant populations from Tunisia, Morocco, Algeria, China, Portugal, Sri Lanka, Zaire, and Turkey. Guichard states, "The need to serve culturally diverse populations has been part of the work of the counselor for many years." Young immigrants coming to the schools have at least one interview with a counselor to help them find where they best fit in the school system.

Continuing education training sessions lasting three to five days are held for counselors working with culturally diverse people. A summer university training program for counselors working with immigrant youth was held from August 30 to September 4, 1993, at Montpellier.

The cultural diversity of France was increased in the 1970s and 1980s when refugees from Southeast Asia fled to France and were granted asylum there. Ninety percent of these refugees were Vietnamese. Counselors were called on to help these refugees through their stages of grief and loss and in adapting to a new culture (Do, 1991).

Germany.[12]   Cultural diversity in Germany is largely a result of the foreigners who have migrated to Germany. The numbers and distribution of foreign people and different cultures vary considerably in the 16 *laender* (states) of Germany.

Martin calls attention to the fact that counselor training in university departments of counseling does not exist in Germany. However, there are a variety of advising and counseling services, such as school psychological services, family and youth counseling services, counseling in labor offices, and counseling for addictions. Most of the people working in these services have been trained as psychologists with basic training in classical psychology. Some have additional training in school psychology and applied psychology.

A second group of people doing counseling are social workers trained in courses concentrating on work with migrants and foreigners at institutions of higher education below the university level preparation. Training programs of this type are located at Munich, Frankfurt/M, Cologne, and Eichstatt/Bavaria.

There is a small group of academics with university training in educational psychology who work as counselors. Their diploma courses may include study of cultures, languages, educational systems, and needs and problems of the culturally different people who live and work in Germany. Some of these courses include a limited amount of guidance and counseling theory and practice. Martin indicates that there is a vast amount of literature published on these topics. However, the ratio of counselors to total population (1 to 10,000 to 50,000 people) is so small that Martin states, "I can hardly say that anybody in this country can really enjoy counselling services, neither the German nor the 'culturally different population.'"

---

[11] From Professor Dr. Jean Guichard, INETOP, University of Paris, the Sorbonne, personal communication, June 30, 1993.

[12] From Professor Dr. Kurt Heller, Director, Institute of Educational Psychology, University of Munich, personal communication, June 30, 1993; and Studien Professor Dr. Lothar R. Martin, Institute of Educational Science, University of Bonn, personal communication, June 28, 1993.

Martin has been operating 2-year, part-time, teacher-counselor courses in Northrhine-Westphalia since 1974 in connection with the NW Institute of Further Education (Martin & Wehrly, 1979). Martin notes, "Teachers who prepare for the certificate are encouraged to specialize on problem areas that are relevant in their situations." As a result, a number of teachers in Martin's courses choose to emphasize counseling with culturally different populations. The students choose from the vast literature on education of migrants and foreigners and discuss the application of general counseling theories and methods to specific situations. "International literature on 'multicultural counseling' is always welcome." On occasion, Martin has also offered courses with similar themes at the University of Bonn Institute of Educational Science.

Heller's most recent work is as director of an international research project on giftedness and talent. The project includes recommendations for counseling programs for gifted youth. Heller's model for counseling the gifted (1992) recognizes the impact of cultural factors from the social environment, especially in diagnosing gifted young people. Heller lists talented immigrants as one of several frequently overlooked or underestimated gifted groups.

For readers interested in counseling psychology in Germany, Nugent (1988) describes his experiences as a Fulbright counseling psychologist in West Germany before the fall of the Berlin Wall.

Greece.[13]   Zanni-Teliopoulos reports that "There is a very small number of counselors in Greece, and they are not serving culturally diverse populations." However, counselors in Greece recognize the need to be culturally sensitive because (1) they are part of the unified European market (EEC), and (2) because there are a great number of migrants of Greek origin returning to Greece from the former Soviet Union and from Albania who need help. At present, no special culturally sensitive training for counselors is offered.

Ireland.[14]   Chamberlain reports that the Republic of Ireland is "relatively free of multicultural ethnic populations. Our cultural differences have more to do with social class and the high level of unemployment (officially 20%, really 28%) which has given rise to a new underclass!" He notes also that a new development is "the adjustment Irish counsellors have to make to the new scenario of a Single Europe."

Chamberlain is "involved with the European Community (EC) programme PETRA 2, Action 3, which is attempting to integrate the Guidance practices of the EC Member States." Chamberlain recognizes that problems that will arise from educational and occupational mobility across the EC member states will inevitably "derive mainly from cultural differences."

---

[13] From Kassandra Zanni-Teliopoulos, Psychologist and Counselor of Vocational Guidance, Institute of Educational and Vocational Guidance, Athens, personal communication, July 15, 1993.

[14] From Dr. James Chamberlain, Senior Lecturer, University College Dublin, Department of Psychology, Guidance and Counselling Unit, personal communication, June 9, 1993.

Lithuania.[15]   According to Valickas, Lithuanian counselors "are called upon to serve patients of diverse ethnic and religious backgrounds. The need to serve culturally diverse populations has never been a sharp one." He also notes that "Under the Communist rule, to treat people in a differentiated way on ethnic or religious grounds was an ideological mistake. Recent changes did bring this issue to the surface."

Minority group, refugee, and rootlessness issues are studied in the Social Psychology course. At present, there is no special training for multicultural counseling, but the need for this special training is acknowledged.

The Netherlands.[16]   The University of Utrecht began preparing school counselors in 1975 under the leadership of Dr. Nathan Deen. Since that time, the population of the Netherlands has continued to become more culturally diverse. The University of Utrecht Department of Counselling Studies gives much consideration to preparing counselors and counselor-teachers to work with students from many cultural backgrounds. Research by Peter DeWeerdt led to the training of counselors and teachers to handle paraprofessionals working with Moroccan and Turkish students. Erika Stern has given leadership to help counselors and other caregivers become aware of and deal with the hidden prejudices and assumptions individuals carry about people of other races and cultures. The department also calls on professionals from other fields, such as sociology, to help in career planning with migrant students.

Spain.[17]   Culturally diverse populations served by Spanish counselors are immigrants from North Africa, working-class immigrants from the South of Spain, and Gypsies. The need to work with culturally diverse clients has increased recently in response to immigration from North African countries and Eastern Europe.

Some recognition of the need for cultural sensitivity in counseling is included in a master's level course as well as in a doctoral level course. At present, no special training is given for cross-cultural counseling.

United Kingdom.[18]   Both Lago and Thorne note that students from throughout the world are now enrolled in higher education in the United Kingdom. There is much other cultural diversity in the United Kingdom with people of Afro-Caribbean (both African and West Indian), Asian (from the Indian subcontinent,

---

[15] From Dr. Gintautas Valickas, Department of Psychology, Vilnius University, personal communication, May 17, 1993.

[16] From the publication, *The Future Needs School Counselling*, Utrecht University Department of Counselling Studies, 1992.

[17] From Dr. Maria Luisa Rodriguez Moreno, Faculty of Education, University of Barcelona, personal communication, June 5, 1993.

[18] From Colin Lago, Head of Counselling Services, The University of Sheffield Counselling Service, Sheffield, personal communication, July 15, 1993; and Dr. Brian Thorne, Director of Student Counselling, University of East Anglia, Norwich, personal communication, June, 22, 1993.

Kenya/Pakistan), European and Eastern European, and Chinese heritages who now make the United Kingdom their home.

Since many of the cultural groups mentioned have had long residency in the United Kingdom, the need to serve culturally diverse populations has existed since counseling began there in the 1960s. Lago notes, however, that the existence of a culturally diverse population "does not necessarily mean they have been served well or skillfully (owing to lack of specific training/sensitivity to issues, etc.)." Thorne states, "There is an ever-increasing need for cross-cultural/multicultural counselling help as ethnic minority groups avail themselves more heavily of the counselling services available."

According to Thorne, the need for multicultural counseling is recognized in all current counselor training in the United Kingdom. However, Lago reports that only one or two specific part-time courses extending over one or two years offer this training. Lago says, "Many courses now try to raise the issues within their overall programmes but such situations may only comprise two or three days' work within a general counselling programme." Recognition of the need for cross-cultural and multicultural counseling help has been stimulated by the work of the Race Awareness in Counsellor Education (RACE) Committee.

Lago explains the growing interest in multicultural counseling thus:

> The RACE Committee has been made a Division of the British Association for Counselling, thus enabling many more persons to become involved. Several major conferences have taken place over the years run by national professional bodies and these have raised a national concern as has the cumulative work of the RACE Division mentioned above. There are, increasingly, articles being written on the subject and many counseling students pursue this subject for their course dissertation.

Lago and his associates have prepared training tapes and trainer's manuals for use in cross-cultural and cross-racial counseling and are currently developing a booklet "to explore the needs of supervisors of counsellors in this field of trans-cultural counselling."

CULTURAL DIVERSITY AND COUNSELOR RESPONSES TO CULTURAL DIVERSITY IN THE MIDDLE EAST

Israel.[19]   Israelashvili reports that "Israel is a nation of immigrants (Jewish) from all over the world. During the last years immigrants from U.S.S.R. and Ethiopia are of central importance for the school counselors. In addition, the living together of the Jew and Muslims is a central topic in the Israeli society."

---

[19] From Dr. Moshe Israelashvili, Director, School of Education Counseling Program, Tel-Aviv University, personal communication, June 28, 1993.

School counselors in Israel have always been aware of the need to serve a culturally diverse population. Israelashvili would like updated information about immigrants from Russia and from Ethiopia to be made available to counselors. He also notes that although there is a growing body of knowledge about the Arabic population within Israel, this knowledge is not offered to counseling students because of budget limitations.

Halpern (1985) discusses the challenges of transporting models of training family therapists from other countries to Israel. Because family therapy is systems based, she sees the need to develop indigenous models for training family therapists. And in another vein, Shechtman (1993) describes the benefits of small-group therapy in an Israeli elementary school.

United Arab Emirates [U.A.E.] and other Arab Countries.[20]   Soliman reports that "There are several culturally diverse populations in the U.A.E. as well as in other Arab countries. . . . Whether counselors are called upon to help these people is not easy to know" because counselors and counseling are not fully understood by the lay public in the Arab countries. "Culturally diverse groups may consult psychiatrists or physicians."

There are not many counselor training programs in the Arab countries. "The Universities of Jordan, Kuwait, Qater, Riyyadh (Saudi Arabia), and Ain Shams (Egypt) offer either a diploma or M.A. degrees in counseling," according to Soliman. He is not sure how aware the faculty in these programs are of the need to train for cultural sensitivity in counseling: "Counseling educators who have degrees in counseling and those who are graduates of American universities are few."

Soliman sees two attitudes prevalent in his culture that work against being sensitive to cultural diversity: the tendency to evaluate and judge others' behavior in an authoritarian way and the tendency to see the negative rather than the positive. He believes these attitudes will need to change before sensitivity to cultural diversity can be attained.

Readers interested in counseling in the Arab countries are referred to Soliman (1981, 1984, 1986, 1987, 1991, 1993, 1994).

CULTURAL DIVERSITY AND COUNSELOR RESPONSES TO CULTURAL DIVERSITY IN THE U.S. BORDER COUNTRIES OF NORTH AMERICA

Canada.[21]   "Canada was colonized and settled by both the French and the British, and politically it is a democratic country based on British tradition"

---

[20] From Dr. Abdalla M. Soliman, Professor and Chair, Department of Psychology, College of Education, United Arab Emirate University, Al Ain (Dr. Soliman has also taught at Kuwait University in Kuwait and at Cairo and Ain Shams universities in Egypt), personal communication, July 2, 1993, and April 26, 1994.

[21] From Dr. William Borgen, Head, Department of Counselling Psychology, and President of the Canadian Guidance and Counselling Association, University of British Columbia, Vancouver, personal

(Robertson & Paterson, 1983, p. 490). Ishiyama notes that "Canada, in general, has been highly multicultural since the 19th century." The pressure to assimilate into one national culture (as existed in the United States for a time) has never been a goal for Canadians.

Canadians of British and French extraction are still numerically the dominant cultural groups in their bilingual nation. The 1991 census report for Canada shows that Canadians of British heritage make up 20.8% and Canadians of French heritage make up 22.8% of the "In Household Census" (personal communication, Statistics Canada, May 8, 1993).

Because of a liberal immigration policy and promotion of multiculturalism, there is now considerable ethnic and cultural diversity in Canada. This diversity varies considerably among the ten provinces and two northern territories. Immigrants and refugees have come from many parts of the world, for the most part settling in the larger cities. Dumont states that

> Montreal has the same diversity of populations that other North American cities have . . . [with] large Portuguese, Hispanic, Italian, Greek, English, Irish, Jewish, Haitian, Chinese, and Caribbean populations (among others) here that speak either English or French, sometimes both, often enough in addition to a different first (mother) language. There is of course the largest ethnic group, that represents the dominant culture of Quebec, the French Canadians.

Dumont also explains that the various ethnic groups in Quebec have "a tendency to seek professional and technical services from members of their own groups."

Ishiyama, reporting from Vancouver, lists these culturally diverse populations that counselors are called upon to serve: "Chinese (from Peoples Republic of China and Hong Kong), Native Indians ('First Nations People'), Japanese, Koreans, Europeans, Vietnamese, Cambodians, South Americans (Spanish-speaking, especially from Chile)." Ishiyama states that, "Especially in British Columbia, there has been a steady increase in the number of Chinese (Hong Kong) immigrants as well as Southeast Asian refugees." Westwood, also from Vancouver, believes that "with the high levels of immigration and refugee settlement, Canada has an additional challenge and that is to teach counsellors components of adaptation to new cultures, needs of newcomers and what are the critical skills for successful adaptation in respect of career and family."

communication, August 4, 1993; Dr. Frank Dumont, McGill University, Department of Educational and Counselling Psychology, Montreal, personal communication, June 15, 1993; Dr. William Hague, Department of Educational Psychology, University of Alberta, Edmonton, personal communication, August 30, 1993; Dr. Ishu Ishiyama, University of British Columbia, Department of Counselling Psychology, Vancouver, personal communication, June 10, 1993; Dr. Walt Pawlovich, Department of Educational Psychology, University of Saskatchewan, Saskatoon, personal communication, August 12, 1993; Dr. Sharon Robertson, Head, Department of Educational Psychology, University of Calgary, and immediate past-president of the Canadian Guidance and Counselling Association, personal communication, August 9, 1993; and Dr. Marvin Westwood, University of British Columbia, Department of Counselling Psychology, Vancouver, personal communication, August 13, 1992.

Robertson, reporting from Calgary, states that "Canadian counsellors are called upon to serve people from various cultural backgrounds: French, English, Scottish, Irish, German, Italian, Slovac, Ukrainian, Spanish, Chinese, Japanese, Vietnamese, East Indian, Aboriginal, Arabic, Jewish." Robertson notes that "over the past years the immigration patterns have changed with an increased proportion of immigrants coming from South East Asia and South America and much lower proportion coming from Europe. There has been increasing recognition of the need to work with Canadian aboriginal peoples."

The University of British Columbia (UBC) Department of Counselling Psychology offers counselor training at the master's level and the doctoral level and offers the Diploma in Guidance Studies. The M.A. and M.Ed. programs in Community Counseling, School Counseling, and Student Personnel Services in Higher Education programs are accredited by CACREP. Within both the community and agency specialty and the school counseling specialty, intercultural counseling is one of the emphases. Borgen stresses that the UBC Counselling Psychology Program works to attain a balance between infusing intercultural counseling into all courses and offering intercultural counseling as an area of emphasis. Westwood states that there is now a required module for "multicultural counselling" in the UBC program. The multicultural module is six weeks long and meets three hours each week. Three courses in particular have an intercultural emphasis: Cross-Cultural Counselling, Supervised Training in Counselling (Counselling Clinic), and the final Practicum. Two faculty members, Ishu Ishiyama and Marvin Westwood, rotate teaching the Cross-Cultural Counseling class. Westwood believes that one of the biggest challenges to be faced is that of developing "the whole faculty in the direction of greater awareness of the value of infusing a multicultural perspective to our program, just as we have been trying to do in the area of gender."

Ishiyama's model of self-validation (Ishiyama & Westwood, 1992) is Ishiyama's

> principal framework for understanding ethnic clients' (including re-entering members of the mainstream culture) cross-cultural or multicultural experience and transition-adjustment process. The training has the following areas of coverage: (a) conceptual understanding of cross-cultural communication and helping processes and research/theory literature; (b) experiential learning; (c) role-play training; (d) communication analysis; (e) case study of an ethnic person or client; (f) supervised clinical training; and (g) research.

As noted in Chapter 3, Ishiyama has specialized in using Morita therapy with Canadian clients (Ishiyama, 1987, 1990).

Westwood's approach includes emphasis on "the 'culture centered' counsellor as referred to by Pedersen and Ivey (1994). . . . To do this one must validate the 'cultural self' to ensure self-confidence and self-respect at the same time we must provide the 'knowledge, awareness and skills' to be successful in the larger society. Universals are stressed at the same time culture specific aspects can't be forgotten." Westwood has a strong background in group work and believes that all people involved in multicultural training can benefit from training in group facilitation.

Westwood stresses the value of the small group for intercultural training because it permits: "(a) exploration of perceptions, ideas, experiences (AWARENESS), (b) analysis of the content of the course (KNOWLEDGE), and (c) development and the practice of application to counselling situations (SKILLS)." Westwood has also specialized in work with and research of international students' adjustment, the impact of peer counseling on this adjustment (Westwood, 1988; Westwood & Barker, 1990), and the process of cross-cultural reentry for returning international students (Greenwood & Westwood, 1992; Westwood, 1986).

The UBC Supervised Training in Counselling (Counselling Clinic) experience is unique in that every week teams of five students and a professor spend a full day at departmental counseling sites in the Vancouver area. At these sites, students work with clients under the direct supervision of their professor. Each term, one team is designated the Intercultural Team. In addition to offering on-site, supervised, cross-cultural counseling training, the Counselling Clinic has served as a way to encourage people from different ethnic groups to apply for training in the UBC program.

The third course in intercultural counseling (as well as in all counseling emphases at UBC) is the final Practicum. In this experiential course, students work largely with a multicultural clientele. UBC Counselling Psychology department members also deal with advocacy issues with the Canadian Native First Nation population.

Hague reports that students at the University of Alberta get special training for cross-cultural counseling in various ways. Segments of courses in the department include cross-cultural content, and students participate in supervised cross-cultural counseling at the departmental counseling clinic and during their field practicum. Hague also states, "Some of our counseling students work in collaboration with Dr. David Baine in our Special Education Area who has a world reputation in cross-cultural education."

Robertson, at the University of Calgary, describes special training at her university and interest in training for cross-cultural counseling among Canadian colleagues from her two years as President of the Canadian Guidance and Counselling Association (CGCA).

> Our own university offers one half course on Intercultural and Gender issues in Counseling as part of our Master's program. We also offer short in-services courses from time to time. The Canadian Guidance and Counselling Association has a continuing education program, and various short courses in this area are recognized by them. The need to heighten awareness of issues in intercultural counselling is finding its way into CGCA conference programs and CGCA publications. The need for training in cross-cultural counselling among counsellors and counsellor educators and supervisors in this country is high.

Pawlovich, Program Chair for the 1993 CGCA meetings at Saskatoon, sent information on the theme of Day 3, Aboriginal Issues, at the national meetings. The day focused on social issues from a First Nations perspective with Canadian aboriginal speakers and session leaders. First Nation Elders opened the day with a prayer. The keynote speaker was Maria Campbell, a community worker with women and children in crisis and with the aboriginal community for 25 years. Other members of the Saskatoon Aboriginal Community led 22 workshops on various topics related to Aboriginal issues. The day concluded with all participants taking part in the Aboriginal Round Dance. The lead article in the July/August, 1993, issue of COGNICA, the newsletter of the CGCA, was a paper presented at the 1993 CGCA meetings, "Healing from a Native Perspective" by Louise Halfe.

Mexico.[22]   In Mexico, there are 56 ethnic groups with their own cultures and languages (from telephone consultation with the National Indian Institute, 15 June, 1993). There are also many foreign minorities in Mexico, and socioeconomic differences make for different cultures as well. Recent internal, external, and international migrations have increased the cultural diversity. Blanco-Beledo notes that "The multicultural phenomenon has always been a reality in Mexico," but he is not aware of special training for multicultural sensitivity in either counseling or psychotherapy in Mexico.

SUMMARY

A summary of the content of returns from counselors in the 22 countries could make for tedious reading and redundant information. Instead, this summary focuses on themes from the respondents and calls attention to components of multicultural training that might be made culturally sensitive for use in other countries.

A major theme that runs through all reports is the recognition of cultural pluralism and diversity within each country's borders. In most of the countries represented, cultural pluralism has been present since the instigation of counseling. The majority of the respondents also reported the worldwide phenomenon of people emigrating to other countries and, in so doing, increasing the cultural pluralism of the receiving country. Many immigrants are refugees who have not left their countries by choice, and counselors have been called on to assist these victims of political and economic oppression. Some of the countries reported that multicultural counselor training is already in place. In other countries, the need for special training to deal with cultural diversity is recognized, but programs to meet this need are incomplete or nonexistent.

Several respondents mentioned the need for special training to work with the native or aboriginal people (Canada, New Zealand, the Philippines, and Taiwan). Suggestions were made to combine multicultural with crisis-oriented training

[22] From Dr. Ricardo Blanco-Beledo, Mexico City, personal communication, June 18, 1993.

where counselors are called on to help disaster victims (such as in the Philippines). Another important issue raised was to include training in group facilitation with training for multicultural counseling (for example, at UBC, Canada). The need to recognize the impact of the prevailing political ideology of a country, as well as what happens to the people when that ideology changes, was called to the readers' attention (Lithuania). Counselor educators trained abroad have a special need to learn how to deliver multicultural counseling and how to train other counselors in their home countries to include cultural sensitivity (Nigeria and the United Arab Emirates).

Many processes for training appear to hold promise for use in other countries, such as having brief immersion experiences in another culture (for example, full day(s) of convention experiences at the 1993 Canadian national meetings and the weekend retreats at Maori lodges in New Zealand); gaining cultural awareness and sensitivity through prepracticum retreats (as in Malaysia); teaching cognitive content through distance education (Germany); taking the counseling practicum (university professor and graduate students) weekly to culturally pluralistic sites (as at UBC, Canada); and networking with professional colleagues who have learned cultural sensitivity through living and working in other cultures (for example, New South Wales, Australia).

The global economy of which we are all now a part can serve as a catalyst for counselors and counselor educators to do more cross-cultural and cross-nation sharing worldwide. We have the opportunity to learn with and from each other in this global village in which we live.

Part Two

*Multicultural Counselor
Preparation: Pathways
from the Present
to the Future*

CHAPTER 6

Introduction to a Developmental Model of Multicultural Counselor Preparation

*P*art II delineates didactic and experiential components for present and future pathways for multicultural counselor preparation. Chapter 6 sets the stage for the developmental model of multicultural counselor preparation introduced in Chapters 7 through 11. Each of the five stages of the model is described in one chapter. The book concludes with a chapter on possible future directions for multicultural counseling.

The purposes of Chapter 6 are: (1) to present information on my experiences in multicultural counselor preparation; (2) to detail goals to promote development in the areas of beliefs and attitudes, knowledge, and skills for each of the five stages of the proposed developmental model; (3) to state assumptions that undergird the model; and (4) to list limitations of the proposed model.

Since 1986, I have taught a graduate class entitled Counseling/Helping in a Multicultural Society, and I have made presentations at state, national, and international professional meetings that use concepts from Carney and Kahn's 1984 stage model (see Table 6.1). Early in 1991, Sabnani, Ponterotto, and Borodovsky published a much more complete stage model for White racial identity development and cross-cultural counselor training (see Appendix B). During the same year, I published my first manuscript outlining a developmental model for multicultural counselor preparation (Wehrly, 1991). In 1992, the Association for Multicultural Counseling and Development of the American Counseling Association published a document detailing 31 multicultural counseling competencies as proposed standards for multicultural counselor accreditation (Sue et al., 1992a, 1992b; see Appendix A). Subsequently, the Ridley, Mendoza, and Kanitz five-stage model was published in 1994. Concepts from all these sources are integrated in the five-stage model described in the next five chapters. Other contributing ideas have come from a host of other authors; from my experiences in teaching and

TABLE 6.1 ■ STAGES OF THE TRAINING DEVELOPMENT AND APPROPRIATE LEARNING ENVIRONMENT

Stage	Trainee Characteristics	Appropriate Learning Environment
1	Limited knowledge of other cultural groups. Views of others based on ethnocentric attitudes. Conflicted by disparity between own ethnocentrism and egalitarian values of the profession. Counseling approaches and goals reflect trainee's world view rather than the client's needs and views.	Highly structured and supportive. Trainer acts as instructor. Readings and lectures are used to provide information on the history of America's cultural groups and social barriers to effective cross-cultural communication. Encourage attitudinal and behavioral self-awareness through structured values clarification activities. Avoid confrontation and moralizing in processing experiential activities. Assess current counseling skills through role plays or other structured formats. Build or enhance active listening skills.
2	Emerging awareness of own ethnocentric attitudes and behaviors. Knowledge of other cultural groups is not organized and is dealt with in a detached manner. Wears a "halo of naivete," believes that his/her basic skills and knowledge are adequate to counsel persons from other cultural groups. Counseling approaches and goals continue to reflect trainee's ethnocentrism and are applied in a rote manner.	Trainer continues to act as instructor by providing information on (1) individual attitudinal barriers to effective cross-cultural counseling; (2) ethnocentrism in the mental health disciplines; and (3) the world views of persons from cultural groups in the trainee's present situation. Use structured activities to examine the source and accuracy of trainee ethnocentric views and behaviors that impede effective cross-cultural communication. Expand counseling skill repertoire using Sue's (1981) cross-cultural counseling critical incident approach, media simulation and role plays. Encourage creative utilization of counseling techniques and counseling goal setting to meet unique needs of culturally different clients. Provide role model of white counselor working in cross-cultural settings.
3	Conflict associated with feelings of guilt and responsibility. For one's ethnocentrism prompts an attitude of "colorblindness" that is expressed either as an active attempt to *deny* cultural differences or an effort to become immersed in another cultural group.	Trainer encourages autonomous self-review and provides a normative structure. Through readings, presentations, simulations and cross-cultural encounters trainees are encouraged to explore the impact of their colorblind attitudes and behaviors of their culturally different individuals.

TABLE 6.1 *(continued)*

Stage	Trainee Characteristics	Appropriate Learning Environment
		Pederson's (1978) triadic counselor training approach is used to reinforce the importance of recognizing and legitimizing attitudinal differences.
4	Emerging self-identity as a cross-cultural change agent and participant. Selectively blends new cross-cultural knowledge, attitudes and skills with desirable features of own reference groups. Creatively applies counseling approaches and selects counseling goals to match the world view of the client.	Trainer acts as a supervisor in helping trainee to clarify and select a personal direction. Information is provided as needed to the trainee. Direct counseling experience is provided in multi-cultural settings under supervision by persons from representative cultural groups. Client load is matched to trainee levels of experience. Varied approaches to cross-cultural counseling are presented, practiced, and critiqued in the light of the trainee's experience.
5	Assumes a self-directed activist posture in expanding own cross-cultural knowledge, attitudes, and skills, and in promoting cultural pluralism in society at large. Challenged by decision regarding nature and extent of personal involvements in cross-cultural counseling situations.	Trainer acts as a peer consultant by helping the trainee clarify his/her future objectives as a counselor. Trainer assists in identifying and/or supplying resources needed for trainee to accomplish personal directions.

SOURCE: From C. G. Carney and K. B. Kahn, "Building Competencies for Effective Cross-Cultural Counseling: A Developmental View," *The Counseling Psychologist, 12*(1), pp. 111–119, copyright © 1984 by Sage Publications, Inc. Reprinted by permission of Sage Publications, Inc.

learning with hundreds of students in my multicultural counseling class and in workshops; and from integrating multicultural components into all the counseling classes that I teach.

I have taught the multicultural counseling class in both on-campus and off-campus locations of Western Illinois University, one of five state universities in the Illinois Board of Governors System. The Western Illinois University campus is located in Macomb, Illinois, a small county seat of fewer than 20,000 people in a very rural part of Illinois. Because of a long history of recruitment of U.S. students of color and international students, the Western Illinois University campus is more culturally pluralistic than might be expected. On-campus enrollment for the 1994-95 academic year was 10,098 students; 15.1% were from minority groups in the

United States, and 4.8% were international students from more than 50 countries. Of the 2501 students registered in off-campus programs, 13.6% were from U.S. minority groups, and 0.4% were international students. Minority and international student enrollment in the Counselor Education Master's Degree Program has been less than 5%, however.

Western Illinois University (WIU) participates in a Graduate Study Center Consortium with nine other universities at the Augustana campus at Rock Island. The complete 48-semester-hour Counseling Program is offered at both the on-campus and the Quad Cities locations. The graduate level multicultural counseling course is taught at least once a year at both the on-campus and Quad Cities locations.

The Quad Cities is an area of more than 250 thousand people and is considerably more culturally pluralistic than the city of Macomb. I mention these facts because I make heavy use of people of color as resources during class sessions at both locations.

The Western Illinois University Counselor Education Master's Degree Program has been approved by the Council for the Accreditation of Counseling and Related Educational Programs since 1987 and requires that counseling students complete the 3-semester-hour class Counseling/Helping in a Multicultural Society. Enrollment in the class is limited to 30 students per term. Graduate students from several other major disciplines (such as College Student Personnel, Communication Sciences and Disorders, Gerontology, Interdisciplinary Studies, and Law Enforcement Administration) as well as nondegree graduate students often enroll in the class. The variety of major interests among class members has posed a challenge to make the course meaningful to all.

Counselor education programs vary in how they incorporate multicultural counseling content into the programs (Copeland, 1982). Much of the content and many of the experiences delineated in the first stages outlined in this section of the book are included in my multicultural counseling class. As stated earlier, the majority of students in the Western Illinois University required multicultural counseling class are White, so the program outlined is probably more appropriate for them than for non-White students.

However, I am very committed to encouraging people of all races and ethnicities to participate in special training for multicultural helping services work. When needed, assignments are tailored to students of color in the class, and special discussion is made where the assignments are different for White and non-White students. I also include observations on the need for integrating multicultural content into all counseling classes.

The Carney and Kahn (1984) model provided the basic outline for the description of stages and within-stage categories, but the paradigm presented in this book has revised the original Carney and Kahn concepts considerably. Implementation of multicultural counselor development is described for each of five stages under these four topics: (1) student characteristics; (2) process guidelines for creating a climate for student growth in beliefs and attitudes, knowledge, and skills; (3) goals to promote development of beliefs and attitudes, knowledge, and skills; and (4) appropriate environments and learning experiences to achieve goals.

Lines or boundaries between stages are flexible, and stage transitions are not abrupt. Many activities described extend over more than one stage. When space limitations preclude complete description of a particular assignment or activity, references are made to sources for additional information.

This section (Part II) is designed for teachers in counselor education and counseling psychology programs, students in these programs, and counselors in the field who are working to improve their multicultural counseling competencies. Throughout Part II, the terms *instructor, trainer,* and *supervisor* are used interchangeably to designate those who facilitate counselor learning and development. The terms *student, trainee,* and *supervisee* are similarly used interchangeably to designate those who are learning either to be counselors or to be better counselors. The goals to promote student development in beliefs and attitudes, knowledge, and skills for each of the five stages of multicultural counselor preparation follow.

STAGE ONE GOALS (CHAPTER 7)

Goal 1: To introduce learners to the field of multicultural counseling and to help learners recognize the male, Euro-Western, culture-bound nature of much of the traditional counseling literature

Goal 2: To create an awareness of the role of culture in the helping and counseling processes

Goal 3: To initiate trainees' study of their own ethnic, cultural, and racial heritages

Goal 4: To initiate learning about the nature of the sociopolitical environment faced by both people of color and White people in the United States

Goal 5: To introduce models for studying culture

Goal 6: To begin multicultural skill development training

STAGE TWO GOALS (CHAPTER 8)

Goal 1: To continue learning about the field of multicultural counseling

Goal 2: To expand awareness of the impact of one's ethnocultural and racial heritage on one's thinking and behavior

Goal 3: To expand knowledge of the historical background of people of color in the United States, including their history of oppression and their history of helping services

Goal 4: To learn procedures for investigating the historical and current value system descriptors for U.S. people of color

Goal 5: To understand the concept of stereotyping, to become aware of the pervasiveness of stereotyping in the current U.S. society, and to become aware of one's own stereotypes about members of other cultures

Goal 6: To realize the within-group variance of personal qualities of people of all ethnic and racial groups

Goal 7: To develop techniques for understanding each client as a unique person within her or his ethnic and racial heritage

STAGE THREE GOALS (CHAPTER 9)

Goal 1: To involve counseling trainees in the application of concepts from racial and ethnic identity development models

Goal 2: To achieve a deeper understanding of the pervasive racism in the United States and to realize one's personal involvement in racist behaviors

Goal 3: To develop a broader understanding of the role of culture in counseling and a wider repertoire of counselor interventions with clients of other cultures, while realizing the limitations of "cookbook" approaches to multicultural counseling

STAGE FOUR GOALS (CHAPTER 10)

Goal 1: To provide supervision by a qualified trainer at an appropriate culturally pluralistic site at which the student can complete a counseling practicum

Goal 2: To challenge the student to continue learning about self in interaction with culturally or racially different clients in the counseling sessions as well as in the clients' own cultural milieus

Goal 3: To provide opportunities for students to develop a broader repertoire of successful multicultural counseling interventions with individuals as well as with families

Goal 4: To initiate application of information from racial and ethnic identity development models in work with clients at various stages of racial and ethnic identity development

STAGE FIVE GOALS (CHAPTER 11)

Goal 1: To provide a supervised internship experience at an appropriate culturally pluralistic site

Goal 2: To assist internship students in learning to work in a variety of roles in the cultural milieus of their clients

Goal 3: To provide support and encouragement for continued student growth in multicultural counseling beliefs, attitudes, knowledge, and skills

ASSUMPTIONS UNDERGIRDING THIS DEVELOPMENTAL MODEL

Before delineating the implementation of the counselor preparation model, it is important to state the following assumptions that undergird the program outlined in the next five chapters. I recognize that these assumptions are influenced by my own ethnic and racial socialization.

1. Faculty in counselor education and counseling psychology programs will have formulated a multicultural training philosophy that is "explicit, coherent, and socially relevant" (Ridley, Mendoza, & Kanitz, 1994, p. 231) before implementing guidelines suggested in the five stages of multicultural counselor preparation (Chapters 7, 8, 9, 10, and 11).

2. Each counselor/helper and each counselee/helpee is unique.

3. Each individual has multiple identities. Some will be personal identities and some will be reference-group orientation identities (Cross, 1987, 1991). The relative salience of each identity to each individual will vary (Cross, 1991; Smith, 1989, 1991).

4. Each counselor (or helper) and each counselee (or helpee) has an ethnic or racial identity. Conscious awareness of reference-group orientation identifications is on a continuum from very limited to highly developed. In addition, the salience of ethnicity or race as a reference group identity will vary from individual to individual (Cross, 1991; Smith, 1989, 1991).

5. Being born and socialized into an ethnic or racial group in and of itself does not qualify an individual to be a culturally skilled counselor with other people of that ethnic or racial group (Harper, 1973; Sue, Arredondo, & McDavis, 1992a, 1992b).

6. The influence of early mental health literature portraying people of color as genetically deficient, culturally disadvantaged, culturally deprived, or rejecting of their own racial or cultural heritage still lingers (Calia, 1966; Cross, 1991; Deutsch, 1966; Riessman, 1962; Sue et al., 1992a, 1992b; Warren, 1966). Being culturally or ethnically different does *not* equate with being genetically deficient, culturally disadvantaged, culturally deprived, or rejecting of one's cultural heritage

(Cross, 1991; Pedersen, 1991; Phinney, 1993; Pinderhughes, 1989; Pine, 1972; Sue et al., 1992a, 1992b).

7. The world views of both counselor and counselee are influenced by the historical and current manifestations of racism and oppression in the total society (Cross, 1991; Helms, 1990, 1992; Smith, 1991; Sue et al., 1992a, 1992b; Sue & Sue, 1990).

8. Counselors need to study the sociopolitical history and values of their own ethnic heritage in order to "own" this heritage and to realize how it can help or hinder multicultural interaction (Pinderhughes, 1989; Sue & Sue, 1990).

9. Knowledge of the sociopolitical history and the values of other cultures, as well as knowledge of ways to learn about other cultures are important; but such knowledge in and of itself is insufficient to develop multicultural counseling competence (Sue & Sue, 1990; Wehrly, 1991).

10. Multicultural counselor development, like human development, occurs in stages or phases that are not necessarily linear (Parham, 1989; Smith, 1989; Wehrly, 1991). A more descriptive model is the spiral model, in which the learner moves upward on the spiral, regresses back down the spiral, gains the courage to try for higher levels of development, and perhaps repeats these movements several times during the learning process (Wehrly, 1991).

11. The acquisition of the beliefs and attitudes, knowledge, and skills needed for multicultural competence is a learning process that includes both cognitive and affective components (Sue et al., 1982; Sue et al., 1992a, 1992b). Growth in one of these domains does not necessarily lead to growth in the others (Carney & Kahn, 1984).

12. Acquisition of the beliefs and attitudes, knowledge, and skills needed for multicultural competence is a learning process that extends for a lifetime (Sue et al., 1992a, 1992b; Sue & Sue, 1990; Wehrly, 1991).

13. Although the empirical research to support the use of certain learning interventions to promote multicultural counselor development is limited, it appears that growth in multicultural counselor competence can occur as a result of involvement in a planned multicultural counselor development program (Helms, 1984).

14. Counselors will enter multicultural training at different levels of racial and ethnic identity development. Assessment of one's own racial and ethnic identity development and learning how to use information on this reference group orientation of both self and of counselee can be useful in counselor-counselee interaction (Helms, 1990).

15. A positive identification with one's own ethnic, cultural, and racial heritage provides a firm base for understanding and respecting the world views of people with different ethnic, cultural, and racial heritages (Banks, 1981; Hoare, 1991; Phinney et al., 1990; Pinderhughes, 1989; Ponterotto & Pedersen, 1993; Smith, 1989).

16. Because each person's ethnic and racial reference group identity is anchored in the ethnic and racial culture in which that person is socialized, no one can be completely objective in attempting to understand the world views of people socialized in other ethnic and racial cultures (Hoare, 1991).

17. There are many ways to obtain cultural knowledge: from books, from audiovisual materials, through direct contact and work with people in the culture being studied, through travel, and through preparation of cultural research reports.

18. Required participation in a multicultural counseling class seems to be an effective way to broaden counseling students' knowledge of the field, to promote development in cultural awareness, and to begin the process of skill development for effective multicultural counseling.

19. Completion of a course in multicultural counseling, in and of itself is not sufficient to make one an effective multicultural counselor. The cultural aspects of counseling need to be included in all didactic and experiential components of counselor education.

20. Multicultural counselor preparation includes learning from both an emic (insider, culture-specific) and etic (outsider, universal) approach (Wehrly, 1991).

21. Because psychologists and clinicians have been trained to look for pathology, mental health professionals may need to be helped to look for the strengths of a cultural, ethnic, or racial group (Cross, 1991; Lee, 1991; Pinderhughes, 1989; Sue et al., 1982).

22. Students vary in learning styles; therefore, a variety of methods are used to facilitate multicultural counselor development.

23. Supervised experiences in multicultural counseling practica and internships at appropriate culturally pluralistic sites and under the supervision of trained multicultural counselors are essential components of multicultural counselor preparation.

24. Counselors and teachers can play important roles in preventing prejudice and expanding tolerance of others in the lives of students with whom they work (Ponterotto & Pedersen, 1993; *Teaching Tolerance*, 1993, 1994).

25. Counselors can learn with and from counselors and helping service colleagues in other countries of the world (Locke, 1992a; Morrissey, 1994; Wehrly & Deen, 1983).

26. Given the prevalence of violent ethnic and racial conflicts in the United States and in other countries, and given the reality that we now live in a global village and operate in a global economy, it is time to begin searching for a broader model of reference group orientation. A positive identification with one's ethnic and racial heritage is the starting point for this broader model, which includes stages leading to understanding and accepting a global reference-group orientation (Banks, 1981; Phinney, personal communication, April 20, 1993; Smith, 1989; *Teaching Tolerance*, 1993, 1994).

LIMITATIONS OF THIS DEVELOPMENTAL MODEL

It is important to recognize that, if this model is applied to groups or classes, not all individuals in any one group at any given time will be at the same stage of readiness to integrate these multicultural learnings into their professional and daily behavior. There will be at least some variance in individuals' readiness to profit from the suggested learning experiences in beliefs and attitudes, knowledge, and skills. This variance in learning readiness is related to the "possibility that counselors within minority groups or the White middle-class majority differ among themselves in terms of their level of readiness for the assimilation of these learnings" (Sabnani et al., 1991, p. 77).

Because much growth in multicultural development takes place through group interactions, I still recommend that the experiential activities take place in a group setting. Once students are aware of differences among themselves in racial and ethnic identity development, they can be more accepting of peers who are at a different level. This awareness can also help students realize the "centrality of the counselor's own racial-identity development to the overall training process" (Sabnani et al., 1991, p. 77).

I recognize that, in many cases, there are more activities and exercises listed than are necessary to achieve the goals of each stage. These activities are suggestions only. Everyone teaching or facilitating growth in multicultural counselor development will need to design and choose activities congruent with the philosophy and goals of their own preparation programs.

SUMMARY

This chapter provided background for the proposed five-stage developmental model of multicultural counseling preparation. Also included were a listing of the goals for each stage of the proposed model and an enumeration of 26 assumptions that undergird the model. The chapter closed with a discussion of limitations of the five-stage developmental model for multicultural counselor preparation.

CHAPTER 7

Multicultural Counselor Preparation: Stage One

The purpose of this chapter is to describe pathways for student growth in beliefs and attitudes, knowledge, and skills in the first stage of multicultural counselor preparation. This developmental process is delineated under four chapter subheadings: (1) student characteristics, (2) process guidelines, (3) goals, and (4) appropriate environments and learning experiences to achieve goals.

Much of this chapter describes content and activities for a class in multicultural counseling. It is important to underscore again that taking a single class in multicultural counseling does not make one a qualified multicultural counselor. All classes (both didactic and experiential) in counselor preparation need to include content and learning from a multicultural perspective.

Chapter 6 emphasized the importance of recognizing individual variances in readiness to profit from suggested learning environments and learning experiences. Given the importance of experiential activities in promoting growth in beliefs and attitudes (Sabnani et al., 1991), group experiential activities are appropriate even though all members may not be at the same level of racial or ethnic identity development and may not profit equally from the experiences.

STUDENT CHARACTERISTICS

Students approach their first multicultural counseling class with a combination of excitement and anxiety. In small-group interaction, the involvement seems to be particularly high and there is much need for processing of the feeling and content of small-group experiences. This high level of participation may be related to the anxiety that surrounds many of the topics presented. Students sometimes comment that they rarely have had the opportunity to talk openly about these topics before.

Many students enter counselor education programs with limited knowledge of other cultural groups and with little awareness of their own racial or ethnic identity (Carney & Kahn, 1984; Christensen, 1989; Helms, 1990; Ponterotto, 1988; Sabnani et al., 1991). Sabnani et al. (1991) call this the *Preexposure/Precontact Stage* for White students. Atkinson, Morten, and Sue (1993) name this the *Conformity Stage* in their Minority Identity Development Model, and Christensen (1989) identifies this as the *Unawareness Stage* in her stage model for the development of cross-cultural awareness. This period of naivete does not last long, however, because some counseling books now include sections on cultural limitations of contemporary counseling theories and techniques (for example, Corey, 1991; Ivey, Ivey, & Simek-Morgan, 1993), and references to the impact of culture on counseling are made in many counseling classes.

Early in their multicultural counselor training, students begin to display a variety of feelings related to what they are studying. For White students, feelings of guilt and confusion are common when they begin to learn the reality of society's oppression of people who are different. Students cope with these feelings in a variety of ways. Some White students deal with the guilt expressed by classmates by relying on old habits like "zapping," kidding, or putting down the person who has shared his or her feelings. Students of color are sometimes surprised to see the racist and oppressive aspects of White culture being described in textbooks and discussed by White people. They may express relief that someone finally understands the struggles that people of their racial and cultural heritages have experienced.

As students participate in the class, they may experience conflicting feelings about retaining their traditional ethnocentric views while recognizing the need for broadening their views of and attitudes toward people of other cultures. Carney and Kahn (1984) state that this dilemma "marks a significant transitional point in the trainee's development" (p. 114), and they caution that moralizing or emotional confronting may cause some students to abandon efforts to change. Students who wish to complete a required course in multicultural counseling do not have the latter option (Ponterotto, 1988).

There are clear parallels between the behavioral descriptors of people in the first stage of racial and ethnic identity development and the descriptors of the behavior of many students as they begin multicultural counselor training. For example:

1. Some people enter the first stage of racial or ethnic identity development with limited awareness of themselves as ethnic or racial beings (Cross, 1991; Helms, 1992; Kim, 1981; Phinney, 1993; Ponterotto, 1988; Ponterotto & Pedersen, 1993; Ruiz, 1990; Sabnani et al., 1991). Students often begin with much naivete about their own racial or cultural heritages and the impact that these reference group orientations have on their lives (Christensen, 1989; Ponterotto, 1988; Sabnani et al., 1991). People of color will probably be more aware of having a

racial or ethnic identity than will White people (Helms, 1984, 1990, 1992; Ponterotto & Pedersen, 1993).

2. Some people of color will show a preference for being White and may depreciate the values of their own racial or ethnic group (Atkinson, Morten, & Sue, 1993; Cross, 1991; Kim, 1981; Ruiz, 1990). Some students of color who have grown up in a predominantly White environment may not have had the opportunity to examine their cultural heritage before they entered multicultural counselor study. Minority students whose parents or grandparents were immigrants and who worked very hard to succeed in the dominant culture may have internalized an idealized view of their environment and may deny experiencing any form of discrimination (Christensen, 1989).

3. Some people at the first stage will show a lack of interest in their own ethnic identity development (Cross, 1991; Phinney, 1993). Early in multicultural counselor training, some students may emphasize that they are just "plain American" and "not into that ethnic stuff." At the onset, they may resist studying their ethnic heritage and view that study as a waste of time.

4. Some people at the first stage of racial or ethnic identity development will have opinions about race and ethnicity but they will be based on the opinions of others. People at this point have not yet gone through a stage of clarifying their own ethnic or racial identity (Cross, 1991; Phinney, 1993; Ponterotto, 1988; Sabnani et al., 1991). Many students enter multicultural counseling training with this lack of ethnic self-awareness.

5. Other people in the first stage of racial or ethnic identity development will show a preoccupation with and a desire to preserve their ethnic self-identity (Smith, 1991). This preoccupation may appear as an ethnocentric attitude in some students.

PROCESS GUIDELINES FOR CREATING A CLIMATE FOR STUDENT GROWTH IN STAGE ONE

Carney and Kahn (1984) recommend a highly structured and supportive training environment at this stage. This structure and support provides a predictable learning environment that can reduce students' anxiety levels. It is important to be accepting of all student responses in exercises on self-awareness, because confrontation may be too threatening for some students and they may stop participating.

It is a challenge for the instructor to create a structured and balanced classroom learning environment for students to experience growth in beliefs and attitudes, knowledge, and skills related to multicultural counseling. Too much structure may squelch learning in either or both the cognitive and the affective domains. Too little structure can turn class sessions into endless rap sessions that do little to help students grow in any of the three domains of beliefs and attitudes, knowledge, or skills. As noted by Westwood (personal communication August 13,

1993) (see Chapter 5), the instructor of the multicultural counseling class needs training in group facilitation.

Sabnani et al. (1991) clarify the different processes needed to accomplish goals related to beliefs and attitudes and goals related to knowledge. To accomplish goals related to beliefs and attitudes, these authors recommend experiential activities. To accomplish goals related to knowledge, the assignments are "more research-oriented, literature-based, nonpersonal-contact tasks" (Sabnani et al., 1991, p. 90). (See Appendix B.)

Because the process is a very important part of multicultural counselor development, attendance at class sessions is required. Students need to understand that there is no way to substitute the value of experiencing a process in which they interact with other students and learn with and from each other. Christensen (1989) emphasizes that the development of cross-cultural awareness "is rooted in knowledge and understanding gained through meaningful, personal experiences (rather than theoretical training only) with culturally dissimilar persons" (p. 274). Small-group interaction with peers of different ethnic and racial heritages in the safety of the multicultural class can provide a starting point for the development of these meaningful cross-cultural experiences.

Some students may need help in understanding the multicultural growth process on which they are embarking. Students' anxieties can be reduced by informing them that they will experience a variety of conflicting emotions on their way to developing multicultural counseling competence. Early in the course, the instructor needs to give an introduction to the process in which students are involved. Giving a brief overview of stages and phases of the models of racial and ethnic identity development is one way to help students understand one aspect of the process. Students will be relieved to know that it is normal to feel a variety of emotions (anxiety, confusion, anger, guilt, joy, relief) while attaining competence in multicultural counseling. For some students, the experiences of the class may resemble a roller-coaster ride of feelings.

Tatum (1992), who teaches classes on the psychology of racism, offers some important guidelines for providing a safe situation in which to discuss emotionally laden issues. These suggestions are appropriate for instructors working with students throughout multicultural training and can be presented at the beginning of the term to help create a classroom climate in which students' growth can take place.

Tatum's first suggestion is to emphasize that students respect other members of the group by maintaining confidentiality of what is disclosed. Tatum also requests that the students not use "zaps," or overt or covert put-downs, in responding to their classmates' openness. She recognizes that these responses may be used "as comic relief when someone is feeling anxious about the content of the discussion" (Tatum, 1992, p. 4). Tatum's third recommendation is that students speak from personal experience using "I believe" or "I feel" statements rather than "People say . . . ".

Student involvement in both small- and large-group discussion seems to be greatly enhanced when they sit in circles (Wehrly, 1991). Tatum (1992) believes that the physical structure of sitting in a circle communicates to the students that they are expected to speak to each other as well as to the instructor.

Westwood believes that it is important for students to recognize the difference between personal opinion and knowledge (M. J. Westwood, personal communication, August 13, 1993). He encourages students to relate the content of classes to their personal experience but to realize that reporting on personal experiences is not to be confused with knowledge. Westwood recommends setting aside some time during each class session for small-group exchange of personal experiences and feelings. When students are aware that they will have time to share these experiences and feelings, they seem more ready to attend to the cognitive content of the class.

Keeping a journal is an effective way for trainees to record their personal reactions to participation in the various class activities. It helps if the instructor can collect the journals periodically and engage in a dialogue with the students through writing responses to feelings expressed or to questions posed by the students (Carney & Kahn, 1984; Tatum, 1992; Wehrly, 1991).

Earlier, I noted the parallels between the behavioral descriptors of people in the first stage of racial and ethnic identity development and the behavioral descriptors of many students as they enter multicultural counselor training. Helms (1984) recognizes that if we assume that racial consciousness models are cognitive developmental models and "that racial consciousness is perceptual in nature" (p. 162), then we cannot expect to change another person's stage of racial consciousness directly. She states, however, that "it seems possible to create an environment in which healthy development can be stimulated" (Helms, 1984, p. 162).

Helms (1984) also posits that racial identity development is a consequence of three factors: the person's readiness or adaptability level, the person's experiences in his or her sociocultural environment, and the person's opportunities for formal education. She sees the third factor, that of educational opportunity, as the one holding the greatest hope for intervening to help a person move to more advanced stages of racial consciousness. Increasing the educational opportunities could impact the other two factors as well. Gaining additional information about self and the world in which one lives may create enough cognitive dissonance to help the individual broaden his or her world views. Helms (1984) emphasizes the importance of augmenting intellectual understanding with affective understanding for the counselor trainee to experience growth.

GOALS TO PROMOTE STUDENT DEVELOPMENT IN BELIEFS AND ATTITUDES, KNOWLEDGE, AND SKILLS IN STAGE ONE

Goal 1: To introduce learners to the field of multicultural counseling and to help learners begin to recognize the male, Euro-Western, culture-bound nature of much of the traditional counseling literature

Goal 2: To create an awareness of the role of culture in the helping and counseling processes

Goal 3: To initiate trainees' study of their own ethnic/cultural and racial heritages

Goal 4: To initiate learning about the nature of the sociopolitical environment faced both by people of color and by White people in the United States

Goal 5: To introduce models for studying culture

Goal 6: To begin multicultural counseling skill development training

APPROPRIATE ENVIRONMENTS AND LEARNING EXPERIENCES TO ACHIEVE GOALS

Goal 1: To introduce learners to the field of multicultural counseling and to help learners begin to recognize the male, Euro-Western, culture-bound nature of much of the traditional counseling literature. Outside readings in current books on cross-cultural counseling and multicultural counseling will introduce students to the field. Some examples of the many contemporary cross-cultural and multicultural counseling books are: Atkinson, Morten, and Sue (1993); Axelson (1993); Baruth and Manning (1991); Ivey, Ivey, and Simek-Morgan (1993); Lee (1995); Lee and Richardson (1991); Locke, (1992b); Pedersen (1988); Pedersen, Draguns, Lonner, and Trimble (1989); Pedersen and Ivey (1994); and Sue and Sue (1990).

Recognizing the cultural limitations of traditional mental health practices (including mental health assessment) will be important for understanding the rationale for multicultural counseling (Axelson, 1993; Lee & Richardson, 1991; Locke, 1992b; Ponterotto & Casas, 1987). In the second chapter of their 1990 book, Sue and Sue address the following culture-bound values that act as barriers to effective cross-cultural counseling: putting the individual at the center of problem resolution; expecting the client to be verbally, emotionally, and behaviorally expressive; emphasizing the importance of insight; expecting the client to be open in self-disclosure; using the linear cause-and-effect model for problem solving; separating mental and physical functioning; and providing an unstructured environment that may seem ambiguous to the client. Sue and Sue also discuss class-bound values and language barriers that inhibit multicultural counseling. These barriers and their impact on cross-cultural counseling are important early topics for student study.

Chapter 2, "History of and Rationale for Multicultural Counselor Preparation," can help students gain a perspective on the origins of and reasons for multicultural counseling training. This history will show students the long pathways traveled by counseling professionals and help students see the impact of culture on the counseling profession. Knowledge of this history can also help students realize that counseling does not take place in a vacuum and that challenging the existing power structure is a time-consuming and complicated process. Class readings and lecturettes can stimulate structured, small-group discussions on any or all these topics.

Early in the multicultural counseling class, students need to be introduced to the terminology of multicultural counseling and the varying definitions of some terms. The changing interpretations of the term *culture*, for example, indicate that some authors limit culture to racial or ethnic heritage, whereas others include all ways of being unique. Waugh's 1991 list of the changes in ethnic minority group names over the years (see Chapter 1) can also be edifying for students.

To help clear the confusion on some of the terms, I have found it useful to define *ethnicity, race*, and *diversity* by drawing a small circle on the chalkboard and writing the terms *ethnicity* and *race* in the center of that small circle. I tell students that we are all born into a racial heritage and also either born or socialized into an ethnic culture, or ethnicity. I then ask students to name other ways that a person can be unique or different. Some of the many words and phrases students volunteer are physical capabilities, age, sex, lifestyle, rural or urban living environments, language(s) spoken, religious or spiritual beliefs, political preferences, and sexual/affectional orientation. Each word or phrase is written outside the periphery of the circle, and by the time this exercise is finished, the chalkboard is full.

This exercise helps show students that each of us is born with a *racial heritage* and is born or socialized into an *ethnic culture* that greatly influences our value systems, attitudes, and behavior. The exercise also calls attention to many other qualities that may be affiliated with but not shared by everyone of a particular ethnicity or race. *Ethnicity* and *race* are thus highlighted as the core of *diversity*. (Refer to Figure 1.1 in Chapter 1 to see a few of the myriad aspects that make up ethnic and cultural diversity.)

Some students may think other descriptors belong at the core of diversity. Discussing the rationale for this difference will help students realize the many ways in which we may feel reference group identity. As Cross (1991) and Phinney (1993) indicate, some people have probably not yet given much thought to their ethnic or racial heritages.

Concurrent with, or prior to, enrollment in the class in multicultural counseling, students have other classes that introduce the cultural limitations of traditional counseling theories. It is especially important that students begin to recognize the dominant Western, White, male influence on traditional theories of counseling, on theories of career development, on assessment instruments and techniques, and on student development theory.

Goal 2: To create an awareness of the role of culture in the helping and counseling processes. Ponterotto and Benesch (1988) believe it is important to be aware of "those elements of the counseling process that may transcend cultural differences [and to learn] how culture and the dynamics of counseling are inextricably interwoven" (p. 237). These authors apply Torrey's conceptual framework for effective helping (1972a, 1972b) to the counseling process.

Torrey's four universal components for curing patients were discussed in Chapter 2: the choice of an appropriate name for the problem, the helper's personal qualities, the patient's expectations, and the helper's credibility. Studying these universals helps students understand the commonalities in problem solving around the world. It will be important, also, to recognize the impact of culture on these universal factors in help giving and help seeking.

Ponterotto and Benesch (1988) elaborate on how these universals apply to counseling and discuss them under five categories. The first factor, that of naming the problem, is greatly impacted by culture; what is considered a problem in one culture may not be considered a problem in another culture. In addition, the ways problems are conceptualized may vary greatly from culture to culture. Culture will also influence the second factor—the desired personal qualities of the counselor. Lack of awareness of client expectations, the third universal in the Torrey paradigm, appears to be a major reason many clients of color terminate counseling. Counselor credibility and how culture establishes the parameters for counselor credibility are the fourth universal aspect. The fifth universal factor is the use of some kind of technique to help the client. Again, a huge cultural component influences techniques selected. Assumptions that underlie any or all of these five factors will be culturally conditioned.

Awareness of these commonalities across cultures in the helping/counseling process can expand one's world views on the helping relationship. Ponterotto and Benesch (1988) propose that "cross-cultural training should stem from a conceptual model such as that posited by Torrey (1972)" (p. 240). They recognize the importance of integrating the components of "defining problems, building rapport, understanding expectations, establishing credibility, and selecting appropriate interventions" (Ponterotto and Benesch, 1988, p. 240) into a coherent model that clearly relates to counseling.

Students need to be introduced to the impact of culture on all aspects of counseling: thinking/cognitive processes, belief systems, definitions and influence of family or kin, definitions of self, decision making and attitudes toward action, time orientation, verbal behavior, and nonverbal behavior (see Chapter 1). Another broad concept to introduce to students (again, see Chapter 1) is the role of the cultural context as a critical factor in understanding self and the person who comes for help.

Goal 3: To initiate trainees' study of their own ethnic/cultural and racial heritages.   Students can begin to learn about their own cultural or ethnic heritage in several ways. A get-acquainted exercise, "What's in a Name," can be used at the first class session. In this exercise, students in small groups share the origins of their names and how their names may have been changed under pressure to conform to the mainstream U.S. society. Students of color often share the importance of their names and who named them. Immigrant or international students, as well as sons and daughters of immigrants, usually have powerful and poignant stories to tell about how someone in their families changed their names to appear more "American." The importance of determining the name by which an individual prefers to be identified is also examined in this exercise.

Other short exercises, such as those in the second chapter of Pedersen's 1988 book, can help students begin the process of self-awareness on cultural topics. The exercise "Categories of Public and Private Self-Disclosure," shown in Exhibit 7.1, introduces students to the impact of culture on their personal perspectives on privacy.

Students are asked to review the list of 30 topics and check whether the topic is *private* (one that they would discuss only with very close friends) or *public* (one that they would discuss with casual friends or strangers).

It is interesting to tabulate the number of public items each person has checked. In most groups, there will be a great spread, and sometimes even a bell-shaped curve, of the number of items checked for public discussion. Students find it interesting to gather in small groups and discuss which items they consider private and which they consider public. The instructor may need to make it very clear that there should be no pressure exerted on any member of the group to justify their *private* choices. Participants then see the need to respect each individual's level of comfort on public and private issues.

Encouraging students to take responsibility for leading self-awareness activities can be beneficial. Most students are willing to work in pairs as facilitators if they are given the opportunity to volunteer at least a week in advance.

Processing of content and feelings after participation in the short exercises is important. Most students find it more meaningful to participate in one or two exercises at each class meeting than to spend the whole 3-hour class period on nothing but awareness exercises. Through these exercises, students begin to explore the origins of their own world views and perceptions of reality and begin to realize that there are multiple world views and ways to perceive reality (Carney & Kahn, 1984).

Goal 4: To initiate learning about the nature of the sociopolitical environment faced both by people of color and by White people in the United States. Ethnic or cultural novels are one way to introduce students to or broaden their awareness of different people's historical and cultural backgrounds. Students realize that the history books they have used omitted much of the history of oppression that people of color experienced. The use of ethnic novels in multicultural counselor training is one technique for expanding both cognitive growth and attitudinal awareness.

A cognitive aspect evident in many ethnic novels is the uniquenesses of the individuals in the stories. Some uniquenesses may result from generational differences in adherence to traditional cultural values, and some may be the result of other factors. Generational differences may be especially evident in novels about immigrant families. For example, Amy Tan's 1989 book *The Joy Luck Club* gives a vivid portrayal of generational differences between the lives of four Chinese women who lived in pre-1949 China and their daughters who were born in California. Rudolfo Anaya's *Bless Me, Ultina* (1972) illustrates generational differences in a family with a long heritage in Southwest United States. Anaya's book also exemplifies the uniquenesses in children whose parents come from different subcultures within an ethnic group, as well as sibling differences that result from

EXHIBIT 7.1

CATEGORIES OF PUBLIC AND PRIVATE SELF-DISCLOSURE

Objective
To compare different rules for public disclosure of private information appropriate to visitor and host culture residents.

Instructions
Please mark each of the following topics as:

Private: if it is comfortable to discuss only with self and intimates;
Public: if it is comfortable to discuss with casual friends, acquaintances, or strangers.

	Public	Private
Attitudes and opinions		
1. What I think and feel about my religion: my personal religious views	_____	_____
2. My views on Communism	_____	_____
3. My views on racial integration	_____	_____
4. My views on sexual morality	_____	_____
5. The things I regard as desirable for a person to be	_____	_____
Tastes and interests		
1. My favorite foods; my food dislikes	_____	_____
2. My likes and dislikes in music	_____	_____
3. My favorite reading matter	_____	_____
4. The kinds of movies and T.V. programs I like best	_____	_____
5. The kind of party or social gathering I like best; the kind that bores me	_____	_____
Work or studies		
1. What I feel are my shortcomings that prevent me from getting ahead	_____	_____
2. What I feel are my special strong points for work	_____	_____
3. My goals and ambitions in my work	_____	_____
4. How I feel about my career; whether I'm satisfied with it	_____	_____
5. How I really feel about the people I work for or with	_____	_____
Money		
1. How much money I make at work	_____	_____

EXHIBIT 7.1 *(continued)*

2. Whether or not I owe money; if so, how much   _____   _____

3. My total financial worth   _____   _____

4. My most pressing need for money right now   _____   _____

5. How I budget my money   _____   _____

Personality

1. Aspects of my personality I dislike   _____   _____

2. Feelings I have trouble expressing or controlling   _____   _____

3. Facts of my present sex life   _____   _____

4. Things I feel ashamed or guilty about   _____   _____

5. Things that make me feel proud   _____   _____

Body

1. My feelings about my face   _____   _____

2. How I wish I looked   _____   _____

3. My feelings about parts of my body   _____   _____

4. My past illnesses and treatment   _____   _____

5. Feelings about my sexual adequacy   _____   _____

Total Private Topics   _____

NOTE: From personal communication with Dr. Dean Barnlund, San Francisco State University. Cited with his permission.
SOURCE: Reprinted from *A Handbook for Developing Multicultural Awareness,* by P. Pedersen, pp. 31–32. © 1988 ACA. Reprinted with permission. No further reproduction authorized without written permission of the American Counseling Association.

the prevailing sociopolitical environments in which different-aged siblings are raised.

Reading these books also allows students to vicariously experience the life of someone whose culture is distinctly different from their own. Because these novels are about other people, reading them is a nonthreatening way to begin the process of seeing the world through different cultural lenses. As readers become engrossed in accounts of people of other cultures, they can begin the process of assessing their own feelings and readiness to work with culturally different people.

Instructors can enhance students' experiences by emphasizing the different purposes for reading and reporting on these novels. Some of these purposes are:

1. To introduce readers to the present or past realities of life for people of color
2. To participate vicariously in the lives of people of color
3. To broaden the reader's world view

4. To help the reader get in contact with the feelings one experiences while reading these novels

A list of novels representing the U.S. people of color groups is distributed. The stories need to portray the values, beliefs, and behaviors of the culture (or cultures) of the people about whom the story is written. The novels should also include descriptors of at least a small slice of the history of the culture described in the novel. Learning about this historical background also broadens readers' perspectives on the sociopolitical environment in which people of color have lived. Not all novels are appropriate for this assignment. Many neither include descriptors of the sociopolitical realities of life for the main character (or characters) nor show how these people's world views differ from those of the majority White culture. A list of some novels appropriate for this assignment is included in Appendix D.

The ethnic or cultural novel requirement is to be used early in the term, and students are given guidelines for what to include in their reports. These reports are quite different from traditional book reports. The ethnic or cultural book reports might include: (1) very brief overviews of the themes of the story, (2) two or three specific anecdotes that illustrate how the main characters in the story view the world from a cultural perspective different from that of the reader, and (3) a record of the feelings students experienced as they read the story.

These brief overviews of themes of the books can be shared orally in small-group class interaction; discussion is facilitated when participants are grouped in small circles. Each small group discusses novels about the same culture, using the topics outlined above. Students detail and discuss the anecdotes that show differing perceptions of reality, giving attention to possible assumptions that underlie the characters' behavior. These discussions help students understand that the assumptions underlying the behavior of the people in the novels may be very different from the assumptions that underlie their own behavior. The discussions also may include aspects of the cultural history of the people in the novel.

Heavy emphasis is placed on talking about feelings students experienced as they read the novels. Students vary greatly on how well they are in contact with and can talk about these feelings. For some people, this is difficult because they are still "totally in their heads" and not yet connecting emotionally with the story content. This is typical behavior for Stage One. Talking about these feelings early in the course helps students begin the process of connecting with their own cultural and racial identity development.

White students who can get in contact with their feelings often use such words and phrases as *appalled* at the oppression suffered, *angry* and *embarrassed* at the majority culture perpetrators' behavior toward the people of color, *disillusioned* with the authors of the traditional history books who have omitted much of the history of oppression of people of color, and *guilty* about being a member of the race responsible for this inhumane treatment. Students of color learn that people of other cultural heritages have also suffered oppression, and they feel empathy for others who have suffered. Students who are able to experience these feelings are moving into Stage Two (Carney & Kahn, 1984).

The ethnic or cultural book assignment carries many of the values that bibliotherapy offers readers. Following are some of the values of using this exercise early in multicultural study.

1. Reading the novels provides the readers vicarious experiences of the lives of people who are of a different ethnic or cultural heritage. Because the experience is vicarious, it poses little or no threat to the reader (Cornett & Cornett, 1980). Through reading, one can learn about a piece of the history of this ethnic group.

2. The content of the novels can help readers learn the many ways of coping with oppression people of color have used. Readers can see the several alternatives that characters in the book have developed for dealing with their problems (Cornett & Cornett, 1980). This exercise also helps readers recognize the strengths of people of color.

3. The reading experience can encourage readers to engage in critical thinking (Cornett & Cornett, 1980) when they begin to realize how selectively some U. S. historical and sociopolitical events have been (and are) reported.

One requirement for a complete bibliotherapeutic experience is for the reader to identify with a lead character in the story and experience an emotional release from perusing the book (Cornett & Cornett, 1980). For students of color, it will probably not be hard to identify with the persons experiencing oppression in the novels and to experience this catharsis. Students of color may feel an emotional release in realizing that others, too, have suffered.

Some White readers who know little of the history of oppression of people of color, and who have suffered little oppression themselves, may have trouble identifying with characters in the books. These readers may not be able to identify fully with what happens to the people in the novels. Most students will, however, experience some strong emotions as they read. Sharing these feelings in writing or orally are important ways for readers to get in contact with their feelings.

An exercise to introduce students to the sociopolitical nature of counseling is to have them study and compare two tables from Katz's 1985 article, "The Sociopolitical Nature of Counseling." The material in Exhibits 7.2 and 7.3 will help students see how traditional counseling theories are imbedded in the dominant White male culture.

In this exercise, students gather in small groups to discuss how their own values compare with the values listed in the tables. For White students, this is also a self-awareness exercise. Students of color will realize how their values may have been influenced by the values of the dominant White culture.

Another assignment that can help students understand different sociopolitical environments is to have them volunteer time working with people of a different cultural group. This is especially valuable for White students who have not lived in, gone to school with, or worked in a culturally pluralistic environment. This volunteer assignment can also help students of color understand the life space in which other people of color live and work. All students can broaden their world

EXHIBIT 7.2

THE COMPONENTS OF WHITE CULTURE: VALUES AND BELIEFS

Rugged individualism
Individual is primary unit
Individual has primary responsibility
Independence and autonomy highly
    valued and rewarded
Individual can control environment

Competition
Winning is everything
Win/lose dichotomy

Action orientation
Must master and control nature
Must always do something about a
    situation
Pragmatic/utilitarian view of life

Decision making
Majority rule when Whites have power
Hierarchical
Pyramid structure

Communication
Standard English
Written tradition
Direct eye contact
Limited physical contact
Control emotions

Time
Adherence to rigid time schedules
Time is viewed as a commodity

Holidays
Based on Christian religion
Based on White history and male leaders

History
Based on European Immigrants'
    experience in the United States
Romanticize war

Protestant work ethic
Working hard brings success

Progress and future orientation
Plan for future
Delayed gratification
Value continual improvement and progress

Emphasis on scientific method
Objective, rational, linear thinking
Cause and effect relationships
Quantitative emphasis
Dualistic thinking

Status and power
Measured by economic possessions
Credentials, titles, and positions
Believe "own" system
Believe better than other systems
Owning goods, space, property

Family structure
Nuclear family is the ideal social unit
Male is breadwinner and the head of the
    household
Female is homemaker and subordinate to
    the husband
Patriarchal structure

Aesthetics
Music and art based on European
    cultures
Women's beauty based on blonde, blue-
    eyed, thin, young
Men's attractiveness based on athletic
    ability, power, economic status

Religion
Belief in Christianity
No tolerance for deviation from single god
    concept

SOURCE: From "The Sociopolitical Nature of Counseling," by J. H. Katz, 1985, *The Counseling Psychologist, 13*, p. 618. Copyright © 1985 Stage Publications. Reprinted by permission.

EXHIBIT 7.3

THE CULTURAL COMPONENTS OF COUNSELING: VALUES AND BELIEFS

The individual in counseling
Individual is the primary focus
Individual has primary responsibility
Individual independence and autonomy
  highly valued
Individual problems are intrapsychic and
  rooted in childhood and family

Action orientation
Client can master and control own life
  and environment
Client needs to take action to resolve own
  problems
Bias against passivity or inaction

Status and power
Belief that Western counseling strategies
  are best
Therapist is expert
Credentials are essential
Therapy is expensive
Licensing used to maintain control of
  profession

Processes (communication)
Verbal communication or talk therapy
Standard monocultural English
Self-disclosure by client
Direct eye contact
Reflective listening

Goals of counseling
Insight, self-awareness, and personal
  growth
Improve social and personal efficiency
Change individual behavior
Increase ability to cope
Adapt to society's values

Protestant work ethic
Work hard in counseling and counseling
  works for you

Goal orientation and progress
Belief in setting goals in counseling
Belief in reaching goals in life

Emphasis on scientific method
Therapist objective and neutral
Rational and logical thought
Use of linear problem solving
Cause and effect relationships
Childhood and family sheds light on
  present behavior
Reliance on quantitative evaluation,
  including psychodiagnostic tests,
  intelligence tests, personal inventories,
  and career placement
Dualism between mind and body
Primary focus on the psychological as
  opposed to the physiological
Label problems using DMS III

Time
Scheduled appointments
Adherence to strict time schedule
  (50-minute hour)

Family structure
Nuclear family is ideal

Aesthetics
YAVIS Client: Young, Attractive, Verbal,
  Intelligent, Successful

SOURCE: From "The Sociopolitical Nature of Counseling," by J. H. Katz, 1985, *The Counseling Psychologist, 13*, p. 620. Copyright © 1985 Sage Publications. Reprinted by permission.

views on how others live by keeping a journal of events and feelings they experience during these volunteer encounters.

The volunteer experience needs to involve at least one hour a week and be ongoing for several weeks. It is more meaningful if the student works with the same individual or group for this extended period. Students may ask whether they can fulfill this requirement by attending different cultural events each week; although that can be educational, the experiences tend to be much more superficial (and sometimes in the realm of the exotic). Those engaging in ongoing experiences with the same cultural group usually develop a much better understanding of both the cognitive and affective realms of the lives of people of color than do people who skip from one cultural event to another.

As noted in Chapter 1, it is also important to study the impact of the sociopolitical environment of the oppression of people of color on White people. In the past, much attention has been given to the impact of oppression on those who are (or have been) oppressed, and this study needs to continue. But we now know that the oppressors also suffer negative consequences (Sue & Sue, 1990). Through autobiographical accounts of oppressors, such as *Killers of the Dream* (Smith, 1961) and *Outside the Magic Circle: The Autobiography of Virginia Foster Durr* (Barnard, 1985), readers of any race can realize that *people who victimize others also hurt themselves.* The TV series, "I'll Fly Away," (Brand, Falsey, & Sander, 1991) also portrays the effects of oppression on both the oppressor and the oppressed.

Goal 5: To introduce models for studying culture.   Currently, there are many formats for beginning the study of culture. Studying culture also involves studying world views because people share many aspects of their world view with other people of the same cultural background. Ibrahim (1985) underscores the critical importance of first understanding our own world view when she states, "It is essential to understand our own cultural heritage and world view before we set about understanding and assisting other people" (p. 635).

One way to introduce the concept of cultural world views is to talk about the hundreds (perhaps thousands) of ethnic cultures on planet Earth. The importance of learning about the values of another culture, while recognizing that it is impossible for each of us to learn the values of all the cultures of the world, is presented. To start the process, students are asked to look at formats for studying culture.

The instructor can explain that anthropologists have been studying culture for many years and can introduce students to the work of Clyde and Florence Kluckhohn. As noted in Chapter 2, Clyde Kluckhohn et al. (1951) conducted an extensive comparative study of values and value orientations in five cultures. F. R. Kluckhohn and F. L. Strodtbeck (1961), using the early work of C. Kluckhohn as a base, conducted additional research on several cultures to test a format for studying the values of cultures and the assumptions that underlie these cultural values. Kluckhohn and Strodtbeck (1961) summarized their research on categories for viewing culture under the following five general areas.

1. How people view human nature (bad, good, or bad and good)
2. The relation of people to nature (in control of, subjugated to, or with respect for living in harmony with)
3. The temporal or time orientation of the cultural group (past, present, future, or a combination of these perspectives)
4. What people believe about human activity (doing, being, or being-in-becoming)
5. The relational orientation of people to other people (lineal, collateral, or individualistic)

Several authors (for example, Ibrahim, 1985; Pedersen, 1988; Stewart, 1972; Stewart & Bennett, 1991; Sue & Sue, 1990) have discussed adaptations and applications of the framework for studying culture presented in the Kluckhohn and Strodtbeck (1961) model. Stewart and Bennett (1991) have adapted the Kluckhohn and Strodtbeck model and discuss American cultural patterns under these categories: (1) form of activity, (2) form of social relations, (3) perception of the world, and (4) perception of self.

In-class, small-group discussions of how each student relates to the Kluckhohn and Strodtbeck model of perspectives on studying culture can help students see commonalities as well as uniquenesses of each group member. Some students reject the model because they believe it portrays only the White male, middle-class values of U.S. society. This can lead to additional discussion of how students who have studied feminist or Afrocentric perspectives might view the world differently. However, most White students, as well as many students of color in the class, realize that they either identify with or have been influenced by many of the dominant societal values. Again, students do become aware of how our mainstream U.S. society has been dominated by White male, middle-class values.

An exercise in which students read vignettes of people experiencing cross-cultural confusion and misunderstandings, combined with the use of an exercise based on Stewart's 1972 adaptation of the Kluckhohn and Strodtbeck model for studying culture, can provide an introduction to how differing world views can lead to a breakdown of communication as well as to stressful cross-cultural encounters. Exhibit 7.4, from Weeks, Pedersen, and Brislin's 1982 *A Manual of Structured Experiences for Cross-Cultural Learning*, lists "American" values and "Contrast-American" values under an adaptation of the five Kluckhohn and Strodtbeck categories; Stewart and Bennett (1991) define *American* as "a short form of 'citizen of the United States of America'" (p. xii).

In the exercise, students are first asked to look at the cultural behaviors listed under each of these five categories: definition of activity, definition of social relations, motivation, perception of the world, and perception of the self and the individual. Next, the descriptors for both the "American" and the "Contrast-American" groups are noted.

EXHIBIT 7.4

SUMMARY OF CULTURAL ASSUMPTIONS AND VALUES

American	Contrast-American
1. Definition of activity	
a. How do people approach activity?	
1) concern with "doing", progress, change	"being"
external achievement	spontaneous expressions
2) optimistic, striving	fatalistic
b. What is the desirable pace of life?	
1) fast, busy	steady, rhythmic
2) driving	noncompulsive
c. How important are goals in planning?	
1) stress means, procedures, techniques	stress final goals
d. What are important goals in life?	
1) material goals	spiritual goals
2) comfort and absence of pain	fullness of pleasure and pain
3) activity	experience
e. Where does responsibility for decisions lie?	
1) responsibility lies with each individual	function of a group or resides in a role (dual contrast)
f. At what level do people live?	
1) operational, goals evaluated in terms of consequence	experimental truth
g. On what basis do people evaluate?	
1) utility (does it work?)	essence (ideal)
h. Who should make decisions?	
1) the people affected	those with proper authority
i. What is the nature of problem-solving?	
1) planning behavior	coping behavior
2) anticipates consequences	classifies the situation
j. What is the nature of learning?	
1) learner is active (student-centered learning)	learner is passive (aerial rote learning)
2. Definition of social relations	
a. How are roles defined?	
attained	ascribed
loosely	tightly
generally	specifically
b. How do people relate to others whose status is different?	
1) stress equality	stress hierarchical ranks
minimize differences	stress differences, especially to superiors

EXHIBIT 7.4 *(continued)*

American	*Contrast-American*
2) stress informality and spontaneity	stress formality, behavior more easily anticipated

c. How are sex roles defined?

similar, overlapping	distinct
sex equality	male superiority
friends of both sexes	friends of same sex only
less legitimized	legitimized

d. What are members' rights and duties in a group?

1) assumes limited liability	assumes unlimited liability
2) joins group to seek own goals	accepts constraint by group
3) active members can influence group	leader runs group, members do not

e. How do people judge others?

1) specific abilities or interests	overall individuality of person and his status
2) task-centered	person-centered
3) fragmentary involvement	total involvement

f. What is the meaning of friendship?

1) social friendship	intense friendship
(short commitment, friends shared)	(long commitment, friends are exclusive)

g. What is the nature of social reciprocity?

1) real only	ideal and real
2) nonbinding (Dutch treat)	binding
3) equal (Dutch treat)	unequal

h. How do people regard friendly aggression in social interaction?

1) acceptable, interesting, fun	not acceptable, embarrassing

3. Motivation

a. What is motivating force?

1) achievement	ascription

b. How is person-person competition evaluated?

1) as constructive, healthy	as destructive, antisocial

4. Perception of the world (world view)

a. What is the (natural) world like?

1) physical	spiritual
2) mechanical	organic
3) use of machines	disuse of machines

b. How does the world operate?

1) in a rational, learnable, controllable manner	in a mystically ordered, spiritually conceivable manner (fate, divination)

(continued)

EXHIBIT 7.4 *(continued)*

American   *Contrast-American*

    2) chance and probability . . . .   no chance or probability

 c. What is the nature of man?
    1) apart from nature or from any hierarchy . . . .   part of nature or of some hierarchy
                           (dual contrast)
    2) impermanent, not fixed, changeable   permanent, fixed, not changeable

 d. What are the relationships between man and nature?
    1) good is unlimited . . . .   good is limited
    2) man should modify nature for his ends . . . .   man should accept the natural order
    3) good health and material comforts expected and desired . . . .   some disease and material misery are
                           natural, to be expected

 e. What is the nature of truth? goodness?
    1) tentative (working type) . . . .   definite
    2) relative to circumstances . . . .   absolute
    3) experience analyzed in separate components dichotomies . . . .   experience apprehended as a whole

 f. How is time defined? Valued?
    1) future (anticipated) . . . .   past (remembrance) or present experi-
                          ence (dual contrast)
    2) precise units . . . .   undifferentiated
    3) limited resource . . . .   not limited (not resource)
    4) lineal . . . .   circular, undifferentiated

 g. What is the nature of property?
    1) private ownership important as extension of self . . . .   use for "natural" purpose regardless of
                          ownership

5. Perception of the Self and the Individual
 a. In what sort of terms is self defined?
    1) diffuse, changing terms . . . .   fixed, clearly defined terms
    2) flexible behavior . . . .   person is located in a social system

 b. Where does a person's identity seem to be?
    1) within the self (achievement) . . . .   outside the self in roles, groups, fam-
                         ily, clan, caste, society

 c. Nature of the individual
    1) separate aspects (intent, thought, act, biographical background) . .   totality of person

 d. On whom should a person place reliance?
    1) self . . . .   status superiors, patron, others
    2) impersonal organizations . . . .   persons

 e. What kind of person is valued and respected? What qualities?
    1) youthful (vigorous) . . . .   aged (wise, experienced)

 f. What is the basis of social control?
    1) persuasion, appeal to the individual . . . .   formal, authoritative
    2) guilt . . . .   shame

EXHIBIT 7.4 *(continued)*

Generalized Forms

a) lineal . . . . (time)   nonlineal

b) efficient and material cause-and-effect thinking . . . . (thinking)   formal causes, correlative thinking

c) material, substantive . . . . (essence and energy)   spirit, energy

d) operationalism (implied observer) . . . .   direct apprehension or formalism (dual contrast)

e) induction . . . .   deduction or transduction (dual contrast)

f) judgment by comparison . . . .   judgment against an absolute standard

g) world stuff expansive (unlimited good) . . . .   world stuff restricted (limited good)

NOTE: Adapted from material by Edward Stewart, who wishes to acknowledge the contributions of Dr. Jasper Ingersoll, Department of Anthropology, Catholic University, to the development of this table.

SOURCE: From *A Manual of Structured Experiences for Cross-Cultural Learning,* by W. H. Weeks, P. B. Pedersen, and R. W. Brislin, pp. 35–39. Copyright © 1982 SIETAR. Reprinted by permission of Intercultural Press, Inc.

The class is then divided into small groups of no more than five or six to study vignettes that portray an "American" facing a problem interacting with someone of a different culture. One possible vignette might be the following:

> "May," a new international student, has begun her studies in counseling at a U.S. university. After a few weeks, May finds herself very curious about certain things that have happened. First, although she always addresses the faculty members by calling them either "Dr." or "Professor," May notices that none of the other students in the class does this.
>
> At the first meeting of the student counseling association, May was the only person who wore formal clothes to the meeting. At the meeting, several students introduced themselves and, after talking with her briefly, many said to her, "We'll have to get together sometime." May responded that she would be happy to do this.
>
> Several weeks passed, but none of the students invited May to join them in their informal meetings. The other students seemed puzzled when May told them she would need to talk with her family before accepting an invitation to participate in a departmental research activity. The use of much small- and large-group discussion in class has also been confusing to May, because she expected that classes would consist of lectures only.

Students are asked to identify specific ways in which the "Contrast-American" is not viewing the situation in the same way as the "American" in the vignette assigned to their group, using Exhibit 7.4 as a guide. In a short space of time, most students are able to identify several cultural behaviors that are being viewed from these contrasting perspectives. Because the events described in the anecdotes are

FIGURE 7.1

Graphic Representation of World Views

SOURCE: Reprinted from "World Views and Counseling," by D. W. Sue, 1978b, *Personnel and Guidance Journal, 56,* pp. 458–462. Copyright © 1978 ACA. Reprinted with permission. No further reproduction authorized without written permission of the American Counseling Association.

```
                                         LOCUS OF CONTROL
                                              Internal

                                 I                              IV
                               IC–IR                          IC–ER

LOCUS OF                       Internal                       External
RESPONSIBILITY
                               (Person)                       (System)

                                 II                             III
                               EC–IR                          EC–ER

                                              External
```

happening to someone else, this exercise shows students, in a nonthreatening way, that cultures do indeed impact behaviors and values.

Some multicultural textbooks include content on paradigms for understanding world views. Pedersen (1988) outlines additional formats for viewing cultures, and Sue and Sue (1990) devote a chapter to a discussion of world views.

Another important world views perspective is the locus of control and locus of responsibility schema presented by D. W. Sue (1978a, 1978b). D. W. Sue was one of the first to research and publish on concepts of world views as they relate to cross-cultural counseling (see Chapter 2). D. W. Sue's early work was based on the locus of control work of Rotter (1966) and the locus of responsibility perspective that comes from attribution theory as discussed by Jones et al. (1972). A discussion of the locus of control and locus of responsibility paradigm is included in Chapter 7 of Sue and Sue's 1990 book.

Sue and Sue (1990) point out that the Kluckhohn and Strodtbeck (1961) model detailing the patterns of American cultural assumptions "are the building blocks of the IC–IR world view and typically guide our thinking about mental health services in Western society" (Sue & Sue, 1990, p. 146). Discussing the four possible quadrants of a person's perspective on locus of control and locus of responsibility paradigm as presented by D. W. Sue (1978a, 1978b) and shown in Figure 7.1 helps students realize the culture-bound nature of much of traditional counseling theory and practice. This framework also helps students understand that people may view their world from a variety of perspectives on personal control and personal responsibility.

Goal 6: To begin multicultural counseling skill development training. Multicultural skill development training is a task that begins in the first stage of building competencies for multicultural counseling and is ongoing during the counselor's lifetime (Carney & Kahn, 1984; Sue, Arredondo, & McDavis, 1992a, 1992b). "Culturally skilled counselors . . . are able to *send* and *receive* both *verbal* and *nonverbal* messages *accurately* and *appropriately*" (Sue, Arredondo, & McDavis, 1992a, p. 486).

An important initial step in the development of multicultural skill development is recognizing that multicultural counseling is a form of cross-cultural communication (Ivey, 1994; Sue, 1992; Sue & Sue, 1990). Crossing cultures in counseling presents myriad challenges to the counselor; cross-cultural communication is fraught with many possible barriers, blunders, or errors that can limit two-way interaction or cause the communication to break down completely. Hall (1976) notes two challenges to cross-cultural communication: "the linearity of language and the deep biases and built-in blinders that every culture provides" (p. 69).

A major goal for students working to attain multicultural counseling competence is to learn many of the basic aspects of communication styles that are influenced by culture (Kochman, 1981; Sue, 1992; Sue & Sue, 1990; Wolfgang, 1985). Topics such as proxemics (the use of space in communication), kinesics (body movements and gestures while interacting), and paralanguage (vocal cues, volume of speech, when to speak and when not to speak) are critical components of this cognitive storehouse of knowledge. Other important components of cross-cultural communication are an understanding of how people interact in high-context cultures as well as in low-context cultures.

In high-context cultures, people communicate by depending on the context or situation and make much use of nonverbal communication and paralanguage cues. In low-context cultures, people depend almost entirely on the verbal part of the communication and give minimal attention to nonverbal or paralanguage cues. Nonverbal communication, also, is influenced by the sociopolitical environment and is less under the control of the speaker than is verbal communication (Sue, 1992; Sue & Sue, 1990). And throughout this wide perspective on how culture impacts communication styles, trainees need to keep in mind the uniqueness of each individual within each cultural group.

Attaining cognitive knowledge of the multitude of factors that influence cross-cultural communication is an important initial step in multicultural skill development. Some of the these aspects of cross-cultural communication were also addressed in Chapter 1 of this book. To gain a wider understanding of the impact of culture on multicultural counseling, students can be encouraged to read widely on the impact of culture on cross-cultural communication (for example, Hall, 1959; Hall, 1976; Kochman, 1981; Sue, 1992; Sue & Sue, 1990; Wolfgang, 1985).

Exhibit 7.5, "How Would You Paraphrase My English?" (Ivey, 1994) is a good example of some of the possible problems encountered in communicating cross-culturally. This excerpt illustrates the challenges faced by Weijun Zhang of Shanghai Teachers University (for whom Chinese is his native language) speaking in English with an African American student in a microcounseling class in the United States. The incident underscores the powerful role that language plays in multicultural communication and counseling.

The nuances of the infinite number of possible dyadic cultural combinations for cross-cultural communication may seem mind-boggling and discouraging to

EXHIBIT 7.5

HOW WOULD YOU PARAPHRASE MY ENGLISH?

by Weijun Zhang

Four years ago, I welcomed two American friends into my home in Shanghai, both of whom had large rips in their jeans. "What's the matter with them?" I thought, "even we poor Chinese do not wear rags like that." To be a good host, I asked if I could help to have them mended. "No, Weijun, these are cool." I responded, "I know it's cool when you have holes in your pants, but this is winter already."

I told the above anecdote to my microcounseling class the other day and it caused a burst of laughter. When I started to boast that I was much more sophisticated nowadays, my good friend Carrie, an African-American, approached me with a mysterious smile. "Make sure that you do the next paraphrasing exercise with me, okay?" she asked. "Sure," I answered, with a question mark in mind.

Carrie (as client): One night, when I was parking in the street, a cat came up to me and said: "Hi, mellow, you got some grass to share, don't you?"

I (as counselor): You mean you are good at cats' nonverbals and imagined that this one was hungry?

Carrie: Don't be smart, Weijun. Just listen. I told that cat, "Get lost, you and I don't have the same program."

I: Sure, humans and animals do not have the same programming. When cats are hungry, they rub against you.

Carrie: Hold your comment, please. The cat, seeing that I had nothing to give, started to call me "bear," which made me mad. So I told him unless he left right away, I would call the pigs.

I: Are you testing my English to understand a fable about animals, Carrie?

Carrie: No, I just wanted to use a true incident to test you ability to paraphrase some Black English. I trust I did not blow your mind completely.

It was only after Carrie's detailed explanation that I understood what her story was about. In Black English, "mellow" means intimate friend, "cat" means man or boy, "grass" means marijuana, "program" means lifestyle or behavior pattern, "bear" means physically repulsive person, and "pig" means racist policeman.

I guess I got Carrie's message: It is far too early for me to boast about my progress in English. In this mulicultural society, I have much more to learn about language in order to be a qualified counselor.

Allen Ivey comments: Language is one of the most powerful, yet most often ignored, multicultural issues. I am glad Weijun touched on the subject.

Not only are there African-Americans who speak Black English, there are also adolescents who speak jargon that is hard for "outsiders" to understand.

EXHIBIT 7.5 *(continued)*

Many minority peoples whose native tongue is not English require you to "tune your ears" into their heavy accents.

If you understand nothing but the "King's English" (in the United States or Canada, standard English), it may render your efforts ineffective when you meet clients such as the one above.

SOURCE: From *Intentional Interviewing and Counseling: Facilitating Client Development in a Multicultural Society,* Third Edition, by A. E. Ivey. Copyright © 1994 Brooks/Cole Publishing Company.

---

beginning multicultural counseling students. This is one of many topics where students can begin to learn how to communicate across cultures and to recognize that this type of learning will be a lifetime endeavor. Learning with and from the client is a powerful tool for expanding one's knowledge of the possible meanings of words the client uses and the meanings of nonverbal communication and paralanguage evident in the counseling session.

Many counselor education programs involve students in some type of active listening or microskills training early in their programs, so most students will be somewhat familiar with this type of learning. It is important that all experiential classes in counselor training include preparation for culturally sensitive use of all the skills of counseling. The multicultural counseling class can offer some initial insights, but there is no way that all instruction and supervision needed can be completed in just one course in multicultural counseling.

The instructor can assess student levels of multicultural counseling development and initiate cultural use of microskills through modeling and participating with students in small-group role play of counseling excerpts or critical incidents in counseling. Some books with the kind of content that can be used for multicultural counselor skill development are: Axelson, 1993; Evans, Hearn, Uhlemann, & Ivey, 1993; Ivey, 1994; Sue & Sue, 1990. Students also can write critical incidents from their own experiences that can be useful in role-play class exercises.

There is a need to be selective, as well as a need to be creative, in using counseling microskills with culturally different people. Ivey is one author who addresses the need for cultural sensitivity in each chapter of the 1994 edition of his book *Intentional Interviewing and Counseling: Facilitating Client Development in a Multicultural Society.* The third edition (1993) of Ivey, Gluckstern, and Ivey's *Basic Attending Skills and Basic Influencing Skills* video includes content regarding culturally sensitive use of the basic attending and influencing skills throughout this micro-training AV series.

SUMMARY

This chapter described some initial pathways for student growth in multicultural beliefs and attitudes, knowledge, and skills. It is important to recognize that student growth in all these areas will be ongoing throughout all stages of multicultural counselor development and does not end abruptly when the individual moves to the next stage.

In addition to including descriptions of student characteristics and process guidelines for people in Stage One of multicultural counselor development, this chapter detailed six goals for this stage and described some of the appropriate environments and learning experiences for achieving these goals. References to many other resources that provide information for student growth in this first stage of multicultural counselor development were also included.

Christensen (1989) contends that "transition to the next stage is sparked by a precipitating event or situation of undeniable import, which jolts the individual's perceptions" (p. 277). This experience may be either positive or negative and usually occurs the first time issues related to racial, cultural, or ethnic differences are examined seriously. This description is similar to the way some racial/ethnic stage theorists describe the movement out of the first stage of reference group identifications (Cross, 1971, 1991; Helms, 1984). As noted in Chapter 6, movement from one stage to another will probably proceed in a spiral manner rather than in a linear fashion.

CHAPTER 8

Multicultural Counselor Preparation: Stage Two

*T*he purpose of this chapter is to outline pathways for student growth in beliefs and attitudes, knowledge, and skills in the second stage of multicultural counselor preparation. The chapter is organized under these subheadings: (1) student characteristics, (2) process guidelines, (3) goals, and (4) appropriate environments and learning experiences to achieve goals.

Much of the content of this chapter could be included in an introductory multicultural counseling class. To maximize student learning in multicultural counseling classes, faculty who teach other counseling courses need to be aware of this multicultural content and to integrate this learning into other counseling classes (both didactic and experiential).

STUDENT CHARACTERISTICS

At this stage, students have a beginning awareness of the impact of culture on behavior and values. Before studying their own cultural heritages, most White students have a limited awareness of the influence their own ethnocultural and racial backgrounds have on their values, beliefs, and behaviors. Many White students also have very little knowledge of the history of oppression of the people of U.S. minority groups. Students of color may or may not know the complete history of their own ethnic group or that of other people of color. Initially, knowledge of other cultures is handled mainly on the cognitive level. In describing student characteristics at this stage, Carney and Kahn (1984) state that "because information about other cultural groups may be new to them, they may lack an organized view of cultural differences and will be inclined to deal with such information in a detached scholarly manner" (p. 114).

Sabnani et al. (1991) have named this the *Conflict Stage*, and Ponterotto (1993) states that, for White counselor education students, "This stage is highlighted by conflict between wanting to conform to majority group norms and wishing to uphold humanistic, egalitarian values" (p. 215). Students experience mixed feelings as they learn about the history of oppression of minority group people in the United States. As students move into this stage, they begin to realize both the falsity of the stereotypes they hold about people of other cultures and the narrowness of their culture-bound perspectives. Many are unaware of their own prejudices and racist behaviors.

After gaining some elementary knowledge about people of other cultures, students may believe that they now need only learn a few counseling skills for working with people cross-culturally to become effective multicultural counselors. This misperception can give students a false sense of accomplishment and cause them to resist exploring their own cultural heritages or their attitudes toward other cultural groups (Carney & Kahn, 1984).

PROCESS GUIDELINES FOR CREATING A CLIMATE FOR STUDENT GROWTH IN STAGE TWO

Students in the second stage still need some structure to promote learning in both the cognitive and affective domains. Offering students options for sources of information on the various topics encourages students to seek information on their own.

In class, students continue to observe Tatum's (1992) guidelines that were presented in Stage One in Chapter 7, (keeping personal information shared in class confidential, refraining from belittling others, and speaking from an "I" perspective). While studying the sociopolitical history of people of color groups, White students often volunteer that they feel guilty about the way the majority White group has treated minority people and about the privileges afforded White people in our society. It is especially important for the instructor to watch and attend to how other students respond to this sharing of feelings. Some students may slip back into old patterns of "zapping" or making fun of students who are open enough to admit their feelings of guilt. Students who regress to this kind of behavior need to be confronted with what they are doing. This can lead to a discussion of the ineffective ways we sometimes handle situations in which we do not feel comfortable and how we deny our own feelings. This discussion provides a good opening to challenge students to explore their inner feelings about people who are different and about their own ethnocentrism.

Students of color enrolled in the multicultural counseling class may also begin to experience strong feelings as they engage in the readings and activities required for the class. Students of color who have grown up in mostly middle-class, White neighborhoods (and gone to middle-class, predominantly White schools) will also confess to feeling guilty as they study the history of racism toward their ethnocultural and racial group and as they realize how much they have denied their true cultural heritages. They may also disclose their feelings of sadness and loss when they realize how much they have let the values of the White middle-class society dominate their value systems. Instructor-modeled recognition of these feelings will help White students in the class be more understanding and supportive of feelings experienced by the students of color.

Through the students' journals, the instructor can continue to respond to students' feelings and questions. It is also important for the instructor to encourage students to think of alternative viewpoints. Caring confrontation will probably be necessary to help student growth in attitudes and beliefs, knowledge, and skills.

Students will begin to realize the ethnocentrism of some or much of their own behavior, and pain or guilt may accompany this recognition. It is important for student growth that the instructor recognize the feelings students are experiencing. Acknowledging that making changes usually means giving up something and is often painful can help students understand what they are experiencing.

Another factor that may influence students in this stage is that they may get excited about what they are learning and want their friends outside of class to experience this excitement, too. However, these students may be rejected or humiliated in their efforts to change others and may come to class wondering what they did wrong. Student growth can lead to feelings of loneliness. The instructor will need to be alert to these possibilities and to help students process their feelings. Some students may need individual therapy to deal with the strong and often conflicting feelings of this stage.

GOALS TO PROMOTE STUDENT DEVELOPMENT IN BELIEFS AND ATTITUDES, KNOWLEDGE, AND SKILLS IN STAGE TWO

Goal 1: To continue learning about the field of multicultural counseling

Goal 2: To expand awareness of the impact of one's ethnocultural and racial heritages on one's thinking and behavior

Goal 3: To expand knowledge of the historical background of U.S. people of color, including their history of oppression and their history of helping services

Goal 4: To learn procedures for investigating the historical and current value system descriptors for U.S. people of color

Goal 5: To understand the concept of stereotyping, to become aware of the pervasiveness of stereotyping in the current U.S. society, and to become aware of one's own stereotypes about members of other cultures

Goal 6: To realize the within-group variance of personal qualities of people of all ethnic and racial groups

Goal 7: To develop techniques for understanding each client as a unique person within her or his ethnic and racial heritage

APPROPRIATE ENVIRONMENTS AND LEARNING EXPERIENCES TO ACHIEVE GOALS

Goal 1: To continue learning about the field of multicultural counseling. Carney and Kahn (1984) suggest the following topics of study for this stage: attitudinal barriers to cross-cultural counseling, ethnocentric perspectives of much of mental health diagnosis and treatment, and perspectives on world views of others. Students were first introduced to these studies in Goal 1 of Stage One.

Some appropriate readings for expanding knowledge on these topics are found in Casas (1984, 1985), D'Andrea and Daniels (1991), Draguns (1989), Hills and Strozier (1992), Lee (1995); Lee and Richardson (1991), Pinderhughes (1989), Ponterotto and Casas (1987), Sue (1978a, 1978b, 1985), and Sue and Sue (1990). The *Journal of Multicultural Counseling and Development* is an especially appropriate professional journal for student use.

Draguns (1989) covers a wide variety of topics and issues on approaches to cross-cultural counseling. In the first chapter of their 1991 book, Lee and Richardson discuss the promises and pitfalls of multicultural counseling.

Pinderhughes (1989) gives a convincing overview of the interplay of race, culture, and power on both the helper and the helpee in the delivery of human services in the first two chapters of *Understanding Race, Ethnicity, and Power*. She presents a strong case for all helping service professionals to first understand their own values, assumptions, and behaviors in order to develop "skills that facilitate empathic interaction with clients and appreciation of culturally different others" (Pinderhughes, 1989, p. 20).

The history and current status of training for multicultural counseling competence has received considerable attention in the cross-cultural literature. In Chapter 2, I gave an overview of professional organizations' efforts to improve multicultural counselor training. For readers interested in additional information, an expansion and review of some of the information from Chapter 2 is included here.

Chapters in Casas' 1984 and 1985 books cover the early history of efforts by APA and ACA to improve racial- and ethnic-minority counseling and provide information on conferences, representations of racial- and ethnic-minority individuals as students and as faculty in counseling psychology and counselor education training programs, numbers of racial- and ethnic-minority practitioners, and descriptions of racial- and ethnic-minority counseling research through the early 1980s. Ponterotto and Casas (1987) reviewed research on training for multicultural competence in counselor education, reported on a survey to identify leading cross-cultural training programs, and made suggestions for improving the status of training for multicultural competence.

D'Andrea and Daniels (1991) used qualitative methods to formulate a theory of levels and stages of multicultural counselor training. From their investigations, D'Andrea and Daniels proposed that counselor education programs are at one of two levels with two distinct stages for each level. At the first level, the training programs are culturally encapsulated and in a stage of cultural entrenchment or in a stage of cross-cultural awakening. At the second level, the level of conscientiously working on multicultural training, the programs are at a cultural integrity stage or at a stage of infusing multicultural training throughout the program.

Hills and Strozier (1992) reported on a 1988-89 survey "to ascertain the response of training programs in counseling psychology to the long history of warnings and recommendations concerning psychology's practical and ethical need to attend to multicultural issues in training" (p. 44). The Hills and Strozier research surveyed the following aspects of multicultural counseling training in the APA accredited programs in counseling psychology: course work, faculty participation, students, and pressure on programs. These authors believe that the results of their survey presented "a generally positive picture" (p. 47) of the state of multicultural counseling in the 49 programs that responded (an 80% response). The study also indicated that, although junior faculty were more heavily involved in various multicultural training activities, it takes the commitment of senior faculty to move multicultural activities to the core of counselor training. Among recommendations made for improving multicultural counselor training was for programs "to expand their practicum sequence to include more multicultural opportunities" (Hills & Strozier, 1992, p. 49) through work to improve relationships with local non-White communities.

Students relate well to Sue's world views concepts on locus of control and locus of responsibility (Sue, 1978a, 1978b; Sue & Sue, 1990) introduced in Stage One. This information seems to have a powerful effect on helping students realize the culture-bound and ethnocentric nature of traditional Euro-Western therapeutic approaches. Pinderhughes (1989) encourages those in the helping services to be aware of how their values concerning locus of responsibility and locus of control compare with those of the client.

Axelson (1993) discusses the application of the world views concepts to the well-being of a client and cautions that "the counselor cannot assume that internality is the only gauge for mental health when reality and experience may demonstrate otherwise" (p. 398). Axelson also points out that, for the client's well-being on the dimension of locus of responsibility, it is unproductive to place blame completely on either the person or the system. He sees locus of control and locus of responsibility as interactive factors and discusses how the counselor needs to look carefully at both factors in assessing the client. Axelson (1993) describes four basic types of world views that emerge from the four possible combinations of the locus of control and locus of responsibility axes.

Type 1. The "pride-in-identity" person who believes in society
Type 2. The marginal person

FIGURE 8.1

Transactional Analysis of
Cultural Identity Quadrants

SOURCE: From *Counseling and
Development in a Multicultural
Society*, Second Edition, by J. A.
Axelson, p. 399. Copyright ©
1993 Brooks/Cole Publishing
Company.

I. (Assertive/Passive)	IV. (Assertive/Assertive)
I'm OK and have control over myself.	I'm OK and have control but need a chance.
Society is OK and I can make it in the system.	Society is not OK and I know what's wrong and seek to change it.
II. (Marginal/Passive)	III. (Passive/Aggressive)
I'm OK but my control comes best when I define myself according to the dominant culture.	I'm not OK and don't have much control; might as well give up or please everyone.
Society is OK the way it is; it's up to me.	Society is not OK and is the reason for my plight; the bad system is all to blame.

> *Type* 3. The "give-up" person who gives up on society
> *Type* 4. The "pride-in-identity" person who is realistic about the
> imperfections of society (p. 398)

Axelson (1993) also applies transactional analysis to Sue's cultural identity quadrants, as shown in Figure 8.1. This explanation of the various combinations of Sue's basic concepts may help some counselors understand the clients who come to them.

At Stage Two, students can use the world views concepts of D. W. Sue and the interpretations of Axelson to assess hypothetical clients. The following hypothetical client, Louisa, could serve as an example.

> You ask me why I came to see you. I'm here because I'm confused. I grew up in a very poor family and married young, so I never had a chance to go to school before. They my husband left me, so I had to apply for ADC. A year ago when they came to our housing project and offered me the chance to go get this special training in using word processors and paid for day care for my children, I thought it was the greatest thing that ever happened to me.
>
> I just graduated from that program at the local community college and have been looking for a job. I have had two offers for jobs, but both are far enough away that I will have to move. The salaries look good; but when I consider the expenses of renting an apartment and dressing up to go to work every day, and the cost of day care, I don't think I will be any better off than when I was on ADC. I'm really proud of what I did to get out and go to school and complete the program, but I'm discouraged. What's wrong with me?

This case can make for a lively discussion among counselors. Is Louisa a Type 2, marginal person (marginal/passive)? Or is Louisa a Type 4, "pride in identity" person, who is realistic about societal imperfections (assertive/assertive)?

Goal 2: To expand awareness of the impact of one's ethnocultural and racial heritages on one's thinking and behavior. The emphasis on learning about the values each of us has acquired through our ethnocultural and racial heritages is relatively new in multicultural counselor preparation. In the early years of cross-cultural and multicultural training, the sole emphasis seemed to be for White counselors to learn about people of color. Now, it is apparent that all people who function as helping services professionals need to learn about their own ethnic heritages (Arciniega & Newlon, 1981; Ibrahim, 1984; Lee, 1984; Parker, 1987, 1988; Pinderhughes, 1989; Sabnani et al., 1991; Sue, 1985, 1993; Sue et al., 1992a, 1992b). As D. W. Sue (1993) stated, "Race, culture, and ethnicity are functions of each and every one of us whether we are African-Americans, American Indians, Asian-Americans, Latino-Americans, or White Americans" (p. 247).

Students of color are encouraged to look beyond the broad categories of African American, Latino American, Asian American, or Native American for self-identification: for example, Caribbean African American, Puerto Rican American, Mexican American, Korean American, or Native American Nation of Lakota. Again, students are encouraged to trace their origins to the part of the world from which their ancestors came. Many African American students can trace their origins to ancestors who were slaves; often, they cannot find more than a few generations of family historical information because of the way families were disrupted under slavery. Awareness of this limitation for African American students seems to have a profound effect on the other members of the class.

I find it useful to have White students trace their ethnic heritage to the countries or parts of the world from which they or their ancestors (or the persons who served as their parents) have come. As mentioned before, some students will object, saying their families are not into that "ethnic stuff" and that they are just plain Americans. A few White students come to the class not knowing the European countries from which their ancestors came. After pursuing information about their own cultural origins and the predominant values of these ethnocultural groups, many students are surprised to find ethnocultural family behaviors that have been passed down for several generations and that have origins in their ethnic and racial heritages.

All students can profit from looking at their ethnocultural and racial heritages and discussing the inherent advantages and disadvantages (Pinderhughes, 1989). A preparatory experience for ethnic and racial self-awareness is the "Cultural Awareness: Ethnicity and Identity" exercise in Green's 1982 book. Before participating orally in this exercise in class, students need out-of-class time to prepare. Students are encouraged to contact older family members to gain historical family information from them. They can investigate such things as where their ancestors came from and why they came to America, an advantage as well as a disadvantage felt by ancestors, and family strengths evident from the heritage. Gathering this information in combination with naming their race of origin helps students develop a racial identity.

In class, students meet in small groups to talk about their ethnocultural and racial histories. As a concluding exercise, students make a statement to the entire class adapting the last guideline of Green's exercise: "In one or two sentences, name your ethnic [and racial] background, and describe one important personal benefit that you enjoy as a consequence of that ethnicity [and racial origin]" (Green, 1982, p. 214). Having all students recognize at least one important personal benefit helps counselors-in-training recognize the strengths of all cultures.

Another short exercise that can help identify cultural values is to ask students to think back about sayings and proverbs they have heard within their families. Students then write these sayings on the chalkboard, study them and note from which ethnic or cultural heritages they come, ask questions about any they do not understand, and look for themes in those listed. Many White students remark that the values represented by their proverbs are the same as those on the "Summary of Cultural Assumptions and Values" (Weeks et al., 1982) used in a previous class (see Chapter 7, Goal 5). A more detailed example of the use of cultural proverbs is provided by Sandra Tjitendero in Hoopes and Ventura's *Intercultural Sourcebook* (1979, pp. 168–169).

Students can also prepare a "roots paper" in which they outline the value system of the ethnocultural and racial heritage(s) they own, support their selection of this value system by anecdotes from past and recent behavior, and speculate on how their own value system might inhibit their working with someone of another culture. In this paper, students include information on the impact of their gender and sexual/affectional orientation, their socioeconomic background, and their spiritual/religious roots in the context of their ethnocultural heritage. Background reading on specific ethnic groups can be found in several sources: Ballantine & Ballantine (1993); *Culturgrams,* Volumes I & II (1994), McGoldrick et al. (1982), National Geographic Society (1989), Peabody (1985), Schaefer (1990), and Thernstrom (1980), for example.

The relatively new *Encyclopedia of World Cultures,* which has nine volumes describing ethnic groups worldwide, can help students who may otherwise have a difficult time tracing their ancestry. These nine volumes are organized by areas of the world: Volume 1, *North America,* edited by O'Leary and Levinson (1991); Volume 2, *Oceania,* edited by Hays (1991); Volume 3, *South Asia,* edited by Hockings (1992); Volume 4, *Europe (Central, Western, and Southeastern Europe),* edited by Bennett (1992); Volume 5, *East and Southeast Asia,* edited by Hockings (1993); Volume 6, *Russia, Eurasia, and China,* edited by Friedrich and Diamond (1994); Volume 7, *South America,* edited by Johannes (1994); Volume 8, *Middle America and the Caribbean,* edited by Dow and Kemper (1995); and Volume 9, *Africa and the Middle East,* edited by Middleton and Rassan (1995). A tenth volume will contain the cumulative indexes and bibliographies.

After preparing their roots paper, students participate in small-group discussions in class, starting with people of similar ethnic heredity and concluding with large-group sharing and processing. Special emphasis is placed on the ownership of values and behaviors from one's ethnic and racial heritage. Students are challenged to speculate on how these values and behaviors might get in their way in counseling and helping people of other ethnic or cultural and racial heritages. Students are, also, encouraged to think about the assumptions about human behavior that are related to their personal value systems and to think about different assumptions that may be held by other people.

The belief by many middle-class White people that hard work leads to success is an example of an assumption that may not be held by many people of color, especially those from lower socioeconomic classes. Students could be encouraged to think about different assumptions related to this work ethic concept that might be held by some people who do not have as much power over their lives as most middle-class White people do.

Some authors refer to the term *cultural baggage* to describe values each of us carries as a result of socialization in an ethnocultural group (or groups). Students sometimes object to the term *cultural baggage* because they view *baggage* negatively; but a few years ago, one student gave an enlightening response to this complaint. He stated that he liked the term *cultural baggage* because to him it implied that, like packing bags for a trip, he had the choice of deciding what he wanted to include in the bags to take with him (Wallace Eddy, personal communication, October 21, 1988). I have found this explanation useful in helping trainees realize that they may choose to change some culture-based values and behaviors that could interfere in cross-cultural interactions. More recently, this former student stated: "I still believe that concept today. I also believe it empowers us to look at our heritage and deal with it honestly in terms of likes and dislikes. After examining our heritage, I feel we are able to make choices and live a more authentic life" (Wallace Eddy, personal communication, September 24, 1994).

During the process of self-study, it is important that all students identify their racial origin(s). As mentioned many times in this book, for many White students, having a racial identity seems to be a new concept, and they may need to be prodded to consider what it means to be White. Recognizing the privileges of being White may also be new to some White students. The instructor needs to challenge these students to think about and move toward "owning" both of these new realizations.

Awareness of the impact of group factors such as racial, ethnic, religious, social class, gender, and generational identifications on self can be expanded in a group like Max Birnbaum's Clarification Group (C Group), described in some detail by Johnson (1990a). The first phase is called the *Recovery of Social Self;* it includes the gathering of life history and experiencing "a structured group interview that focuses on reference group factors in the development of individual group members" (Johnson, 1990a, p. 136). From this phase, students move to the second phase in which they are asked "to examine their views of the social world, especially the perceptual linkages between themselves and others who are socially and culturally different" (Johnson, 1990a, p. 136). At this point, students begin to recognize their ethnocentric viewpoints and can be challenged to move into the third phase in which present feelings are explored and confronted.

Goal 3: To expand knowledge of the historical background of U.S. people of color, including their history of oppression and their history of helping services.
A recurring theme in the multicultural literature is the critical need for all counselors to understand the sociopolitical history that people of color have

experienced in the United States. (Arciniega & Newlon, 1981; Harper, 1973; Parker, 1987, 1988; Sabnani et al., 1991; Sue & Sue, 1990; Sue et al., 1992a, 1992b). Outside readings are a good way to start learning about the history and value systems of cultures. Some of the many good sources of information on the history and values of U.S. minority groups are Axelson (1993), Ballantine and Ballantine (1993); Daniels (1988); McGoldrick et al. (1982), National Geographic Society (1989), Schaefer (1990), Sue & Sue (1990); Thernstrom (1980), Wilkinson (1986), and the nine volumes of *The Encyclopedia of World Culture* referred to under Goal 2.

Students choose an ethnic culture distinctly different from the one in which they were socialized, do library research, and prepare a short paper on the history of that cultural group in the United States. In that paper, those studying African Americans, Hispanic/Latino Americans, and Asian Americans summarize the circumstances that brought the first members of the group to the United States, describe how they were treated as immigrants or slaves, and report on who performed the helping service needs of these people throughout their history in this country. Those studying the history of the American Indians/Native Americans are asked to summarize the history of the selected tribe or nation from the time of first contact with White European immigrants, explaining how the White immigrants treated that tribe or nation, and determine who performed the helping service needs for that group throughout its recorded history.

White students are urged to select a people of color group so they can gain a broader picture of the sociopolitical history of these people. Students of color select a different people of color group to gain perspectives on that ethnocultural and racial group's sociopolitical heritage.

Because compiling a written record of the history of any people of color group can be tedious, I encourage students to shorten their record by making a time line of important historical events. In addition to naming the event and the approximate date of its occurrence, I ask students to write brief notes to highlight the particular significance of this event for the people of that group.

After completing this library research, students meet for in-class group reporting. Students first divide into small groups with others who have studied the same people of color group, and they prepare summary reports of their findings to share with the large group. Again, everyone talks about feelings experienced as they learned of the oppression suffered by all the minority group people and the behavior of the perpetrators of oppression.

Goal 4: To learn procedures for investigating the historical and current value system descriptors for U.S. people of color. Following, or concurrent with, the study of the history of oppression and helping services of U.S. minority people, students examine the traditional and present values considered representative of the majority of people of one ethnic minority group. Learning the value systems for all U.S. people of color groups would be a formidable and probably an impossible task. It is for this reason that it helps for learners to begin with the study of one U.S. people of color group. Using the models for studying culture introduced in

Chapter 7, students can begin to apply these paradigms to the study of one ethnic minority group's culture.

At this point in the multicultural counseling class, students are encouraged to narrow the focus of study of a cultural ethnic group through adding other cultural and diversity descriptors and focusing on the study of this group. Some examples are African American professional women, gay White students, Latino lesbians, Native American Sioux Nation children, Mexican American college students, and Chinese American adolescents. Sources of information for this study of culture are many: printed resources, audio visual resources, and people resources. Narrowing the focus of the study can make for more meaningful research, because students often have a keen interest in one or more of the other diversity descriptors. Encouraging students to combine the focus of at least one other diversity descriptor with the focus on one cultural group often leads to a better understanding of the meaning of multiple oppressions.

The importance of people resources is emphasized. Inviting people of color to interact with the class is a good way to initiate this interaction. At least three resource people from each people of color group take part in this class interaction. Class members are urged to invite resource people to join the class for open sharing. Having class members do the inviting serves at least two purposes: (1) students feel more "ownership" of the activity when they do the inviting, and (2) it encourages cross-cultural interaction outside of class.

The availability of people of color to invite will vary depending on whether the class meets in an urban or a rural setting. With on-campus classes, finding people of color to meet with the class will probably be easy because many students will be working with or have friendships with students of color on campus. It may help to keep a list of minority resource consultants who are available at a given location. The students who do the inviting also introduce the resource people to the class.

A few years ago, some of the resource people asked for guidelines about what they should talk about with the class. Our class then spent time brainstorming on the type of questions they might ask, and they are listed in Exhibit 8.1. The questions were selected on the basis of information needed to help prospective counselors better understand people of color.

We keep copies of these questions on file, and classes update them regularly. The printed questions are then sent to resource consultants prior to their meeting with our class. The resource people have the freedom to choose questions to which they respond. In addition, class members will have many other questions to ask the resource people. It is important to communicate to the resource people that they are not expected to represent, or speak for, their entire cultural group.

I developed the "Culture—The Silent Partner Worksheet" (Wehrly, 1990) for students to have in front of them when they interact with guests in the people of color panels (see Exhibit 8.2). The worksheet gives students ideas for additional questions they could ask to help them understand how important culture is in the lives of the people with whom they are interacting. Students also find the worksheet helpful in additional interviews for their final paper in the Counseling/Helping in a Multicultural Society class. The information on this worksheet underscores how knowledge of the importance of culture in a person's life can serve as a silent but powerful partner to the counselor or helper (a concept introduced in Chapter 1 of this book).

We concentrate on different people of color groups at different class sessions. Students are expected to make additional contacts with members of the ethnic or cultural group they have elected to study. Some White students may feel threatened because they have had so little contact with people of other cultural groups.

Students who are involved in the ongoing volunteer contacts with people of a different cultural group described under Goal 4 in Stage One (Chapter 7) will find the interaction with people of color panel members especially interesting. By the time panel members interact with the class, the people who have engaged in regular cross-cultural encounters will already have learned much about the cultural values of this group. Mio (1989) underscores the values of regular one-to-one exchanges of ideas with members of another cultural group as students begin the study of multicultural counseling and describes a qualitative study of the significance of this kind of assignment. Mio found that knowledge gained through direct

EXHIBIT 8.2

CULTURE—THE SILENT PARTNER WORKSHEET

Some aspects of life that are impacted by culture	Implications for helping service professionals
Language	
Rituals observed	
Perspectives on work and activity	
Pace of life—perspectives on relaxing	
Celebrating holidays	
Expressions of emotions	
Feelings about life, death, and illness	
Definitions of the family and meanings of "family"	
Attitudes toward help seeking	
Sex role definitions	
Meaning of friendship	
Perspectives on control of nature	
Perspectives on time	
Perceptions of individual identity	
Approaches to decision making	
Nonverbal communication	

SOURCE: From "Culture—The Silent Partner Worksheet," by B. Wehrly. In M. Woodside and T. McClam, *Instructor's Manual for an Introduction to the Human Services*, pp. 46–47. Copyright © 1990 Brooks/Cole Publishing Company.

contacts is more meaningful and seems to be learned on a deeper level than knowledge obtained from books, lectures, and the media.

Presenting critical incident cases related to the people of color panel group discussions can help students apply values descriptive of that cultural group. One such example is the case of Mr. Fox and his challenges with motivating Native American students described in the following exercise.

> George Fox is a first-year, sixth-grade elementary school teacher in an area of Arizona where most of the children are of Native American heritage. From Mr. Fox's perspective, the children seem to lack motivation.

To help the children become more motivated, Mr. Fox has instituted contests in spelling and arithmetic classes. He offers prizes for students who receive the top grades in weekly tests in both classes. The prizes offered are special stickers to place after their names on a poster on the front bulletin board and bonus points to be added toward a weekend trip to California at the end of the term.

Each Friday, Mr. Fox has a special ceremony at which he awards certificates to the winning students and gives them stickers to put on the front bulletin-board poster. Students seem reluctant to come to the front of the classroom to receive these awards, and the whole plan has not been very successful in getting these students to work harder in their spelling and arithmetic classes.

Can you help Mr. Fox understand what traditional Native American cultural values may be incongruent with his use of these contests as motivational devices?

In small-group discussion of Mr. Fox's dilemma, students may note that the traditional value systems of many American Indians encourage cooperation rather than competition, group rather than individual efforts, anonymity rather than individual visibility, submissiveness rather than aggression, humility rather than assertiveness about one's accomplishments, and a present time orientation rather than a future time orientation. Fox's contest does not take these traditional values into consideration.

After students have researched a culture through their library investigations and people resource contacts, they again meet in small-group discussions, report to the entire class, and process the information. The focus of these discussions is on the traditional values associated with people of this cultural group, calling attention to the fact that no one individual of any cultural group will display all the values of her or his cultural heritage. Johnson (1990b) notes that "the individual shares the group in a unique way, but the individual context is never the same as the context of a group" (p. 44). It is very important to emphasize this point, so that counselors-in-training will not stereotype people of a different cultural group on the basis of the knowledge gained about this group.

Goal 5: To understand the concept of stereotyping, to become aware of the pervasiveness of stereotyping in the current U.S. society, and to become aware of one's own stereotypes about members of other cultures. Kleinman (1985) warns that we may insult and demean clients if we treat them according to our stereotypes of their culture. Students begin learning about the concept of stereotyping early in the multicultural counseling class. In an introductory lecture, the dangers of stereotyping people based on their ethnic or cultural heritage are emphasized. At this point, the concept is often understood more on a cognitive than on an affective level. We "walk a tightrope" in our use of the knowledge we gain about a cultural group. Without this knowledge, we may make enormous blunders that can serve as barriers to multicultural counseling. With the knowledge of cultural values of groups with which we work, we must be very careful to view each individual as a unique person and find out how important the traditional values of that person's cultural heritage are to the individual.

Many of us are not aware of the stereotypes we hold about people of other cultural groups. Unless we become aware of these stereotypes and confront the assumptions we make based on these stereotypes, we may have great difficulties in effective cross-cultural interpersonal communication. Study and discussion of the history of minority group people can help dispel stereotypes that are carried from childhood. Direct contact with people of other cultures also helps us realize the erroneous nature of many of our stereotypes. After the people of color panel discussions, students will sometimes volunteer stereotypes they have held that they now realize are inaccurate.

Oral sharing of stereotypes can be an effective way for class members to begin the process of understanding stereotypes. After the instructor models one or more examples of stereotypes held, some class members will share their stereotypical views.

Exhibit 8.3 (from Ponterroto & Pedersen, 1993) describes an experiential activity to help students become aware of stereotyped expressions about other groups that are frequently heard or implied but not necessarily believed by the individual naming the stereotype. Note the *Objective, Procedure, Debriefing,* and *Learning Principle* sections listed for this exercise.

A variation of the stereotypes exercise is to have the stereotypes listed by students for the different ethnic, racial, and cultural groups written in felt pen on large sheets of newsprint (one sheet for each group) that are mounted around the room. Debriefing should also be done after the total group views each list of cultural group stereotypes. As Ponterotto and Pedersen (1993) point out, it is important to realize how emotion-laden the small- and large-group discussions may become. It is especially important that lists of stereotypes be composed for *all* cultural groups represented in the class. This exercise is one in which it would be beneficial to underscore the fact that the content is *not* factual knowledge but *opinion*. The fact that *people do stereotype others* is in the realm of knowledge of the powerful impact that the agents of socialization have on all people.

Parker (1988) has a chapter that could help students understand and "own" stereotypes. Other structured exercises on stereotypes are described in Paradis (1981) and in Weeks, Pedersen, and Brislin (1982). Participation in these experiential activities can also heighten self-awareness of stereotypes.

Goal 6: To realize the within-group variance of personal qualities of people of all ethnic and racial groups. Open sharing among members of the multicultural counseling class probably does the most to help students see the great within-group variance among ethnic groups. This occurs most naturally in classes that are culturally pluralistic. In addition, class interaction with resource people of color highlights the great variations within each group. Another way to encourage learning about the variance within cultural groups is to require that each student interview more than one member of the ethnic or cultural group selected for study.

EXHIBIT 8.3

STEREOTYPES

Objective

Sometimes, by focusing on stereotypes directly and explicitly, it is possible to increase our control over the ways that stereotypes shape our lives. This exercise provides the opportunity for persons to describe "typical" or "frequently expressed" stereotypes about different groups, even though the participant does not believe that stereotype. Students from different ethnic, racial, and cultural groups will probably identify different patterns of stereotypes. By testing these stereotypes against persons actually from the different groups, it should be possible to demonstrate the dangers of stereotyping.

Procedure

1. Assemble a group of students willing to look at stereotypes regarding different ethnic, racial, and cultural groups. Because the topic is sensitive, it would be useful to keep the groups small, from 5 to 10 persons, for instance. It would also be useful to include different ethnic, racial, and cultural group members among the participants.
2. Each participant will be asked to complete a checklist indicating different ethnic, racial, and cultural groups at the top of the page and a list of adjectives along one side of the page.

Adjectives			Groups		
	A	B	C	D	E
Not at all aggressive					
Conceited about appearance					
Very ambitious					
Almost always acts as a leader					
Very independent					
Does not hide emotions					
Very active					
Very logical					
Not at all competitive					
Feelings easily hurt					
Not at all emotional					
Very strong need for security					
Easily influenced					

154 ■ CHAPTER 8

EXHIBIT 8.3 *(continued)*

Adjectives	Groups				
	A	*B*	*C*	*D*	*E*
Very objective					
Very self-confident					
Easy going					
Has difficulty making decisions					
Dependent					
Likes math and science					
Very passive					
Very direct					
Knows the ways of the world					
Excitable in a minor crisis					
Very adventurous					
Very submissive					
Hard-working and industrious					
Not comfortable with aggression					

Debriefing:
Students may work in small groups to compare patterns of similarity and differences as they identify stereotypes typically held regarding one or another ethnic, racial, or cultural group. Because stereotypes tend to be volatile and emotion-laden, it is not necessary for individual participants to indicate whether or not they themselves agree with the stereotypes—although their acceptance or rejection of the stereotype may well come out in the discussion. It would be useful to test these stereotypes against actual persons who are members of the ethnic, racial, cultural groups being mentioned. It might also be useful to search through magazines or publications to find pictures or word descriptions that do or do not support the stereotypes.

Learning principle:
Stereotypes are most powerful when they are unexamined and untested against the reality of the ethnic, racial, or cultural groups being represented.

Individual differences are what you were born with. Ethnic, racial, and cultural differences are the result of everything that has happened to you since then. It is especially crucial to prevent prejudice in the adolescent years when identity is being shaped and where ethnic, racial, and cultural differences have such a profound impact. In Exercise #6, we look at the unfolding process by which a person's ethnic, racial, and cultural identity is developed.

SOURCE: From *Preventing Prejudice: A Guide for Counselors and Educators,* by J. G. Ponterotto and P. B. Pedersen, pp. 106–108. Copyright © 1993 Sage Publications. Reprinted by permission.

Goal 7: To develop techniques for understanding each client as a unique individual within her or his ethnic and racial heritage. Learning about the sociopolitical history and values of people of another culture is a large task. An even larger task is translating learning about people of other cultures to culturally sensitive work with these people. Many people find it helpful to learn how to integrate cultural knowledge in the counseling process through working on one aspect at a time.

In an early session with a client, it is usually important to recognize the difference in cultural heritages between the counselor and the counselee. Self-disclosing any feelings you, the counselor, have relative to this difference and asking clients how they feel about this may be helpful.

Simply stating that you need help understanding the role that culture plays in the life of your client can be an effective way to learn the importance of the cultural heritage in that person's life. If the client seems hesitant to respond to open questions about her or his culture, it might help to ask about some of the items listed on the "Culture—The Silent Partner Worksheet" (Wehrly, 1990) introduced under Goal 4. The counselor needs to be sensitive to the client's reluctance to respond to cultural questions and should postpone further discussion related to cultural heritage if the topic seems threatening to the client.

To help understand the client's problem from the client's cultural perspective, an adaptation of Kleinman's explanatory medical model (1980, 1985, 1986, 1988) can be helpful. "Explanatory models are the notions about an episode of sickness and its treatment that are employed by all those engaged in the clinical process" (Kleinman, 1980, p. 105). Kleinman discusses the values of obtaining the patient's perceptions of sickness and comparing these perspectives with those of the doctor (explanatory models of both patient and doctor).

As modified for appropriate use in counseling, the explanatory medical model questions consist of the counselor asking the client for help in understanding his or her problem. Open questions such as the following (as modified from Kleinman, 1980) are appropriate to use in enlisting the client's help.

1. What name do you give to your problem?
2. What caused your problem?
3. When and how did your problem begin?
4. How serious is your problem?
5. How does this problem affect your life?
6. How does this problem affect the lives of those around you?
7. What worries you about this problem?
8. (For clients who are immigrants or who are not living with the natural support system in which they were socialized): How would you solve this problem if you were living back in _____?
9. What kind of help or treatment do you think you should receive?

These questions can be used effectively only after establishing trust and rapport with the client. The establishment of a meaningful cross-cultural working relationship may involve several sessions and will be described in greater detail in Stage Three. The counselor must allow time for discussing or elaborating on responses; it is possible that not all questions will be covered in one session. If the counselor is also working with other members of the family, their answers to the same Kleinman explanatory model questions can be compared with the answers of the person who has the problem.

After instructor modeling, role playing (including role reversal) with counseling trainees can be an effective way to learn to use the explanatory model questions as a technique in understanding clients' perspectives on their problems. Individuals interested in learning more about using explanatory models are referred to some of Kleinman's writing on the subject (for example, 1980, 1985, 1986, 1988).

Another helpful model is the Comas-Diaz and Jacobsen (1987) model for assessing ethnocultural identification. "The ethnocultural assessment may be particularly useful in the evaluation and treatment of minority group members and ethnocultural translocated individuals, and in cross-cultural psychotherapy" (Comas-Diaz & Jacobsen, 1987, p. 233). The assessment consists of obtaining information on five stages of the client's ethnocultural identity development. Much of the information is obtained directly from the client, but additional information can be obtained from family members and from study of the literature on client's culture(s).

Comas-Diaz and Jacobsen underscore the importance of the therapist's study and understanding of her or his own ethnocultural identity development. The authors point out the critical importance of therapists' coming to terms with the feelings they have about their own ethnocultural heritages, which supports the activities of Goal 2 of this chapter. Actual implementation of the complete assessment procedure will probably occur later in a student's multicultural development and will be described in Stage Four. Introducing students to the model at this time can help them see the multiplicity of forces that may impact people in transition, the uniqueness among people that result from these many influences, and the importance of counselor self-awareness of ethnocultural identity development.

Any or all of the 18 critical incident cases in Sue and Sue's 1990 book can help students apply knowledge they have learned about different cultures. Sue and Sue suggest several ways in which the critical incident cases may be used cognitively, in addition to role playing alternative counselor interventions. The authors also suggest having class members write their own critical incidents to use for classroom learning experiences.

At the Stage Two level, most students will be more ready for cognitive discussions of the critical incidents than for role playing alternative counselor interventions. Nevertheless, role playing should be tried to encourage class members to "stretch" and not let themselves "stall" at the level of talking about, rather than trying out, new behaviors. Attention is called to the aspects of cross-cultural communication introduced in Stage One. In role-play practice, it may be more effective to practice one aspect of cross-cultural communication at a time, such as concentrating on either proxemics, kinesics, paralanguage, high-/low-context communication, sociopolitical aspects of nonverbal communication, or nonverbals as a reflection of our biases and fears (Sue, 1992; Sue & Sue, 1990).

SUMMARY

This chapter described student characteristics and process guidelines for counselors in the second stage of the development of multicultural counseling competency. The appropriate environments and learning experiences to achieve seven goals were discussed.

Stage Two was described as one in which individuals feel much inner conflict because of the added knowledge they have gained about themselves and about the past and present prejudice and racism of the "real world" toward people who are different in our society. Ponterotto (1993) states that White counselors choose one of two options to deal with this inner conflict: (1) take a prominority/antiracism stance, or (2) retreat into White culture. Ponterotto also emphasizes that counselors must be exposed to culturally diverse faculty, administrators, peers, a multicultural curriculum, and have ongoing interracial interactions and discussions in order to move forward in the stages of racial identity development.

Sources for additional information and for experiential activities were cited in this chapter. A listing of appropriate Stage Two cross-cultural counseling training goals and tasks for White counselors from the 1991 Sabnani et al. model is included in Appendix B. With some modifications, most of these training goals and tasks are also appropriate for use with counselors of color.

CHAPTER 9

Multicultural Counselor Preparation: Stage Three

*T*he purpose of this chapter is to outline pathways for student growth in beliefs and attitudes, knowledge, and skills in the third stage of multicultural counselor preparation. Chapter 9 is organized under these subheadings: (a) student characteristics, (b) process guidelines, (c) goals, and (d) appropriate environments and learning experiences to achieve goals.

Much of the content of this chapter is appropriate for a class in multicultural counseling. As noted in the previous chapters, it is especially important for other faculty members to be aware of the content of the multicultural counseling class so that all other classes, both didactic and experiential, in the counselor training program reinforce the learning from the multicultural counseling class. It will be important for the experiential classes to build and expand on the initial attempts to teach the culturally sensitive skills introduced in the multicultural counseling class.

The content described in Stages One, Two, and Three may be the extent of the content that can be taught in a multicultural counseling class if the class is composed of students from a variety of disciplines. If the class is limited to counseling majors, and if students have completed an introductory culturally sensitive experiential course in counseling, it may be possible to incorporate more training in multicultural counseling techniques in the multicultural counseling class. The background in cultural awareness and sensitivity in interpersonal relations that students bring to the class will influence the way the multicultural counseling class is taught. Departments that have done considerable professional development work on diversity will be prepared to include more in the multicultural counseling class.

STUDENT CHARACTERISTICS

Students who have been able to relate both cognitively and affectively to the experiences of the first two stages of multicultural counselor development will feel strong, often mixed, feelings by the third stage. Sabnani et al. (1991) have labeled Stage Three the *Prominority/Antiracism Stage* for White counselors. Carney and Kahn (1984) describe the third stage as the most complex—one in which students feel an increased sense of personal responsibility and guilt "because the perceived locus of responsibility has begun to shift from external authority to themselves" (p. 115). Christensen (1989) notes that this stage "is an especially painful and often prolonged period in which the emphasis is really on self-awareness in relation to cross-cultural experiences and events" (p. 279). Coping with the feelings that accompany this new awareness of self and of the "real world" may result in a sense of disequilibrium.

Christensen (1989) describes the affective states the Stage Three majority individual may feel as curiosity, denial, guilt, fear, powerlessness, and anger. The affective states of the Stage Three minority individual are excitement, denial, rejection, sadness, powerlessness, and anger. It is common for both the majority and minority individuals to vacillate between these feelings or seem to remain stuck in a particular state for some time.

Students who have not had a previous introduction to the models of racial and ethnic identity development may experience strong feelings as they study these models. Many will begin serious examination of their own attitudes, beliefs, and behaviors and will discuss at what stage or level they place themselves. Some trainees may reject these concepts completely; others may find it very difficult to see themselves at anything but the highest level of racial or ethnic identity development.

White students may talk more about these feelings than students of color do in large-group discussions. Students of color may share their feelings in small-group discussions, depending on the trust-level that they feel with the members of the small group. At this stage, it is not uncommon for students of color to come to the instructor individually or to write notes to the instructor and share the feelings they are experiencing.

Pinderhughes (1989) describes the heavy emotions that people of any ethnic background feel as they work to understand race and their personal involvement in racism: "A sense of fatigue and exhaustion can surface as a result of the struggle to understand the many complexities, to tune in on the sadness, frustration, fear, and anger previously hidden, unarticulated and/or unexpressed; the old denial and ignorance that maintained tranquility and stability have now broken down" (p. 106).

Carney and Kahn (1984) propose that taking on an attitude of color blindness is one way many students deal with these strong feelings. Color blindness behavior may take one of two directions: denial or immersion. People using denial will play down the importance of race and culture and will emphasize the commonalities of people of all races and cultures. Pinderhughes (1989) warns that taking the stance that all people are alike "protects those holding it from awareness of their ignorance of others and the necessity of exerting the energy and effort to understand and bridge the differences" (p. 44). Ridley (1989) lists color blindness as a racist process variable in counseling; he states that color blindness "disregards the central importance of color in the psychological experience of the client" (p. 72).

White students who choose immersion tend to blame society and express anger toward their cultural origins. They often become deeply involved with the plight of a particular cultural or ethnic group and may behave very paternally toward people of color in their attempts to "help" cross culturally. Immersing oneself in activities to "help" people of color may be a way of working out feelings of guilt over what White people have done to people of color. Sometimes White people also become patronizing in their work with people of color. Sabnani et al. (1991) state that White counselors at this stage may find themselves overidentifying with people of color.

Maintaining the attitude of denial of differences is difficult, because the individual will be confronted with differences daily. Maintaining immersion and overidentification with people of another culture is also difficult, because members of the other culture will eventually reject the person as an outsider. People of color will also reject the paternal and patronizing behaviors of White people. To continue multicultural counselor development, counselor trainees are required to move beyond these stances (Carney & Kahn, 1984; Ponterotto, 1988; Sabnani et al.; 1991).

PROCESS GUIDELINES FOR CREATING A CLIMATE FOR STUDENT GROWTH IN STAGE THREE

It is especially important that instructors monitor student reactions to learning experiences in the third stage so that instructors can respond with either the support or the challenges needed. White students often need help in their journeys toward owning their personal racial and ethnic identities. Students of color who have been socialized in a mostly White environment may be shocked to realize how they have identified with and been influenced by the majority White society. Most students will need help in acquiring knowledge about contemporary racial and ethnic identity development models. They will also need assistance in using the information from these models in multicultural counseling.

The instructor who works with counseling students at this stage will find training in group facilitation particularly valuable for helping students deal with the intensity of their feelings and keeping the class sessions moving in a productive manner. It may not be easy to combine both teaching cognitive content and attending to students' feelings.

In their study of racial and ethnic identity development models, students may experience strong emotions. The feelings of denial, fear, guilt, anger, rejection, sadness, and powerlessness—which are common reactions of both White students and students of color—may be intense and need to be processed. Positive feelings of excitement and curiosity will also need to be acknowledged to legitimize them. It will be important for the instructor to monitor the way the students experience these feelings and to intervene when members of the class try to "Band Aid" or respond inappropriately to the feelings of their peers. To move ahead on the multicultural counseling developmental continuum, people need the opportunity to experience these feelings fully. The instructor will also need to show cultural sensitivity toward people of color who have been socialized to refrain from showing their feelings publicly.

White counselors may need assistance in recognizing when they act in a paternal or patronizing manner toward people of color. Open discussion of how and when White people act paternally or patronizingly is one way to help White trainees learn when they use these behaviors and how trainees of color receive these behaviors. Addressing paternal or patronizing behaviors when they occur in class is another way to assist students in this learning.

GOALS TO PROMOTE STUDENT DEVELOPMENT IN BELIEFS AND ATTITUDES, KNOWLEDGE, AND SKILLS IN STAGE THREE

Goal 1: To involve counseling trainees in the application of concepts from racial and ethnic identity development models

Goal 2: To achieve a deeper understanding of the pervasive racism in the United States and to realize one's personal involvement in racist behaviors

Goal 3: To develop a broader understanding of the role of culture in counseling and a wider repertoire of counselor interventions with clients of other cultures while realizing the limitations of "cookbook" approaches to multicultural counseling

APPROPRIATE ENVIRONMENTS AND LEARNING EXPERIENCES TO ACHIEVE GOALS

Goal 1: To involve counseling trainees in the application of concepts from racial and ethnic identity development models. The experiences of Goal 1 lay the groundwork for the achievement of Goal 2. Knowledge of one's own level of racial and ethnic identity developmental level is fundamental to understanding one's personal involvement in racism.

In recent years, much work has been done on formulating and testing minority, White, and generic models of racial and ethnic identity development (for example, Atkinson, Morten, & Sue, 1979, 1983, 1989, 1993; Carter, 1990; Christensen, 1989; Cross, 1971, 1991; Helms, 1984, 1985, 1990; Katz & Ivey, 1977; Kim, 1981; Parham & Helms, 1981; Phinney, 1989, 1993; Ponterotto, 1988; Ruiz, 1990; Sabnani et al., 1991; Smith, 1991; Sue & Sue, 1990). Counseling students need to become cognizant of the growing literature in this field and learn the application of concepts from models of racial and ethnic identity development. It is especially important that students face and "own" their own racial identity.

The content of Chapter 3, models of racial identity development, and the content of Chapter 4, models of ethnic identity development, are basic to an introduction to racial and ethnic identity development. One way to learn to apply knowledge of racial and ethnic identity development is to discuss how the behavior of individuals described in vignettes (or critical incidents) fits the descriptors of a particular stage of racial or ethnic identity development. Along with out-of-class study of the content of Chapters 3 and 4, students can write a vignette describing an individual in one stage of one of these theories. The class can divide up the assignment so that the vignettes written will be representative of all the theories.

Counselor trainees need to understand that applying these models to descriptions of hypothetical people involves speculation, not factual information. Again, it is important to remember that no single individual will show all the characteristics listed in the stage models. The information from the racial and ethnic identity development models can help trainees understand the reference-group orientation behaviors that both the counselor and the counselee bring to the counseling situation.

Following are examples of some vignettes that describe individuals in one stage of each of several racial and ethnic identity development models. The task of the reader is to refer back to the models of racial or ethnic identity development described in Chapters 3 and 4 and to decide which stage the individuals described represent.

Enrico is a Mexican American whose parents emigrated to California in the early 1950s. Enrico was born two years after his parents arrived in the United States. He dropped out of high school in his third year and went to work with a trucking agency making deliveries in the Los Angeles area to help support his family. Enrico is proud of his Mexican American heritage, and he participates regularly in Latino festivities in the area.

Recently, Enrico has heard rumors that the trucking firm for which he has worked for nearly 20 years may be bought out by a larger company and may be laying off some of its workers. His high-school-age daughter has been challenging him to attend night school to earn his GED so that he can improve

Minority Identity Development (MID) Model
From Atkinson, Morten, & Sue, 1993, described in Chapter 3 of this book.

his chances of keeping his job, or even be promoted in his company. Enrico's philosophy, and that of many of his Mexican American family and friends, has always been "que será será" ("whatever will be, will be"). But when he tells his daughter this, she tells him that this is not necessarily true. Some of his family and friends have teased Enrico about thinking he is better than they are to even consider going back to school.

Discuss at which level of the MID you might place Enrico. Is he in Stage 2 or Stage 4 of the MID? ■

The Cross Model of Black Identity Development
From Cross, 1991, delineated in Chapter 3.

Brenda is an African American teenager whose parents experienced the Civil Rights movement of the 1960s and 1970s. Brenda is intensely proud of her Black heritage. She makes sure that her hairstyles, dress, and manners are congruent with Blackness. Brenda is considering changing her name to one that is considered Afrocentric because she wants to be sure that people are aware of her pride in her African heritage. In the past, the clique Brenda was in at her interracial high school was composed of females from three racial heritages. Recently, Brenda dropped out of this clique and now makes sure her close friends are African Americans. When her White English teacher encourages Brenda to use standard English in her written compositions, Brenda becomes angry at this attempt to force her to cease using Black English.

At which stage of Cross' theory of Black identity development is Brenda operating? ■

The Kim Model of Asian American Racial Identity Development
From Kim, 1981, described in Chapter 3.

Eloise is a sansei (third generation) Japanese woman. Her grandparents were interned at the Manzanar Japanese Internment Camp in the mountains of California during World War II. Eloise's mother was born at the camp. Family members have always been very proud of being Americans and have played down their Japanese heritage. An uncle who served with the famed U.S. 100/442nd Regimental Combat Team in Italy during the war is still viewed as a family hero.

Recently, Eloise became aware of the humiliation and economic losses her grandparents suffered during and following their internment. It all started when she found a copy of a *National Geographic* that featured a story on the West Coast Japanese during World War II (Zich & Yamashita, 1986). Eloise is beginning to feel very angry toward the White people who treated her grandparents in this degrading manner, and she believes her grandparents' internment in this concentration camp was very unfair and a violation of their constitutional and human rights. Eloise does not understand why her grandparents do not complain about what happened to them.

Discuss the different levels of racial identity development that Eloise and her grandparents may represent according to the Kim model of Asian American racial identity development. ■

Arturo is a Latino teenager whose father worked hard to rise out of poverty and complete medical school. As a young man, Arturo's father changed his last name to Jones. After receiving his M.D., Arturo's father brought his family to a small, rural Midwestern town because the community offered to finance a clinic where he could practice medicine. Since moving to this part of the United States, Arturo's family insists that he go by the name of Art and become as "Americanized" as possible. The family members worked hard to lose their Latino accent and they use English in all their family interactions. They rarely mention and never visit relatives who live in a poor area of New York City. Art has heard his parents worry about the possibility of experiencing poverty and prejudice if the local community learns about their true racial heritage. All of Art's friends at the local high school are White. When another Latino teenager transfers to the local high school, Art shows no interest in befriending him.

Using Ruiz's model, discuss the level at which this family seems to be operating. ■

The Ruiz Model of Chicano-Latino Identity Development
From Ruiz, 1990, described in Chapter 3.

Marilyn is a White female in her mid-thirties. She has worked in an insurance company home office for 12 years. An African American male, James, who has worked in the same division with her for several years, has recently been turned down for a promotion he requested. Marilyn does not understand why James is upset that the person who got the promotion is as qualified as James but is a White male.

At which of Hardiman's levels of White racial identity development does Marilyn seem to be operating? ■

Hardiman's Model of White Racial Identity Development
From Hardiman, 1982, described in Chapter 3.

Janice is another White female who works in the same office as Marilyn in the previous vignette (Hardiman's model). When the office supervisor was out of town, Janice was in charge of the division in which Marilyn and James work. Unlike Marilyn, Janice is upset that James did not receive the promotion. Janice believes that racism may have been one reason James was not promoted. Janice remembers that she was called in by one of the personnel officers before the promotion was made and was asked for input on how well James and the other man did their work. Janice worries that she may have said something that caused James not to get the promotion.

According to Helms' model, at what level of White racial identity development is Janice functioning? ■

Helms' Model of White Racial Identity Development
From Helms, 1990, described in Chapter 3.

Ponterotto's White Racial Consciousness Development Model

From Ponterotto, 1988, described in Chapter 3.

Chris is a White, male, high school teacher in his second year of teaching at a large suburban high school in the eastern United States. Chris is taking evening classes and is currently enrolled in a multicultural counseling class at a nearby university. Recently, a male refugee student from Somalia enrolled in one of the history classes Chris teaches. Chris has become excited about learning as much as he can about the Somalis and has voraciously read a recent publication on the history and culture of the people of this country (Putman & Noor, 1993). Chris is attempting to learn some of the language and the proverbs of Somalia in order to help his new refugee student. In the multicultural counseling class, Chris is eager to share his newfound learning about the culture of the Somalis.

In which of Ponterotto's stages of White racial consciousness development is Chris operating? ■

Phinney's Theory of Adolescent Identity Development

From Phinney, 1993, as described in Chapter 4.

Kevin is a 16-year-old high school student in the U.S. Pacific Northwest. Kevin's mother is Native American and his father is White. For most of his life, Kevin has lived in a White, middle-class neighborhood. Recently, Kevin has become very interested in his Native American heritage and has been researching that side of his biracial heritage. Kevin has attended meetings of the Native American group in his area and participated in their cultural events. Kevin is attempting to decide how he identifies himself according to ethnic heritage. Is is White? Is he Native American? Or is he of interracial, or mixed, heritage (both Native American and White)? Kevin is still searching for the ethnic identity with which he can feel comfortable.

According to Phinney's three-stage model of ethnic identity development in adolescence, at what stage is Kevin operating? ■

Smith's Theory of Ethnic Identity Development within the Context of Majority/Minority Status

From Smith, 1991, as described in Chapter 4.

Louise is an African American who works full-time as a reservation clerk with a major airline. Louise is attending night school to improve her writing skills because she aspires to become a recognized poet. The White instructor of Louise's class has given her positive feedback on the quality of her poems and has encouraged Louise to begin submitting her poems for publication. Louise asked two of her African American friends for feedback on her poems, and, with their encouragement, Louise began submitting poems for possible publication in several popular magazines.

Louise has become accustomed to receiving rejection slips about the poems submitted, but recently a publisher invited Louise to come discuss her work. At the interview, Louise felt exploited when the White publisher stated that he is searching for writing by an African American to feature in his monthly publication. The man seemed doubly pleased to realize he might be able to publish the work of an African American female poet. Louise also felt that this man behaved in a paternal manner in his interview with her. Louise wants to have her writing published on its own merits, and she does not like the idea of getting published just because she is African American and female. At the moment, Louise is trying to decide whether to agree to write for this magazine or to turn down the offer. She is also considering changing her writing style or giving up writing completely.

In terms of Smith's concepts of ethnic identity development within the context of majority/minority status, at what ethnic identity status might Louise be functioning? ■

Students can use these vignettes or those they have written themselves for small-group discussion. In some cases, it may be difficult to place the main character in one specific stage or phase. This dilemma shows that in many cases it is not easy to place an individual neatly in just one category. Students could also see whether they can determine the racial or ethnic identity development of the people in these vignettes on a different racial or ethnic identity development theory.

After discussing the various vignettes, trainees can discuss where they place themselves on racial and ethnic identity development. There are enough models offered that students might consider their own racial and ethnic identity development in terms of more than one model.

This small-group discussion can lead to an in-depth exploration of racial and cultural identity development for all counselor trainees. Exploring ethnic and racial identity development can be helpful for all group members, even though this self-disclosure may be a threatening experience. In these small-group discussions, students name the stage at which each believes she or he is and also describe past and current behaviors that support this self-assessment. Honest but caring feedback from peers and the instructor may be needed, especially for persons who believe they are at a level of racial or ethnic identity development that seems to be incongruent with their behaviors.

An alternative use of the vignettes might be to role play how the main characters in these short stories might describe their problem or situation if they came to a counselor. The role plays could be short but still include trying out interventions the counselors could use in initial assessment of these people.

Current racial identity research also provides clues to appropriate matching of counselors and counselees. Helms (1984) introduces four types of counseling relations based on racial consciousness stages. The Counseling Racial Simulators in Appendix I of Helms' 1990 book provide materials for in-class simulations between dyads at different levels of racial identity development. As racial identity/consciousness development research continues and expands, additional information on matching counselees to counselors will be available. More details on training counselors for working with clients at different levels of racial and ethnic identity development is also included in Chapter 10, Stage Four, Goal 4.

Goal 2: To achieve a deeper understanding of the pervasive racism in the United States and to realize one's personal involvement in racist behaviors. Racism is a practice that serves an individual's purpose by protecting privileges (Green,

1982). "Power is a force that is absolutely essential to perpetuate racism" (Ridley, 1989, p. 58). The perpetrator of racism has the power to control, for his or her own benefit, those who have less power. In the cross-cultural therapeutic relationship, power is given to the counselor by virtue of both the clinical role and the cultural dynamics (Pinderhughes, 1989).

Ponterotto and Pedersen (1993) reviewed the history of the use of the term *racism* and noted that it came into popular use during the height of the Civil Rights movement of the late 1960s. Ponterotto and Pedersen clarify three forms or levels of racism based on the work of Jones (1972, 1981). *Individual racism* is the discriminatory behavior individuals show that is based on biological considerations. *Institutional racism* includes the enforcement of policies that unfairly restrict the opportunities of certain groups, and may be either intentional or unintentional. *Cultural racism* is more subtle, but it is "the most pervasive and insidious. . . . [It] includes the individual and institutional expression of the superiority of one race's cultural heritage (and concomitant value system) over that of other races" (Ponterotto & Pedersen, 1993, p. 11).

Ponterotto and Pedersen (1993) reviewed the prevalence of racism in contemporary United States and concluded that, because of the stigma attached, overt racism is declining. However, newer forms of covert racism abound, and recent conceptions of prejudice hold that racist attitudes and beliefs lie outside most people's conscious awareness. These authors discuss the consequences of racism and emphasize that racism affects everyone whether victim or perpetrator. The subtle but pervasive effect of the practice of any kind of racism seems to lead to a duality of consciousness or a compartmentalization of our lives (as emphasized by Sue & Sue, 1990, and in Lillian Smith's autobiography, *Killers of the Dream* [1961] cited earlier in this book).

Pinderhughes (1989) describes racism as entrapment for everyone and considers freedom from this entrapment essential to successful psychotherapy. Pinderhughes (1989) states that "practitioners need to (1) understand their responses to racism and the consequences of them, (2) understand how they may threaten the cross-racial encounter, and (3) learn to manage them effectively" (p. 72).

Pinderhughes gives a detailed description of the painful process of confronting and understanding race and racism in self and others and gives insight into the negative consequences of denying race in cross-cultural therapy. She describes working with helping service personnel of all races to assist them in understanding their racial identities and personal racism and includes descriptive vignettes to illustrate the anxiety, fear, anger, guilt, loss, and hostilities that accompany this difficult process for both Whites and people of color. Understanding the distinction between prejudice and racism and coming to an understanding of how we all collude to perpetuate racism are among many important concepts presented by Pinderhughes (1989).

Ridley (1989) also addresses the topic of the subtle but devastating effect of racism in the helping process. Ridley states that the criteria for judging racist behavior lies in the consequences of behavior and not in the intentions or causes.

Ridley discusses overt and covert racism as they relate to individual and institutional racism; covert racism may be either intentional or unintentional. Ridley (1989) describes seven racism process variables in counseling: color blindness, color consciousness, cultural transference, cultural countertransference, cultural ambivalence, evoking pseudotransference, and misinterpreting client nondisclosure. To prepare counselors for these challenges, Ridley (1989) recommends that the counselor have individual counseling with a therapist of another culture who is skilled in cross-cultural therapy. "Cross-cultural pairing in a counseling dyad can illuminate derogatory stereotypes by analyzing resistance or overcompensation in the counselor" (Ridley, 1989, p. 69).

Corvin and Wiggins (1989) describe an antiracism model based on Hardiman's theory of White racial identity development, for White professionals and recommend that it be experienced over a period of several weeks. Their model outlines appropriate goals and activities for the four racial identity developmental stages of acceptance, resistance, redefinition, and internalization (Corvin & Wiggins, 1989). Among the many purposes of this developmental model are: (1) to heighten the emotional sensitivity of White people to the full meaning of being White in the United States; (2) to become aware of stereotypes held of other groups (similar to the exercise described in Chapter 8, Stage Two, Goal 5); (3) to come to terms with the privileges of being White and of being a member of the White racist system in the United States; and (4) to develop strategies to combat racism on all levels.

In their 1993 book *Preventing Prejudice: A Guide for Counselors and Educators*, Ponterotto and Pedersen present an overview of the multiple factors related to prejudice and racism in contemporary United States society. They also offer detailed guidelines and exercises for counselors to use to reduce prejudice and racism in schools, on college and university campuses, and in the community. In addition, Ponterotto and Pedersen review racism and prejudice assessment instruments and include a resource guide on race awareness for counselors and educators.

The exercise, "Cultural Awareness and Racism," in Green's 1982 book (pp. 216–219) has been effective in helping members of my classes initiate an awareness of some ways in which they support racism. Green (1982) includes Wellman's "five kinds of rationales by which inequality is explained and ultimately explained away by people who do not normally consider themselves bigots" (p. 217). Following are abbreviated descriptions of the five rationales for supporting inequality presented by Wellman (in Green, 1982, pp. 217–218).

1. *Balance Sheet Justice.* According to this rationale to justify inequality, resources are scarce, priorities have to be established, and decisions need to be made. Sometimes minorities get shortchanged in this process. People subscribing to this rationale believe that, if minorities can "get their act together," they can put pressure on the system to get what is rightly theirs. "But things being as they are, it seems inevitable that the gains of some will be the loss of others" (Green, 1982, p. 217).

2. *Changing Others.* This rationale accepts the fact that it is wrong to discriminate in hiring but being zealous in affirmative action alienates people. Having better education for minorities would help, but we must at the same time maintain

standards. Many difficulties and contradictions will be solved if better ways can be found to improve education for minorities and help them into the mainstream.

3. *Individualized Action.* According to the third rationale, inequalities do exist, but many people from disadvantaged groups do not take advantage of what they have. People need to take control of their lives and show some initiative and assertiveness. Then they can "pull themselves up by their own bootstraps."

4. *Improving Communication.* Race, class, and ethnic origin make little difference because all people are the same from the perspective of this rationale. When people run into trouble trying to work together, the problem is due to a failure of communication, not to bad intentions. We all need to work to improve communication so people will have fewer difficulties.

5. *Learning to Think Straight.* The fifth rationale that supports inequality states that racism causes confusion and people get strange ideas and "get paranoid." Our perspectives are all limited, and race and culture only make a complex situation more difficult. "If people could only straighten out their thoughts and unravel all their feelings about this, it would help a lot" (Green, 1982, p. 218).

After experimenting with several ways to use and process this exercise, I have found that a structured format is most effective in helping people confront their own racist behaviors. Students are required to study the five rationales in the "Cultural Awareness and Racism" exercise before oral class participation. In class, students form five groups, and three tasks are given to each group.

The first task is to go through the five rationales, discuss ownership of each rationale, and share personal blocks students felt while studying and discussing the five rationales. Processing of feelings is important. Sometimes White students have difficulty understanding how any of these rationales support inequality because the rationales are such a strong part of their value systems. The third rationale, Individualized Action, is the one that most White students, and some students of color, can own.

The second task for each group is to take one of the five rationales and brainstorm on the hidden assumptions that underlie that rationale. Examples of an assumption related to each of the five rationales are: (1) minorities have the power to put pressure on the system; (2) all minorities want to enter the mainstream; (3) all people have enough power to take control of their lives; (4) improving communication will act as a panacea for all problems of inequality; and (5) straight thinking will solve the problems of race and culture.

The third task is to brainstorm on ways to go beyond guilt and formulate concrete actions to take in daily life that will change one's ongoing support of racism. Students often mention that they can start by getting in contact with the statements they make and the excuses they give themselves for not speaking up when they hear others make racist statements.

Discussion of these tasks leads to much verbalization in which group participants find it easier to talk about institutional racism and racist behavior in others than in themselves. Pinderhughes (1989) calls attention to the need to go beyond this level and move group participants to the point of personal racial identification and personal ownership of racist behaviors; my experience in using Green's exercise confirms Pinderhughes' warning. Ideally, these behaviors will be confronted in all classes in the counseling curriculum.

Sue et al. (1992a) state that "Culturally skilled counselors possess knowledge and understanding about how oppression, racism, discrimination, and stereotyping affect them personally and in their work" (p. 482). A developmental task of this stage is for the counselor to reach the point of acknowledging his or her racist attitudes, beliefs, and behaviors. For White counselors, this includes understanding how they have personally benefitted from individual, institutional, and cultural racism. Pinderhughes (1989) challenges people of color to examine how they collude in reinforcing prejudices against their own people based on skin color, noting that this behavior is readily engaged in by people of several color groups. Counselors of any racial heritage may need to recognize the racist tendency of wanting to protect counselees of color and to hold lower expectations for them (Pinderhughes, 1989). Ridley (1989) maintains that overlooking real psychopathology and applying relaxed standards of treatment to counselees of color can be a result of making the racist assumption that all the client's problems come from being a member of a people of color group.

Other authors also underscore the importance of addressing racism in multicultural counselor preparation. Casas and San Miguel (1993) emphasize that racism is *not* a thing of the past but a very present issue that counselors and counselor educators sorely need to address. Sue (1993) issued several warnings to White multicultural researchers that apply also to multicultural counselor preparation. Sue addressed the critical need for White professionals to view themselves as racial beings and to look at practices in counselor training that take the focus off racism, prejudice, and discrimination. Sue views the practice of focusing on international multiculturalism and the practice of defining culture so broadly that all differences are reduced to individual differences as two examples of taking the focus off the self of the counselor so that issues related to racism are avoided.

Perhaps one of the most urgent reasons counselors need to address their own racism and prejudice is that *counselors serve as gatekeepers* in the lives of the people with whom they work. Recognition of the role of the counselor as gatekeeper has been limited; perhaps counselors find it difficult to recognize the power they often hold over other people. Reports of people of color being assigned to counselors with limited experience and training and the high attrition that occurs after one or two sessions for counselees of color attest to the power of the counselor as gatekeeper.

Two additional books may be of interest to readers. In *Race Matters* (1993), Cornel West combines his background of theologian, philosopher, and activist to address the problems of race in the United States. Robert Miles' *Racism* (1989) presents a perspective on the history and current status of racism in Europe from a sociological perspective.

Goal 3: To develop a broader understanding of the role of culture in counseling and a wider repertoire of counselor interventions with clients of other cultures

while realizing the limitations of "cookbook" approaches to multicultural counseling. There is an abundance of information on how to counsel with people of each of the U.S. minority groups. Witness the number of multicultural counseling books with chapters or sections on ways of working more effectively with people in minority groups, the number of articles in recent professional journals on these topics, the many professional development sessions at counseling conventions on working with people of color groups, and the one- or two-day workshops on this topic.

There is danger in wholesale adoption of any of these guidelines or techniques, which are sometimes called "cookbook" approaches (Wehrly, 1991). One danger is that students will "buy into" content of a particular manuscript or "expert" and think they now have the "how to do it" with people of a cultural group. As noted in Chapter 8, some students adopt this stance in the early stages of multicultural counseling development.

Counselors who adopt en masse the multicultural counseling techniques of a perceived expert in the field often fail to get to know the clients as individual members of their cultural groups, often stereotyping clients on the basis of their cultural heritage. Another part of the problem may be the lack of awareness students have of the impact of culture on *both* counselor and counselee. Sensitive cross-cultural counseling requires a real depth of counselor self-awareness (as described in Goal 2). The process of attaining this self-awareness is usually painful; time is needed to process and integrate learning needed into one's values and beliefs, attitudes, and behaviors. It is much easier to concentrate on the client than to concentrate on self.

Students become aware of the "tightrope" we all walk in applying cultural knowledge while making sure we get to know each client as an individual. As mentioned earlier in this book, having little or no cultural knowledge can lead to enormous blunders in our interactions with culturally different clients; but ascribing cultural traits without discretion can lead to clients' being insulted.

Sue and Zane (1987) state that knowledge of the client's culture is not helpful in and of itself; techniques based on this presumed knowledge may be applied very inappropriately. In their discussion of the need for therapists to provide culturally responsive treatment, Sue and Zane (1987) emphasize two critically important basic counseling processes—credibility and giving. "Credibility refers to the client's perception of the therapist as an effective and trustworthy helper. Giving is the client's perception that something was received from the therapeutic encounter" (p. 40). The authors discuss the importance of both ascribed and achieved credibility in work with ethnic minority people. Examples of gifts Sue and Zane (1987) discuss are "anxiety reduction, depression relief, cognitive clarity, normalization, reassurance, hope and faith, skills acquisition, a coping perspective, and goal setting" (p. 42). Draguns (1981) made a similar observation, underlining the importance of the counselor as a catalytic agent in the life of any client, regardless of culture.

Chapter 8 included an introduction to some general guidelines to improve client perceptions of counselor credibility and trustworthiness in cross-cultural counseling. To reiterate, during the first counseling session, it is very important for the counselor to address differences in race or culture between counselor and counselee. The counselor could say something like this to the counselee: "You and I are from different ethnic backgrounds. This sometimes means that we may have to work extra hard to understand each other. I am wondering how you feel about working with me as a counselor of a different ethnic heritage." Then, the counselee is given the opportunity to voice his or her reactions to this difference. One aspect of cultural differences that may cause client or counselor discomfort is use of physical space during the counseling session. Much more threatening, however, may be negative stereotypes that both counselee and counselor may bring to the session. If these stereotypes become evident, it sometimes helps to address them openly as well.

During the first session, it is also important to speak directly to the client's issues to "find out clearly what is wanted and to frame the goals clearly in the patient's [client's] terms" (D. Brown, personal communication, June 2, 1991). The client is the best source of this information. Kleinman's explanatory model paradigm introduced under Goal 7 of Stage Two (Chapter 8), is one model for obtaining this information. It is appropriate to ask the client for information on how the client's culture influences what she or he wants. It is not appropriate to continue asking questions about the client's culture just to satisfy the counselor's curiosity (Draguns, 1981).

The task of translating the meaning and implications of cultural knowledge into culturally sensitive counseling interventions is a large one. Appropriate use of cultural knowledge includes the ability to assess client levels of acculturation and ethnocultural identification. Counselor trainee involvement in these tasks was initiated in the second stage when students researched their own cultural heritages and were introduced to Kleinman's explanatory models. An additional aspect that needs to be assessed is the racial or ethnic identity development level of the client. (Considerable discussion of identifying stages of racial or ethnic identity of both the counselor and counselee was included under Goal 2 of this chapter.)

A very important task for all counselors in all sessions is to develop a trusting relationship with the client. This must occur before meaningful dialogue can take place in the counseling session. If the counselor and the client are of different cultural and racial backgrounds, developing a working relationship may be quite challenging. White counselors may need to go beyond simply confronting the racial and ethnic differences during the first counseling session if they want to take the first steps to gain credibility with African American counselees (Poston, Craine, & Atkinson, 1991). The reverse situation, in which counselors of color are assigned to White clients, may also be problematic. It may be very challenging for a counselor of color to gain credibility with a White client, but this situation is rarely addressed in the literature.

In Chapter 3, I briefly discussed Gibbs' 1985 developmental model for establishing White/Black relationships in social work practice. The microanalysis of the stages Black clients go through in developing a relationship with a White helper and the helper's stage-appropriate behavior responses can be translated to counselor/client interactions.

Although Gibbs built her model on White helper–Black helpee relationships, she suggests that the interpersonal relationship may be important in cross-cultural work with other ethnic minority clients, especially with people of Latin heritage for whom *personalismo* is very important. Interpersonal relationships may also be important in work with people who function from a disadvantaged status. I believe that many aspects of this model are appropriate for relationship building in any session where the counselor and client come from different cultural heritages or different socioeconomic backgrounds.

Gibbs (1985) states that "The model of an interpersonal orientation to treatment proposes that the initial phase of the treatment relationship can be broken down into five microstages in which the client is evaluating the worker while the worker is attempting to establish a relationship and to assess the client's problems" (p. 188). Gibbs' Model of Interpersonal Orientation (1985) consists of five stages in which themes of client evaluation of the helper are given. In addition, Gibbs lists appropriate helper behavior responses for each stage. The following overview of Gibbs' cross-cultural social work model adapts this process to counselor and counselee interactions.

Stage I: Appraisal Stage.　This is the "sizing up" stage, during which the client is generally polite but guarded while he or she waits for the counselor to initiate the session. Beneath what may appear to be a client's pleasant manner may be feelings of mistrust or suspiciousness. The client is waiting to see whether the counselor is genuine and approachable.

Counselor competence is judged on the counselor's ability to show *personal authenticity*. The counselor will be judged on "the degree to which he or she projects the qualities of being warm, 'real,' and 'down-to-earth'" (Gibbs, 1985, p. 190).

Stage II: Investigation Stage.　In this stage, the client continues to evaluate the counselor. The client may ask the counselor questions about his or her background, values, opinions, or professional qualifications. The client is checking out the counselor's previous counseling experience with minority clients and attempting to determine whether the counselor can equalize differences between self and clients of color.

In this stage, counselor competence is assessed by the ability to show *egalitarianism*. Can the counselor equalize status and power differences between self and client by using language that is not professional jargon and by acting in a nonauthoritarian and democratic manner? If so, the client will judge the counselor positively.

Stage III: Involvement Stage.　Client/counselor relationships will progress to this stage only if the client receives positive "vibes" from the counselor in Stages I and II; if not, the client will terminate the sessions. If the counselor passes the tests of the first two stages and the client feels a positive identification with the counselor, the client will begin to open up and self-disclose. Because she or he feels a sense of mutuality with the counselor, the client may attempt to establish a more personal relationship with the counselor, inviting the counselor to attend a community ethnic event or special family function. These invitations are a form of testing whether the counselor really identifies with the client.

Identification on the part of the counselor is extremely important to continuing the working relationship. The client is testing (1) whether the counselor can really identify with his or her ethnic or socioeconomic background and is willing to work as a change agent in the client's life space, or (2) whether the counselor merely represents the status quo. The counselor will be assessed on the ability to help clients within their own cultural milieu without expecting them to give up their own sense of ethnic identity and ethnic values.

It may not be ethical for the counselor to accept all invitations. In these instances, the counselor needs to explain the ethics of the profession to the client.

Stage IV: Commitment Stage. This stage will follow if the counselor was flexible enough and sensitive in establishing a more personal relationship with the counselee in the first three stages. The client's defensiveness will decrease considerably, and the client will become actively involved in the treatment process. The initial commitment to working with the counselor will be based more on a personal regard for the counselor than on client belief in the effectiveness of treatment. "At this point the client feels that the worker has demonstrated *acceptance* of him or her as a unique individual through empathic and supportive behaviors" (Gibbs, 1985, p. 189).

Acceptance is the counselor behavior response that is key to the success of this stage. Clients at this stage continue to evaluate the counselors on the degree to which counselors show empathy and understanding of sociocultural factors that impact the clients' views of their problems. The key elements of appropriate counselor behavior are responding in a nonjudgmental manner and showing understanding of the conflicts the clients bring.

Stage V: Engagement Stage. In this stage, the client becomes fully involved in the counseling process and will work with the counselor to identify problems, define goals, and reach these goals. The client has acknowledged (albeit, silently) that the counselor has interpersonal competence and that the counselor can be trusted to help in problem resolution.

The focus has been shifted from the counselor's interpersonal abilities to the counselor's instrumental abilities to do the job. Counselor *performance* is the key factor to success in fully engaging the client in a mutual working relationship.

Gibbs suggests that this sequence of events may take place over two or three sessions, but there may be elements of each of the five microstages in the first session. The counselor will need to be alert to these stage shifts in order to respond appropriately to the client and prevent the client from terminating prematurely.

Gibbs' model outlines the need to personalize the counseling relationship at the outset. To many counselors trained in keeping the relationship "professional," stressing the interpersonal aspect may seem antithetic to the delivery of profes-sional services and may suggest the possibility of dual relationships. At times, the counselor may have to point out the inappropriateness of some interpersonal relationships so the client will not feel that he or she is being rejected. In an internship student discussion of the appropriateness of accepting counselees' invitations to personal events, one student suggested asking the question, "Whose needs are being met if I accept the invitation?" (V. Rosenkoetter, personal commu-nication, February 14, 1994). She believed that in some cases it could be helpful, as long as the clients' needs were the only reason to participate.

Skills in interpersonal relationships are different from instrumental skills in counseling. Interpersonal relationship skills are those that enable the counselor to develop the personal relationship in counseling described in Gibbs' model. Instru-mental skills include all counseling skills that may be effective in multicultural counseling. Counselors will need to pay attention to developing both kinds of skills for cross-cultural work.

If problems arise in building a cross-cultural relationship, Gibbs' model can help the counselor identify whether the problem is caused by a breakdown in interpersonal relationships. If such a breakdown has occurred, these problems will need to be dealt with quickly, before the client terminates the counselor/client relationship. The development of appropriate interpersonal relationships in cross-cultural counseling appears to be the real test of whether a counselor can truly accept clients as they are, show genuine understanding, and thus gain their trust and respect.

People who are working to improve multicultural counseling skills often wonder whether there are certain aspects of the counseling process that can be applied universally, regardless of culture. In Chapter 2, I discuss Torrey's (1972a, 1972b) four universal components for curing patients and his challenge to the ethnocentric perspective of Western psychotherapy. Ponterotto and Benesch's (1988) translation of Torrey's universals to cross-cultural counseling was included in Chapter 7, Stage One of multicultural counselor preparation. At this point, it may be wise to review the following universals: naming the problem brought by the client, considering the personal qualities of the helper, being aware of expectations brought by the client, and using some kind of technique to help the client. In addition, review how the client's culture will influence each of these "universals."

In 1989, Draguns expressed a slightly different perspective when he stated, "We do not yet have a catalog of universal, culture-free elements of counseling" (p. 16). Draguns recommended that counselors be prepared to adapt several aspects of the counseling process to the client's cultural background: for example, counseling activity levels, content and mode of verbal interaction, and tone of voice. Other suggestions Draguns (1989) offered are to show acceptance of clients within their cultural frames of reference and be open to using more direct interventions than are customary within Western psychotherapy. In essence, however, Draguns is referring to many of the elements discussed by Torrey (1972a, 1972b), Ponterotto and Benesch (1988), and Gibbs (1985).

Other counselor trainees may want to see how the many components of cross-cultural counseling fit together. Table 9.1 presents a picture of the variables involved in multicultural counseling. Ponterotto and Casas (1991) developed this table as an expansion of an earlier model of Casas and Vasquez (1989). The variables are arranged in columns from left to right, starting with those that are the most covert or distal to the counseling process and moving to the variables that become central during counseling. Those listed on the left are the counselor's personal sociocultural and professional variables; these Selective Counselor Variables have the potential for greatly influencing the counseling process. The middle columns focus on Selective Client Variables. This listing of client variables "identifies personal sociocultural characteristics and variables including beliefs and attitudes and life experiences that *must* be understood and appropriately addressed in the counseling process" (Ponterotto & Casas, 1991, p. 74). The Selective Counseling Process Variables on the right include client and counselor variables that interact during the counseling process. Again, it is important for the counselor to understand how these variables may play out in counseling.

Readers may recognize that many of the variables presented by Ponterotto and Casas (1991) are included in the cubical models introduced in Chapter 3. The largest difference between the model presented here and the cubical models is that Ponterotto and Casas' paradigm for understanding the counseling process includes emphasis on both counselor and client variables as well as on the interaction of these variables in the counseling process. The cubical models reviewed in Chapter 3 present three-dimensional frameworks for viewing the sociocultural settings and problems brought by clients, with little attention given to counselor variables.

Pedersen's 1977 triad model has been widely used in cross-cultural training. In this model, a coached client and anti-counselor pair from one ethnic culture interact with a counselor trainee from another culture. The anti-counselor is encouraged to be deliberately subversive and point out mistakes and aspects that would not be voiced in a cross-cultural dyadic session. Sessions are videotaped for replay, debriefing, and discussion among the three participants and the counselor trainer.

Pedersen (1978) states, "A counselor-client coalition against the problem or anti-counselor becomes the vehicle of effective counseling, whereas ineffective counseling results in a client-problem coalition that isolates the counselor" (p. 480). Pedersen (1978, 1988) sees four skill areas in which this type of training can be used: to articulate the problem, to anticipate the resistance, to diminish defensiveness, and to teach recovery skills. Pedersen modified the triad model and developed a procounselor format in which a counselor ally acts as a supportive and facilitative co-worker with the counselor.

Neimeyer, Fukuyama, Bingham, Hall, and Mussenden (1986) reported on research on both forms of the triad model with 20 volunteer counselor education graduate students. The results of this research "suggest that the two training procedures have a different impact on trainees" (p. 439). Tentative recommendations from the Neimeyer et al. (1986) study were to use the pro-counselor model with beginning counselors to provide them with more successful cross-cultural counseling experiences. The authors stated that "the use of the more confrontive

TABLE 9.1 ■ THEORETICAL FRAMEWORK FOR UNDERSTANDING THE CROSS-CULTURAL COUNSELING PROCESS

Selective Counselor Variables		Selective Client Variables		Selective Counseling Process Variables	
Personal Socio-Cultural	*Professional*	*Personal Socio-Cultural*	*Life Experiences*	*Client*	*Counselor (Setting and Treatment)*
Biological/psychological predisposition	Culture	Biological/psychological predisposition	Place of birth	Expectations of counseling process	Setting
Gender	Assumptions	Gender	Nationality- immigrant status (for	Counselor role/attributes	Location, accessibility
Race	Beliefs	Race	self and family	Client role	Ambience
Sexual preference	Values	Sexual preference	members)	Preferences for counselor	Staffing; racial, ethnic, gender, linguistic
	Attitudes		Reasons for	approach/technique	composition
Life experiences		Culture	immigrating	Race-level of racial	
Culture	Training	Assumptions/world	Ethnicity-visible	identity	Level of sensitivity to
Assumptions/world views	Philosophy	views	characteristics	Ethnicity-level of	personal and professional
Beliefs	Theoretical orientation	Beliefs	Socio-economic status	acculturation	biases and stereotypes
Values	Basic counseling skills	Values	Employment history	Personality attributes	
Attitudes	Cross-cultural counseling skills	Attitudes	Family characteristics	Attitudes toward	Understanding and respecting client's culture
			Level of	counseling process	
Cognitive styles	Behaviors	Cognitive styles	acculturation	Counselor race/ethnicity	Understanding client's
Information processing		Information processing	Type: single/two	and personal attributes	expectations, preferences, and attitudes
Biased thinking		Biased thinking	parent, extended	Credibility attributed to	
Stereotyping		Stereotyping	Number of children	counseling process	Accepting the intra and extra psychic nature of
			Child-rearing	Counselor	presenting problems
Self-perception		Self-perception	practices	Perceived nature of	
Racial identity		Self-esteem		presenting problem	Establishing credibility
Acculturation level		Self-efficacy	Living environment	Follow-through,	
		Racial identity	Stability and type:	termination, outcome	Building rapport
Racial consciousness and sensitivity		Acculturation level	urban/rural segregated/integrated		Selecting effective/ appropriate interventions
		Aptitudes, abilities, interests	Safety Available support		
Behaviors			systems		Follow-through, termination, outcome
		Hopes and expectations	Educational history		
		Behaviors	Social/political/ economic stressors		
			Health status: physical and mental access to and use of relevant services		

SOURCE: From J. G. Ponterotto and J. M. Casas, *Handbook of Racial/Ethnic Minority Counseling Research*, 1991, p. 75. Courtesy of Charles C Thomas, Publisher, Springfield, Illinois.

anti-counselor model may be better suited to the advanced student who has already developed some level of confidence and skill in cross-cultural interactions" (p. 439). Translating this for use in the stage model of counselor education means that students could start with the pro-counselor triad model soon after completing the active listening training of Stages One and Two. The anti-counselor triad model could then be used as soon as students feel some comfort using the pro-counselor model.

I have found a modification of the model to be at least somewhat effective in settings in which the availability of non-White people to act as counselees and anti-counselors for all people of color cultures is limited. Toward the end of the semester's multicultural counseling class, students have participated in many cognitive and affective cultural awareness activities, including in-depth research of their own cultural or ethnic heritages and study of the history, current status, and modes of helping of culturally different groups. At this point, many students can role play persons of the other cultures they have studied or worked with, thus taking the parts of the client and anti-counselor. In this role play, White students taking the part of non-White students are able to provide enough challenge to the counselor trainees to help introduce them to this type of interaction. For many White trainees, such a role play is much less threatening than when the client and anti-counselor really *are* people of color. It does, however, seem to be one way to help White students begin to cross the threatening threshold of counseling someone of a different culture.

In one respect, Pedersen's triad (or quadruple) model for cross-cultural training helps prepare counselors for culture shock. Many people think of culture shock as occurring only when one travels to another country or when one interacts at home with someone from another country. However, much cross-cultural interaction within the borders of one's own country may result in a form of culture shock to either or all the parties involved.

Merta, Stringham, and Ponterotto (1988) describe a bipartite culture shock learning exercise designed for a special seminar to help counseling trainees become more sensitive to cultural differences. This training paradigm included cognitive, behavioral, and evaluative components. Although the participants were international students, this exercise could be repeated in many counseling classes by recruiting culturally different students or community residents to enact problems they might bring to a counselor. These micro approaches to integrating multicultural counseling aspects into classes such as marriage and family counseling, individual counseling, assessment, and career counseling could provide valuable learning experiences that would support and extend the basic content of the multicultural counseling class.

SUMMARY

Chapter 9 gave an overview of the third stage of the development of multicultural counselor competence. This stage is often described as the most complex of the stages, and the chapter began with a description of the conflicting and painful feelings that students may experience as they examine their own racial and ethnic identity development and realize the impact that individual racism, institutional racism, and cultural racism have had on their personal behavior. Process guidelines for helping students deal with these conflicting feelings were included. The implementation of Stage Three was discussed under three broad goals: to apply racial and ethnic identity theory to self and to clients; to gain a broader understanding of both the racism that is pervasive in the United States and one's personal involvement in racist behaviors; and to continue growth in learning the use of culturally sensitive counseling techniques.

Counselor trainees' abilities to apply the theories of racial and ethnic identity development presented in Chapters 3 and 4 were tested by applying each theory to a descriptive vignette. The importance of helping counselor trainees apply the theories of racial and ethnic identity development to themselves was emphasized, as was understanding that one's racial and ethnic identity development is basic to comprehending one's role in racism. This chapter also underscored the critical importance of realizing the pervasiveness of racism and one's personal involvement in subtle forms of racism. Exercises to heighten awareness of personal support of racism were included, as well as references to additional perspectives on racism and other models of antiracism training.

Chapter 9 also covered the application of cultural knowledge to the ongoing development of appropriate counseling skills, and trainees were cautioned against using "cookbook approaches." This chapter stressed the importance of both interpersonal and instrumental counseling skills in establishing a relationship with clients of a different culture. Models for the development of a trusting cross-cultural relationship were introduced.

As noted earlier, it is evident that movement from stage to stage in gaining multicultural counseling competence is not abrupt. Because Stage Three is built on Stages One and Two, many of the activities and much of the learning of this stage are a continuation of what was begun in previous stages.

CHAPTER 10

Multicultural Counselor Preparation: Stage Four

The purpose of this chapter is to outline pathways for supporting students in their continuing growth in beliefs and attitudes, knowledge, and skills in multicultural competence during Stage Four of their preparation program. At Stage Four, the counseling students participate in counseling practicum experiences. The chapter also is organized under these four subheadings: (1) student characteristics, (2) process guidelines, (3) goals, and (4) appropriate environments and learning experiences to achieve goals.

To achieve the full benefits of the counseling practicum, the campus supervisor(s) and the off-campus supervisor(s) (if the practicum experiences are off campus) will need to have appropriate background and training in multicultural counseling. It will also be important for the student to have access to a culturally pluralistic client population.

STUDENT CHARACTERISTICS

Students entering the counseling practicum are expected to have completed basic course work in such classes as Introduction to the Helping Services, Counseling Theories, Group Counseling (including participation in an ongoing growth group), Multicultural Counseling, Marriage and Family Counseling, Assessment, Lifestyle and Career Development, and a laboratory in counseling techniques. Students who reach this level of multicultural counselor preparation have an initial awareness of their own racial and cultural identities, have considerable knowledge of general (as well as some specific) guidelines for multicultural counseling, and have an awareness of how culture impacts the many facets of counseling. In addition, they know how to seek out additional information to improve their counseling effectiveness.

The students' personal perspectives on their own identities in relation to people who are different have changed greatly since entering multicultural counselor preparation. Students now view these differences from a more flexible viewpoint rather than in terms of rigid categories.

Christensen (1989) calls the fourth stage of cross-cultural awareness development the *Consolidated Awareness Stage*. By this time, counseling students have established a sense of balance based on acceptance of themselves and of others who are different. Trainees have studied the historical and current sociopolitical factors that have impacted (and are impacting) the lives of people of color. They have an understanding of how race, ethnicity, and culture influence the treatment, status, and life chances of all people.

Majority individuals in this stage understand the role their group has played in dominating minority individuals. These students have identified with the White race. Friendship choices for majority individuals are no longer based on cultural or racial background, and there is a commitment to work to achieve better understanding across groups (Christensen, 1989).

Minority individuals at this stage are fully identified with their own groups but at the same time are willing to show acceptance of the majority group. They also show "an appreciation of how people's life experiences may lead to attitudes with which they do not agree" (Christensen, 1989, p. 282). At this stage, minority individuals are actively seeking ways to bring about greater intergroup understanding and social change.

According to the 1993 revision of the Minority Identity Development (MID) Model of Atkinson, Morten, and Sue, minority students at Stage 5, the *Synergistic* stage, would be comfortable in a multicultural counseling practicum. At this level, the minority trainees have resolved conflicts experienced in the fourth stage and feel a sense of self-fulfillment. They can objectively examine values of their own groups as well as of people of other cultural groups. "Desire to eliminate *all* forms of oppression becomes an important motivation for the individual's behavior" (Atkinson, Morten, & Sue, 1993) in this last stage of minority identity development.

In terms of the model of White racial identity development presented by Sabnani et al. (1991), White students who have reached Stage 5, *Redefinition and Integration,* have the potential to function well in a multicultural counseling practicum. The newfound White identity has been internalized. The stage is "marked by a culturally transcendent world view and by a balance of multicultural interests and respect for cultural differences" (Sabnani et al., 1991, p. 82).

Some degree of apprehension and anxiety regarding one's potential to function effectively in multicultural counseling may still be present for students of any ethnic background, but increased flexibility will give students the freedom and courage to test and create counseling interventions appropriate for culturally different clients. These students are ready for supervised counseling practicum experiences at culturally pluralistic sites.

PROCESS GUIDELINES FOR CREATING A
CLIMATE FOR STUDENT GROWTH IN STAGE FOUR

Creating a climate for growth will be the biggest challenge for the counseling practicum supervisor. This climate will need to include challenges to keep the student interested in growth in self-awareness, cognitive knowledge, and multicultural counseling competencies. Along with challenges to these kinds of trainee growth will be a need for continued support for and recognition of trainee efforts.

Supervisors of counseling practicum students need a full awareness of the trainees' competency levels to see that the trainees are assigned clients with whom they can work effectively, particularly in the initial phase of the Counseling Practicum. It can be very discouraging, and even overwhelming, for beginning counseling trainees to be assigned only very challenging cases. As the term progresses and multicultural counseling competency levels increase, "the trainee's caseload may be increased in complexity of client and stage of ethnic identity consistent with the stage of the trainee's level of development" (Carney & Kahn, 1984, p. 116).

If the counseling trainees are working at off-campus sites, creating a climate and atmosphere conducive to student growth may require that the university supervisor work closely with the off-campus site supervisors at the onset of the counseling practicum. When the counseling practicum is carried out in a clinic setting within the university facility, clients need to be screened for appropriate involvement in a counselor training facility. The amount of faculty time allotted to supervising the counseling clinic will play a large role in the number and types of clients that can be accepted. Some people who come to university counselor training clinics may need to be referred for therapy at other mental health settings.

For trainees in a practicum setting such as that described at the University of British Columbia in Vancouver, Canada (see Chapter 5), the supervisor and students meet at a community site where area clients come for counseling. Having the supervisor present to model counseling and to serve as a consultant for trainees in the beginning stages of counseling provides strong support for student growth. Problems and issues can be addressed "in the here and now" rather than waiting for consultation at a later time.

At this stage in multicultural counselor competency development, the trainer's role moves from that of instructor to that of supervisor and mentor. Counseling students need to have opportunities to select and try their own directions in work with clients. Part of the supervisor's role will be to help the trainee get the information he or she requests. For cognitive information, the trainees may need to learn more sources of information so they can acquire a process they can apply later.

Once they begin direct counseling with clients of a different culture, the counseling trainees will gain a wider perspective on how many clients' problems are issues that are exacerbated by limits and regulations of the larger society. It will become very obvious to the student counselor that the clients' issues are not all intrapersonal issues. It may also become evident that many clients are suffering from multiple oppressions. A beginning counselor trying to work with a client who has brought multiple issues may soon feel as overwhelmed as the client. Help may be needed from the supervisor to work with the client to "sort out" and prioritize problems.

Student realization of the many sources of problems can lead to a real sense of frustration on the part of the counselor trainee since he or she may feel an urgency to go out and change that environment *for* the client. Counselor trainees may need much help in learning how to work *with* the client to assist that individual in learning how to impact his or her environment. There is the danger of the counselor wanting to do for rather than to do with the client. There is also the danger of the trainee wanting to push the client to move faster than the client is ready to move.

Trainees who have established good cross-cultural client relationships (as detailed in the adaptation of Gibbs' 1985 Model of Interpersonal Orientation presented in Chapter 9), are aware that clients expect counselors to be ready to work in the clients' cultural milieus. At this point, counselor trainees may need much support and assistance in choosing appropriate interventions so the client and counselor are working together toward goals that are mutually agreed upon by both the counselor and the counselee.

Another issue that may arise in the counseling practicum is that students feel reasonably confident in cross-cultural work with people of one cultural group but have less confidence in working with people of different cultural heritages. If possible, it will be helpful for students to work with clients of more than one cultural heritage.

Details of some appropriate supervisor interventions to help trainees successfully complete the fourth stage of multicultural counseling competence are included as they apply to implementing the goals of Stage Four. Helping the counseling trainee deal appropriately with frustrations brought on by the environment of the client increases the trainee's readiness to move into the fifth stage of multicultural counselor preparation (Carney & Kahn, 1984).

Appendix E contains sample items the counseling practicum supervisor can use to evaluate the student's multicultural counseling competence. Appendix F lists sample multicultural items counseling practicum students can use to evaluate their counseling site and counseling practicum site supervisor.

GOALS TO PROMOTE STUDENT DEVELOPMENT IN BELIEFS AND ATTITUDES, KNOWLEDGE, AND SKILLS IN STAGE FOUR

Goal 1: To provide supervision by a qualified trainer at an appropriate culturally pluralistic site at which the student can complete a counseling practicum

Goal 2: To challenge the student to continue learning about self in interaction with culturally or racially different clients in the counseling session, as well as in the clients' own cultural milieus

Goal 3: To provide opportunities for students to develop a broader repertoire of successful multicultural counseling interventions with individuals as well as with families

Goal 4: To initiate application of information from racial and ethnic identity development models in work with clients at various stages of racial and ethnic identity development

APPROPRIATE ENVIRONMENTS AND LEARNING EXPERIENCES TO ACHIEVE GOALS

Goal 1: To provide supervision by a qualified trainer at an appropriate culturally pluralistic site at which the student can complete a counseling practicum. In some areas of the United States, students will have difficulty receiving on-site supervision by counselors trained in multicultural counseling. A major reason for this deficiency is that many current counselors were trained in the traditional monocultural theoretical base of the first several decades of U.S. counselor training. This paucity of site supervisors who are qualified to supervise the student in multicultural counseling can result in the supervision being handled directly by the on-campus instructor. At least part of the supervisory work should be provided by people of different cultural groups, either at the practicum site or in the university counselor education department.

Ashby and Cheatham (1994) emphasize that all supervision is cross-cultural. Issues of supervision become complex when the varying levels of supervision include supervisors and counselors-in-training with different racial or cultural backgrounds and training and clients who may also be from different racial and cultural backgrounds (Bernard, 1994; Leong, 1994; Leong & Wagner, 1994; Priest, 1994). As an example, the supervisor may be White, the counselor-in-training may be a person of color, and the client may be White. Different information processing and differential power elements may come into play. The process becomes even more complicated in work with gays or lesbians who may be struggling with identity issues where the cultural components are not obvious. Exploration of the many and complex dimensions of multicultural supervision is in its infancy (Bernard, 1994; Leong & Wagner, 1994).

Selection of a site that serves clients of different cultures is also important. To serve culturally diverse clients, students at rural university locations may need to commute to a more urban area for at least part of their counseling practicum experiences.

Hills and Strozier (1992), in their national study of multicultural counseling training in APA-approved counseling psychology programs, found that non-White communities have not put pressure on their local university counselor preparation programs to serve the people of their areas. These authors recommend that departments "seeking to expand their practicum sequence to include more multicultural opportunities may need to work on their relationship with the non-White community in the area" (Hills & Strozier, 1992, p. 49). Opportunities for multicultural counseling may be present in areas near universities, but leadership is needed to develop positive relationships between the university training programs and these non-White communities. The University of British Columbia Counseling Psychology Program's practice of taking a team of counselors to the area might be one model for developing better relations with non-White communities (see Chapter 5).

Supervision of the counseling practicum student is usually shared by the on-campus counseling practicum instructor and an on-site supervisor. A supervisor of supervisors adds an additional level of supervision at some sites. As noted earlier in this chapter, supervisors need a background of education and experience in multicultural counseling. At this point in the development of the counselor-in-training, supervisors provide a balance of support and challenge to the student.

Counseling students need the opportunity to observe productive multicultural counseling sessions at their counseling practicum site, to spend many hours in direct counseling with culturally different clients, and to participate in individual and group supervision of their work. Cameras, videotapes, and one-way mirrors are essential for high-quality supervision.

Goal 2: To challenge the student to continue learning about self in interaction with culturally or racially different clients in the counseling session, as well as in the clients' own cultural milieus.   One of the three major sections of the Association for Multicultural Counseling and Development (AMCD) position paper on multicultural counseling competencies is devoted to "counselor awareness of own assumptions, values, and biases . . . [as they relate to] beliefs and attitudes, knowledge, and skills" (Sue et al., 1992a, p. 482). Among the several clarifying guidelines is this statement: "Culturally skilled counselors are constantly seeking to understand themselves as racial and cultural beings and are actively seeking a nonracist identity" (Sue et al., 1992a, p. 482).

Understanding oneself as an ethnic and racial being is a process that will be ongoing throughout life. The counselor trainee's self-understanding of the impact that the trainee's racial and ethnic heritage and racial and ethnic identity development have on the trainee's behavior in counseling has been the focus of much of the work in Stages One through Three.

By this stage in multicultural development, students have an initial awareness of self in the role of multicultural counselor, are able to identify some areas in which they need assistance, and know when they need to request help from supervisors. Practicum students also need a sense of self-confidence to be able to deal with challenges to change that will occur as they engage in counseling culturally different clients.

If counseling students seem unaware of their own impact on the dyadic experience, the practicum supervisors' roles are to confront and challenge the students while also providing support for continued student development. Helping students move from cognitive awareness of issues to application of cognitive knowledge in appropriate counseling behavior is an ongoing task for the supervisors. Interaction with students during the weekly supervisory sessions is a time when challenges to and support for student growth are present.

One way to expand trainee and supervisor interaction is through the use of journaling. Students make journal entries after each counseling session and after each supervisory session. Journals submitted for supervisor review and reactions on a weekly basis give the supervisor a more complete picture of the student's comfort level with multicultural and other counseling issues. This review also allows supervisors an opportunity to give the student additional feedback and support.

In the AMCD position paper on multicultural counseling competencies, Sue et al. (1992a, 1992b) recommend that culturally skilled counselors learn about themselves and the milieu of culturally different others by becoming "actively involved with minority individuals outside the counseling setting . . . so that their perspective of minorities is more than an academic or helping exercise" (p. 70). Some of the activities in which counselors may participate are community events, political and social functions, celebrations, and neighborhood meetings. This suggestion is similar to Gibbs' (1985) recommendation in her model of interpersonal orientation to relationship building in the initial stages of cross-cultural counseling (see Chapter 9, Goal 3). As counselors begin to work with the culturally different in the counseling practicum, they will need to get out into the community of their counselees to gain this broader perspective.

Goal 3: To provide opportunities for students to develop a broader repertoire of successful multicultural counseling interventions with individuals as well as with families.   Practicum trainees can see how to apply what they have learned in the academic environment by observing on-site counselors working cross-culturally with individuals and families. Practicum students can be eased into taking full responsibility for counseling sessions through co-counseling with experienced therapists before implementing counseling on their own. Student participation in case conferences on culturally different clients can also be helpful in building trainee self-confidence.

In addition to participating in the activities listed above, practicum supervisors will be involved in weekly individual supervisory sessions with practicum students. The major focus of these individual sessions will be to review and discuss students' videotaped counseling sessions. Student interest in refining special techniques often leads to questions about counseling interventions. Supervisors need to be prepared to respond to these questions by discussing or modeling appropriate techniques. In addition, students may ask where to get more information on specific techniques or models.

A number of models for multicultural counselor preparation were reviewed in the first section of Chapter 3 of this book. Detailed information from these models may be helpful for practicum students. Some of these models will be referred to in this section.

Atkinson, Thompson, and Grant (1993) recommend that counselors examine three factors in choosing counselor roles and interventions: "(a) the client's level of acculturation, (b) the locus of the problem's etiology, and (c) the goals of helping" (p. 259).

Acculturation of minority clients refers to the extent to which these people have taken on the beliefs, values, and behaviors of the dominant White society. Behavioral manifestations of acculturation may vary according to the environment in which the person is functioning and according to the individual's adaptability. Some people learn to live biculturally or multiculturally and adjust their behaviors according to the environmental situation.

Culture-specific instruments have been developed for assessing levels of acculturation and have been used in research to measure attitudes toward mental health services (see, for example, Atkinson & Gim, 1989; Atkinson, Whiteley, & Gim, 1990; Gim, Atkinson, & Whiteley, 1990; and Ponce & Atkinson, 1989). Instruments used by these researchers are the Acculturation Rating Scale for Mexican Americans (ARSMA) for both normal and clinical populations developed by Cuellar, Harris, and Jasso in 1980; and the Suinn-Lew Asian Self-Identity Acculturation Scale (SL-ASIA) developed by Suinn, Rickard-Figueroa, Lew, and Vigil in 1987. Sabnani and Ponterotto (1992) and Ponterotto and Casas (1991) describe the Acculturation Rating Scale for Mexican Americans (ARSMA) as the most researched of the acculturation rating scales. Sabnani and Ponterotto (1992) state, "There seems to be adequate evidence for the construct-related, content-related, and criterion-related validity of the ARSMA" (p. 176), and they state the major drawback of the ARSMA "is that it does not measure the other dimensions that are assumed to be concomitants of acculturation (e.g., worldviews), so that the use of other scales to make up for this gap is advised" (p. 176).

Atkinson, Thompson, and Grant (1993) reviewed research indicating the impact acculturation has on cross-cultural counseling with Latinos, Native Americans, and Asian Americans. Less acculturated Latino American and Native American clients showed a preference for counselors who are ethnically similar to them. The less acculturated Latino American clients also expected counselors to be directive and empathic. Less acculturated Native American clients had expectations for nurturance and expert techniques to facilitate the session. Less acculturated Asian American clients showed more resistance to coming to counselors and being open to self-disclosure in counseling. No research was found on the effects of acculturation on African Americans in counseling. Atkinson, Thompson, and Grant (1993) propose that, because African Americans have been on the North American continent for a long time, many of them have learned to live biculturally to survive.

Ponterotto and Casas (1991) warn against predicting a client's attitude toward counseling solely on the basis of the client's level of acculturation. The great variance within each cultural group underscores the need to view each client as a unique individual in that cultural group.

For the practitioner interested in less formal procedures for assessing accultur-ation levels of minority clients, several methods and techniques introduced in Stages One, Two, and Three (Chapters 7, 8, and 9) give clues about clients' acculturation level. Various adaptations of the Kluckhohn and Strodtbeck (1961) model for studying culture and world views (see Chapter 7, Goal 5 of Stage One) can give initial indications of how much a client's world view may differ from those of the dominant, White U.S. society. The discussion of Goal 6 of Stage One highlighted some aspects of cross-cultural communication that may give clues as to levels of acculturation (such as use of space, body movement and gesturing, and paralanguage).

The counselor can get an idea of the importance of the client's traditional culture by utilizing the "Culture—The Silent Partner Worksheet" introduced in Chapter 8 (Goal 4 of Stage Two). Kleinman's explanatory model discussed under Goal 7 of Stage Two is another possibility for gaining clues on clients' acculturation levels. Acculturation also impacts levels of racial and ethnic identity development discussed in Chapter 9 (Goal 1 of Stage Three). More on the application of racial and ethnic identity development levels to counseling is included in a subsequent section of this chapter.

The *locus of the client's problem etiology* could be conceptualized on a contin-uum from internal to external, according to Atkinson, Thompson, and Grant (1993). They believe it would be rare for the locus of the problem to be completely internal or completely external; Axelson (1993) also cautions against viewing the locus of the problem as completely internal or completely external. Examples of problems generally thought to have an internal etiology are problems of mood swings, impulse control, and irrational fears. Examples of problems with an external locus are those resulting from job discrimination, sexual harassment, or post-traumatic stress (Atkinson, Thompson, & Grant, 1993).

In many cases, problem manifestation is influenced by both internal and external factors. For example, suppose Maria, a young Latino female client, says she receives no recognition for the high-quality work she believes she has been doing as a laboratory technician. The counselor may need to help Maria investigate how her supervisors and co-workers are treating her and how she responds to feedback from them. Without knowledge of Maria's present and past experiences in handling feedback and her experiences in dealing with oppression and discrimi-nation, the counselor may have difficulty pinpointing the locus of Maria's problem. In addition to giving clues on the client's acculturation level, Kleinman's explana-tory model (Goal 7 of Stage Two in Chapter 8) can provide perspectives on how clients view the locus of their problems.

Goals of counseling are often influenced by the route the client takes to the counselor (Atkinson, Thompson, & Grant, 1993). If a client is referred by another person or by an institution, that other person or institution may have already set goals for the client. It may be very difficult to convince a client to work on goals set by others unless the client willingly accepts them as goals on which he or she chooses to work. When this happens, the client has, in essence, turned into a self-referral. Atkinson, Thompson, and Grant (1993) note that goals of prevention are usually established by the counselor, and goals of remediation are frequently established by the client. However, my experiences in cross-cultural counseling indicate some clients *are* interested in learning how to handle problems proactively in order to prevent future occurrences of these problems.

The client's willingness to set long-term goals may be influenced by the time perspective of the client's culture. One of the five Kluckhohn and Strodtbeck (1961) categories for studying cultures is the temporal orientation of the cultural group. (This concept was introduced in Chapter 7, Goal 5 of Stage One.) Whether an individual's temporal orientation is dominated by the past, the present, the future, or a combination of these perspectives can influence the client's participation in goal setting. Socioeconomic level can also greatly influence the client's readiness to set goals. People in poverty who live a day-to-day, "hand-to-mouth" existence often have difficulty setting long-term goals because their mode of functioning is to survive on a day-to-day basis. Middle-class White counselors, in particular, need to be aware of these strong influences on client goal setting during counseling.

Another perspective for learning about the impact of culture on the client is to do an assessment of *ethnocultural identification*. The Comas-Diaz and Jacobsen (1987) model of ethnocultural identification assessment was introduced in Chapter 8, in Goal 7 of Stage Two. These authors define ethnocultural identification as "a process whereby patients attribute ethnocultural characteristics to their therapists . . . [and] a therapeutic process that fosters an identification in which the therapist reflects pieces of the patient's fragmented self" (Comas-Diaz & Jacobsen, 1987, p. 236). This type of assessment can be especially helpful in working with people who have moved from their original cultural setting, whether from inside or outside their home country.

Comas-Diaz and Jacobsen (1987) describe five stages of counselor assessment of client ethnocultural identification.

1. Obtaining an ethnocultural history
2. Focusing on circumstances of the translocation of the client and his or her family
3. Assessing how the client perceives the family's ethnocultural identity since the translocation
4. Assessing the client's personal perception of his or her ethnocultural adjustment
5. Considering the counselor's own ethnocultural adjustment to see any areas that overlap those of the client to determine how this might affect transference and countertransference

Comas-Diaz and Jacobsen (1987) discuss the process of transference and countertransference between client and counselor and possible problems of over-identification with the client by the counselor. Kleinman (1985, 1988) also addresses problems in counselor overidentification with clients; Kleinman calls this the "cultural blind spot." Ethnocultural identification is used "as an auxiliary therapeutic tool to facilitate coping with changing cultural values and transitional experiences" (Comas-Diaz & Jacobsen, 1987, p. 232).

In a presentation at the 1994 Winter Roundtable on Cross-Cultural Counseling and Psychotherapy at Teachers College, Columbia University, Comas-Diaz discussed how women of color first develop an identity based on race, then develop an identity based on gender, and finally develop an integrated identity. She views women of color as having been colonized and having to live with a pervasive identity conflict. Therapists need to recognize the collective effects of colonization that have led to dichotomous thinking for women of color. Counselors can work to empower women of color to find for themselves how to overcome colonization. Comas-Diaz (1994) cautioned therapists to be more aware of the following dyadic variables in cross-cultural psychotherapy: empathy, ethnocultural identification, intuition, and the attribution of the other. She stated that therapists are involved in family therapy whenever they work with anyone whose identity extends beyond the self. The 1994 book edited by Comas-Diaz and Greene, *Women of Color: Integrating Ethnic and Gender Identities in Psychotherapy*, addresses many ethnic and gender identity psychotherapeutic issues for women of color.

Practicum students interested in additional information on cross-cultural counseling with people of specific populations have a wealth of information available in the current professional literature. There are chapters devoted to counseling with people of special cultural groups in several multicultural counseling textbooks (for example, Atkinson, Morten, & Sue, 1993; Lee, 1995; Lee & Richardson, 1991; Locke, 1992b; Pedersen et al., 1989; Sue & Sue, 1990). In addition, the number of articles in the professional counseling journals devoted to counseling with specific populations continues to increase.

To continue to improve students' multicultural counseling skills, the practicum students and their supervisors work together to monitor the students' caseloads. As the practicum students gain confidence in their cross-cultural work and their competency increases, they can take on more difficult counseling cases.

Goal 4: To initiate application of information from racial and ethnic identity development models in work with clients at various stages of racial and ethnic identity development.
Application of information from racial and ethnic identity development models parallels the expansion of counseling interventions discussed in Goal 3. Because this is such an important topic, I have elected to discuss this application here, under a separate goal. The major topics addressed under Goal 3 (assessment of clients' levels of acculturation, assessing the locus of the client's problem etiology, and establishing goals of counseling) all relate to understanding and applying information on clients' levels of racial and ethnic identity development to the counseling process.

Atkinson, Morten, and Sue (1993) and Helms (1984, 1985, 1990) emphasize that their minority and racial identity development models are intended not as theories of personality but as paradigms to help counselors understand clients' attitudes and behaviors. The Minority Identity Development Model (MID) (Atkinson, Morten, & Sue, 1993) is presented to help counselors become more sensitive to:

1. The role oppression has played in the minority individual's identity development
2. The many differences in cultural identity that exist among members of the same minority
3. The potential each minority individual has for changing his or her cultural identity

Hardiman (1982), Helms (1984, 1985, 1990, 1992), Ponterotto (1988), Ponterotto and Pedersen (1993), Sabnani et al. (1991), and Sue and Sue (1990) present White racial identity development models that describe the process White people experience in acknowledging that:

1. They have a racial identity.
2. White people are privileged because of the power that their group has had in the United States.
3. There are social implications and obligations of being born into a privileged group that has used (and is continuing to use) its power to oppress people of color.

Helms (1984) gives a detailed description of the "counseling attitudinal and behavior predispositions" (p. 156) of Black dyads, White dyads, and mixed dyads. Helms (1984) also addresses what may happen in a counseling situation when the counselor and the client are at "parallel, crossed, progressive, and regressive" (p. 159) stages. In the parallel relationship, client and counselor are at the same stage of racial identity development. In the crossed relationship, client and counselor are in stages that represent opposing attitudes about Blacks and Whites. The progressive relationship is one in which the counselor is at least one stage more advanced on racial identity development than the client. The regressive relationship occurs when the client's stage of racial identity development is ahead of the counselor's. The progressive relationship is the only one in which the counselor would be able to help the client move ahead; and unless the counselor had reached the highest level of racial identity development, the counselor might not be able to do much to help the client move forward because the relationship would soon be a parallel one.

Helms' concepts reinforce the need for counseling practicum students to have reached the highest level of racial or ethnic identity development in order to be ready to cope with the cross-cultural challenge of clients at different levels of racial or ethnic identity development. The old adage that we cannot help people move beyond the level that we as counselors have attained seems to apply in determining the impact of the counselor's racial identity development on the client. After studying how to determine clients' levels of racial and ethnic identity development (Chapter 9, Goal 1 of Stage Three), a next step for counseling trainees is to gain perspectives on counseling interventions that are appropriate for clients at various levels of racial and ethnic identity development.

Taking client needs into consideration is important in designing treatment interventions in counseling. Several authors have hypothesized on the needs of clients in the various stages of racial and ethnic identity development (Atkinson, Morten, & Sue, 1993; Helms, 1984, 1985, 1990, 1992; Parham & Helms, 1981; Phinney, 1989, 1993; Ponterotto, 1988; Ponterotto & Pedersen, 1993; Sabnani et al., 1991; Sue & Sue, 1990). Considerably more is written about counselor interventions to meet the racial and ethnic identity stage needs of clients of color than about counselor interventions to meet the racial and ethnic identity stage needs of White clients.

The following sections address meeting the needs of people of color and the needs of White people in the various stages of racial and ethnic identity development. Authors differ as to whether racial and ethnic identity development is a process that extends over three, four, five, or six stages. The model presented here integrates a brief overview of needs and suggested counselor interventions for five stages of racial and ethnic identity development for clients of color and for White clients. Empirical research to assess the effectiveness of these counselor interventions is still *very* limited, particularly research on appropriate counselor cross-cultural interventions with White people. (To some, it appears to be another case of majority White professionals denying the reality of the changing cultural pluralism within our ranks.)

Clients of color in the first stage of racial identity development still identify primarily with the majority White race; they accept the standards of the White majority as the way to measure themselves. Minority clients at this level are unlikely to seek counseling for problems related to cultural identity. Clients will probably present problems that are amenable to solution through goal-oriented techniques (Atkinson, Morten, & Sue, 1993).

At the first stage, clients of color may be insulted if assigned to a counselor of color and may request to see a White counselor (Atkinson, Morten, & Sue, 1993). If assigned to a White counselor, minority clients' needs to please the White counselor may become very evident because the clients strive to identify themselves as White. If assigned to a counselor of color, the client of color's displeasure with being assigned a minority counselor may surface in the counseling session. Attempts by either minority or majority counselors to help these clients of color explore racial or ethnic identity issues may be met with considerable resistance, because this exploration "may eventually touch upon feelings of low self-esteem, dissatisfaction with personal appearance, vague anxieties, racial self-hatred, and challenge the clients' self-conception that he/she is not like the other members of his/her own race" (Sue & Sue, 1990, p. 108).

Sue and Sue (1990) recommend that a counselor of any race begin the process of helping his or her minority clients sort out conflicts related to racial and cultural identity development through a reeducative process. This reeducation may include an integrated discussion of majority-minority relations, cultural racism, self-hatred on the basis of race, and belief that one is different from others of the same race.

Counselors will need to be very sensitive to the first-stage clients' readiness to deal with feelings related to racial and cultural identity development (Sue & Sue, 1990). Work with some clients will start more on the cognitive rather than on the affective level. A goal of these interventions will be to help clients understand the difference between positive and negative adoption of White majority values, beliefs, and behaviors. The negative adoption of majority values in the first stage includes rejecting the traditional values, beliefs, and behaviors of their own minority culture. Positive adoption of values from other cultures comes after thoughtful consideration of these values for their own lives and movement to a stage of integrative awareness.

Sue and Sue (1990) also call attention to the need for majority and minority counselors to work in a different manner with minority clients in the first stage. Minority counselors will probably have to help minority clients deal with their resistance and hostility to working with other minority individuals and help them understand the source of this resistance and hostility. An accepting and nonjudgmental minority counselor can serve as a positive role model to the minority client. Majority counselors, on the other hand, may have to help the minority clients understand their need to please and overidentify with majority individuals. An accepting and nonjudgmental majority counselor can model the importance of cultural diversity. Counselors of any race will find it important to guard against subtle reinforcement of the client's rejection of his or her own racial and cultural identity.

Ponterotto and Pedersen (1993) reviewed several studies with minority individuals that show a negative correlation with the first stage of racial or ethnic identity development and positive mental health indices. On the basis of these findings, these authors predict that "These individuals are clearly more in danger of being racist toward their own group than toward White persons" (Ponterotto & Pedersen, 1993, p. 58).

Minority adolescents in the first stage of Phinney's 1993 three-stage model of adolescent ethnic identity development are in one of two substages of the *Unexamined Ethnic Identity* development stage. These adolescents may show a complete lack of interest in learning about their ethnic or cultural heritage (the *Diffuse* substage); or, their views on ethnic identity may be dominated by the views of significant others in their lives (the *Foreclosed* substage). These young people do not necessarily hold negative views toward their own ethnic heritage, nor do they always show preferences for being White.

On the basis of her research, Phinney (1993) states that "subjects with an unexamined ethnic identity had the lowest ego-identity scores" (p. 73). Phinney believes that some minority adolescents in the first stage of ethnic identity development may have internalized preconceived negative notions of their ethnicity from their parents or the larger society. At this point, these young people might profit from beginning the process of active exploration of their ethnic heritage to learn the strengths of this heritage and to take the first steps toward a positive identification with their ethnicity. Since Phinney and her associates found that ethnic identity development was related to ego identity development, self-esteem, and psychological functioning (Phinney, 1989, 1992; Phinney & Alipuria, 1990), counselor interventions to help minority adolescents in the *Unexamined Ethnic Identity* gain pride in their heritage could improve their success in coping with the wider world.

White clients in the first stage of racial identity development show very ethnocentric attitudes about being White. White clients may not view themselves as having a racial identity (Helms, 1984, 1985, 1990, 1992; Katz & Ivey, 1977; Ponterotto, 1988; Sabnani et al., 1991). In their 1993 integration of concepts from White identity models, Ponterotto and Pedersen state that Whites at this stage may be oblivious to their role in cultural and racial issues and to any cultural and racial stereotypes that they hold. If first-stage White clients show resistance to working with a counselor of color, this resistance would be an issue to explore in counseling. It might be well, however, to first help the White clients explore the strengths of their own White ethnic heritages. This, then, could serve as a positive base for accepting others who are different.

A reeducative process to help White individuals understand the privileges of being White (McIntosh, 1990) and the real historical backgrounds for U.S. people of color could be another route for broadening the White person's ethnocentric perspective. Helms' 1992 book, *A Race is a Nice Thing to Have,* can serve as a workbook for use both in the counseling sessions and as homework between counseling sessions. Chapters 1 through 6 of Helms' 1992 book could serve as a starting point for first-stage White clients to discover their Whiteness. As a conclusion to this section, Helms (1992) states: "The remedy for the Contact stage is more information and more exposure to cultural diversity" (p. 39).

Several activities in which counselor trainees were involved in the first stages of multicultural counselor development could be applied to work with first-stage White clients (such as reading ethnic novels; exploring one's own ethnic, racial, and cultural identity; studying the descriptors of people of a variety of heritages; learning about differences in world views).

Clients of color in the second stage of racial or ethnic identity development show a willingness to begin discussing issues of self-identity and self-esteem. Interest in learning more about their own racial or ethnic identity usually leads to a preference for a counselor who is knowledgeable about the client's racial or ethnic heritage (Atkinson, Morten, & Sue, 1993). Although a counselor of the same heritage as the client may be the one who has the broadest background to help the minority client, the client's conflicting feelings and beliefs may still surface during the sessions. Sue and Sue (1990) suggest that the counselor capitalize on the client's receptivity to self-exploration and help the second-stage client of color "come to grips with his/her identity conflicts" (p. 109). Helms (1984) recommends that the counselor help the client of color at the early stages "test out new skills for interacting with both races" (p. 162).

Phinney, Lochner, and Murphy (1990) encourage counselors to continue to support adolescent minority clients in the *Ethnic Identity Search/Moratorium* stage to "explore their feelings and attitudes regarding their ethnicity" (p. 68) and to learn about their history in a multicultural society. These authors also recommend that counselors help adolescent minority clients reevaluate negative images they may hold toward people of their own group. Living biculturally is another area for counselors to explore with minority adolescents. Phinney et al. (1990) recognize that this may be a difficult and somewhat disturbing process, but it is a process that "can be expected to lead ultimately to a more secure sense of self and more healthy adjustment" (p. 68). Because Phinney's model includes only three stages, the work described in this paragraph will continue through Stages Three and Four of the model presented in this chapter.

One finding from the research of Phinney and her associates is worthy of repeating. The interviews with eighth-graders in the middle stage of ethnic identity development (Phinney & Tarver, 1988) and with tenth-graders (Phinney, 1989) did not reveal the intense emotions described by some authors of racial identity development models. It is important to underscore that the Phinney researchers worked with eighth- and tenth-graders in their study of ethnic identity development, and the racial identity theorists worked mainly with students of college age. This age difference may account for some of the differences in findings.

One-third of the eighth-graders and over half of the tenth-graders in Phinney's studies were actively involved in some kind of search to learn more about their own culture through activities like talking with family and friends, going to cultural events and museums, and reading books about their culture. Phinney (1993) noted that these young people "had thought about the effects of their ethnicity on their life, in the present and in the future" (p. 67). Phinney hypothesized that what may be most important is how minority adolescents view themselves as members of their ethnic group and how this group membership may influence their career and life options. These issues are important ones for counselors to explore with minority adolescents in the middle stage of ethnic identity development.

White clients in the second stage of racial and ethnic identity development begin to feel conflict over their increasing knowledge of the realities of racism and racial relations in the larger society and their involvement in maintaining the status quo (Ponterotto, 1988; Sabnani et al., 1991). They begin to realize how they have compartmentalized or denied information related to race relations, and they begin to recognize their personal involvement in supporting racism (Sue & Sue, 1990). Ponterotto and Pedersen (1993) state, "The central feature of this stage is conflict between wanting to conform to majority norms (i.e., peer pressure from White acquaintances) and wishing to uphold humanistic, nonracist values" (p. 77). At this stage, White clients may feel confusion, shame, guilt, depression, and anger.

Counselor interventions with White clients in the second stage of racial and ethnic identity development may include support for openness to self and explorations of what the individual wants to do about these conflicting feelings. The process of reeducation to the full meaning of being White needs to continue. One activity might be to discuss McIntosh's (1990) 26 daily benefits of White privilege and the feelings associated with recognizing that being White means having an "unearned advantage and conferred dominance" (p. 35). Chapter 7, "How Can I Be White?" in Helms' 1992 book also provides content for discussing the dilemmas second-stage White clients experience.

Clients of color in the third stage of minority identity development will pose a special challenge, especially if the counselor is White (Sue & Sue, 1990). Any counselor (majority or minority) will be viewed with suspicion and seen as part of "the Establishment." Minority clients at this stage tend to view all problems as products of their oppression and rarely come to counseling except when they experience a crisis (Atkinson, Morten, & Sue, 1993). If third-stage minority clients do come for counseling, they usually prefer to work with an ethnically similar counselor and in a group setting with other minority clients with similar cultural and racial issues.

Counselors working with third-stage minority clients must be ready to be tested, to deal with hostility, and to not personalize the attacks and become defensive. Clients of color may need much help to deal with their anger. Counselor self-disclosure can be an important technique to develop rapport with minority clients at this stage (Sue & Sue, 1990). Counseling approaches that tend to be action oriented and directed toward external change usually work best. Sue and Sue (1990) recommend "that the counselor help the culturally different client explore new ways of relating to both minority and White persons" (p. 111).

White clients at the midpoint of racial and ethnic identity development begin to question and challenge their own racism (Sue & Sue, 1990). They may see racism everywhere on a daily basis. Many Whites at this stage feel anger at White family, friends, and institutions and experience guilt over being a part of an oppressive system. To compensate for these feelings of guilt, White individuals may choose one of two different paths. Some White people may become zealous in their work to improve the plight of minority individuals (Ponterotto, 1988), and in so doing they may behave in a paternalistic or patronizing way toward people of color. Some White people may attempt to try to identify with members of a particular minority group (Sue & Sue, 1990) and attempt to take on behaviors of the group.

The result of either of these behavioral choices may not be as positive as the White individual had hoped. She or he will probably feel dejected over a lack of appreciation of all-out efforts to "help" people of color or feel rejected in efforts to identify with people of color. These feelings will need to be dealt with during counseling and alternative behavioral choices explored.

Helms (1992) describes people in the third stage of White racial identity development somewhat differently, with a different progression through the stages. Helms views this stage as one in which the general theme "is idealization of Whites and White culture and denigration of peoples of color and their culture" (p. 53). She notes that feelings of White superiority may be expressed overtly or covertly by White people in this stage. Telling a racist joke is an example of overt expression; listening to or not challenging a racist joke is an example of covert racism. Helms believes White people in this stage of racial identity development are strongly represented in White society. She also views this stage as "a stable and consistent stage because cultural and institutional racism are so firmly established in American society" (Helms, 1992, p. 54).

Chapter 8 in Helms 1992 book, "Reintegration: 'We have the best because we are the best!'" (pp. 53–57) gives additional descriptors for people in the third stage of her White racial identity development model. Because Helms believes it is crucial that White people recognize what they are doing in the *Reintegration* stage in order to encourage them to abandon this stage, she includes a self-assessment exercise, "How much Reintegration do you have?" (p. 56) for Whites to "be able to recognize the subtle and not so subtle ways Reintegration can be expressed" (Helms, 1992, p. 55). Introduction to and study of the models of White racial and ethnic identity development could be another self-assessment exercise for White people.

Fourth-stage clients of color begin to feel more comfortable with their own racial and ethnic heritage. Concurrently, however, they grow uncomfortable with the rigidly held views of the third stage and realize they are expending too much effort directing anger at another group (Atkinson, Morten, & Sue, 1993; Sue & Sue, 1990). They may feel torn between loyalty to their own group and the desire for more freedom to be themselves.

Sue and Sue (1990) caution that minority individuals in the fourth stage may resemble minority individuals in the first stage in that they appear to move away from members of their own group. The dynamics of what is going on within minority individuals in the first and fourth stages are quite different, however. Minority individuals in the first stage are motivated by total self-hatred and hatred of everything associated with their racial group. Minority individuals in the third stage have worked through and no longer have global negative feelings and beliefs toward their own racial group. Fourth-stage minority persons feel positively about their own racial group and move away selectively on certain issues. Sue and Sue (1990) recommend that the counselor help the fourth-stage minority client through "self exploration approaches aimed at helping the client integrate and incorporate a new sense of identity" (p. 111).

Fourth-stage White clients may chose to retreat into White culture rather than continue to experience the intense conflicts of the third stage (Ponterotto & Pedersen, 1993; Sabnani et al., 1991). They may feel anger and fear related to the rejection they experienced in their zealous prominority efforts of the previous stage. They may also feel pressures from White peers about their prominority "White liberal" views and behaviors. The pressures from both minority and majority people may feel so intense that fourth-stage White clients may retreat into the safety of their White cultural cocoons for safe haven. Ponterotto and Pedersen (1993) state that this stage "is characterized by an over-identification with whiteness and by a defensiveness about White culture" (p. 78).

Helms (1992) believes White people go through two additional stages before they reach the highest level. She labels the first stage "Pseudo-Independent: 'Let's help them become more like Whites'" (Helms, 1992, p. 59). This phase of White identity development involves the first major step toward development of a nonracist White identity, and in Chapter 9 of her 1992 book, Helms lists nine characteristics of this stage. Racism is addressed mainly on a cognitive rather than on a cognitive and affective level. White individuals may remain in this stage indefinitely if no racial events touch them personally. They will expend energies that focus on defining how people of color should think, feel, and act to be more like White people. Detailed descriptions of White people at this stage are included in Helms' exercise, "Rediscovering my feelings about my race" (1992, p. 69).

Helms (1992) calls the next level "Immersion/Emersion: I'm White!" (p. 73). She believes that most White people do not progress very far in developing this type of identity because the stage "requires one to assume personal responsibility for racism and to understand one's role in perpetuating [racism] . . . [and to face] feelings of guilt, anger, and anxiety that were pushed out of awareness during earlier stages of development" (Helms, 1992, p. 74).

Sabnani et al. (1991) recommend that White people in their *Retreat into White Culture* stage participate in cross-cultural encounter groups "so that feelings of anger from perceptions of rejection, or other such feelings, may be worked through" (p. 92). Participation in cross-cultural groups seems to help White clients in their feelings toward and relationships with both minority and majority peers.

Fifth-stage clients of color in the Minority Identity Development Model (Atkinson, Morten, & Sue, 1993) are in the *Synergistic* stage. These authors describe them as having a sense of minority identity that is "well balanced by an appreciation of other cultures" (Atkinson, Morten, & Sue, 1993, p. 36). Although discrimination and oppression are still part of their lives, these clients have developed inner resources to deal actively with problems. For minority clients at this stage, attitudinal similarity with the counselor is more important than same minority-group membership.

Sue and Sue (1990) named this stage *Integrative Awareness*. Minority individuals at this level feel a sense of security and have moved to being able to "own and appreciate unique aspects of their culture as well as those of U.S. culture" (Sue & Sue, 1990, p. 106). Major conflicts related to cultural identity have been resolved and individuals are able to see positive aspects of all cultures. They are also able to select and reject aspects of any culture they find undesirable. Sue and Sue (1990) believe that minority individuals at this stage will have "a strong commitment and desire to eliminate all forms of oppression" (p. 106).

Phinney (1993) states, "The ideal outcome of the identity process is an achieved identity, characterized by a clear, confident sense of one's own ethnicity" (p. 71). As examples of minority adolescents in the *Ethnic Identity Achievement* stage, Phinney (1993) includes statements made by an Asian male and a Black female: " 'My culture is important and I am proud of what I am. Japanese people have so much to offer.' . . . 'It used to be confusing to me, but it's clear now. I'm happy being black' " (pp. 71–72).

Counseling with minority individuals at this level often involves working with clients through a systems approach to develop strategies for bringing about change in their communities and in society (Sue & Sue, 1990). Counselor interest in counseling for systems change will be an important factor in the fifth-stage minority client's preferences for a counselor. Positive reinforcement for minority clients' behavioral changes helps support them in their lifelong racial identity development.

Fifth-stage White clients are in the stage of *Redefinition and Integration*, according to Ponterotto and Pedersen's (1993) integrated model of White identity development. The transition has been made to a more balanced identity. White people at this stage are aware of their responsibility for perpetuating racism as they take on a healthy, nonracist White identity. Similar to minority individuals at the same identity level, Whites are able to see positive and negative factors in all races and groups. They are able to work to fight racist activities and remain open to continued learning about people of other cultures.

The final stage in Helms' 1992 model of White identity development is named "Autonomy: 'I see color and like it'" (p. 87). Similar to Ponterotto and Pedersen (1993), Helms sees the White individual as having an ideal view of a nonracist White person and as having a commitment to work to reach that ideal. Helms describes the White person in this stage as a person who has embarked on "a lifelong process of discovery and recommitment to defining oneself in positive terms as a White person" (p. 87). She also emphasizes that attaining this level of reference group orientation does not change one's basic personality characteristics.

For the White person at the highest level of racial identity development, counselor preference will be based on feelings of congruence with a counselor who will help them work toward a nonracist society. Helping this White client plan and implement activities to reduce racism and oppression for all people who are different may be major tasks for the counselor.

Sabnani et al. (1991) underscore the importance of giving feedback to White people in this stage regarding their changes in behavior. Such feedback can serve as reinforcement of difficult behavior changes and help White individuals continue their lifelong racial identity searches.

SUMMARY

Chapter 10 addressed counselor trainee development in the fourth stage of multicultural counselor development, the stage in which the trainee participates in a counseling practicum experience. After describing practicum student characteristics and process guidelines for creating a climate for practicum student growth in beliefs and attitudes, knowledge and skills, appropriate multicultural environments and learning experiences for practicum students were delineated under four goals.

Goal 1 discussed the challenges of obtaining supervision by qualified supervisors at appropriate culturally pluralistic sites, given the current state of multicultural counselor training. The second goal addressed the challenges of assisting practicum students to continue to learn about themselves in interaction with culturally different clients during the counseling session as well as in the clients' own cultural milieus. Goal 3 dealt with helping the practicum student develop a broader repertoire of successful multicultural counseling interventions. Counseling with either minority or majority clients in the various stages of racial and ethnic identity development was addressed under Goal 4. The importance of students' reaching the highest level of racial and ethnic identity development by the time they participate in the counseling practicum was underscored.

To aid the counseling practicum supervisor in evaluating the multicultural counseling competencies of the practicum student, Appendix E lists sample items for evaluating these multicultural counseling competencies. Appendix F lists sample multicultural items for counseling practicum students to evaluate their practicum site and their practicum site supervisor.

CHAPTER 11

Multicultural Counselor Preparation: Stage Five

T he purpose of this chapter is to outline pathways for supporting counseling trainees in their ongoing development in beliefs and attitudes, knowledge, and skills in multicultural competence during Stage Five of their preparation program. In Stage Five, counseling students will participate in appropriate off-campus internship experiences. This chapter is organized under these four subheadings: (1) student characteristics, (2) process guidelines, (3) goals, and (4) appropriate environments and learning experiences to achieve goals.

STUDENT CHARACTERISTICS

Kiselica (1991) gives a vivid description of the anxieties and fears he, a White male of European ancestry, felt as he began his internship experience with "troubled African American and Hispanic American families with histories of poverty, tragedy, and oppression" (p. 127). Kiselica also describes how he conquered these fears and developed a new understanding of his clients, learned to use culturally appropriate interventions along with learning from his mistakes, and experienced joy and inspiration in discovering the beauty of his clients' culture.

Carney and Kahn (1984) describe students in the fifth stage of multicultural counselor development as being excited about their capabilities and having a desire to go on learning. Fifth-stage students are able to accept and celebrate cultural differences and make a real commitment to work to bring about changes in society. Christensen (1989) names this the stage of *Transcendent Awareness* and describes both majority and minority individuals in this stage as "spontaneously able to establish rapport with members of various groups" (p. 383) and having no hesitation to work with dissimilar clients.

Having successfully completed their supervised counseling practicums by this stage, students will have more confidence in their abilities to do multicultural counseling. By virtue of their physical location, many counseling centers serve one or two people of color groups. As a result, students may be somewhat limited in their range of experiences with people of other ethnic or racial groups. Students may also feel somewhat limited in counseling experiences with clients who bring other diversity issues, such as socioeconomic levels, gender, religious and spiritual beliefs, sexual/affectional orientations, physical challenges, language, and so on.

At this stage of multicultural counselor development, the counseling student "assumes a self-directed activist posture in expanding own cross-cultural knowledge, attitudes, and skills, and in promoting cultural pluralism in society at large" (Carney & Kahn, 1984, p. 113). Students are ready to meet the challenge of various kinds of involvement in addition to counseling at their supervised internship sites.

PROCESS GUIDELINES FOR CREATING A CLIMATE FOR STUDENT GROWTH IN STAGE FIVE

The way supervision is implemented at this level is crucial to the counseling student's continued growth. The internship student will have at least two and maybe as many as four levels of supervision, depending on the site and on-campus circumstances. More on the critical importance of supervision is discussed in Goal 1; supervision is addressed here because it impacts heavily on student growth in beliefs and attitudes, knowledge, and skills in Stage Five.

There are "teachable moments" that supervisors need to recognize and capitalize on for students to experience growth. Internship students will profit from having the freedom to try interventions they deem appropriate, but it is important for interns to have a supervisor to consult when they have questions or feel "stuck." Depending on the circumstances, interns can benefit from the supervisor's use of support, encouragement, information, modeling, and confrontation.

Regular group meetings of internship students can provide many "teachable moments." Here, the counseling trainees take turns presenting cases and showing video clips to illustrate their work with clients. Other members of the internship group join the on-campus supervisor in discussing, critiquing, supporting, and making recommendations for possible future interventions. Keeping the internship supervision groups small (no more than five or six people) allows students ample time to discuss each case.

One topic that surfaces repeatedly during the group internship sessions is ways to help bring about change in the clients' behaviors. This can lead to an in-depth exploration of the internship students' individual perceptions of change. A review of sources of client etiology, such as that discussed under Goal 3 of Chapter 10, may be beneficial. Up to this time in their trainee development, some internship students may have concentrated more on intrapsychic sources of client etiology than on external forces that impinge on the client.

As noted earlier, many counseling trainees recognize rather early in their experiential training that the sources of clients' problems are not limited to intrapsychic forces. Unless the students have had courses or training in social change, consultation, mediation, or change agentry skills, they will probably need supervisor assistance when working with their clients to bring about change in their clients' cultural milieus. More details on training internship students to expand the interventions they may use with their clients is given in Goal 2.

Appendix G contains sample items for the evaluation of the intern's multicultural counseling competence by the counseling internship supervisor. Appendix H lists sample multicultural items for evaluation of the internship site and the internship supervisor by the counseling intern.

GOALS TO PROMOTE DEVELOPMENT IN BELIEFS AND ATTITUDES, KNOWLEDGE, AND SKILLS IN STAGE FIVE

Goal 1: To provide a supervised internship experience at an appropriate culturally pluralistic site

Goal 2: To assist internship students in learning to work in a variety of roles in their clients' cultural milieus

Goal 3: To provide support and encouragement for continued student growth in multicultural counseling beliefs and attitudes, knowledge, and skills

APPROPRIATE ENVIRONMENTS AND LEARNING EXPERIENCES TO ACHIEVE GOALS:

Goal 1: To provide a supervised internship experience at an appropriate culturally pluralistic site. University supervisors of internship experiences are responsible for helping students locate internship sites where they can work with culturally pluralistic populations under the supervision of qualified professionals. As discussed in Stage Four, finding locations may be a challenge in rural areas, and the student may need to participate in internship experiences some distance from campus.

The internship setting should be one that specializes in the type of counseling the internship student wishes to engage in after completing the counseling program (elementary school, secondary school, college counseling, mental health, community agency, rehabilitation, hospital, and so on). As noted before, supervisors should have appropriate background, training, and experiences in multicultural counseling. It is also important for the internship student to work with a culturally pluralistic staff.

Involvement in a supervised internship experience at an appropriate culturally pluralistic site requires that the student make a heavy commitment of at least 600 clock-hours of on-site service. In addition to many hours of direct counseling with individuals, families, and groups, the internship student will participate in all other work normally undertaken at the site.

Individual supervision is provided at the internship site. On-campus group supervision is required but may also be available at the internship location. In many situations, group supervision is available for interns at both locations. In consultation with their internship supervisors, counseling interns learn to design appropriate interventions "that . . . match the culture or life-style of the clients" (Sue, Akutsu, & Higashi, 1985, p. 279).

One type of work that may be undertaken at the internship site is diagnostic intakes. Diagnostic intakes with people who have been socialized outside the dominant White society may present special challenges to beginning internship students. The section "Ethical and Cultural Considerations" in the Introduction to the *Diagnostic and Statistical Manual of Mental Disorders,* Fourth Edition (American Psychiatric Association, 1994) notes that the authors of the DSM-IV are aware that the manual is used with people from culturally diverse populations in the United States and internationally. Clinicians are apprised of the challenge of using the DSM-IV criteria in evaluating persons whose ethnic or cultural heritage is different from the clinician's.

> A clinician who is unfamiliar with the nuances of an individual's cultural frame of reference may incorrectly judge as psychopathology those normal variations in behavior, belief, or experience that are particular to the individual's culture. For example, certain religious practices or beliefs (e.g., hearing or seeing a deceased relative during bereavement) may be misdiagnosed as manifestations of a Psychotic Disorder. Applying Personality Disorder criteria across cultural settings may be especially difficult because of the wide cultural variation in concepts of self, styles of communication, and coping mechanisms. (American Psychiatric Association, 1994, p. xxiv)

The DSM-IV includes three types of culturally relevant information for use in diagnoses.

1. A new section discussing culture-related features is included for each disorder. Each section describes how culture may influence the content and form of symptom presentation and the course of the disorder.
2. Culture-bound syndromes, those that have been described in only one or a few societies of the world, are presented in two ways. The *Not Otherwise Specified* categories include some examples of culture-bound syndromes. Appendix I of DSM-IV includes a glossary of 25

of the best-studied culture-bound syndromes. The Glossary of Culture-Bound Syndromes in Appendix I names the condition, lists the cultures in which it has been described, and includes a brief description of the psychopathology.
3. An *Outline for Cultural Formulation* is also included in Appendix I. This outline provides a systematic way for the clinician to evaluate and report the impact of the client's cultural context.

Sue et al. (1992a, 1992b) also caution counselors about the potential bias in assessment instruments and implore counselors to keep the cultural background and linguistic characteristics of the client in mind when interpreting results of cross-cultural assessments. An additional challenge of cross-cultural assessment is that of "determining the degree to which cultural conflict constitutes a major source of difficulty" (Pinderhughes, 1989, p. 18).

Internship students may need to work closely with psychotherapists and psychiatrists who have experience and training in assessing and diagnosing people of different cultural and racial backgrounds. Students may be introduced to some of the newer instruments for assessing the mental health states of culturally different people, such as the depression scales developed and normed on the Southeast Asian refugee population.

Culturally pluralistic internship sites may use paraprofessional "front line" personnel to provide the immediate service for people who come for help. For some internship students, working with paraprofessionals and being involved in their training will be a new experience.

Another experience that may be new to interns is using interpreters or translators. Kleinman (1985) and Sue and Sue (1990) discuss the challenges of counseling through interpreters. Sue et al. (1992a, 1992b) state that it is the counselor's responsibility to interact in the client's preferred language. If the counselor does not speak the client's language, the counselor is advised to engage the services of a translator who has an appropriate professional background as well as knowledge of the client's culture. If the services of a qualified translator are not available, it is the counselor's responsibility to refer the client to a competent bilingual counselor.

There is a great need for interpreters or translators who have background in basic terms and processes of counseling. Esquivel and Keitel (1990) outline training interpreters need. At some large metropolitan mental health facilities, special training for interpreters may be available; but in small cities and rural locations, interpreters with a knowledge of professional terminology are a rarity. Many colleges and universities have faculty and staff who are fluent in more than one language. Depending on the nature of the case, and with the consent of the client, the counselor may need to call on individuals who speak the client's language to help with translation. These individuals will need to be apprised of the necessity to maintain confidentiality in doing this translation.

In the mid-1980s, I worked with Southeast Asian refugee students and their families in the rural area local schools. I used respected members of the refugee community with English skills to schedule the sessions and to serve as interpreters during family conferences with non-English-speaking refugee parents (Wehrly, 1991). Although the arrangement had many limitations, this method was better than having no school contact with newly arrived refugee parents.

Sue and Sue (1990) state that the shortage of bilingual counselors can seriously impede the counseling process, because many clients who are limited to speaking the counselor's language cannot communicate their thoughts and feelings fully. Ishiyama and Westwood (1992) and Westwood and Ishiyama (1990, 1991) recommend that when the client's mother tongue is not the same as the counselor's, clients should be encouraged to express feelings and ideas in their own languages. Clients feel an emotional release when they express their feelings in their mother tongues, and the counselor can learn by watching the nonverbal aspects for later feedback. Sometimes, it may be helpful for counselors to use a bilingual dictionary to check out feelings clients express in their own language and help them expand their vocabularies (Ishiyama & Westwood, 1992). These techniques may be of particular value for internship counselors working in settings that serve recent immigrants, refugees, or international students.

Participation in outreach activities is also expected at many internship sites. Interns may be involved in presenting educational programs for the populations being served. At other times, interns may be called on to go with a team for home visits or to participate in conferences at other social service sites. Some of the activities discussed under Goal 2 may be considered by some professionals as outreach activities.

Goal 2: To assist internship students in learning to work in a variety of roles in their clients' cultural milieus. As noted in earlier chapters, counseling students begin to realize rather early in their training that not all problems brought by clients are intrapsychic problems. Several authors address the need for expanding the roles of counselors working cross-culturally (Atkinson, Morten, & Sue, 1993; Atkinson, Thompson, & Grant, 1993; Axelson, 1993; Lee, 1995; Ponterotto & Pedersen, 1993; Sue & Sue, 1990; Westwood and Ishiyama, 1990).

In their three-dimensional model for counseling racial and ethnic minorities, Atkinson, Thompson, and Grant (1993) suggest eight roles for the counselor, depending on where the three-dimensional axes intersect for the level of acculturation, the locus of problem etiology, and the goals of helping. The eight counselor roles proposed by these authors are adviser, advocate, facilitator of indigenous support systems, facilitator of indigenous healing systems, consultant, change agent, counselor, and psychotherapist (Atkinson, Thompson, & Grant, 1993). For all these roles, the authors emphasize the importance of first establishing a good working relationship with clients.

Atkinson, Thompson, and Grant (1993) also caution that the eight counseling roles seem to be defined by the extremes of the three continua. It is highly unlikely that clients will be totally acculturated or totally unacculturated, will have problem etiologies that are totally external or totally internal, or will need to set goals that are totally preventive or totally remediative. For these reasons, the authors recognize that it may be appropriate to combine two or more roles. As an example, the racial or ethnic minority student client who is discriminated against in the classroom may need counselor help in both the adviser and the counselor roles to determine how to react to this oppression. The same student may also need the counselor to serve as a change agent to meet with the people who are discriminating against him or her, as well as with the people in power in the school, to encourage training to stop discrimination and oppression of the racial/ethnic minority students.

The *adviser* role is recommended for low-acculturated clients who have limited experience in dealing with the U.S. mainstream population and whose problems stem largely from external sources. Atkinson, Thompson, and Grant (1993) recommend this role for work with recently arrived immigrants and with people who are moving out of the support of their own racial or ethnic community. The counselor uses the role of adviser to help these clients realize the stressful situations they may experience as they move into the larger society. First-generation minority students planning to attend predominantly White universities might profit from advance warning and preparation for dealing with the stresses of functioning at these universities. Recently arrived immigrants might be helped by advising them to join a community support group.

Atkinson, Thompson, and Grant (1993) view the *advocate* role as appropriate "for clients who are low in acculturation and who need remediation of a problem that results from oppression and discrimination" (p. 265). When the client has limited English-speaking skills, the counselor may have to literally speak for the client. In the advocate role, the counselor may need to go with the client to help the people in power realize the impact their actions have on the client. In a school situation, the counselor as advocate might need to monitor the placement of students with limited English in appropriate classes and to help obtain English tutoring for these students. School counselors can also serve as advocates for immigrant children by organizing parent-training programs to prepare immigrant parents to make better use of resources in the community (Esquivel & Keitel, 1990). Another example of the advocate role would be for college counselors to meet with campus law enforcement officials who apply university rules more rigidly to students of color than to White students. In the advocate role, the counselor can help campus law enforcement personnel see how they are discriminating against students of color.

As a *facilitator of indigenous support systems*, the counselor can be instrumental in helping low-acculturated clients whose intrapersonal and interpersonal problems appear to have an internal locus and are not the direct result of oppression or discrimination. The counselor can help these clients join an appropriate indigenous support group for dealing with these problems. This skill requires that counselors have awareness of and a working relationship with the community elders or religious leaders.

Atkinson, Thompson, and Grant (1993) state that, in some cases, service to counselees with problems of the type just discussed may best be remediated through the counselor's acting as a *facilitator of indigenous healing systems*. The authors view two ways in which a counselor can serve as a facilitator of indigenous healing systems for clients who are low in acculturation. One way is to refer the client to a healer in the client's culture. The second way is for the counselor to use indigenous healing techniques directly, providing the counselor is thoroughly trained in indigenous healing techniques and is able to "honestly defer to the belief system inherent in these methods" (Atkinson, Thompson, & Grant, 1993, p. 267). Sue et al. (1992a, 1992b) state that, when appropriate, culturally skilled counselors will consult with traditional healers or religious or spiritual leaders and practitioners in the treatment of culturally different clients.

The counselor as *consultant* works with highly acculturated clients who seek to prevent externally caused problems. The counselor works with clients of color to set up preventive programs that could ward off or minimize problems resulting from discrimination and oppression. Parents of color who request that their child join a counselor-led, stress-inoculation group would be seeking the consultant services of the school counselor.

Atkinson, Thompson, and Grant (1993) note that the consultant role is most appropriate for organizational consulting. Among several multicultural issues in organizational consultation discussed by Jackson and Hayes (1993) are differences in high- and low-context cultures, differences in how time is perceived, and cultural misunderstandings that can occur when the managers are of a different culture than the rest of the people in the organization.

Gibbs (1980) proposes a five-stage consultant model with an interpersonal orientation for use with African American consultees. She emphasizes that the consultant needs to employ techniques that equalize the differences between the consultant and the African American consultee. Gibbs' 1980 model is the one on which she built her 1985 developmental model for White/Black relationship establishment discussed in Chapter 9.

The counselor as *change agent* is the sixth role proposed by Atkinson, Thompson, and Grant (1993). In the role of change agent, the counselor works with highly acculturated clients to help them change something in the environment that serves to discriminate against, or oppress, these clients. One way the counselor change agent role is frequently implemented is in working with racial- or ethnic-minority political groups to bring about changes in the system. Another counselor change agent role is to organize neighborhood groups to discuss and decide how to work to eradicate, or at least ameliorate, negative circumstances in the environment. Supervisors should be prepared for questions and concerns related to ways to help the student trainees serve as change agents in their clients' milieus.

The *counselor* role is defined by Atkinson, Thompson, and Grant (1993) as a preventive and developmental role in which counselors focus on the developmental and educational needs of highly acculturated clients. School, college, and community agency counselors can implement this role when they work with groups of students in development programs with a proactive focus. The current professional literature includes much support for counselor involvement in the developmental role. Following is an overview of some of these proactive programs.

Liu and Baker (1993) outline a 12-session friendship training program for preschool children in a daycare center. Although the program was designed to remediate problems manifested by a newly arrived, non-English-speaking, immigrant child, the authors describe the possible benefits of this type of cultural adaptation program for children experiencing culture shock. Esquivel and Keitel (1990) give an overview of several preventive and intervention programs in their manuscript on counseling with immigrant children in the schools.

The work of Phinney and her associates (Phinney, 1989, 1990, 1992, 1993; Phinney & Alipuria, 1990; Phinney & Chavira, 1992; Phinney, Lochner, & Murphy, 1990; Phinney & Tarver, 1988) delineated in Chapter 4 and referred to in Chapters 9 and 10 of this book supports counselor work with both minority and majority adolescents to help them realize the importance of developing an ethnic identity as a correlate of overall healthy functioning. Counselors could work with interested teachers and their classes or lead their own discussion groups with youth to help adolescents experience a planned, developmental ethnic identity search that would take place over the course of several weeks. Some components of such an ethnic identity search might be a study of the ethnic history of adolescents' own families, a reevaluation of any negative images that society may hold toward their ethnic groups, discussions of the challenges of living biculturally or multiculturally, and an exploration of ways to combat racism.

Originally, Phinney et al. (1990) recommended the activities described above for counselor work with minority youth. Given the rapidly changing demographics of our society and Phinney's 1992 research—showing that White students who were a minority in their high school also showed high correlations between ethnic identity achievement and overall psychological adjustment—I recommend that counselors work with both minority and majority students in developmental ethnic identity search programs.

The multicultural counseling literature includes manuscripts that outline developmental programs to help minority youth achieve bicultural competence. After describing the rationale for services that meet the human needs of American Indians, LaFromboise and Rowe (1983) outline the development and implementation of culturally sensitive social skills training for American Indians. LaFromboise and Rowe developed their assertion skills training program through a year's work with 30 tribal groups and agencies. The program targeted the need for appropriate assertion skills in eight situations. A key element was teaching participants the situation-specific nature of assertiveness. Pretest and posttest differences in participants' performance were assessed through ratings of videotapes and were significant at the .001 level.

Schinke et al. (1988) detail developing and researching a controlled design, bicultural competence skills approach to preventing substance abuse among American Indian adolescents. Adolescents assigned to the prevention condition groups participated in ten group sessions that used cognitive and behavioral methods. The six authors concluded that their research lent "modest support to a bicultural competence skills intervention approach for preventing substance abuse among American-Indian youth" (Schinke, et al., 1988, p. 89).

Szapocznik, Kurtines, and Fernandez (1980) discuss biculturalism and adjustment for Hispanic American youth, and they recommend counselor-led group sessions that focus on ethnic values clarification. These sessions help Hispanic American youth explore the positive and negative aspects of both the Hispanic and the Anglo cultures. Other bicultural group training could include sessions addressing differences in communication skills, differences in negotiation skills, and differences in survival skills in the two cultures. Szapocznik et al. (1980) emphasize that "Bicultural students must be aware of these differences and need to develop the flexibility to implement different survival skills according to the cultural context in which they function" (p. 374). Ruiz (1984) describes the use of the sentence completion method in cross-cultural group counseling. Ruiz (1984) has designed eight sentence stems that introduce emotion-laden topics and lead to much participation among the group members.

Locke and Faubert (1993) describe a "Getting on the Right Track" developmental program that provided "African American high school students with opportunities to esteem their African roots" (p. 129) and that served to strengthen students' ego identity through an African-centered perspective. The program was a joint endeavor between a state university and an area high school. The school counselor, a graduate assistant, and mentor-teachers worked with African American students who had the potential to be successful in high school and college. Student interests and hobbies were identified and turned into research questions that were investigated through the use of scientific methods of inquiry.

Developmental programs for work with gifted African American students are reviewed by Ford-Harris, Schuerger, and Harris (1991) and Ford, Harris, and Schuerger (1993). These authors detail the impact of racial identity stage development on the behavior of gifted Black students and make recommendations for counselor interventions to address the possible negative impact of the Black experience on gifted students. Among counselor interventions suggested are the use of role models and mentors, open discussions about racial issues, role playing, group counseling, and family counseling. An additional technique not mentioned by these authors is the use of bibliotherapy with gifted African American students. Bibliotherapy can help African American students realize they are not alone with their dilemmas and can help them gain a sense of hope through the vicarious experiences that may occur during the bibliotherapeutic process.

Ponterotto and Pedersen's *Preventing Prejudice: A Guide for Counselors and Educators* (1993) provides both the theoretical rationale for and pragmatic application of prejudice prevention theory in work with students, faculty, staff, and parents. In their Chapter 6, "Counselor Roles in Prejudice Prevention and Race Relations," Ponterotto and Pedersen (1993) delineate roles and strategies for counselor involvement with school and college faculty and students in preventing prejudice. Some of the many ways in which the counselor can get involved are through facilitating healthy ethnic identity development, fostering critical thinking skills, promoting multicultural and nonsexist education, facilitating interracial contact, and focusing on transforming negative racial attitudes. Ponterotto and Pedersen (1993) also discuss the following counselor roles in prejudice prevention: parent training, faculty and administration consultant work, group counseling and support, individual and group counseling, and acting as an activist for prejudice prevention.

Other chapters in Ponterotto and Pedersen's 1993 book include discussions and exercises for use with various populations: for example, Chapter 7, "Race Relations in the Schools," Chapter 8, "Race Relations on the College Campus," and Chapter 9, "Race Relations in the Community." Information on assessment of prejudice and racial identity is included in Chapter 10. Also, Helms' 1992 book *A Race is a Nice Thing to Have* can be used as a discussion guide for work with both individuals and groups to help White people understand their own racial identity development and to help people of color understand the White people in their lives.

The counselor's role in cross-cultural work in family therapy is somewhat difficult to place within the framework presented by Atkinson, Thompson, and Grant (1993). The term *therapy* itself indicates that this is part of the work of the psychotherapist. Because family therapy deals with interventions to help members improve their functioning as a family unit and not solely with problems with an internal etiology, family therapy probably comes more within the counselor role. In their listing of multicultural counseling competencies, Sue et al. (1992a) recommend that counselors have "knowledge of minority family structures, hierarchies, values, and beliefs . . . [and] are knowledgeable about the community characteristics and the resources in the community as well as the family" (p. 482). This recommendation underlines the critical need to look for strengths in the family system and to build on these strengths.

After reviewing the literature on family training and supervision, Arnold (1993) stated, "The literature on training for a multiethnic perspective in marital and family therapy is limited, conflicting, and not empirically based" (p. 142). Arnold notes, however, that there are a few outstanding volumes that include theoretical and methodological discussions of multiethnic training for family therapists, (for example, Arnold cites Boyd-Franklin, 1989a; Falicov, 1983; Ho, 1987; McGoldrick et al., 1982; and Papajohn & Spiegel, 1975).

Several other manuscripts addressing the importance of ethnic issues in family therapy have also been published. The *Journal of Psychotherapy & the Family* published a special issue with eleven articles devoted to "Minorities and Family Therapy" (Saba, Karrer, & Hardy, 1989). The following summaries represent just a few current manuscripts in professional journals that discuss therapy with families of color.

Hong and Ham (1992), Kim (1985), and Berg and Jaya (1993) discuss culturally sensitive counseling with Asian American families. Hong and Ham (1992) address the stresses of immigration for Chinese Americans and discuss how these stresses impact the various stages of the family life cycle. Kim (1985) presents a strategic-structural framework for family therapy with Asian Americans. Berg and Jaya (1993) underscore the importance of helping Asian families solve problems through attention to the way cultural values guide family therapy interventions: (1) using negotiation and mediation instead of direct confrontation; (2) understanding why "grounding" (restricting out-of-home activities) will not work as a discipline measure with Asian youth; (3) having an awareness of the special role of the mother with her children; (4) making suggestions to help individuals perform their roles as family members; (5) recognizing the hierarchy in all levels of society and in the family in particular; (6) knowing the pervasiveness of putting the family first and the individual second; and (7) remembering the importance of helping family members save face by not embarrassing them in front of each other.

Sciarra and Ponterotto (1991) discuss the challenges of counseling the Hispanic bilingual family in which different levels of acculturation and different types of bilingualism that influence the therapeutic process are present. Three measures for assessing acculturation levels are described. Language is viewed as a decisive factor that affects the acculturation process. The authors discuss the problems of working with subordinate bilinguals (who show different levels of competence in Spanish and English) and also "show different levels of affect depending on which language they are speaking" (Sciarra & Ponterotto, 1991, p. 475). Feelings expressed in English are often verbalized more as an intellectual or cognitive task because of the extra involvement in encoding in the English language. Pros and cons of working in the mother tongue or the second language with Hispanic clients are addressed.

Sciarra and Ponterotto (1991) note that it is very difficult to conduct a family therapy session in one language even when all family members speak that language. It is important for the therapist to understand the dynamics of language switching and its therapeutic implications. Note which language is used by which family member and when each language is used by the various family members. "The cross-cultural bilingual therapist may want to consider initiating language switching with bilingual clients as part of the therapeutic process" (Sciarra & Ponterotto, 1991, p. 486).

Boyd-Franklin (1989b) recognizes the cultural diversity among African American families and discusses five factors and their subcategories that she considers crucial in the treatment of African American families. Boyd-Franklin presents these factors from the perspective of using them as strengths in family therapy: (1) the extended family bond (including the use of genograms), (2) the adaptability of roles (the parental child system and the three-generational system), (3) the strengths of religious orientations (with outlets for leadership, creative talents, and emotional catharsis as well as the possibility of using the family minister as a co-therapist), (4) the values of the work ethic and education (and the expectation that the children will surpass parents in their careers), and (5) the many coping skills African American families use to survive. Boyd-Franklin discusses her nontraditional treatment approach from the perspective of a multisystems model.

Tafoya (1989) uses a traditional Sahaptin legend to serve as a paradigm "for the way many Native Americans conceptualize relationships, responsibilities, learning, and teaching, . . . [the aspects that Tafoya sees as] core elements in Family Therapy" (p. 72). Tafoya discusses traditional healing approaches in Native American cultures, cross-cultural concerns, concerns related to spouse interactions, and family therapy issues. He discusses the importance of the circle as a sacred symbol and model for relationships and asks therapists: "How can you assist your clients and patients to creatively complete their circles?" (Tafoya, 1989, p. 97).

Problems and therapeutic issues of Black-Hispanic families are discussed by

Baptiste (1990). It is important for counselors to determine whether members are Black-Hispanic immigrants or Black-Hispanic Americans and to understand the possible identity confusion, depreciated self-image, and feelings of loss, ostracism, and isolation that all members of these biracial families may experience. Problems for Black-Hispanic people are often magnified because both ethnic identities are devalued and stigmatized by the larger society, and members of the two groups may be in conflict. Baptiste recommends that therapists help Black-Hispanic families recognize and cherish the strengths of both heritages while fusing a single racial identity with which they can live. This process will also include acknowledging the reality of societal ambivalence about people of biracial heritage and sorting through and rejecting the limitations of societal stereotypes about biracial people. Another point emphasized by Baptiste is the importance of the therapist's examining his or her own feelings, beliefs, and attitudes about biracial people before beginning this type of family therapy.

The eighth counselor role described by Atkinson, Thompson, and Grant (1993) is that of *psychotherapist*. The authors view the psychotherapist role as appropriate for the highly acculturated client who is looking for relief from a problem that has an internal etiology. They underscore the need for cross-cultural counselors "to be trained in (and to internalize) the requisite knowledge, skills, and attitudes to enable them to be sensitive to cultural influences and ever vigilant to the impact of external forces (discrimination and oppression) on the problem" (Atkinson, Thompson, & Grant, 1993, p. 270).

Axelson (1993) describes how the role of counselors in school or college settings is maximized when counselors apply and generalize the fundamentals of counseling "to all aspects of the personal, intellectual, and social development of students within the total school or college environment" (p. 321). Exhibit 11.1 lists these eight roles for counselors in educational settings: intercultural communicator, student advocate, crisis intervenor, developmental facilitator, information processor, career guide, interpreter of the bureaucratic system, and in-service staff consultant. Several of Axelson's eight functional roles of counselors in a multicultural educational environment are similar to the eight roles just described of Atkinson, Thompson, and Grant (1993).

Goal 3: To provide support and encouragement for continued student growth in multicultural counseling beliefs and attitudes, knowledge, and skills.
The overview of a variety of roles in which internship counselors may function gives some indication of the breadth of activities in which interns may be involved. One responsibility not delineated specifically under Goal 2 is that of writing reports. Paperwork at many agencies (especially those with financial support from various governmental sources) sometimes seems burdensome. Internship students may be heavily involved in writing clinical assessments and reporting on follow-up work with clients, in addition to assisting in preparing reports for governmentally funded projects. Internship supervisors can provide support to internship students by volunteering suggestions for report writing and continuing to offer encouragement.

FUNCTIONAL ROLES OF COUNSELORS IN A MULTICULTURAL EDUCATIONAL ENVIRONMENT

Intercultural communicator
Shows and shares cultural awareness. Fosters intergroup understanding. Facilitates cross-cultural communication and works against alienation.

Student advocate
Understands and interprets the needs, experiences, and situations of students in order to protect them from unresponsive, unrealistic, unreasonable, or harmful aspects of the educational environment.

Crisis intervenor
Takes thoughtful risks in doing what is necessary and best for student development outside the educational environment.

Developmental facilitator
Creates and applies experiences and activities that will help students with issues that most share in common. Some concerns that many students confront are starting school and college, peer relations and pressures, parent and family relations, male-female relations, parenting, generational conflicts, and self-concept. Some concerns faced by youth are also reflective of current issues in the society at large, such as the responsible use of drugs and issues related to abortion.

Information processor
Screens, interprets, and uses subjective information and objective standardized data about students in ways that emphasize their motivations, strengths, and resources in balance with their weaknesses, problems, and points for improvement.

Career guide
Uses and applies reality testing, appropriate role models, and nonbiased information with an optimistic attitude toward assisting students in expanding their possibilities of attaining career goals that best fulfill their personalities and potentials.

Interpreter of the bureaucratic system
Assists in decoding the social, political, and class factors embedded both in the educational system and in the society at large. Functions as a type of intermediary who emphasizes the needs of individuals and cultural groups in an impersonal system. At times, he or she will seek to effect change in the system when administrative needs take precedence over individual needs.

In-service staff consultant
Interprets immediate and long-range needs and experiences of students in interaction with staff goals through consultative counseling with individual staff members and staff groups.

SOURCE: From *Counseling and Development in a Multicultural Society*, Second Edition, by J. A. Axelson, pp. 221–222. Copyright © 1993 Brooks/Cole Publishing Company.

Carney and Kahn (1984) suggest that one role of the trainer supervisor at this stage is to help students clarify their future objectives as counselors. Supervisor interactions with internship trainees can be both direct (through supervision) and indirect (through journal interactions). Internship students will probably have a choice of supervisors with whom they wish to carry on these important life career planning sessions, because they have at least one on-site supervisor and at least one campus supervisor. Encouraging students to talk with professionals at a variety of multicultural counseling sites may be useful. An additional setting for interacting with peers is at professional development gatherings.

Another avenue for student growth in multicultural counseling competence is participation in appropriate sessions at state, regional, and national professional organizational meetings. Taking part in multicultural counseling professional development institutes now can also lead to a continuation of this lifelong learning process. Supervisor modeling of this type of involvement is encouraging to students, and, when appropriate, the supervisor and internship student may present programs together at professional meetings. Assistance in securing financial support for these professional development experiences may be vital to student participation.

SUMMARY

Chapter 11 addressed the roles and challenges internship students and their supervisors face in the fifth stage of multicultural counselor development. At this, the last stage of formal multicultural counselor training, students assume a much more self-directed posture and participate in all the activities carried out at the site at which they do their Counseling Internship. The role of the internship supervisor turns to that of mentor for the students.

After discussing student characteristics and process guidelines for creating a climate for student growth in beliefs and attitudes, knowledge, and skills, this chapter's content was organized under three goals. The first goal discussed the challenges of locating and functioning at a culturally pluralistic site where both counselors and clients are representative of the cultural pluralism of the larger society.

The second goal delineated counselor work in a variety of roles. Atkinson, Thompson, and Grant's (1993) eight counselor roles (adviser, advocate, facilitator of indigenous support systems facilitator of indigenous healing systems, consultant, change agent, counselor, and psychotherapist) were used as an organizational framework for this discussion.

The chapter closed with a discussion of the importance of providing support and encouragement for counseling interns and challenging them to continue this lifelong learning process of gaining multicultural counseling competence.

To aid the counseling internship supervisor in evaluating the intern's multicultural competencies, Appendix G contains sample items for evaluating these multicultural counseling internship competencies. Appendix H lists sample multicultural items for counseling interns to evaluate their internship site and their internship site supervisor.

CHAPTER 12

The Possible Futures: Moving Beyond the Incomplete Status of Multicultural Counselor Preparation

"*I*ncomplete" was the answer given by a freshman student when asked to grade the current status of American civilization in an Occidental College class titled "The American Dream" (Farney, 1992). Professionals in multicultural counseling might well give the same grade—incomplete—to the current status of multicultural counselor preparation in the United States. As we look at the prodigious efforts of many people in the past two decades, it is evident that we have traveled many and long pathways toward the goal of training competent multicultural counselors to serve the increasing culturally pluralistic population of our country. Our task, however, is incomplete.

The purpose of this chapter is to give a brief overview of the unfinished business—the incomplete status of progress toward the realization of multiculturalism as the Fourth Force in Counseling. Challenges and issues are reviewed, and the continued work for those interested in furthering the cause of multicultural counselor training is delineated.

Lee (1991) argued for a dramatic shift in mental health interventions, one in which counseling services "must be delivered in the belief that people from diverse backgrounds are psychologically healthy, undergo normal developmental experiences, and have dynamics and resources indigenous to their culture to deal with problem solving and decision making completely" (pp. 212–213). Pedersen (1991) stated, "Until and unless the multicultural perspective can be understood as not only generic to all counseling but also increasing the accuracy of counseling, culture will remain an exotic concept" (p. 250). Pedersen also noted that until we can help counselors realize that multiculturalism makes their work easier and more fun, not much change is likely to occur.

How, then, do we help the counseling profession understand the new focus on recognizing the mental health strengths of all cultures and the pervasiveness of culture in all counseling? How do we convince counselors that their jobs will be easier and more enjoyable when they attain multicultural counseling competence? How do we convince the counseling profession that multiculturalism *is* the Fourth Force in Counseling?

The preceding eleven chapters attempted to shed light on several of the pathways traveled to gain multicultural counseling competence. Concepts from a host of counseling professionals were synthesized to delineate a five-stage developmental model of attaining multicultural counseling competence. What, then, remains to be done? Why do I say that our task is incomplete? What are the possible goals for multicultural counseling, and how do we attain them?

This chapter is organized under two general areas: (1) the need for continuing and expanded professional organization leadership to improve multicultural counselor preparation, and (2) the need for continuing and expanded work on research and development of models of multicultural counseling and multicultural counselor preparation. The issues and tasks discussed are *not* mutually exclusive; there is overlap and need for concurrent teamwork on many of these tasks. The old "chicken or the egg" metaphor applies here; it is very difficult to say which needs to come first. The challenges are raised again to encourage ongoing and expanded work to improve multicultural counseling competence.

THE NEED FOR CONTINUING AND EXPANDED PROFESSIONAL ORGANIZATION LEADERSHIP TO IMPROVE MULTICULTURAL COUNSELOR PREPARATION

Efforts by professional organizations to meet this challenge are discussed under "Ethical and Training Standards and Issues" in Chapter 2 of this book. Continuing and expanded professional organization leadership is needed to establish more explicit expectations for multicultural counselor preparation in guidelines used by accrediting, licensing, and certification boards (Ponterotto & Casas, 1987, 1991; Sabnani et al., 1991; Sue et al., 1992a, 1992b). Several initial steps have been taken by the ACA and the APA and their subdivisions to provide guidelines for multicultural counseling (for example, Sue et al., 1982; Sue et al., 1992a, 1992b). The task now is to move toward operationalizing these guidelines.

As Casas and San Miguel (1993) noted (see Chapter 2), the APA and ACA multicultural counseling mandates issued to date are really guiding principles and recommendations, not mandates. In addition, until accrediting bodies can be convinced to include guidelines with more specificity for multicultural training, progress toward recognizing multiculturalism as a Fourth Force in Counseling may be slow.

Chapter 2 also discussed the inappropriateness of many counselor education programs for U.S. students of color (Gutierrez, 1982) and for international students who come to study in the United States (Saleh, 1989). Major revisions are needed in many existing counselor training programs to make these programs culturally sensitive. Students of color and international students need to feel that their cultures are worthy of recognition and that White people can learn with and from them on how other cultures meet helping service needs. Much of the challenge of attracting students of color into some of the current counselor education programs may be related to the cultural insensitivity of the programs and the need to attract more faculty of color to teach and mentor in these programs.

At the 1993 ACA national meetings in Atlanta, a volunteer group, Advocates for Multicultural Counseling, gathered to expedite the movement toward incorporating a multicultural perspective into the training and practice of counseling. The group met again at the Multicultural Leadership Conference at ACA headquarters in late August of 1993 and at the ACA 1994 national meetings in Minneapolis. Subcommittees are actively at work; motions to further multicultural counseling have been presented to the ACA Governing Council to expand multicultural counselor training and multicultural considerations in all of the ACA's operations.

A symposium at the 1993 annual convention of the American Psychological Association addressed the topic of multicultural training. Following the symposium, three participants published a process model for developing multicultural training programs (Ridley, Mendoza, & Kanitz, 1994), designed "to facilitate a pedagogically sound, intentional, stagewise process of MCT program development" (Ridley et al., 1994, p. 283). The five stages delineated are (1) training philosophy, (2) learning objectives, (3) instructional strategies, (4) program designs, and (5) evaluation.

Professional organization leadership is needed not only to present guidelines for revising current counselor and counseling psychology training programs but also to provide more opportunities for nationwide multicultural counseling training. Such training is especially needed to help update practitioners who did not receive multicultural counselor training in their counselor preparation programs to ethically serve a culturally pluralistic population. The need for in-the-field supervisors of counseling practicum and internship students to receive multicultural training is especially urgent (Bernard, 1994).

I facilitated a 1993 discussion group, "Next Steps in Training for Cross-Cultural Competence," at the 10th Annual Teachers College Winter Round Table (which focused on Training for Cross-Cultural Competence). Participants there stated that integration of cross-cultural curriculum into all areas of counseling psychology and counselor training programs would be an important next step. Participants also emphasized retraining existing faculty to be able to implement and integrate cross-cultural content throughout the training programs, and they suggested making these competencies a part of tenure consideration for faculty members. The forty-one participants in the discussion also spoke of the urgent need to retrain many in-the-field counseling supervisors for cross-cultural competence.

The complexities of cross-cultural and multicultural counseling supervision are discussed in a special section, "Cross-Cultural Counseling Supervision," in *Counselor Education and Supervision* (Bernard, 1994; Cook, 1994; Fukuyama, 1994; Leong, 1994; Leong & Wagner, 1994; Priest, 1994). Leong (1994) introduced the series of articles that followed from a 1993 American Psychological Association convention symposium. Leong and Wagner (1994) provided a critical review of the limited theoretical and empirical cross-cultural supervision literature. Cook (1994) hypothesized cross-cultural interactions between supervisors and supervisees using Helms' model of racial identity development. The potential usefulness of critical incidents for studying multicultural supervision was discussed by Fukuyama (1994). Issues that may emerge when supervisors are ethnic minority members and supervisees are ethnic majority members were the focus of Priest's (1994) discussion.

Bernard (1994) closed the special ACES section with a discussion and commentary of the preceding articles. Her comment on the importance of the level of racial identity development of the supervisor in determining "the sophistication of the discourse in supervision about racial issues" (Bernard, 1994, p. 163) adds weight to the concerns voiced by participants in the 1993 Teachers College Winter Roundtable. Bernard's views on the critical importance of addressing multicultural supervision are clear: "I do not consider it an overstatement that the development of the profession and the relevance of counselor education programs will be severely compromised if we do not advance the knowledge and practice of multicultural supervision" (Bernard, 1994, p. 170).

Increased dialogue with counselor educators in other countries is needed to provide guidelines for preparing counselors for the multicultural global society in which we live (Wehrly & Deen, 1983). Chapter 5 addressed efforts to train for multicultural counseling competence in many areas of the world. More cross-national cooperation is needed with professional organizations in other countries to share multicultural counseling model development and research. A few of the many questions that might be discussed cross-nationally are: How are counselors working to deal with prejudice and racism in other countries? How are ethnic conflicts dealt with in other countries? What training efforts are underway to prepare counselors for cultural pluralism? What have counselors in other countries done to develop and research models of racial and ethnic identity development?

In North America, some cross-national sharing of professional ideas is taking place among members of the American Counseling Association and the Canadian Guidance and Counselling Association at their respective national meetings. On the international scene, the International Round Table for the Advancement of Counselling (IRTAC) conclaves have had ongoing sessions where counseling professionals from thirty or more countries engage in cross-cultural sharing during working groups since the first IRTAC was held in Neuchatel, Switzerland, in 1966. The theme for the 1995 IRTAC conclave at the University of Malta was "Counseling for Tolerance." With the advent of electronic mail, perhaps even more professionals can get involved in cross-national sharing.

THE NEED FOR CONTINUING AND EXPANDED WORK ON RESEARCH AND DEVELOPMENT OF MODELS OF MULTICULTURAL COUNSELING AND MULTICULTURAL COUNSELOR PREPARATION

Every chapter in this book has referred to models of multicultural counseling or models of multicultural counselor preparation. Some of these models are based on research, but many are based on the authors' professional and clinical observations, not on empirical research. There is a great need for expanding the research of existing models, replicating the research of existing models, and developing and researching new models. Both quantitative and qualitative research of multicultural counseling are needed (Ponterotto & Casas, 1991; Sabnani et al., 1991; Wehrly & Watson-Gegeo, 1985).

Sabnani et al. (1991) recommend that their model of White counselor racial identity development be implemented and researched. The developmental model I present in this book is in need of implementation and research.

Ponterotto and Casas' 1991 *Handbook of Racial/Ethnic Minority Counseling Research* is the first book to focus exclusively on racial and ethnic minority counseling research. This book can serve as a guide for students, practitioners, researchers, and counselor educators. In their concluding chapter, Ponterotto and Casas (1991) "outline and clarify twelve topical areas for further research" (p. 152). In abbreviated form, the 12 areas where additional research is needed are the following:

1. Accurate epidemiological data on how prevalent psychological problems are among the various racial and ethnic groups
2. Additional research of minority identity models to expand knowledge of the heterogeneity within all racial and ethnic groups
3. Intensified research on how the Eurocentric corporate, political, and educational systems impact racial and ethnic minority individuals in these systems
4. Research on institutional racism and bias to determine the effects of interventions (such as prejudice prevention programs) to reverse the White, middle-class, status quo attitudes and behaviors
5. Continued research of White racial identity development
6. Research on how minority mental health strengths enable minority racial and ethnic people to function as well as they do
7. Research on how intragroup racial and ethnic variability is influenced by factors such as socioeconomic level, geographic area, religion and spiritualism, acculturation or racial/ethnic identity levels, generational status, and so on
8. Systematic qualitative and quantitative research on the effects of the variations in and the process of bicultural identity development
9. More focus on researching racial and ethnic youth, older people, and family systems

10. More research on primary prevention and training programs for parents of all racial and ethnic groups
11. Research on instrumentation for assessing and testing racial and ethnic minority populations
12. More research on both etic and emic aspects of cross-cultural counseling, including more research of indigenous models of mental health.

After presenting their White racial identity development model for counselors, Sabnani et al. (1991) discuss identity development and other cross-cultural training research needs. They note that research on minority identity development, especially for African Americans, is ahead of research on White identity development. They also review existing instruments and propose the possibility of using assessment devices to assign students to sequentially organized cross-cultural training. Sabnani et al. (1991) underscore the need to address and measure other cross-cultural training variables such as cognitive styles, personality characteristics, and the relationship between stated beliefs or attitudes and actual behavior.

The rest of this chapter highlights some of the research areas presented by Ponterotto and Casas (1991) and by Sabnani et al. (1991) and proposes additional areas for multicultural research.

Extend research to assess the effectiveness of multicultural counselor training programs. Currently, there is no consensus on what components make up a quality multicultural training program; neither are there clear guidelines for empirically assessing these programs (Ponterotto, Rieger, Barrett, & Sparks, 1994; Sabnani et al., 1991). Ponterotto et al. (1994) review four new instruments for assessing multicultural counseling competence: The Cross-Cultural Inventory—Revised; the Multicultural Counseling Awareness Scale—Form B: Revised Self-Assessment; the Multicultural Counseling Inventory; and the Multicultural Awareness-Knowledge-and-Skills Survey. Each instrument is reviewed in terms of description and development, psychometric properties, and evaluation.

In their discussion of the four instruments, Ponterotto et al. (1994) state that "Perhaps the major conclusion we can draw from this review is that as compared with instrumentation in other counseling areas, such as career development and personality, multicultural instrumentation is in its infancy with regard to empirical validation" (p. 321). The authors conclude their article by discussing these five directions for further research: "Defining Multicultural Counseling Competence," "Outcome Studies," "Concurrent Validity Studies," "Instrument Stability Over Time," and "Need for Expanded Evaluation Methods" (Ponterotto et al., 1994, pp. 321–322).

Atkinson, Casas, and Neville (1994) studied the involvement of ethnic minority psychologists in mentoring students and novice professionals to determine their perceptions of benefits received from these efforts. The ethnic minority clinical, counseling, and school psychologists who participated were heavily involved in mentoring activities, and they perceived that the benefits outweighed the added responsibilities. Research is also needed on how students, interns, and novice professionals who are involved as mentees perceive their mentoring experiences. In addition, research is needed to determine whether the availability of faculty of color to mentor students helps attract and retain students of color in counselor training programs.

Increase development and research of models of racial and ethnic identity development. As noted by Ponterotto and Casas (1991) and by Sabnani et al. (1991), work is still needed on the models of racial and ethnic identity development. One of the few theoretical models that has already undergone rigorous development and research is Phinney's adolescent ethnic identity model (Phinney, 1989, 1990, 1991, 1992, 1993; Phinney & Alipuria, 1990; Phinney & Chavira, 1992; Phinney, Lochner, & Murphy, 1990; Phinney & Tarver, 1988). Phinney is interested in having her model researched and tested in geographic regions beyond the Los Angeles metropolitan area and with people of other developmental age levels.

Rios (1994) presented a revision of the Atkinson et al. (1989) Racial/Cultural Identity Development Model with culturally-sensitive variations for the Latino/Latina of Color and the White Latino/Latina (Crillo) at the 11th annual Teachers College Winter Roundtable on Cross-Cultural Counseling. Rios also proposed implications of the model for Latino/Latina identity, implications for counseling, and implications for additional research.

Rowe, Bennett, and Atkinson (1994) present a critique of current White racial identity models and propose an alternative paradigm, White Racial Consciousness Statuses. The Rowe et al. conceptualization is based on Phinney's (1989) model of adolescent ethnic identity development and includes two statuses of White racial consciousness with four types of attitudes related to each status. Rowe et al. question the validity of describing the racial identity models as developmental.

A question that needs clarification in the current critique of racial identity/consciousness models is how the term *developmental* is interpreted. The question of whether or not models are developmental may be related to confusion over interpretation of *developmental*. I propose that this is an issue that needs to be addressed by multicultural authors and researchers.

As noted in Chapter 3, current models of minority and racial identity development are viewed as inappropriate for people of more than one racial heritage (Kerwin & Ponterotto, 1994; Kerwin, Ponterotto, Jackson, & Harris, 1993; Poston, 1990; Reynolds & Pope, 1991; Root, 1990, 1992). Current models of racial and ethnic identity development also fail to address the complexities faced by people experiencing multiple oppressions, such as gender, race, sexual/affectional orientation, and religion (Reynolds & Pope, 1991).

Reynolds and Pope (1991) challenge the current simplicity of existing models of multicultural counseling and discuss how these linear models are inadequate for work with people suffering multiple oppressions. Reynolds and Pope propose a paradigm based on Root's (1990) biracial identity model. Their Multidimensional Identity Model (MIM) includes "four possible options for identity resolution that occur within a dynamic process of self-growth and exploration" (Reynolds & Pope, 1991, pp. 70–71). One option is to passively accept society's definition of self. A second option is to consciously choose to identify with one aspect of self. A third option is to identify with all options of self in a segmented manner. The fourth option is to identify with all options by identifying as a new group. All four options are acceptable; and the individual may move among the options depending on personal needs and reference group orientation in various situations.

The interaction of gender and ethnic identity issues in multicultural counseling is another area in need of additional attention (Comas-Diaz & Greene, 1994; Davenport & Yurich, 1991). Davenport and Yurich (1991) explore multicultural gender issues through interweaving the "self-in-relation theory" with status as it relates to gender. The impact of gender and status is illustrated through case examples of Mexican Americans and African Americans. These authors conclude that "As both researchers and practitioners, we need to move beyond our preference for looking at others through a singular lens such as gender, or ethnicity and instead examine the interactive nature of various influences" (Davenport & Yurich, 1991, p. 70).

As proposed in Assumption 26 in Chapter 6, I believe it is time to search for identity models that transcend identification with one's racial and ethnic heritage. Hoare (1991) proposed the need to look again at the meaning of identity when she said, "Accepting that a mature, connected identity is fundamental to acceptance of self and others and to rejection of prejudice, there is a clear need to revisit the meaning of identity and to discern how those who are identity achieved tend to include and accept others who hold different cultural values and perspectives" (p. 46).

The individual's positive identification with his or her ethnic or racial heritage will be the starting point for developing this more inclusive identity model. Banks (1981) proposed such a six-stage model for multiethnic education. In the Banks model, the individual reaches ethnic identity clarification at Stage 3. At Stage 4, the person is capable of functioning in a biethnic environment (within her or his own ethnic group and within the environment of another ethnic culture). The individual in Stage 5 "has reflective ethnic and national identifications and the skills, attitudes, and commitment needed to function within a range of ethnic and cultural groups within his or her nation" (Banks, 1981, p. 220). The individual who is functioning at Stage 6 is able to identify positively at the ethnic, national, and global levels. The Stage 6 individual has the abilities and commitment to function within any culture of the world. If we as a profession truly believe in the universality of human rights, a model of multicultural counselor racial and ethnic identity development is needed that includes these additional levels of identification.

Refine and research developmental models of supervising counseling students and integrate these with developmental models of multicultural counselor preparation. Developmental models of counseling student supervision are in need of additional theoretical development and research (Joy, 1992; Loganbill,

Hardy, & Delworth, 1982; Stoltenberg, 1981; Stoltenberg & Delworth, 1987; Stoltenberg & Delworth, 1988). Joy (1992) succinctly summarizes the challenges in gaining a broader understanding of developmental supervision when she states, "a great deal more information is needed to clarify the ways the developmental transitions occur between stages of counselor development, what supervisory interventions will engage supervisees at differing levels of training, and which will maximize trainee growth" (p. 31).

Models to integrate developmental multicultural counselor preparation with developmental models of counselor education supervision are needed (Sabnani et al., 1991; Wehrly, 1991). Descriptors of student needs, process guidelines, and appropriate learning environments from these models can be delineated and integrated. A cursory examination of the descriptors from developmental multicultural counselor preparation and developmental models of counselor education supervision shows the need for different types of supervision as counseling students progress in their training to be counselors. During the early stage or level of multicultural counselor training, supervision is mainly from a structured, leader-directed relationship between the counseling supervisor and the counseling student. As the student progresses in gaining competencies in multicultural counseling, the supervisor/student relationship moves toward one in which the supervisor and advanced student interact as co-professionals.

Stoltenberg and Delworth (1988) propose that the person/environment relationship in which the counseling student learns is a critical element in student growth. I also believe that the person/environment relationship is a critical factor for the student learning to be a multicultural counselor. The profession of training counselors and psychotherapists will take a giant step forward when we delineate and research the factors that promote counseling and psychotherapist student growth at the various stages or levels of development.

SUMMARY

This chapter addressed the unfinished business—the incomplete status—of multicultural counselor preparation. Chapter content was organized under two main headings: (1) the need for continuing and expanded professional organization leadership to improve multicultural counselor preparation, and (2) the need for continuing and expanded work on research and development of models of multicultural counseling and multicultural counselor preparation. Readers were challenged to continue work to reach the goal of making multiculturalism *the Fourth Force* in Counseling.

Among several issues and unfinished business highlighted in this chapter was the need to develop and research models of racial and ethnic identity that transcend identification with one's own racial and ethnic identification. These models will include positive identification with self and with people of other racial and ethnic groups in one's own nation and throughout the world. More cross-national professional sharing among counselors and human service personnel in other countries was also encouraged. Perhaps cross-national professional sharing could lay the groundwork for building the wider racial and ethnic identity models.

Appendixes

Appendix A details the Proposed Cross-Cultural Competencies and Objectives found in Appendix A of the Association for Multicultural Counseling and Development (AMCD) position paper, "Multicultural Counseling Competencies and Standards: A Call to the Profession," (Sue, Arredondo, & McDavis, 1992a, 1992b).

Appendix B presents Cross-Cultural Counseling Training Goals and Tasks for White racial identity development (Sabnani, Ponterotto, & Borodovsky, 1991). The authors list goals and tasks for beliefs and attitudes, knowledge, and skills for the five-stage model they propose.

Appendix C is a copy of the one-page questionnaire used to gather information from international colleagues for Chapter 5 of this book, "Multicultural Counseling on the International Scene."

Appendix D is a suggested readings list of cultural and ethnic novels and other books for broadening cultural awareness.

Appendixes E, F, G, and H contain sample items for use in evaluating the Counseling Practicum and the Counseling Internship. The items included are not exhaustive; these evaluations need to be adapted to comply with one's departmental goals and objectives for multicultural counselor preparation.

APPENDIX A

Proposed Cross-Cultural Competencies and Objectives

I. COUNSELOR AWARENESS OF OWN CULTURAL VALUES AND BIASES

A. *Attitudes and Beliefs*
1. Culturally skilled counselors have moved from being culturally unaware to being aware and sensitive to their own cultural heritage and to valuing and respecting differences.
2. Culturally skilled counselors are aware of how their own cultural backgrounds and experiences and attitudes, values, and biases influence psychological processes.
3. Culturally skilled counselors are able to recognize the limits of their competencies and expertise.
4. Culturally skilled counselors are comfortable with differences that exist between themselves and clients in terms of race, ethnicity, culture, and beliefs.

B. *Knowledge*
1. Culturally skilled counselors have specific knowledge about their own racial and cultural heritage and how it personally and professionally affects their definitions of normality-abnormality and the process of counseling.
2. Culturally skilled counselors possess knowledge and understanding about how oppression, racism, discrimination, and stereotyping affects them personally and in their work. This allows them to acknowledge their own racist attitudes, beliefs, and feelings. Although this standard applies to all groups, for White counselors it may mean that they understand how they may have directly or indirectly benefitted from individual, institutional, and cultural racism (White identity development models).

3. Culturally skilled counselors possess knowledge about their social impact on others. They are knowledgeable about communication style differences, how their style may clash or foster the counseling process with minority clients, and how to anticipate the impact it may have on others.

C. *Skills*
1. Culturally skilled counselors seek out educational, consultative, and training experience to improve their understanding and effectiveness in working with culturally different populations. Being able to recognize the limits of their competencies, they (a) seek consultation, (b) seek further training or education, (c) refer out to more qualified individuals or resources, or (d) engage in a combination of these.
2. Culturally skilled counselors are constantly seeking to understand themselves as racial and cultural beings and are actively seeking a nonracist identity.

II. COUNSELOR AWARENESS OF CLIENT'S WORLDVIEW

A. *Attitudes and Beliefs*
1. Culturally skilled counselors are aware of their negative emotional reactions toward other racial and ethnic groups that may prove detrimental to their clients in counseling. They are willing to contrast their own beliefs and attitudes with those of their culturally different clients in a nonjudgmental fashion.
2. Culturally skilled counselors are aware of their stereotypes and preconceived notions that they may hold toward other racial and ethnic minority groups.

B. *Knowledge*
  1. Culturally skilled counselors possess specific knowledge and information about the particular group they are working with. They are aware of the life experiences, cultural heritage, and historical background of their culturally different clients. This particular competency is strongly linked to the "minority identity development models" available in the literature.
  2. Culturally skilled counselors understand how race, culture, ethnicity, and so forth may affect personality formation, vocational choices, manifestation of psychological disorders, help-seeking behavior, and the appropriateness or inappropriateness of counseling approaches.
  3. Culturally skilled counselors understand and have knowledge about sociopolitical influences that impinge upon the life of racial and ethnic minorities. Immigration issues, poverty, racism, stereotyping, and powerlessness all leave major scars that may influence the counseling process.

C. *Skills*
  1. Culturally skilled counselors should familiarize themselves with relevant research and the latest findings regarding mental health and mental disorders of various ethnic and racial groups. They should actively seek out educational experiences that foster their knowledge, understanding, and cross-cultural skills.
  2. Culturally skilled counselors become actively involved with minority individuals outside of the counseling setting (community events, social and political functions, celebrations, friendships, neighborhood groups, and so forth) so that their perspective of minorities is more than an academic or helping exercise.

III. CULTURALLY APPROPRIATE INTERVENTION STRATEGIES
  A. *Attitudes and Beliefs*
  1. Culturally skilled counselors respect clients' religious and/or spiritual beliefs and values, including attributions and taboos, because they affect worldview, psychosocial functioning, and expressions of distress.
  2. Culturally skilled counselors respect indigenous helping practices and respect minority community intrinsic help-giving networks.
  3. Culturally skilled counselors value bilingualism and do not view another language as an impedi-

ment to counseling (monolingualism may be the culprit).

B. *Knowledge*
  1. Culturally skilled counselors have a clear and explicit knowledge and understanding of the generic characteristics of counseling and therapy (culture bound, class bound, and monolingual) and how they may clash with the cultural values of various minority groups.
  2. Culturally skilled counselors are aware of institutional barriers that prevent minorities from using mental health services.
  3. Culturally skilled counselors have knowledge of the potential bias in assessment instruments and use procedures and interpret findings keeping in mind the cultural and linguistic characteristics of the clients.
  4. Culturally skilled counselors have knowledge of minority family structures, hierarchies, values, and beliefs. They are knowledgeable about the community characteristics and the resources in the community as well as the family.
  5. Culturally skilled counselors should be aware of relevant discriminatory practices at the social and community level that may be affecting the psychological welfare of the population being served.

C. *Skills*
  1. Culturally skilled counselors are able to engage in a variety of verbal and nonverbal helping responses. They are able to *send* and *receive* both *verbal* and *nonverbal* messages *accurately* and *appropriately*. They are not tied down to only one method or approach to helping but recognize that helping styles and approaches may be culture bound. When they sense that their helping style is limited and potentially inappropriate, they can anticipate and ameliorate its negative impact.
  2. Culturally skilled counselors are able to exercise institutional intervention skills on behalf of their clients. They can help clients determine whether a "problem" stems from racism or bias in others (the concept of health paranoia) so that clients do not inappropriately personalize problems.
  3. Culturally skilled counselors are not averse to seeking consultation with traditional healers and religious and spiritual leaders and practitioners

in the treatment of culturally different clients when appropriate.

4. Culturally skilled counselors take responsibility for interfacing in the language requested by the client and, if not feasible, make appropriate referral. A serious problem arises when the linguistic skills of a counselor do not match the language of the client. This being the case, counselors should (a) seek a translator with cultural knowledge and appropriate professional background and (b) refer to a knowledgeable and competent bilingual counselor.

5. Culturally skilled counselors have training and expertise in the use of traditional assessment and testing instruments. They not only understand the technical aspects of the instruments but are also aware of the cultural limitations. This allows them to use test instruments for the welfare of the diverse clients.

6. Culturally skilled counselors should attend to as well as work to eliminate biases, prejudices, and discriminatory practices. They should be cognizant of sociopolitical contexts in conducting evaluation and providing interventions and should develop sensitivity to issues of oppression, sexism, elitism, and racism.

7. Culturally skilled counselors take responsibility in educating their clients to the processes of psychological intervention, such as goals, expectations, legal rights, and the counselor's orientation.

SOURCE: Reprinted from "Multicultural Counseling Competencies and Standards: A Call to the Profession," by D. W. Sue, P. Arredondo, and R. J. McDavis, 1992, *Journal of Counseling and Development, 70*, pp. 484–486. Copyright © 1992 ACA. Reprinted with permissions. No further reproduction authorized without written permission of the American Counseling Association.

APPENDIX B
Cross-Cultural Training Goals and Tasks

	Beliefs/Attitudes	
	Goals	*Tasks*
Stage 1: Preexposure/precontact	Awareness of one's own cultural heritage Awareness of the cultural heritage of minority groups	Awareness group experience "Ethnic dinners"[b] Tours/exhibits of other cultures' crafts/areas Intercultural sharing[c] Multicultural action planning (low level of active involvement)[c] Free drawing test[h] Public and private self-awareness exercise[g] Value statements exercise[h] Decision awareness exercise
Stage 2: Conflict	Awareness of one's stereotypes and prejudicial attitudes and the impact of these on minorities Awareness of the conflict between wanting to conform to White norms while upholding humanitarian values Dealing with feelings of guilt and depression or anger	Critical incidents exercise[h] Implicit assumptions checklist exercise[h] We and you exercises[h] Exercise for experiencing stereotypes[c] Stereotypes awareness exercise[g] Less structured cross-cultural encounter groups
Stage 3: Prominority/antiracism	Awareness of overidentification and of paternalistic attitudes, and the impact of these on minorities	Interracial encounters[m] Cross-cultural encounter groups Responsible feedback exercise[h] Anonymous feedback from the group exercise[h]
Stage 4: Retreat into White culture	Awareness of and dealing with one's own fear and anger	Cross-cultural encounter groups Lump sum[h]
Stage 5: Redefinition and integration	Develop an identity which claims Whiteness as a part of it	Feedback-related exercises (see Stage 3)

NOTE: References for exercises suggested in [this] table are indicated by letters, as follows: a. Parker & McDavis, 1979; b. McDavis & Parker, 1977; c. Parker, 1988; d. Ivey & Authier, 1978; e. Egan, 1982; f. Carkhuff & Anthony, 1979; g. Pedersen, 1988; h. Weeks et al., 1977; i. Brislin et al., 1986; j. Albert, 1983; k. Merta, Stringham, & Ponterotto, 1988; l. Sue, 1981; m. Katz & Ivey, 1977.

Knowledge		Skills	
Goals	*Tasks*	*Goals*	*Tasks*
Knowledge of the cultural heritage of other minority groups	Research into the history of other cultures Intercultural sharing[c] Multicultural action planning (low level of active involvement)[c] Ethnic literature reviews Field trips Case studies[g] Culture assimilator[ijk]	Beginning development of counseling skills	Regular counselor training tasks (micro-skills training)[def]
More extensive knowledge of other cultures Knowledge of the concepts and prejudice and racism Knowledge of the impact of racism on minorities and the privileges of being White	MAP—investigative[c] Tours to other communities Research on racism in the past and present Classes in multicultural issues presenting survey data on minorities Films	Develop more client-specific methods of intervention	Critical incidents method[l] Role-playing exercise[h] Role-playing a problem in a group[h]
Further immersion into other cultures	Guided self-study Exposure to audiovisual presentations[g] Interviews with consultants and experts[g] Lectures Minority student panels[b] Research into the impact of race on counseling	Continue developing culturally emic and etic approaches to counseling	Role-playing exercises Communication skills training Facilitating interracial groups (FIG)[b] Counseling ethnic minorities (CEMI)[b]
Knowledge of the development of minority identity and White identity	Research into minority identity development models Research into White identity development models	Building culturally etic (transcendent) approaches	Microskills training Ponterotto and Benesch (1988)
Expand knowledge on racism in the real world Expand knowledge on counseling methods more appropriate to minorities	Visits to communities with large minority populations Research on ways to transform White-based counseling methods to one more credible to minorities	Deepen more culturally emic approaches Face more challenging cross-cultural counseling interactions	Facilitating interracial groups (FIG)[h] Counseling ethnic minorities individually (CEMI)[b] Triad model[g] Cross-cultural practica

SOURCE: From "White Racial Identity Development and Cross-Cultural Counselor Training: A Stage Model," by H. B. Sabnani, J. G. Ponterotto, and L. G. Borodovsky, 1991, *The Counseling Psychologist, 19*(1), pp. 86–89, copyright © 1991 by Sage Publications. Reprinted by permission of Sage Publications, Inc.

APPENDIX C

International Colleague Questionnaire

Western Illinois University
BOARD OF GOVERNORS UNIVERSITIES

COUNSELOR EDUCATION AND
COLLEGE STUDENT PERSONNEL

College of Education
74 Horrabin Hall
Macomb, Illinois 61455-1396

309/298-1529

March 15, 1993

Dear International Colleague in Counseling: I am currently under contract with the Brooks/Cole Publishing Company to author a book that describes the process of attaining multicultural counseling competence. Since counselors in many countries of the world are now working with culturally diverse populations, I would like to share information on cross-cultural or multicultural counseling outside of the U.S.A. in this book.

I would appreciate your responding to the questions below and returning this sheet to me at the address on the attached mailing label at your earliest convenience. (Continue on back or add sheets as needed.) My FAX number is 309-298-2222 if you prefer to respond that way.

Name _____

Complete address _____

_____

_____ FAX # _____

1. What kind of culturally diverse populations are counselors called upon to serve in your country?

2. Has this need to serve culturally diverse populations always been part of counselor work in your country or have recent changes in the populations of your country contributed to the need for cross-cultural/multicultural counseling help?

3. What type of training is now being offered (or is needed) for counselors in your country to deliver culturally sensitive counseling?

(Please include any descriptive information on cross-cultural/multicultural counselor training offered in your country as well as names and addresses of others to contact in your country. *If no special training is provided, I would still like to hear from you.*)

4. May I have permission to quote you in my book?   Yes_____ No_____

Thank you very much!

Bea Wehrly, PhD, NCC, Professor

APPENDIX D

Cultural and Ethnic Novels and Other Books for Broadening Cultural Awareness

Black Americans/African Americans

Angelou, M. (1970). *I know why the caged bird sings*. New York: Random House.

Angelou, M. (1974). *Gather together in my name*. New York: Random House.

Angelou, M. (1981). *The heart of a woman*. New York: Random House.

Bowen, E. (1954). *Return to laughter*. New York: Harper.

Brown, C. (1976). *The children of Ham*. New York: Stein & Day.

Brown, C. (1965). *Manchild in the promised land*. New York: Grove Press.

Delaney, S., & Delaney, A. E. (1993). *Having our say— The Delaney sisters' first 100 years*. New York: Kadansha International.

Freedman, S. G. (1993). *Upon this rock: The miracles of a Black church*. New York: Harper Collins.

Haley, A. (1976). *Roots*. Garden City, NY: Doubleday.

Haley, A. (1965). *The autobiography of Malcolm X*. New York: Grove Press.

Kotlowitz, A. (1991). *There are no children here—The story of two boys growing up in the other America*. New York: Doubleday.

Morrison, T. (1987). *Beloved*. New York: Plume.

Morrison, T. (any edition). *The bluest eye*. (any publisher).

Myers, W. D. (1981). *Hoops*. New York: Delacorte Press.

Naylor, G. (1983). *Women of Brewster Place*. New York: Penguin.

Naylor, G. (1989). *Mama Day*. New York: Vintage Books.

Njeri, I. (1990). *Every goodbye ain't gone*. New York: Times Books.

Porter, C. (1991). *All-bright court*. Boston: Houghton Mifflin.

Sterling, D. (1984). *We are your sisters*. New York: W. W. Norton.

Walker, A. (1982). *The color purple*. New York: Harcourt Brace Jovanovich.

Walker, A. (1992). *Possessing the secret joy*. New York: Harcourt Brace.

Wideman, J. E. (1984). *Brothers and keepers*. New York: Holt, Rinehart & Winston.

Asian and Asian Americans

Benedict, R. (1946). *The chrysanthemum and the sword: Patterns of Japanese culture*. Boston: Houghton Mifflin.

Chang, J. (1991). *Wild swans: Three daughters of China*. New York: Simon & Schuster.

Houston, J. W., & Houston, J. D. (1974). *Farewell to Manzanar*. Boston: Houghton Mifflin.

Kingston, M. (1976). *The woman warrior: Memories of a girlhood among ghosts*. New York: Random House.

Markandaya, K. (1954). *Nectar in a sieve*. New York: John Day.

Mukherjee, B. (1989). *Jasmine*. New York: Grove Press.

Ngor, H. (1987). *A Cambodian odyssey*. New York: Macmillan.

Okado, J. (1957). *No-no boy*. Seattle, WA: University of Washington Press.

Tan, A. (1989) *The joy luck club*. New York: Putnam.

White, M. (1987). *The Japanese educational challenge: A commitment to children*. New York: Free Press.

Hispanic/Latino

Anaya, R. (1973). *Bless me Ultima*. Berkeley, CA: Quinto Sol Publications.

Anaya, R. (1976). *Heart of Aztlan*. Editorial Justa.

L'Engle, M. (1976). *Dragons on the waters*. New York: Farrar Straus Giroux.

Lewis, O. (1961). *The children of Sanchez*. New York: Random House.

Lewis, O. (1966). *La vida: A Puerto Rican family in the culture of poverty—San Juan and New York*. New York: Random House.

Morago, C. (1983). *Loving in the war years*. Boston: South End Press.

Nichols, J. (1974). *The Milagro beanfield war*. New York: Holt, Rinehart & Winston.

Native American/American Indian/Eskimo American

Borland, H. (1963). *When the legends die*. Philadelphia: Lippincott.

Briggs, J. (1970). *Never in anger*. Cambridge: Harvard University Press.

Brown, D. (1971). *Bury my heart at Wounded Knee: An Indian history of the American West*. New York: Holt, Rinehart & Winston.

Dorris, M. (1989). *The broken cord*. New York: Harper & Row.

Fire, J./Lame Deer, & Erdoes, R. (1972). *Lame Deer: Seeker of visions*. New York: Simon & Schuster.

George, J. C. (1983). *The talking earth*. New York: Harper & Row.

Herbert, F. (1984). *Soul catcher*. New York: Avenel Books.

Houston, J. A. (1983). *Eagle song*. New York: Harcourt Brace.

Neihardt, J. (1932). *Black Elk speaks*. New York: Simon & Schuster.

Neihardt, J. (1951). *When the tree flowered*. New York: Macmillan.

Jewish

Appleman-Jurman, A. (1988). *Alicia: My story*. New York: Bantam.

Hertzberg, A. (1989). *The Jews in America: Four centuries of an uneasy encounter: A history*. New York: Simon & Schuster.

Hoffman, E. (1989). *Lost in translation—A life in a new language*. New York: E. P. Dutton.

Lasky, K. (1984). *Prank*. New York: Macmillan.

Middle Eastern

Mackey, S. (1987). *The Saudis—Inside the desert kingdom*. New York: Meridian.

Mahmoody, B. (1987). *Not without my daughter*. New York: St. Martin's Press.

Uris, L. (1984). *The Haj*. New York: Bantam.

Interracial/Biracial/Multiracial Relationships

Mathabane, M., & Mathabane, G. (1992). *Love in black and white: The triumph of love over prejudice and taboo*. New York: Harper & Collins.

APPENDIX E

*Sample Items for Evaluation of the Practicum
Student's Multicultural Counseling Competence
by the Counseling Practicum Supervisor*

Directions
Circle the number that best represents how you, *the supervisor* of the counseling practicum student,
evaluate the trainee's performance during the term you served as the practicum supervisor.

The counseling practicum student:	Rarely		Sometimes		Consistently	
displays an awareness of his or her own racial and cultural identity development and its impact on the counseling process.	1	2	3	4	5	6
is aware of his or her own values, biases, and assumptions about other racial and cultural groups and does not let these biases and assumptions impede the counseling process.	1	2	3	4	5	6
exhibits a respect for cultural differences among clients.	1	2	3	4	5	6
is aware of the cultural values of each client as well as of the uniquenesses of each client within the client's racial and cultural group identification.	1	2	3	4	5	6
is sensitive to nonverbal and paralanguage cross-cultural communication clues.	1	2	3	4	5	6
demonstrates the ability to assess the client's level of acculturation and to use this information in working with the client to implement culturally sensitive counseling.	1	2	3	4	5	6
displays an understanding of how race, ethnicity, and culture influence the treatment, status, and life chances of clients.	1	2	3	4	5	6
is able to help the client sort out the degree to which the client's issues or problems are exacerbated by limits and regulations of the larger society.	1	2	3	4	5	6

(continued)

The counseling practicum student:	Rarely		Sometimes		Consistently	
is able to assess and identify the locus of the client's problem etiology.	1	2	3	4	5	6
is able to help the client deal with environmental frustration and oppression.	1	2	3	4	5	6
is able to recognize and work with the client dealing with multiple oppressions.	1	2	3	4	5	6
works with the client to bring about change rather than *doing for* the client.	1	2	3	4	5	6
and client *work together* to determine mutually acceptable and culturally sensitive goals.	1	2	3	4	5	6
demonstrates appropriate behavior in work outside of the counseling office in the cultural milieu of the client.	1	2	3	4	5	6
demonstrates the ability to assess the racial and ethnic identity developmental level of clients and use counseling interventions that are appropriate for work with the client at the following levels of racial and ethnic identity development:						
Stage 1	1	2	3	4	5	6
Stage 2	1	2	3	4	5	6
Stage 3	1	2	3	4	5	6
Stage 4	1	2	3	4	5	6
Stage 5	1	2	3	4	5	6
demonstrates an awareness of appropriate times to request help from supervisor.	1	2	3	4	5	6

APPENDIX F

Sample Multicultural Items for Evaluation of the Practicum Site and Supervisor by the Counseling Practicum Student

Directions

Circle the number that best represents how you, *the counseling practicum student*, evaluate your counseling practicum site and your counseling practicum site supervisor.

My counseling practicum site:	No		Somewhat		Yes	
serves a client population that is representative of the cultural diversity of the area.	1	2	3	4	5	6
is a setting that welcomes practicum students training for multicultural counseling.	1	2	3	4	5	6
provides opportunities for me to engage in multicultural counseling.	1	2	3	4	5	6
provides the opportunity for me to participate in case conferences on culturally different clients.	1	2	3	4	5	6
is committed to team efforts to train multicultural counselors.	1	2	3	4	5	6
provides me with opportunities to work with supervisors and other counselors whose ethnic or cultural heritage is different from my own.	1	2	3	4	5	6

My counseling practicum site supervisor:	Rarely		Sometimes		Consistently	
demonstrates effective and culturally sensitive counseling.	1	2	3	4	5	6
provides opportunities for me to engage in co-counseling with clients whose cultural heritage is different from my own.	1	2	3	4	5	6
assists me in broadening my knowledge and skills in application of racial and ethnic identity development theory to multicultural counseling.	1	2	3	4	5	6

(continued)

My counseling practicum site supervisor:	Rarely		Sometimes		Consistently	
assists me in learning to work with clients to develop culturally sensitive goals.	1	2	3	4	5	6
monitors my caseload to maintain a balance of comfort and challenge in my practicum in multicultural counseling.	1	2	3	4	5	6
assists me in participating in appropriate cross-cultural activities in the cultural milieus of my clients.	1	2	3	4	5	6
provides support and encouragement in my efforts to gain competence in multicultural counseling.	1	2	3	4	5	6

APPENDIX G

Sample Items for Evaluation of the Intern's Multicultural Counseling Competence by the Counseling Internship Supervisor

Directions
Circle the number that best represents how you, *the supervisor* of the counseling intern, evaluate the trainee's performance during the term when you served as the counseling internship supervisor.

The counseling intern:	Rarely		Sometimes		Consistently	
displays an active interest in increasing her or his cross-cultural knowledge, attitudes, and skills.	1	2	3	4	5	6
has developed a personal philosophy of change that is congruent for work with diverse clients.	1	2	3	4	5	6
exhibits growth in learning to integrate cultural knowledge in internship responsibilities.	1	2	3	4	5	6
recognizes the multiple oppressions brought by many clients and helps clients deal with these effectively.	1	2	3	4	5	6
is able to formulate culturally sensitive diagnoses using the DSM-IV.	1	2	3	4	5	6
is an effective participant in the outreach activities of our counseling center.	1	2	3	4	5	6
exhibits the desire to promote cultural pluralism in the larger society.	1	2	3	4	5	6
knows when to let the client communicate in his or her mother tongue.	1	2	3	4	5	6
knows when to ask for help from the supervisor.	1	2	3	4	5	6
capitalizes on strengths in multicultural work with individuals and families.	1	2	3	4	5	6
is proficient in writing clinical assessments and/or reports required at our counseling center.	1	2	3	4	5	6

(continued)

The counseling intern:	Rarely		Sometimes		Consistently	
is able to implement the following counselor roles appropriately:						
adviser	1	2	3	4	5	6
advocate	1	2	3	4	5	6
facilitator of indigenous support systems	1	2	3	4	5	6
facilitator of indigenous healing systems	1	2	3	4	5	6
consultant	1	2	3	4	5	6
change agent	1	2	3	4	5	6
counselor	1	2	3	4	5	6
psychotherapist	1	2	3	4	5	6
displays an interest in participating in ongoing multicultural counseling professional development.	1	2	3	4	5	6

APPENDIX H

Sample Multicultural Items for Evaluation of the
Counseling Internship Site and Supervisor by the
Counseling Intern

Directions

Circle the number that best represents how you, *the counseling intern*, evaluate your counseling internship site and your counseling internship site supervisor.

My internship site:	No		Somewhat		Yes	
serves a client population that is representative of the cultural diversity of the area.	1	2	3	4	5	6
is a setting that welcomes counseling interns training for multicultural counseling.	1	2	3	4	5	6
is committed to team efforts to train multicultural counselors.	1	2	3	4	5	6
provides opportunities to be an active participant in outreach activities of the center.	1	2	3	4	5	6
provides me the opportunity to participate in all of the counseling-related activities of the center.	1	2	3	4	5	6
provides me with opportunities to work with supervisors and other counselors whose ethnic or cultural heritage is different from my own.	1	2	3	4	5	6
provides appropriate background training in basic terms and processes of counseling for the people serving as interpreters or translators during counseling sessions.	1	2	3	4	5	6
has helped me to learn how to use the services of a qualified interpreter or translator during a counseling session.	1	2	3	4	5	6

(continued)

My internship site supervisor:	Rarely		Sometimes		Consistently	
assisted me in conquering the anxieties and concerns I brought to the internship experience.	1	2	3	4	5	6
capitalized on "teachable moments" to help me increase my multicultural competence during my counseling internship.	1	2	3	4	5	6
assisted me in learning to formulate culturally appropriate diagnoses using the DSM-IV.	1	2	3	4	5	6
worked with me when I needed assistance in designing counseling interventions that were appropriate for the culture and lifestyle of my clients.	1	2	3	4	5	6
has given me helpful supervision in implementing these counseling intern roles with culturally different clients:						
adviser	1	2	3	4	5	6
advocate	1	2	3	4	5	6
facilitator of indigenous support systems	1	2	3	4	5	6
facilitator of indigenous healing systems	1	2	3	4	5	6
consultant	1	2	3	4	5	6
change agent	1	2	3	4	5	6
counselor	1	2	3	4	5	6
psychotherapist	1	2	3	4	5	6
supported my ongoing professional development	1	2	3	4	5	6

REFERENCES

Abel, T. M. (1956). Cultural patterns as they affect psychotherapeutic procedures. *American Journal of Psychotherapy, 10*, 728–740.

Aboud, F. E. (1987). The development of ethnic self-identification and attitudes. In J. S. Phinney & M. J. Rotheram (Eds.), *Children's ethnic socialization: Pluralism and development* (pp. 32–55). Newbury Park, CA: Sage.

Akbar, N. (1989). Nigrescence and identity: Some limitations. *The Counseling Psychologist, 17,* 258–263.

Akhtar, S. (1984). The syndrome of identity diffusion. *American Journal of Psychiatry, 141,* 1381–1385.

Albert, R. D. (1983). The intercultural sensitizer or culture assimilator: A cognitive approach. In D. Landis & R. W. Brislin (Eds.), *Handbook of intercultural training: Vol. 2. Issues in training methodology* (pp. 86–217). New York: Pergamon.

American Psychiatric Association. (1987). *Diagnostic and statistical manual of mental disorders* (3rd ed., rev.). Washington, DC: Author.

American Psychiatric Association. (1994). *Diagnostic and statistical manual of mental disorders* (4th ed.). Washington, DC: Author.

Ampadu, M. (1992, March). *Traditional healing in Africa: Implications for cross-cultural counseling.* Paper presented at the annual meeting of the American Association for Counseling and Development, Baltimore, MD.

Anaya, R. A. (1972). *Bless me, Ultima.* Berkeley, CA: Tonatuh-Quinto Sol International.

Arbuckle, D. S. (1972). Counseling with members of minority groups. *Counseling and Values, 16,* 239–246.

Arciniega, M., & Newlon, B. J. (1981). A theoretical rationale for cross-cultural family counseling. *School Counselor, 27,* 89–96.

Arnold, M. S. (1993). Ethnicity and training marital and family therapists. *Counselor Education and Supervision, 33,* 139–147.

Arredondo, P., Psalti, A., & Cella, K. (1993). The woman factor in multicultural counseling. *Counseling and Human Development, 25*(8), 1–8.

Arredondo-Dowd, P. M., & Gonsalves, J. (1980). Preparing culturally effective counselors. *The Personnel and Guidance Journal, 58,* 657–661.

Ashby, J. S., & Cheatham, H. E. (1994, February). *Developing competencies for cross-cultural supervision.* Workshop presented at the Eleventh Annual Teachers College Winter Roundtable on Cross-Cultural Counseling and Psychotherapy, New York, NY.

Atkinson, D. R. (1993). Reaction. Who speaks for cross-cultural counseling research? *The Counseling Psychologist, 21,* 218–224.

Atkinson, D. R., Casas, A., & Neville, H. (1994). Ethnic minority psychologists: Whom they mentor and benefits they derive from the process. *Journal of Multicultural Counseling and Development, 22,* 37–48.

Atkinson, D. R., & Gim, R. H. (1989). Asian-American cultural identity and attitudes toward mental health services. *Journal of Counseling Psychology, 36,* 209–219.

Atkinson, D. R., Morten, G., & Sue, D. W. (1979). *Counseling American minorities: A cross-cultural perspective.* Dubuque, IA: W. C. Brown.

Atkinson, D. R., Morten, G., & Sue, D. W. (1983). *Counseling American minorities: A cross-cultural perspective* (2nd ed.). Dubuque, IA: W. C. Brown.

Atkinson, D. R., Morten, G., & Sue, D. W. (1989). *Counseling American minorities: A cross-cultural perspective* (3rd ed.). Dubuque, IA: W. C. Brown.

Atkinson, D. R., Morten, G., & Sue, D. W. (1993). *Counseling American minorities: A cross-cultural perspective* (4th ed.). Dubuque, IA: Brown & Benchmark.

Atkinson, D. R., Thompson, C. E., & Grant, S. K. (1993). A three-dimensional model for counseling racial/ethnic minorities. *The Counseling Psychologist, 21,* 257–277.

Atkinson, D. R., Whiteley, S., & Gim, R. H. (1990). Asian-American acculturation and preferences for help providers. *Journal of College Student Development, 31,* 155–161.

Attneave, C. L. (1969). Therapy in tribal settings and urban network intervention. *Family Process, 8,* 192–210.

Attneave, C. (1982). American Indians and Alaska native families: Emigrants in their own homeland. In M. McGoldrick, J. K. Pearce, & J. Giordana (Eds.), *Ethnicity and family therapy* (pp. 55–83). New York: Guilford.

Aubrey, R. F. (1977). Historical developments of guidance and counseling and implications for the future. *Personnel and Guidance Journal, 55,* 288–295.

Axelson, J. A. (1993). *Counseling and development in a multicultural society* (2nd ed.). Pacific Grove, CA: Brooks/Cole.

Ballantine, B., & Ballantine, I. (Eds.). (1993). *The Native Americans: An illustrated history.* Atlanta: Turner Publishing, Inc.

Banks, J. A. (1981). *Multiethnic education: Theory and practice.* Boston: Allyn & Bacon.

Banks, J. A. (1988). Ethnicity, class, cognitive, and motivational styles: Research and teaching implications. *Journal of Negro Education, 57,* 452–466.

Baptiste, D. A. (1990). Therapeutic strategies with Black-Hispanic families: Identity problems of a neglected minority. *Journal of Family Psychotherapy, 1*(3), 15–38.

Barnard, H. F. (Ed.). (1985). *Outside the magic circle: The autobiography of Virginia Foster Durr.* Tuscaloosa, AL: University of Alabama Press.

Baruth, L. G., & Manning, M. L. (1991). *Multicultural counseling and psychotherapy: A lifespan perspective.* New York: Merrill.

Bateson, G. (1979). *Mind and nature: A necessary unity.* New York: E. P. Dutton.

Beauvais, F. (1977). Counseling psychology in a cross-cultural setting. *The Counseling Psychologist, 7*(2), 80–82.

Bennett, L. A. (Ed.). (1992). *Encyclopedia of world cultures: Vol 4. Europe (central, western, and southeastern Europe).* Boston: G. K. Hall.

Berg, I. K., & Jaya, A. (1993). Different and same: Family therapy with Asian-American families. *Journal of Marital and Family Therapy, 19,* 31–38.

Bernal, G. (1982). Cuban families. In M. McGoldrick, J. K. Pearce, & J. Giordana (Eds.), *Ethnicity and family therapy* (pp. 187–207). New York: Guilford Press.

Bernard, J. M. (1994). Multicultural supervision: A reaction to Leong and Wagner, Cook, Priest, and Fukuyama. *Counselor Education and Supervision, 34,* 159–171.

Bojuwoye, O. (1992). The role of counseling in developing countries: A reply to Soliman. *International Journal for the Advancement of Counseling, 15,* 3–16.

Bowen, E. S. (1954). *Return to laughter.* New York: Harper & Brothers.

Boyd-Franklin, N. (1989a). *Black families in therapy.* New York: Guilford.

Boyd-Franklin, N. (1989b). Five key factors in the treatment of Black families. *Journal of Psychotherapy and the Family, 6*(1/2), 53–69.

Brand, J., Falsey, J., & Sander, I. (Executive Producers) & Sander, I. (Director). (1991). *I'll fly away* [Video]. Burbank, CA: Brand-Falsey Production in association with Lorimar Television.

Brinson, J., & Kottler, J. (1993). Cross-cultural mentoring: A strategy for retaining minority faculty. *Counselor Education and Supervision, 32,* 241–253.

Brislin, R. W., Cushner, K., Cherrie, C., & Yong, M. (1986). *Intercultural interactions: A practical guide.* Newbury Park, CA: Sage.

Calia, V. F. (1966). The culturally deprived client: A reformulation of the counselor's role. *Journal of Counseling Psychology, 13,* 100–105.

Carkhuff, R. R., & Anthony, W. A. (1979). *The skills of helping.* Amherst, MA: Human Resource Development Press.

Carney, C. G., & Kahn, K. B. (1984). Building competencies for effective cross-cultural counseling: A developmental view. *The Counseling Psychologist, 12*(1), 111–119.

Carter, R. T. (1990). The relationship between racism and racial identity among White Americans: An exploratory investigation. *Journal of Counseling and Development, 69,* 46–50.

Carter, R. T., & Helms, J. E. (1992). The counseling process as defined by relationship types: A test of Helm's interactional model. *Journal of Multicultural Counseling and Development, 20,* 181–201.

Casas, J. M. (1984). Policy, training, and research in counseling psychology: The racial/ethnic minority perspective. In S. D. Brown & R. W. Lent (Eds.), *Handbook of counseling psychology* (pp. 785–831). New York: Wiley.

Casas, J. M. (1985). The status of racial- and ethnic-minority counseling: A training perspective. In P. Pedersen (Ed.), *Handbook of cross-cultural counseling and therapy* (pp. 267–273). Westport, CT: Greenwood.

Casas, J. M., & San Miguel, S. (1993). Reaction. Beyond questions and discussions, there is a need for action: A response to Mio and Iwamasa. *The Counseling Psychologist, 21,* 233–239.

Casas, J. M., & Vasquez, J. T. (1989). Counseling the Hispanic client: A theoretical and applied perspective. In P. B. Pedersen, J. G. Draguns, W. J. Lonner, and J. E. Trimble (Eds.), *Counseling across cultures* (3rd ed.) (pp. 153–175). Honolulu: University of Hawaii Press.

Cheatham, H. E., Ivey, A. E., Ivey, M. B., & Simek-Morgan, L. (1993). Multicultural counseling and therapy: Changing the foundations of the field. In A. E. Ivey, M. B. Ivey, & L. Simek-Morgan, *Counseling and psychotherapy: A multicultural perspective* (3rd ed.) (pp. 93–123). Boston: Allyn & Bacon.

Cheek, D. K. (1976). *Assertive Black . . . puzzled White.* San Luis Obispo, CA: Impact Publishers.

Christensen, C. P. (1989). Cross-cultural awareness development: A conceptual model. *Counselor Education and Supervision, 28,* 270–287.

Clark, A., Hocevar, D., & Dembo, M. H. (1980). The role of cognitive development in children's explanations and preferences for skin color. *Developmental Psychology, 16,* 332–339.

Cohen, D. (Ed.). (1991). *The circle of life: Rituals from the human family album*. San Francisco: Harper.

Comas-Diaz, L. (1994, February). *Race and gender in psychotherapy with women of color*. Paper presented at the Eleventh Annual Teachers College Winter Roundtable on Cross-Cultural Counseling and Psychotherapy, New York, NY.

Comas-Diaz, L., & Greene, B. (Eds.). (1994). *Women of color: Integrating ethnic and gender identities in psychotherapy*. New York: Guilford.

Comas-Diaz, L., & Jacobsen, F. M. (1987). Ethnocultural identification in psychotherapy. *Psychiatry, 50*, 232–241.

Cook, D. A. (1994). Racial identity in supervision. *Counselor Education and Supervision, 34*, 132–141.

Copeland, E. J. (1982). Minority populations and traditional counseling programs: Some alternatives. *Counselor Education and Supervision, 21*, 187–193.

Copeland, E. J. (1983). Cross-cultural counseling and psychotherapy: A historical perspective, implications for research and training. *The Personnel and Guidance Journal, 62*, 10–15.

Corey, G. (1991). *Theory and practice of counseling and psychotherapy*. Pacific Grove, CA: Brooks/Cole.

Cornett, C. E., & Cornett, C. F. (1980). *Bibliotherapy: The right book at the right time*. Bloomington, IN: Phi Delta Kappa Educational Foundation.

Corvin, S., & Wiggins, F. (1989). An antiracism training model for white professionals. *Journal of Multicultural Counseling and Development, 17*, 105–114.

Council for Accreditation of Counseling and Related Educational Programs. (1993). *CACREP Accreditation Standards and Procedures Manual*. Alexandria, VA: Author.

Cross, W. E. (1971). The Negro-to-Black conversion experience: Toward a psychology of Black liberation. *Black World, 20*, 13–17.

Cross, W. E. (1978). The Thomas and Cross models of psychological nigrescence: A review. *The Journal of Black Psychology, 5*, 13–31.

Cross, W. E. (1987). A two-factor theory of Black identity: Implications for the study of identity development in minority children. In J. S. Phinney & M. J. Rotheram (Eds.), *Children's ethnic socialization: Pluralism and development in minority children* (pp. 117–133). Newbury Park, CA: Sage.

Cross, W. E. (1989). Nigrescence: A nondiaphonous phenomenon. *The Counseling Psychologist, 17*, 273–276.

Cross, W. E. (1991). *Shades of Black: Diversity in African-American identity*. Philadelphia: Temple University Press.

Cross, W. E., Parham, T. A., & Helms, J. E. (1991). The stages of Black identity development: Nigrescence models. In R. L. Jones (Ed.), *Black psychology* (3rd ed.) (pp. 319–338). Berkeley, CA: Cobb & Henry.

Cuellar, I., Harris, L. C., & Jasso, R. (1980). An acculturation scale for Mexican American normal and clinical populations. *Hispanic Journal of Behavioral Sciences, 2*, 199–217.

Culturgrams: The nations around us: Vol. 1. North America and South America; Western and Eastern Europe. (1994). Garrett Park, MD: Garrett Park Press.

Culturgrams: The nations around us: Vol 2. Middle East, Asia, Africa, and Pacific areas. (1994). Garret Park, MD: Garrett Park Press.

D'Andrea, M., & Daniels, J. (1991). Exploring the different levels of multicultural counseling training in counselor education. *Journal of Counseling and Development, 70*, 78–85.

Daniels, R. (1988). *Asian America: Chinese and Japanese in the United States since 1850*. Seattle: University of Washington Press.

Das, A. K. (1987). Indigenous models of therapy in traditional Asian societies. *Journal of Multicultural Counseling and Development, 15,* 25–36.

Das, A. K., & Littrell, J. M. (1989). Multicultural education for counseling: A reply to Lloyd. *Counselor Education and Supervision, 29,* 7–15.

Davenport, D. S., & Yurich, J. M. (1991). Multicultural gender issues. *Journal of Counseling and Development, 70,* 64–71.

Deen, N. (Ed.). (1986a). 1985 Consultation, "Counselling and Ethnic Minorities," [Special issue, I]. *International Journal of the Advancement of Counselling, 9*(3).

Deen, N. (Ed.). (1986b). 1985 Consultation, "Counselling and Ethnic Minorities," [Special issue, II]. *International Journal for the Advancement of Counselling, 9*(4).

Deutsch, M. (1966). Some psychosocial aspects of learning in the disadvantaged. *Teachers College Record, 67,* 260–265.

Do, C. L. (1991). *Adaptation of young Vietnamese refugees in France.* Unpublished manuscript.

Dow, J., & Kemper, R. V. (Eds.). (1995). *Encyclopedia of world cultures: Vol. 8: Middle America and the Caribbean.* Boston: G. K. Hall.

Draguns, J. G. (1977). Mental health and culture. In D. S. Hoopes, P. B. Pedersen, & G. Renwick (Eds.), *Overview of intercultural education, training and research* (Volume I, Theory, pp. 57–73). Washington, DC: Society for Intercultural Education, Training, and Research.

Draguns, J. G. (1981). Cross-cultural counseling and psychotherapy: History, issues, current status. In A. J. Marsella & P. B. Pedersen (Eds.), *Cross-cultural counseling and psychotherapy.* New York: Pergamon.

Draguns, J. G. (1989). Dilemmas and choices in cross-cultural counseling: The universal versus the culturally distinctive. In P. B. Pedersen, J. G. Draguns, W. J. Lonner, & J. E. Trimble (Eds.), *Counseling across cultures* (3rd ed.). Honolulu: University Press of Hawaii.

Durie, M., & Hermansson, G. (1990). Counseling Maori people in New Zealand [Aotearoa]. *International Journal for the Advancement of Counselling, 13,* 107–118.

Egan, G. (1982). *The skilled helper* (2nd ed.). Pacific Grove, CA: Brooks/Cole.

Erikson, E. H. (1950). *Childhood and society.* New York: Norton.

Erikson, E. H. (1963). *Childhood and society* (2nd ed.). New York: Norton.

Erikson, E. H. (1964). *Insight and responsibility.* New York: Norton.

Erikson, E. H. (1968). *Identity: Youth and crisis.* New York: Norton.

Esquivel, G. B., & Keitel, M. A. (1990). Counseling immigrant children in the schools. *Elementary School Guidance and Counseling, 24,* 213–221.

Evans, D. R., Hearn, M. T., Uhlemann, M. R., & Ivey, A. E. (1993). *Essential interviewing: A programmed approach to effective communication* (4th ed.). Pacific Grove, CA: Brooks/Cole.

Everts, J. F. (1988). The Marae-based Hui: An indigenous vehicle to address cross-cultural discrimination in New Zealand. *The Journal for Specialists in Group Work, 13,* 130–134.

Falicov, C. J. (1982). Mexican families. In M. McGoldrick, J. K. Pearce, & J. Giordana (Eds.), *Ethnicity and family therapy* (pp. 134–163). New York: Guilford Press.

Falicov, C. J. (Ed.). (1983). *Cultural perspectives in family therapy.* Rockville, MD: Aspen Publications.

Farney, D. (1992, December 2). Mosaic of Hope: Ethnic identities clash with student idealism at a California college. *The Wall Street Journal,* pp. 1, 2, 3.

Ferguson, M. (1985). *The Aquarian conspiracy.* Los Angeles: Tarcher.

Ford, D. Y., Harris, J. J., & Schuerger, J. M. (1993). Racial identity development among gifted Black students: Counseling issues and concerns. *Journal of Counseling and Development, 71,* 409–417.

Ford-Harris, D. Y., Schuerger, J. M., & Harris, J. J. (1991). Meeting the psychological needs of gifted Black students: A cultural perspective. *Journal of Counseling and Development, 69,* 577–580.

Friedrich, P., & Diamond, N. (Eds.). (1994). *Encyclopedia of world cultures: Vol. 6. Russia, Eurasia, and China.* Boston: G. K. Hall.

Fukuyama, M. A. (1990). Point/counterpoint. Taking a universal approach to multicultural counseling. *Counselor Education and Supervision, 30,* 6–17.

Fukuyama, M. A. (1994). Critical incidents in multicultural counseling supervision: A phenomenological approach to supervision research. *Counselor Education and Supervision, 34,* 142–151.

Garcia-Preto, N. (1982). Puerto Rican families. In M. McGoldrick, J. K. Pearce, & J. Giordana (Eds.), *Ethnicity and family therapy* (pp. 164–186). New York: Guilford Press.

Gehrie, M. J. (1979). Culture as an internal representation. *Psychiatry, 42,* 165–170.

Gibbs, J. (1980). The interpersonal orientation in mental health consultation. Toward a model of ethnic variations in consultation. *Journal of Community Psychology, 8,* 195–207.

Gibbs, J. T. (1985). Treatment relationships with Black clients: Interpersonal vs. instrumental strategies. In C. B. Germain, P. Caroff, P. L. Ewalt, P. Glasser, & R. Vaughan (Eds.), *Advances in clinical social work practice* (pp. 184–195). Silver Springs, MD: National Association of Social Workers.

Gim, R. H., Atkinson, D. R., & Whiteley, S. (1990). Asian-American acculturation, severity of concerns, and willingness to see a counselor. *Journal of Counseling Psychology, 37,* 281–285.

Gothard, W. P., & Bojuwoye, O. (1992). Counsellor training in two different cultures. *International Journal for the Advancement of Counselling, 15,* 209–219.

Green, J. W. (1982). *Cultural awareness in the human services.* Englewood Cliffs, NJ: Prentice-Hall.

Greenwood, A., & Westwood, M. J. (1992). *Returning home: A group program to assist persons returning home after living/studying/working abroad.* Canadian Bureau for International Education (CBIE), Ottawa, 94 pp. Published in French also.

Gutierrez, F. J. (1982). Working with minority counselor education students. *Counselor Education and Supervision, 21,* 218–226.

Halfe, L. (1993, July/August). Healing from a Native perspective. *COGNICA,* p. 1.

Hall, E. T. (1959). *The silent language.* Garden City, NY: Doubleday.

Hall, E. T. (1976). *Beyond culture.* New York: Anchor Press/Doubleday.

Halpern, E. (1985). Training family therapists in Israel: The necessity of indigenous models. *The American Journal of Family Therapy, 13,* 55–60.

Hardiman, R. (1982). *White identity development: A process oriented model for describing the racial consciousness of White Americans.* Unpublished Doctoral Dissertation. University of Massachusetts, Amherst.

Harper, F. D. (1973). What counselors must know about the social sciences of black Americans. *Journal of Negro Education, 42,* 109–116.

Harper, F. D., & Stone, W. O. (1986). A multimodal model for multicultural counseling. *International Journal for the Advancement of Counselling, 9,* 251–263.

Hays, T. E. (Ed.). (1991). *Encyclopedia of world cultures: Vol. 2. Oceania.* Boston: G. K. Hall.

Heller, K. A. (1992, November). *Identifying and counseling gifted students.* Invited lecture at the International Conference on Counseling and Guidance, Athens, Greece.

Helms, J. E. (1984). Toward a theoretical explanation of the effects of race on counseling: A Black and White model. *The Counseling Psychologist, 12*(4), 153–165.

Helms, J. E. (1985). Cultural identity in the treatment process. In P. Pedersen (Ed.), *Handbook of Cross-Cultural Counseling and Therapy* (pp. 239–245). Westport, CT: Greenwood Press.

Helms, J. E. (1989). Considering some methodological issues in racial identity counseling research. *The Counseling Psychologist, 17,* 227–252.

Helms, J. E. (Ed.). (1990). *Black and white racial identity: Theory, research, and practice.* New York: Greenwood Press.

Helms, J. E. (1992). *A race is a nice thing to have.* Topeka, KS: Content Communications.

Helms, J. E. (1993). Reaction. I also said, "White racial identity influences White researchers." *The Counseling Psychologist, 21,* 240–243.

Herbert, F. (1984). *Soul catcher.* New York: Simon & Schuster.

Herr, E. L. (1979). *Guidance and counseling in the schools: The past, present, and future.* Falls Church, VA: American Personnel and Guidance Association.

Herskovits, M. J. (1956). *Man and his works: The science of cultural anthropology.* New York: Knopf.

Hickson, J., & Kreigler, S. (1991). Childshock: The effects of apartheid on the mental health of South Africa's children. *The International Journal for the Advancement of Counseling, 14,* 141–154.

Hills, H. I., & Strozier, A. L. (1992). Multicultural training in APA-approved counseling psychology programs: A survey. *Professional Psychology, 23,* 43–51.

Hines, P. M., & Boyd-Franklin, N. (1982). Black families. In M. McGoldrick, J. K. Pearce, & J. Giordana (Eds.), *Ethnicity and family therapy* (pp. 84–107). New York: Guilford Press.

Ho, M. K. (1987). *Family therapy with ethnic minorities.* Newbury Park, CA: Sage.

Hoare, C. H. (1991). Psychosocial identity development and cultural others. *Journal of Counseling and Development, 70,* 45–53.

Hockings, P. (Ed.). (1992). *Encyclopedia of world cultures: Vol. 3. South Asia.* Boston: G. K. Hall.

Hockings, P. (Ed.). (1993). *Encyclopedia of world cultures: Vol. 5. East and southeast Asia.* Boston: G. K. Hall.

Hodgkinson, H. L. (1985). *All one system. Demographics of education, kindergarten through graduate school.* Washington, DC: The Institute for Educational Leadership, Inc.

Hodgkinson, H. (1991). Reform versus reality. *Phi Delta Kappan, 73*(1), 8–16.

Hollis, J. W., & Wantz, R. A. (1990). *Counselor preparation, 1990–1992: Programs, personnel, trends* (7th ed.). Muncie, IN: Accelerated Development, Inc.

Hong, G. K., & Ham, M. A. D-C. (1992). Impact of immigration on the family life cycle: Clinical implications for Chinese Americans. *Journal of Family Psychotherapy, 3*(3), 27–40.

Hood, A. B., & Arceneaux, C. (1987). Reaction: Multicultural counseling: Will what you don't know help you? *Counselor Education and Supervision, 26,* 173–175.

Hoopes, D. S., & Ventura, P. (Eds.). (1979). *Intercultural sourcebook: Cross-cultural training methodologies.* Yarmouth, ME: Intercultural Press.

Hopson, D. P., & Hopson, D. (1990). *Different and wonderful: Raising Black children in a race-conscious society.* New York: Simon & Schuster.

Ibrahim, F. A. (1984). Cross-cultural counseling and psychotherapy: An existential-psychological approach. *International Journal for the Advancement of Counselling, 7,* 159–169.

Ibrahim, F. A. (1985). Effective cross-cultural counseling and psychotherapy: A framework. *The Counseling Psychologist, 13,* 625–638.

Ibrahim, F. A., & Arredondo, P. M. (1986). Ethical standards for cross-cultural counseling: Counselor preparation, practice, assessment, and research. *Journal of Counseling and Development, 64,* 349–352.

Ishiyama, F. I. (1987). Use of Morita therapy in shyness counseling in the West: Promoting clients' self-acceptance and action taking. *Journal of Counseling and Development, 65,* 547–551.

Ishiyama, F. I. (1990). A Japanese perspective on client inaction: Removing attitudinal blocks through Morita therapy. *Journal of Counseling and Development, 68,* 566–570.

Ishiyama, F. I., & Westwood, M. J. (1992). Enhancing client-validating communications: Helping discouraged clients in cross-cultural adjustment. *Journal of Multicultural Counseling and Development, 20,* 50–63.

Ivey, A. E. (1977). Cultural expertise: Toward systematic outcome criteria in counseling and psychological education. *Personnel and Guidance Journal, 55,* 296–302.

Ivey, A. E. (1987). Reaction: Cultural intentionality: The core of effective helping. *Counselor Education and Supervision, 26,* 168–172.

Ivey, A. E. (1991). *Developmental strategies for helpers.* Pacific Grove, CA: Brooks/Cole.

Ivey, A. E. (1993). Reaction. On the need for reconstruction of our present practice of counseling and psychotherapy. *The Counseling Psychologist, 21,* 225–228.

Ivey, A. E. (1994). *Intentional interviewing and counseling: Facilitating client development in a multicultural society* (3rd ed.). Pacific Grove, CA: Brooks/Cole.

Ivey, A. E., & Authier, J. (1978). *Microcounseling: Innovations in interview training.* Springfield, IL: Charles C Thomas.

Ivey, A., Gluckstern, N., & Ivey, M. (1993). *Basic attending skills and basic influencing skills* (3rd ed.) [Videotapes and manuals]. North Amherst, MA: Microtraining Associates.

Ivey, A. E., Ivey, M. B., & Simek-Morgan, L. (1993). *Counseling and psychotherapy: A multicultural perspective* (3rd ed.). Boston: Allyn & Bacon.

Jackson, D. N., & Hayes, D. H. (1993). Multicultural issues in consultation. *Journal of Counseling and Development, 72,* 144–147.

Johannes, W. (Ed.). (1994). *Encyclopedia of world cultures: Vol. 7. South America.* Boston: G. H. Hall.

Johnson, S. D. (1990a). Applying socio-identity analysis to counseling practice and preparation: A review of four techniques. *Journal of Multicultural Counseling and Development, 18,* 133–143.

Johnson, S. D. (1990b). Toward clarifying culture, race, and ethnicity in the context of multicultural counseling. *Journal of Multicultural Counseling and Development, 18,* 41–50.

Jones, E. E., Kanouse, D. E., Kelley, H. H., Nisbett, R. E., Valins, S., & Weiner, B. (1972). *Attribution: Perceiving the causes of behavior.* Morriston, NJ: General Learning Press.

Jones, J. M. (1972). *Prejudice and racism.* Reading, MA: Addison-Wesley.

Jones, J. M. (1981). The concept of racism and its changing reality. In B. J. Bowser & R. G. Hunt (Eds.), *Impacts of racism on white Americans* (pp. 27–49). Newbury Park, CA: Sage.

Joy, S. (1992). Supervising the experienced student counselor. *IACD Quarterly, No. 125,* 24–33.

Kaplan, R. B. (1989). Cultural thought patterns in inter-cultural education. In J. S. Wurzel (Ed.), *Toward multiculturalism: Readings in multicultural education* (pp. 207–221). Yarmouth, ME: Intercultural Press, Inc.

Katz, J. H. (1985). The sociopolitical nature of counseling. *The Counseling Psychologist, 13,* 615–624.

Katz, J. H., & Ivey, A. (1977). White awareness: The frontier of racism awareness training. *The Personnel and Guidance Journal, 55*, 485–489.

Katz, P. A. (1987). Developmental and social processes in ethnic attitudes and self-identification. In J. S. Phinney & M. J. Rotheram (Eds.), *Children's ethnic socialization: Pluralism and development* (pp. 92–99). Newbury Park, CA: Sage.

Katz, R. (1982). *Boiling energy: Community healing among the Kalahari Kung.* Cambridge, MA: Harvard University Press.

Kelly, E. W. (1992). *Religious and spiritual issues in university-based counselor education programs: A national survey of current status. Summary of a report of a research project sponsored by the Counseling and Human Development Foundation.* Unpublished manuscript.

Kelley, G. A. (1955). *The psychology of personal constructs* (Vols. 1–2). New York: Norton.

Kennedy, S., Scheirer, J., & Rogers, A. (1984). The price of success: Our monocultural science. *American Psychologist, 39*, 996–997.

Kerwin, C., & Ponterotto, J. G. (1994, May). Counseling multiracial individuals and their families—Don't believe all myths. *Guidepost*, pp. 1, 10, 11.

Kerwin, C., Ponterotto, J. G., Jackson, B. L., & Harris, A. (1993). Racial identity in biracial children: A qualitative investigation. *Journal of Counseling Psychology, 40*, 221–231.

Khan, J. A. (1983). The evolution of counseling and guidance in Australia: Or, as yet no counseling kangaroos? *The Personnel and Guidance Journal, 61*, 469–472.

Kim, J. (1981). *Processes of Asian-American identity development: A study of Japanese American women's perceptions of their struggle to achieve positive identities as Americans of Asian ancestry.* Unpublished Doctoral Dissertation. University of Massachusetts, Amherst.

Kim, S. C. (1985). Family therapy for Asian Americans: A strategic-structural framework. *Psychotherapy, 22*, 342–356.

Kim, Y. M. (1993). Helping health professionals with the human factor. *American Counselor, 2*(3), 22–24.

Kingston, H. (1976). *The woman warrior: Memories of a girlhood among ghosts.* New York: Random House.

Kinzie, J. D. (1978). Lessons from cross-cultural psychotherapy. *American Journal of Psychotherapy, 32*, 510–520.

Kiselica, M. S. (1991). Reflections on a multicultural internship experience. *Journal of Counseling and Development, 70*, 126–130.

Kleinman, A. (1980). *Patients and healers in the context of culture.* Berkeley: University of California Press.

Kleinman, A. (1985, February). *Culture in the clinic.* Paper presented at the Third annual Teachers College Roundtable for Cross-Cultural Counseling, Teachers College, Columbia University, New York.

Kleinman, A. (1986). *Social origins of distress and disease.* New Haven: Yale University Press.

Kleinman, A. (1988). *Rethinking psychiatry.* New York: Free Press.

Kluckhohn, C., et al. (1951). Values and value-orientations in the theory of action. In T. Parsons & E. A. Shils (Eds.), *Toward a general theory of action* (pp. 388–433). Cambridge, MA: Harvard University Press.

Kluckhohn, F., & Strodtbeck, F. (1961). *Variation in value orientations.* Evanston, IL: Row Petersen.

Kochman, T. (1981). *Black and White: Styles in conflict.* Chicago: University of Chicago Press.

Kohout, J., Wicherski, M., & Cooney B. (1992). *Characteristics of graduate departments of psychology: 1989–90*. Washington, DC: American Psychological Association.

LaFromboise, T. D., & Rowe, W. (1983). Skills training for bicultural competence: Rationale and application. *Journal of Counseling Psychology, 30,* 589–595.

Lee, C. C. (1991). New approaches to diversity: Implications for multicultural counselor training and research. In C. C. Lee & B. L. Richardson (Eds.), *Multicultural issues in counseling: New approaches to diversity* (pp. 209–214). Alexandria, VA: AACD.

Lee, C. C. (Ed.). (1995). *Counseling for diversity: A guide for school counselors and related professionals*. Boston: Allyn & Bacon.

Lee, C. C., Oh, M. Y., & Mountcastle, A. R. (1992). Indigenous models of helping in nonwestern countries: Implications for multicultural counseling. *Journal of Multicultural Counseling and Development, 20,* 3–10.

Lee, C. C., & Richardson, B. L. (Eds.). (1991). *Multicultural issues in counseling: New approaches to diversity*. Alexandria, VA: AACD.

Lee, J. D. (1984). Counseling and culture: Some issues. *Personnel and Guidance Journal, 62,* 592–597.

Leong, F. T. L. (1994). Emergence of the cultural dimension: The roles and impact of culture on counseling supervision. *Counselor Education and Supervision, 34,* 114–116.

Leong, F. T. L., & Wagner, N. S. (1994). Cross-cultural counseling supervision: What do we know? What do we need to know? *Counselor Education and Supervision, 34,* 117–131.

Le Vine, P. (1991). Morita psychotherapy: A theoretical overview for Australian consideration. *Australian Psychologist, 26,* 103–106.

Le Vine, P. (1993). Morita-based therapy and its use across cultures in the treatment of bulimia nervosa. *Journal of Counseling and Development, 72,* 82–90.

Liu, Y. C., & Baker, S. B. (1993). Enhancing cultural adaptation through friendship training: A single-case study. *Elementary School Guidance and Counseling, 28,* 92–103.

Livingstone, B. J. (1989). Counseling in South Africa: The challenge of apartheid. *Journal of Multicultural Counseling and Development, 17,* 171–179.

Lloyd, A. (1987a). Stimulus paper: Multicultural counseling: Does it belong in a counselor education program? *Counselor Education and Supervision, 26,* 164–167.

Lloyd, A. (1987b). Response: Multicultural counseling: Lloyd's reply. *Counselor Education and Supervision, 26,* 181–183.

Locke, D. C. (1990). Point/counterpoint: A response. A not so provincial view of multicultural counseling. *Counselor Education and Supervision, 30,* 18–25.

Locke, D. C. (1991). The Locke paradigm of cross cultural counseling. *International Journal for the Advancement of Counseling, 14,* 15–25.

Locke, D. C. (1992a). Counseling beyond U.S. borders. *American Counselor, 1* (2), 13–16.

Locke, D. C. (1992b). *Increasing multicultural understanding: A comprehensive model*. Newbury Park, CA: Sage.

Locke, D. C., & Faubert, M. (1993). Getting on the right track: A program for African American high school students. *The School Counselor, 41,* 129–133.

Loden, M., & Rosener, J. B. (1991). *Workforce America: Managing employee diversity as a vital resource*. Homewood, IL: Business One Irwin.

Loganbill, C., Hardy, E., & Delworth, V. (1982). Supervision: A conceptual model. *The Counseling Psychologist, 10,* 3–42.

Makinde, O. (1987). African urbanism: Preparation for multi-ethnic schools' counselors. *Journal of Multicultural Counseling and Development, 15,* 38–44.

Manthei, R. J. (1993). Recent developments and directions in counselling in New Zealand. *International Journal for the Advancement of Counselling, 16,* 135–144.

Marcia, J. E. (1966). Development and validation of ego-identity status. *Journal of Personality and Social Psychology, 3,* 551–558.

Marcia, J. E. (1980). Identity in adolescence. In J. Adelson (Ed.), *Handbook of adolescent psychology* (pp. 159–187). New York: Wiley.

Marsella, A. J., & Pedersen, P. B. (Eds.). (1981). *Cross-cultural counseling and psychotherapy.* New York: Pergamon Press.

Martin, L., & Wehrly, B. (1979). Counseling, school and society: Interdependent systems —The example of the Federal Republic of Germany. *Counseling and Human Development, 12*(2), 1–12.

Maslow, A. H. (1954). *Motivation and personality.* New York: Harper.

McDavis, R. J., & Parker, M. (1977). A course on counseling ethnic minorities: A model. *Counselor Education and Supervision, 17,* 146–149.

McFadden, J. (1986). Stylistic dimensions of counseling minorities. *International Journal for the Advancement of Counselling, 9,* 209–219.

McGoldrick, M., Pearce, J. K., & Giordano, J. (Eds.). (1982). *Ethnicity and family therapy.* New York: Guilford Press.

McIntosh, P. (1990, Winter). White privilege: Unpacking the invisible knapsack. *Independent School, 49,* 31–36.

McWhirter, J. J. (1988). Counseling psychology and the Fulbright program: The Australian connection. *The Counseling Psychologist, 16,* 303–306.

Mead, G. H. (1934). *Mind, self, and society.* Chicago: University of Chicago Press.

Merta, R. J., Stringham, E. M., & Ponterotto, J. G. (1988). Simulating culture shock in counselor trainees: An experiential exercise for cross-cultural training. *Journal of Counseling and Development, 66,* 242–245.

Middleton, J., & Rassan, A. (Eds.). (1995). *Encyclopedia of world cultures: Vol. 9. Africa and the Middle East.* Boston: G. K. Hall.

Miles, R. (1989). *Racism.* New York: Routledge.

Mio, J. S. (1989). Experiential involvement as an adjunct to teaching cultural sensitivity. *Journal of Multicultural Counseling and Development, 17,* 38–46.

Mio, J. S., & Iwamasa, G. (1993). To do, or not to do: That is the question for White cross-cultural researchers. *The Counseling Psychologist, 21,* 197–212.

Mio, J. S., & Morris, D. R. (1990). Cross-cultural issues in psychology training programs: An invitation for discussion. *Professional Psychology, 21,* 434–441.

Morrissey, M. (1994, September). Giving back more than you got. *Counseling Today, 37*(3), 9.

National Geographic Society. (1989). *The world of the American Indian.* Washington, DC: Author.

Navin, S. (1989). Guidance and counseling program development in Botswana. *International Journal for the Advancement of Counselling, 12,* 199–201.

Navin, S. L. (1992). Feasibility study of a university counseling center in Botswana: Innovative response to boundary changing worldwide. *International Journal for the Advancement of Counselling, 15,* 103–111.

Neimeyer, G. J., Fukuyama, M. A., Bingham, R. P., Hall, L. E., & Mussenden, M. E. (1986). Training cross-cultural counselors: A comparison of the pro-counselor and the anti-counselor triad models. *Journal of Counseling and Development, 64,* 437–439.

Newlon, B. J., & Arciniega, M. (1983). Counseling minority families: An Adlerian perspective. *Counseling and Human Development, 16*(4), 1–12.

Nobles, W. W. (1989). Psychological Nigrescence: An Afrocentric review. *The Counseling Psychologist, 17,* 253–257.

Nugent, F. A. (1988). Counseling psychology and the West German Fulbright program. *The Counseling Psychologist, 16,* 293–296.

Nwachuku, U. T., & Ivey, A. E. (1991). Culture-specific counseling: An alternative training model. *Journal of Counseling and Development, 70,* 106–111.

Okon, S. E. (1980). Counselling in the faculty of education of Ahmadu Bello University: Progress report 1980. *International Journal for the Advancement of Counselling, 4,* 227–239.

Okon, S. E. (1983). Guidance and counseling services in Nigeria. *The Personnel and Guidance Journal, 61,* 457–459.

O'Leary, T. J., & Levinson, D. (Eds.). (1991). *Encyclopedia of world cultures: Vol. 1. North America.* Boston: G. K. Hall.

Papajohn, J., & Spiegel, J. (1975). *Transactions in families.* San Francisco: Jossey-Bass.

Paradis, F. E. (1981). Themes in the training of culturally effective psychotherapists. *Counselor Education and Supervision, 21,* 136–151.

Parham, T. A. (1989). Cycles of psychological Nigrescence. *The Counseling Psychologist, 17,* 187–226.

Parham, T. A. (1993). Reaction. White researchers conducting multi-cultural counseling research: Can their efforts be "Mo Betta"? *The Counseling Psychologist, 21,* 250–256.

Parham, T. A., & Helms, J. E. (1981). The influence of black students' racial identity attitudes on preferences for counselor's race. *Journal of Counseling Psychology, 28,* 250–257.

Parham, T. A., & Helms, J. E. (1985). Relation of racial identity attitudes to self-actualization and affective states of Black students. *Journal of Counseling Psychology, 32,* 431–440.

Parker, M., & McDavis, R. J. (1979). An awareness experience: Toward counseling minorities. *Counselor Education and Supervision, 18,* 312–327.

Parker, W. M. (1987). Reaction: Flexibility: A primer for multicultural counseling. *Counselor Education and Supervision, 26,* 176–180.

Parker, W. M. (1988). *Consciousness-raising: A primer for multicultural counseling.* Springfield, IL: Charles C Thomas.

Patterson, C. H. (1958). The place of values in counseling and psychotherapy. *Journal of Counseling Psychology, 5,* 216–223.

Peabody, D. (1985). *National characteristics.* Cambridge: Cambridge University Press.

Pedersen, P. B. (1977). The triad model of cross-cultural counselor training. *Personnel and Guidance Journal, 56,* 94–95, 98–100.

Pedersen, P. B. (1978). Four dimensions of cross-cultural skill in counselor training. *Personnel and Guidance Journal, 56,* 480–484.

Pedersen, P. (1988). *A handbook for developing multicultural awareness.* Alexandria, VA: AACD.

Pedersen, P. B. (1991). Concluding comments to the special issue. *Journal of Counseling and Development, 70,* 250.

Pedersen, P. B. (Ed.). (1991). Multi-culturalism as a fourth force in counseling [Special issue]. *Journal of Counseling and Development, 70*(1), 4–250.

Pedersen, P. (1993). Reaction. The multicultural dilemma of White cross-cultural researchers. *The Counseling Psychologist, 21,* 229–232.

Pedersen, P. B., Draguns, J. G., Lonner, W. J., & Trimble, J. E. (Eds.). (1981). *Counseling across cultures* (rev. ed.). Honolulu: University Press of Hawaii.

Pedersen, P. B., Draguns, J. G., Lonner, W. J., & Trimble, J. E. (1989). *Counseling across cultures* (3rd ed.). Honolulu: University Press of Hawaii.

Pedersen, P., & Ivey, A. (1994). *Culture-centered counseling and interviewing skills.* Westport, CT: Praeger.

Pedersen, P., Lonner, W. J., & Draguns, J. G. (Eds.). (1976). *Counseling across cultures.* Honolulu: University Press of Hawaii.

Phinney, J. S. (1989). Stages of ethnic identity development in minority group adolescents. *Journal of Early Adolescence, 9,* 34–49.

Phinney, J. S. (1990). Ethnic identity in adolescence and adults: Review of research. *Psychological Bulletin, 108,* 499–514.

Phinney, J. S. (1991). Ethnic identity and self-esteem: A review and integration. *Hispanic Journal of Behavioral Sciences, 13,* 193–208.

Phinney, J. S. (1992). The multigroup ethnic identity measure: A new scale for use with diverse groups. *Journal of Adolescent Research, 7,* 156–176.

Phinney, J. S. (1993). A three-stage model of ethnic identity in adolescence. In M. E. Bernal & G. P. Knight (Eds.), *Ethnic identity: Formation and transmission among Hispanics and other minorities* (pp. 61–79). Albany, NY: SUNY Press.

Phinney, J. S., & Alipuria, L. L. (1990). Ethnic identity in college students from four ethnic groups. *Journal of Adolescence, 13,* 171–183.

Phinney, J. S., & Chavira, V. (1992). Ethnic identity and self-esteem: An exploratory longitudinal study. *Journal of Adolescence, 15,* 271–281.

Phinney, J. S., Lochner, B. T., & Murphy, R. (1990). Ethnic identity development and psychological adjustment in adolescence. In A. R. Stiffman & L. E. Davis (Eds.), *Ethnic issues in adolescent mental health* (pp. 53–72). Newbury Park, CA: Sage.

Phinney, J. S., & Rotheram, M. J. (Eds.). (1987a). *Children's ethnic socialization: Pluralism and development.* Newbury Park, CA: Sage.

Phinney, J. S., & Rotheram, M. J. (1987b). Children's ethnic socialization: Themes and implications. In J. S. Phinney & M. J. Rotheram (Eds.), *Children's ethnic socialization: Pluralism and development* (pp. 274–292). Newbury Park, CA: Sage.

Phinney, J. S., & Tarver, S. (1988). Ethnic identity search and commitment in Black and White eighth graders. *Journal of Early Adolescence, 8,* 265–277.

Pinderhughes, E. (1989). *Understanding race, ethnicity, and power: The key to efficacy in clinical practice.* New York: Free Press.

Pine, G. J. (1972). Counseling minority groups: A review of the literature. *Counseling and Values, 17,* 35–44.

Ponce, F. Q., & Atkinson, D. R. (1989). Mexican-American acculturation, counselor ethnicity, counseling style, and perceived counselor credibility. *Journal of Counseling Psychology, 36,* 203–208.

Ponterotto, J. G. (1987). Counseling Mexican Americans: A multimodal approach. *Journal of Counseling and Development, 65,* 308–312.

Ponterotto, J. G. (1988). Racial consciousness development among white counselor trainees: A stage model. *Journal for Multicultural Counseling and Development, 16,* 146–156.

Ponterotto, J. G. (1989). Expanding directions for racial identity research. *The Counseling Psychologist, 17,* 264–272.

Ponterotto, J. G. (1993). Reaction. White racial identity and the counseling professional. *The Counseling Psychologist, 21,* 213–217.

Ponterotto, J. G., & Benesch, K. F. (1988). An organizational framework for understanding the role of culture in counseling. *Journal of Counseling and Development, 66,* 237–241.

Ponterotto, J. G., & Casas, J. M. (1987). In search of multicultural competence within counselor education programs. *Journal of Counseling and Development, 65,* 430–434.

Ponterotto, J. G., & Casas, J. M. (1991). *Handbook of racial/ethnic minority counseling research*. Springfield, IL: Charles C Thomas.

Ponterotto, J. G., & Pedersen, P. B. (1993). *Preventing prejudice: A guide for counselors and educators*. Newbury Park, CA: Sage.

Ponterotto, J. G., Rieger, B. P., Barrett, A., & Sparks, R. (1994). Assessing multicultural counseling competence: A review of instrumentation. *Journal of Counseling and Development, 72,* 316–322.

Pope-Davis, D. B., & Ottavi, T. M. (1992). The influence of White racial identity attitudes on racism among faculty members: A preliminary examination. *The Journal of College Student Development, 33,* 389–394.

Poston, W. S. C. (1990). The biracial identity development model: A needed addition. *Journal of Counseling and Development, 69,* 152–155.

Poston, W. S. C., Craine, M., & Atkinson, D. R. (1991). Counselor dissimilarity confrontation, client cultural mistrust, and willingness to self-disclose. *Journal of Multicultural Counseling and Development, 19,* 65–73.

Pratomthong, S. J., & Baker, S. (1983). Overcoming obstacles to the growth and development of guidance and counseling in Thailand. *The Personnel and Guidance Journal, 61,* 466–469.

Prediger, D. J. (1993). *Multicultural assessment standards: A compilation for counselors*. Alexandria, VA: The Association for Assessment in Counseling.

Priest, R. (1994). Minority supervisor and majority supervisee: Another perspective of clinical reality. *Counselor Education and Supervision, 34,* 152–158.

Putman, D. B., & Noor, M. C. (1993). *The Somalis: Their history and culture*. (CAI Refugee Fact Sheet #9). Washington, DC: The Refugee Service Center, Center for Applied Linguistics.

Quevodo-Garcia, E. L. (1987). Facilitating the development of Hispanic college students. In D. J. Wright (Ed.), *Responding to the needs of today's minority students* (pp. 49–63). San Francisco: Jossey-Bass.

Ramsey, P. G. (1987). Young children's thinking about ethnic differences. In J. S. Phinney & M. J. Rotheram (Eds.), *Children's ethnic socialization: Pluralism and Development* (pp. 56–72). Newbury Park, CA: Sage.

Reynolds, A. L., & Pope, R. L. (1991). The complexities of diversity: Exploring multiple oppressions. *Journal of Counseling and Development, 70,* 174–180.

Ridley, C. R. (1989). Racism in counseling as an adversive behavioral process. In P. B. Pedersen, J. G. Draguns, W. J. Lonner, & J. E. Trimble (Eds.), *Counseling across cultures* (3rd ed., pp. 55–77). Honolulu: University Press of Hawaii.

Ridley, C. R., Mendoza, D. W., & Kanitz, B. E. (1994). Multicultural training: Reexamination, operationalization, and integration. *The Counseling Psychologist, 22,* 227–289.

Riessman, F. (1962). *The culturally deprived child*. New York: Harper & Row.

Rios, P. (1994, February). *Racial/cultural diversity among Latinos: Implications for minority development models*. Paper presented at the Eleventh Annual Teachers College Winter Roundtable on Cross-Cultural Counseling and Psychotherapy, New York, NY.

Robertson, S. E., & Paterson, J. G. (1983). Characteristics of guidance and counseling services in Canada. *The Personnel and Guidance Journal, 61,* 490–493.

Rollin, S. A., & Witmer, M. (1992). Integrating guidance, counselling, and counsellor education in Botswana: A consultation model. *International Journal for the Advancement of Counselling, 15,* 113–122.

Root, M. P. P. (1990). Resolving "other" status: Identity development of biracial individuals. In L. Brown & M. P. P. Root (Eds.), *Complexity and diversity in feminist theory and therapy* (pp. 185–205). New York, Halworth.

Root, M. P. P. (Ed.). (1992). *Racially mixed people in America*. Newbury Park, CA: Sage.

Rosenthal, D. A. (1987). Ethnic identity development in adolescents. In J. S. Phinney & M. J. Rotheram (Eds.), *Children's ethnic socialization: Pluralism and development* (pp. 156–179). Newbury Park, CA: Sage.

Rosqueta-Rosales, L. (1989). *Counseling in perspective: Theory, process, and skills*. Quezon City, Philippines: The University of the Philippines Printery.

Ross, J. R. (1985). The cross-cultural context: Some issues for counsellors in New Zealand. *New Zealand Counselling and Guidance Association Journal, 7*(1), 39–49.

Rotheram, M. J., & Phinney, J. S. (1987a). Introduction: Definitions and perspectives in the study of children's ethnic socialization. In J. S. Phinney & M. J. Rotheram (Eds.), *Children's ethnic socialization: Pluralism and development* (pp. 10–28). Newbury Park, CA: Sage.

Rotheram, M. J., & Phinney, J. S. (1987b). Ethnic behavior patterns as an aspect of identity. In J. S. Phinney & M. J. Rotheram (Eds.), *Children's ethnic socialization: Pluralism and development* (pp. 201–218). Newbury Park, CA: Sage.

Rotter, J. B. (1966). Generalized expectancies for internal versus external control of reinforcement. *Psychological monographs: General and applied, 80*(1), 1–28.

Rowe, W., Bennett, S. K., & Atkinson, D. R. (1994). White racial identity models: A critique and alternative proposal. *The Counseling Psychologist, 22*, 129–146.

Ruiz, A. S. (1984). Cross-cultural group counseling and the use of the sentence completion method. *Journal for Specialists in Group Work, 9*, 131–136.

Ruiz, A. S. (1990). Ethnic identity: Crisis and resolution. *Journal of Multicultural Counseling and Development, 18*, 29–40.

Saba, G. W., Karrer, B. M., & Hardy, K. V. (Eds.). (1989). Minorities and family therapy [Special issue]. *Journal of Psychotherapy and The Family, 6*(1/2).

Sabnani, H. B., & Ponterotto, J. G. (1992). Racial/ethnic minority-specific instrumentation in counseling research: A review, critique, and recommendations. *Measurement and Evaluation in Counseling and Development, 24*, 161–187.

Sabnani, H. B., Ponterotto, J. G., & Borodovsky, L. G. (1991). White racial identity development and cross-cultural counselor training: A stage model. *The Counseling Psychologist, 19*, 76–102.

Saleh, M. A. (1989). The cultural milieu of counseling. *International Journal for the Advancement of Counselling, 12*, 3–11.

Schaefer, R. T. (1990). *Racial and ethnic groups* (4th ed.). Glenview, IL: Scott Foresman/ Little, Brown.

Schechtman, Z. (1993). School adjustment and small-group therapy: An Israeli study. *Journal of Counseling and Development, 72*, 77–81.

Schinke, S. P., Botvin, G. J., Trimble, J. E., Orlandi, M. O., Gilchrist, L. D., & Locklear, V. S. (1988). Preventing substance abuse among American Indian adolescents: A bicultural competence skills approach. *Journal of Counseling Psychology, 35*, 87–90.

Sciarra, D. T., & Ponterotto, J. G. (1991). Counseling the Hispanic bilingual family: Challenges to the therapeutic process. *Psychotherapy, 28*, 473–479.

Shon, S. P., & Davis, Y. J. (1982). Asian families. In M. McGoldrick, J. K. Pearce, & J. Giordana (Eds.), *Ethnicity and family therapy* (pp. 208–228). New York: Guilford Press.

Smith, E. J. (1991). Ethnic identity development: Toward the development of a theory within the context of majority/minority status. *Journal of Counseling and Development, 70,* 181–188.

Smith, E. M. J. (1985). Ethnic minorities: Life stress, social support, and mental health issues. *The Counseling Psychologist, 13,* 537–579.

Smith, E. M. J. (1989). Black racial identity development: Issues and concerns. *The Counseling Psychologist, 17,* 277–288.

Smith, L. (1961). *Killers of the dream.* New York: Norton.

Soliman, A. (1981). The counselor as an agent of change: Some implications for developing countries. *International Journal for the Advancement of Counselling, 4,* 215–225.

Soliman, A. M. (1984, Spring). Why is counseling developing slowly in developing countries? *Internationally Speaking,* p. 8.

Soliman, A. M. (1986). The counseling needs of youth in the Arab countries. *International Journal for the Advancement of Counselling, 9,* 61–72.

Soliman, A. M. (1987). Status, rationale and development of counseling in the Arab countries: View of participants in a counseling conference. *International Journal for the Advancement of Counselling, 10,* 131–141.

Soliman, A. M. (1991). The role of counseling in developing countries. *International Journal for the Advancement of Counselling, 14,* 3–14.

Soliman, A. M. (1993). Choice of helpers, types of problems and sex of helpers of college students. *International Journal for the Advancement of Counselling, 16,* 67–79.

Soliman, A. M. (1994, April). *Helpers and characteristics of the helping relationship as perceived by college students in the United Arab Emirates.* Paper presented at the 1994 American Counseling Association Convention, Minneapolis, MN.

Steele, S. (1988). On being Black and middle class. *Commentary, 85*(1), 42–47.

Steele, S. (1990). *The content of our character: A new vision of race in America.* New York: Harper Perennial.

Stewart, E. C. (1972). *American cultural patterns: A cross-cultural perspective.* Yarmouth, ME: Intercultural Press.

Stewart, E. C., & Bennett, M. J. (1991). *American cultural patterns: A cross-cultural perspective* (rev. ed.). Yarmouth, ME: Intercultural Press.

Stewart, L. H. (1983). On borrowing guidance theory and practice: Some observations of an American participant in the British guidance movement. *Personnel and Guidance Journal, 61,* 507–510.

Stoltenberg, C. (1981). Approaching supervision from a developmental perspective: The counselor complexity model. *Journal of Counseling Psychology, 28,* 59–65.

Stoltenberg, C. D., & Delworth, U. (1987). *Developmental supervision: A training model for counselors and psychotherapists.* San Francisco: Jossey-Bass.

Stoltenberg, C. D., & Delworth, U. (1988). Developmental models of supervision: It is development—Response to Holloway. *Professional Psychology: Research and Practice, 19,* 134–137.

Sue, D. W. (1978a). Eliminating cultural oppression in counseling: Toward a general theory. *Journal of Counseling Psychology, 25,* 419–428.

Sue, D. W. (1978b). World views and counseling. *Personnel and Guidance Journal, 56,* 458–462.

Sue, D. W. (1981). *Counseling the culturally different.* New York: Wiley.

Sue, D. W. (1985, June). The counselor of tomorrow: A multicultural perspective. *ACES Newsletter,* pp. 11–12.

Sue, D. W. (1992). Culture-specific strategies in counseling: A conceptual framework. *Professional Psychology, 21,* 424–433.

Sue, D. W. (1993). Reaction. Confronting ourselves: The White and racial/ethnic-minority researcher. *The Counseling Psychologist, 21,* 244–249.

Sue, D. W., Arredondo, P., & McDavis, R. J. (1992a). Multicultural counseling competencies and standards: A call to the profession. *Journal of Counseling and Development, 70,* 477–486.

Sue, D. W., Arredondo, P., & McDavis, R. J. (1992b). Multicultural counseling competencies and standards: A call to the profession. *Journal of Multicultural Counseling and Development, 20,* 64–88.

Sue, D. W., Bernier, J. E., Durran, A., Feinberg, L., Pedersen, P., Smith, E. J., & Vasquez-Nuttal, E. (1982). Position paper: Cross-cultural counseling competencies. *The Counseling Psychologist, 10,* 45–52.

Sue, D. W., & Sue, D. (1990). *Counseling the culturally different: Theory and practice* (2nd ed.). New York: Wiley.

Sue, S., Akutsu, P. D., & Higashi, C. (1985). Training issues in conducting therapy with ethnic-minority-group clients. In P. Pedersen (Ed.), *Handbook of cross-cultural counseling and therapy* (pp. 275–280). Westport, CT: Greenwood.

Sue, S., & Zane, N. (1987). The role of culture and cultural techniques in psychotherapy: A critique and reformulation. *American Psychologist, 42*(1), 37–45.

Suinn, R. M., Rickard-Figueroa, K., Lew, S., & Vigil, P. (1987). The Suinn-Lew Asian Self-Identity Acculturation Scale: An initial report. *Educational and Psychological Measurement, 47,* 401–417.

Super, D. E. (1983). Synthesis: Or is it distillation? *Personnel and Guidance Journal, 61,* 511–514.

Szapocznik, J., Kurtines, W. M., & Fernandez, T. (1980). Bicultural involvement and adjustment in Hispanic-American youths. *International Journal of Intercultural Relations, 4,* 353–365.

Tafoya, T. (1989). Circles and cedar: Native Americans and family therapy. *Journal of Psychotherapy and the Family, 6*(1/2), 71–98.

Tainsri, R., & Axelson, J. A. (1990). Group sensitivity training with Thai workers and managers as a process to promote inter- and intrapersonal relations, and work performance. *International Journal for the Advancement of Counseling, 13,* 219–226.

Tajfel, H. (1970). Experiments in intergroup discrimination. *Scientific American, 223*(5), 96–102.

Tajfel, H. (Ed.). (1982). *Social identity and intergroup relations.* New York: Cambridge University Press.

Tan, A. (1989). *The joy luck club.* New York: Random House.

Tatum, B. D. (1992). Talking about race, learning about racism: The application of racial identity development theory in the classroom. *Harvard Educational Review, 62*(1), 1–24.

Taub, D. J., & McEwen, M. K. (1992). The relationship of racial identity attitudes to autonomy and mature inter-personal relationships in Black and White undergraduate women. *Journal of College Student Development, 33,* 439–446.

Teaching Tolerance. (1993, Spring). Montgomery, AL: Southern Poverty Law Center.

Teaching Tolerance. (1993, Fall). Montgomery, AL: Southern Poverty Law Center.

Teaching Tolerance. (1994, Spring). Montgomery, AL: Southern Poverty Law Center.

Thernstrom, S. (Ed.). (1980). *Harvard encyclopedia of American ethnic groups.* Cambridge, MA: Belknap Press of Harvard University.

Thompson, C. L., & Rudolph, L. B. (1992). *Counseling children* (3rd ed.). Pacific Grove, CA: Brooks/Cole.

Tokar, D. M., & Swanson, J. L. (1991). An investigation of the validity of Helm's (1984) model of White racial identity development. *Journal of Counseling Psychology, 38,* 296–301.

Torrey, E. F. (1972a). *The mind game: Witchdoctors and psychiatrists.* New York: Emerson Hall.

Torrey, E. F. (1972b). What western psychotherapists can learn from witchdoctors. *American Journal of Orthopsychiatry, 42*(1), 69–76.

Triandis, H. (1985). Some major dimensions in cultural variation in client populations. In P. Pedersen (Ed.), *Handbook of cross-cultural counseling and therapy* (pp. 21–28). Westport, CT: Greenwood Press.

U.S. Bureau of the Census. (1992). *Statistical abstract of the United States. The national data book* (112th ed.). Washington, DC: Bureau of the Census.

Unnithan, G. J. (1986). Counselling services in Indian educational institutions: Needs and challenges. *International Journal for the Advancement of Counselling, 9,* 197–203.

Utrecht University Department of Counselling Studies. (1992). *The future needs school counselling.* Department of Counselling Studies, Faculty of Social Sciences, Utrecht University, The Netherlands.

Vacc, N. A., & Wittmer, J. P. (1980). *Let me be me: Special populations and the helping professional.* Muncie, IN: Accelerated Development.

Vaughan, G. M. (1987). A social psychological model of ethnic identity development. In J. S. Phinney & M. J. Rotheram (Eds.), *Children's ethnic socialization: Pluralism and development* (pp. 73–91). Newbury Park, CA: Sage.

Vontress, C. E. (1966a). Counseling and the culturally different adolescent: A school community approach. In J. C. Gowan & G. D. Demos (Eds.), *The disadvantaged and potential dropout* (pp. 357–366). Springfield, IL: Charles C Thomas.

Vontress, C. E. (1966b). The Negro personality reconsidered. *Journal of Negro Education, 35,* 210–217.

Vontress, C. E. (1967). Counseling Negro adolescents. *The School Counselor, 15,* 86–91.

Vontress, C. E. (1970). Counseling blacks. *Personnel and Guidance Journal, 48,* 713–719.

Vontress, C. E. (1971a). *Counseling Negroes.* Boston: Houghton Mifflin.

Vontress, C. E. (1971b). Racial differences: Impediments to rapport. *Journal of Counseling Psychology, 18,* 7–13.

Vontress, C. E. (1985). Existentialism as a cross-cultural counseling modality. In P. Pedersen (Ed.), *Handbook of cross-cultural counseling and therapy* (pp. 207–212). Westport, CT: Greenwood.

Vontress, C. E. (1988). An existential approach to cross-cultural counseling. *Journal of Multicultural Counseling and Development, 16,* 73–83.

Vontress, C. E. (1991). Traditional healing in Africa: Implications for cross-cultural counseling. *Journal of Counseling and Development, 70,* 242–249.

Waldegrave, C., & Tapping, C. (1990, No. 1). Just therapy. *Dulwich Centre Newsletter,* pp. 6–46.

Walz, G. R., & Benjamin, L. (1978). *Transcultural counseling: Needs, programs and techniques.* New York: Human Sciences Press.

Warren, P. (1966). Guidelines for the future: An educational approach for the culturally disadvantaged. *Journal of Negro Education, 35,* 282–286.

Waugh, D. (1991, September 2). Facts about group names: Ethnic groups change names with the times. *San Francisco Examiner,* p. A6.

Webster, A. C., & Hermansson, G. L. (1983). Guidance and counseling in New Zealand. *The Personnel and Guidance Journal, 61,* 472–476.

Weeks, W. H., Pedersen, P. B., & Brislin, R. W. (Eds.). (1977). *A manual of structured experiences for cross-cultural learning.* Yarmouth, ME: Intercultural Press.

Weeks, W. H., Pedersen, P. B., & Brislin, R. W. (Eds.). (1982). *A manual of structured experiences for cross-cultural learning.* Yarmouth, ME: SIETAR.

Wehrly, B. (1990). Culture—The silent partner worksheet. In M. Woodside & T. McClam, Instructor's manual for *An introduction of human services* (pp. 46–47). Pacific Grove, CA: Brooks/Cole.

Wehrly, B. (1991). Preparing multicultural counselors. *Counseling and Human Development, 24*(3), 1–24.

Wehrly, B., & Deen, N. (1983). Counseling and guidance issues from a worldwide perspective: An introduction. *Personnel and Guidance Journal, 61,* 452.

Wehrly, B., & Deen, N. (Eds.). (1983). International guidance and counseling [Special issue]. *The Personnel and Guidance Journal, 61*(8).

Wehrly, B., & Watson-Gegeo, K. (1985). Ethnographic methodologies as applied to the study of cross-cultural counseling. In P. Pedersen (Ed.), *Handbook of cross-cultural counseling and therapy* (pp. 65–71). Westport, CT: Greenwood.

Weinreich, P. (1986). The operationalisation of identity theory in racial and ethnic relations. In J. Rex & D. Mason (Eds.), *Theories of race and ethnic relations* (pp. 299–320). New York: Cambridge University Press.

West, C. (1993). *Race matters.* Boston: Beacon Press.

Westwood, M. J. (1986). *Returning home: A program for persons assisting international students with the re-entry process.* Canadian Bureau for International Education (CBIE), 26 pages. Published in French also.

Westwood, M. J. (1988). *Peering up: A manual for developing a peer program to assist the adjustment of the international student.* Canadian Bureau for International Education (CBIE), Ottawa, 25 pages. Published in French also.

Westwood, M. J., & Barker, M. (1990). Academic achievement and social adaption among international students: A comparison groups study of the peer-pairing program. *International Journal of Intercultural Relations, 14,* 251–263.

Westwood, M. J., & Ishiyama, I. (1990). The communication process as a critical intervention for client change in cross-cultural counseling. *Journal of Multicultural Counseling and Development, 18,* 163–171.

Westwood, M. J., & Ishiyama, F. I. (1991). Challenges in counseling immigrant clients: Understanding intercultural barriers to career adjustment. *Journal of Employment Counseling, 28,* 130–143.

Wilkinson, C. B. (Ed.). (1986). *Ethnic psychiatry.* New York: Plenum.

Wohl, J. (1982). Eclecticism and Asian counseling: Critique and application. *International Journal for the Advancement of Counselling, 5,* 215–222.

Wolfgang, A. (1985). The function and importance of nonverbal behavior in intercultural counseling. In P. Pedersen (Ed.), *Handbook of cross-cultural counseling and therapy* (pp. 99–105). Westport, CT: Greenwood Press.

Wrenn, C. G. (1962). The culturally encapsulated counselor. *Harvard Educational Review, 32,* 444–449.

Yusuf, O. A. (1990, June). *Counseling psychology in Ethiopia—A discipline in search of identity.* Paper presented at the International Round Table for the Advancement of Counseling, Helsinki, Finland.

Zich, A., & Yamashita, M. S. (1986). Japanese Americans: Home at last. *National Geographic, 169,* pp. 512–539.

NAME INDEX

Deutsch, M., 27, 109
DeWeerdt, P., 93
Diamond, N., 146
Do, C. L., 91
Dodson, Jualyne, 4
Dow, J., 146
Draguns, J. G., 29–30, 31, 80, 118, 142, 172, 173, 176
Dumont, F., 96
Durie, M., 89
Durr, V. F., 21, 128
Durran, A., 20

Eddy, W., 147
Erikson, E. H., 70–71, 72
Esquivel, G. B., 207, 211
Evans, D. R., 137
Everts, J. F., 89

Falicov, C. J., 17, 18, 213
Falsey, J., 128
Farney, D., 219
Faubert, M., 212
Feinberg, L., 20
Ferguson, M., 22
Fernandez, T., 211
Ford, D. Y., 55, 212
Ford-Harris, D. Y., 212
Friedrich, P., 146
Fukuyama, M. A., 44, 177, 222

Garcia-Preto, N., 17
Gibbs, J. T., 48, 173–176, 187, 210
Gim, R. H., 188
Giordano, J., 31, 146
Gluckstern, N., 137
Gonsalves, J., 44
Gothard, W. P., 83
Grant, S. K., 46, 188, 189, 208–210, 213, 215, 217
Green, J. W., 145, 168, 169–170
Greene, B., 191, 226
Greenwood, A., 98
Guichard, J., 91
Gutierrez, F. J., 40, 220

Halfe, L., 99
Hall, E. T., 25, 135
Hall, L. E., 177
Halpern, E., 95
Ham, M. A., 213
Hardiman, R., 59, 66, 165, 192
Hardy, E., 42, 227

Hardy, K. V., 213
Harper, F. D., 29, 45, 109, 148
Harris, A., 62, 70, 225
Harris, J. J., 55, 212
Harris, L. C., 188
Hayes, D. H., 210
Hays, T. E., 146
Hearn, M. T., 137
Heller, K., 91–92
Helms, J. E., 5, 27, 34, 49, 52, 54–55, 58, 59–60, 72, 110, 114, 115, 117, 138, 163, 165, 167, 191, 192, 193, 195, 197–198, 199, 200, 213
Herbert, F., 11
Hermansson, G. L., 80, 89–90
Herr, E. L., 24
Herskovits, M. J., 4, 8
Hickson, J., 84
Higashi, C., 37, 206
Hills, H. I., 41, 142, 143, 185
Hines, P. M., 17
Ho, M. K., 213
Hoare, C. H., 3, 16, 19, 22, 110, 226
Hocevar, D., 68–69
Hockings, P., 146
Hodgkinson, H. L., 34
Hollis, J. W., 41
Hong, G. K., 213
Hood, A. B., 32
Hoopes, D. S., 146
Hopson, D., 68
Hopson, D. P., 68

Ibrahim, F. A., 37, 44, 128, 129, 145
Ingersoll, J., 133
Ishiyama, F. I., 45, 96, 97, 208
Israelashvili, M., 94–95
Ivey, A. E., 3, 22, 29, 30, 32, 33, 34, 40, 45–46, 47, 50, 58, 79, 84, 97, 114, 118, 134, 135, 137, 163, 195, 235
Ivey, M. B., 33, 46, 47, 114, 118, 137
Iwamsasa, G., 34

Jackson, B. L., 46, 62, 70, 225
Jackson, D. N., 210
Jacobsen, F. M., 157, 190, 191
Jasso, R., 188
Jaya, A., 213
Jiang, S., 86
Johannes, W., 146
Johnson, S. D., 4, 6, 18, 147, 152
Jones, J. M., 134, 168
Joy, S., 226, 227

Kahn, K. B., 47, 48, 103, 104–105, 106, 110, 114, 115, 117, 121, 124, 134, 139, 140, 160, 161, 183, 184, 203, 204, 217
Kakar, S., 16
Kanitz, B. E., 103, 109, 221
Kaplan, R. B., 8, 9
Karrer, B. M., 213
Katz, J. H., 58, 125, 126–127, 163, 195, 235
Katz, P. A., 66, 68
Katz, R., 82
Keitel, M. A., 207, 211
Kelly, E. W., 11
Kelly, G. A., 26
Kemper, R. V., 146
Kennedy, S., 34
Kerwin, C., 62, 70, 225
Khan, J. A., 80, 88
Khapklomsong, P., 87
Kim, J., 49, 55–57, 66, 72, 73, 114, 115, 163, 164–165, 213
Kim, Y. M., 81
King, M. L., Jr., 53
Kingston, H., 11
Kinzie, J. D., 11, 18
Kiselica, M. S., 203
Kleinman, A., 152, 156, 157, 173, 190, 207
Kluckhohn, C., 25, 44, 128
Kluckhohn, F., 25, 29, 44, 128, 129, 134, 189, 190
Knight, G. P., 74
Kochman, T., 17, 135
Kohout, J., 41
Kottler, J., 42
Kreigler, S., 84
Kurtines, W. M., 211

LaFromboise, T. D., 211
Lago, C., 93–94
Lee, C. C., 82, 111, 118, 142, 191, 208
Lee, J. D., 31, 145, 219
Leong, F. T. L., 185, 222
Le Vine, P., 45, 87–88
Levinson, D., 146
Lew, S., 188
Littrell, J. M., 5, 6, 19, 32
Liu, Y. C., 210
Livingstone, B. J., 84
Lloyd, A., 31–32
Lochner, B. T., 49, 72, 195–196, 211, 225
Locke, D. C., 44, 79, 111, 118, 191, 212
Loden, M., 4

Sue, D. W., 10, 17, 20, 21, 24, 27, 30, 31,
    34, 35, 37, 38, 39, 43, 44, 47, 49, 50,
    51, 52, 72, 103, 109, 110, 111, 114,
    115, 118, 128, 129, 133, 134, 135,
    137, 142, 143, 144, 145, 148, 157,
    158, 163–164, 168, 171, 182, 186,
    187, 191, 192, 193–194, 195, 196,
    197, 198, 199, 200, 207, 208, 213,
    220, 229, 233
Sue, L., 235
Sue, S., 6, 11, 20, 37, 38, 172, 206
Suinn, R. M., 188
Super, D. E., 23, 40
Swanson, J. L., 55
Szapocznik, J., 211, 212

Tafoya, T., 214
Tainsri, R., 87
Tajfel, H., 72
Tan, A., 19, 121
Tapaninen, A., 90
Tapping, C., 90
Tarver, S., 72, 196, 211, 225
Tatum, B. D., 116, 117, 140
Taub, D. J., 55
Thernstrom, S., 146, 148
Thompson, C. E., 46, 188, 189, 208–210,
    213, 215, 217
Thompson, C. L., 66

Thorne, B., 93–94
Tjitendero, S., 146
Tokar, D. M., 55
Torrey, E. F., 28–29, 119–120, 176
Triandis, H., 9, 18, 19, 20
Trimble, J. E., 31, 118

Uhlemann, M. R., 137
Unnithan, G., 84–85
U. S. Bureau of the Census, 36

Vacc, N. A., 31
Valickas, G., 93
Vasquez, J. T., 177
Vasquez-Nuttall, E., 20
Vaughan, G. M., 67
Ventura, P., 146
Vigil, P., 188
Vontress, C. E., 27, 45, 82

Wagner, N. S., 185, 222
Waldegrave, C., 90
Walz, G. R., 31
Wantz, R. A., 41
Warren, P., 27, 109
Watson-Gegeo, K., 223
Waugh, D., 5, 8, 119
Webster, A. C., 80, 90

Weeks, W. H., 129, 133, 146, 153, 235
Wehrly, B., 31, 103, 110, 111, 116, 117,
    149, 151, 156, 172, 208, 222, 223,
    227, 236
Weinreich, P., 69
Wellman, 169
West, C., 171
Westwood, M. J., 96, 97–98, 115, 117, 208
Whiteley, S., 188
Wicherski, M., 41
Wiggins, F., 169
Wilkinson, C. B., 148
Witmer, M., 83
Wittmer, J. P., 31
Wohl, J., 40
Wolfgang, A., 135
Woodside, M., 151
Wrenn, C. G., 26, 29
Wurzel, J. S., 9

Yamashita, M. S., 164
Yurich, J. M., 226
Yusuf, O. A., 82, 83

Zane, N., 6, 11, 20, 172
Zanni-Telipoulos, K., 92
Zhang, W., 135, 136–137
Zich, A., 164

SUBJECT INDEX

AACD (American Association for Counseling and Development), 37–38
Abandonment of racism phase, 59–60
Aboriginal people, 86, 88
Abstractive-pragmatic information processing, 9–10
ACA. *See* American Counseling Association
Acceptance stage, 59
Acculturation, client, 188–189, 208, 214, 215
Acculturation Rating Scale for Mexican Americans (ARSMA), 188
Acculturation rating scales, 188
ACES (Association for Counselor Educators and Supervisors), 41
Achieved credibility, 172
Achieved ethnic identity stage, 73, 74
Achieved identity status, 71
Action-orientation, 16–17
Adlerian psychology, 45
Adolescents, racial and ethnic identity development in, 69–75, 166, 225
Adults, racial and ethnic identity development in, 75–78
Adviser role, 208, 209
Advocate role, 208, 209
Advocates for Multicultural Counseling, 221
Africa, multicultural counseling in, 82–84
African Americans. *See also* People of color
acculturation assessment of, 188
Civil Rights movement and, 27
cultural and ethnic literature on, 238
defined, 7
developmental programs for, 212
ethnic heritage of, 145
racial and ethnic identity development models for, 52–55, 74, 164, 191–200
African-centered perspective, 212

Afrocentric, 52, 53, 54
Agnosticism, 15
AMCD. *See* Association for Multicultural Counseling and Development
American Association for Counseling and Development (AACD), 37–38
American Counseling Association (ACA), 37–39, 41, 103, 142, 220–221, 222
American Cultural Patterns: A Cross Cultural Perspective (Stewart), 29
American Indians. *See* Native Americans
American Personnel and Guidance Association (APGA), 35, 37
American Psychological Association (APA), 33–34, 35, 37–39, 142–143, 220–222
American Psychologist, 34
"American" vs. "Contrast-American" assumptions and values, 129, 130–133
AMHCA Journal, 31
Ancestral heritage exercise, 145–146
Anglo, 7
Animism, 15
Anthropologists, 25
Antiracism stage, 62
APA. *See* American Psychological Association
Apartheid, 84
APGA (American Personnel and Guidance Association), 35, 37
Appraisal stage, 174
Aquarian Conspiracy, The (Ferguson), 22
Arab countries, multicultural counseling in, 95
ARSMA (Acculturation Rating Scale for Mexican Americans), 188
Ascribed credibility, 172
Ascribed role or status, 16, 130
Ascription, 131
Asia, multicultural counseling in, 84–87

Asian Americans. *See also* People of color
acculturation assessment of, 188
cultural and ethnic literature on, 238
defined, 7
family therapy with, 213–214
racial and ethnic identity development model for, 55–57, 164–165
Assessment, ethnocultural, 157, 188
Assimilation, cultural, 24–25
Association for Assessment in Counseling, 40
Association for Counselor Educators and Supervisors (ACES), 41
Association for Multicultural Counseling and Development (AMCD), 38, 43, 103, 186–187
Associative information processing, 9–10
Assumptions, cultural, 130–133, 146–147
Atheism, 15
Australia, multicultural counseling in, 80, 87–89
Autonomy stage, 60, 200
Awakening to social political consciousness stage, 56–57

Balance sheet justice, 169
Banks model for multiethnic education, 226
Basic Attending Skills and Basic Influencing Skills video (Ivey, Gluckstern, & Ivey), 137
Behavior
cross-cultural communication and, 135, 136–137
cultural context and, 18–21
impact of culture on, 8–18, 151
Belief systems
counselor awareness of, 231–232
cultural impact on, 11, 12–15
Biases, cultural. *See* Cultural biases

Bibliography, 238–239
Bibliotherapy, 125, 212
Biculturalism, 70, 196, 212
Bilingual counselors, 207–208, 214
Biracial, 62, 70, 166, 215, 225, 238
Black Americans. *See* African Americans
Black and White Racial Identity: Theory,
    Research, and Practice (Helms), 55
Black-Hispanic families, 214–215
Black Racial Identity Attitude Scale
    (RIAS-B), 54–55
Black World, 52
Bless Me, Ultima (Anaya), 121
Blind spot, cultural, 190
Books, ethnic/cultural, 121, 123–124,
    238–239
Buddhism, 13
Bulimia nervosa, 45

CACREP. *See* Council for Accreditation of
    Counseling and Related Educational
    Programs
Canada, multicultural counseling in, 95–99
Canadian Guidance and Counselling
    Association (CGCA), 98–99, 222
Canadian Native First Nation, 96, 98–99
Career counseling, 83
Career guide role, 215, 216
Carney and Kahn's developmental model,
    47, 104–105, 106
"Categories of Public and Private Self-
    Disclosure" exercise, 121, 122–123
Caucasians. *See* Whites
Causal stage, 57
Census, U.S. ethnic, 36
CGCA (Canadian Guidance and
    Counselling Association), 98–99, 222
Change agent role, 208, 209, 210
Chicanos. *See* Latinos
Childhood and Society (Erikson), 70
Children, racial and ethnic identity
    development in, 66–69
Children's Ethnic Socialization (Phinney &
    Rotheram), 65
Christensen's developmental model, 48
Christianity, 12
Civil Rights movement, 27, 168
Clarification Group (C Group), 147
Classroom climate (multicultural counselor
    preparation)
    stage one, 115–117
    stage two, 140–141
    stage three, 161–162

stage four, 183–184
    stage five, 204–205
Classroom panels, 149–152
Cognitive processes, 8–11
Cognitive stage, 58
Collectivist cultures, 19–20
Colonization, 191
Color blindness, 160–161, 169
Color consciousness, 169
Comas-Diaz & Jacobsen model for
    ethnocultural assessment,157, 190
Commitment stage, 175
Communication skills
    bicultural group training and, 212
    cross-cultural, 134–137, 157–158
Competencies, multicultural, 35, 38–39,
    231–233
Conflict resolution, 77–78
Conflict stage, 62, 140, 234
Conformity stage, 114
Confucianism, 13
Consequence stage, 58
Consolidated awareness stage, 182
Consultant role, 208, 210
Contact stage, 59, 195
Context, culture as, 18–21
Contextual identification, 19
"Contrast-American" vs. "American"
    assumptions and values, 129, 130–133
"Cookbook" approaches, 172
Council for Accreditation of Counseling and
    Related Educational Programs
    (CACREP), 38–39, 97, 106
Counseling. *See also* Multicultural
    counseling; Psychotherapy
    cultural biases in, 21–22, 118–119,
        126–127, 231–233
    goals of, 189–190
    historical origins of, 23–25
    international acceptance of, 79–81
    multiculturalism and, 32–33
    racism in, 167–171
    role of culture in, 6, 29–30, 119–120
    values and beliefs in, 127
Counseling and Psychotherapy: A
    Multicultural Perspective (Ivey, Ivey, &
    Simek-Morgan), 33
Counseling and Values, 28
Counseling in Perspective—Theory, Process
    and Skills (Rosqueta-Rosales), 86
Counseling practicum. *See also* Internship
    experience applying models of racial
    and ethnic identity
    development in, 191–200

developing repertoire of interventions in,
    187–191
    goals for, 184–185
    process guidelines for, 183–184
    student characteristics and, 181–182
    student self-understanding and, 186–187
    student's evaluation of (form), 242–243
    supervision of, 185–186
    supervisor's evaluation of (form), 240–241
Counseling Psychologist, The, 31, 34, 35
Counseling Racial Simulators, 167
Counseling the Culturally Different (Sue &
    Sue), 20
Counselor Education and Supervision, 31,
    222
Counselor education programs. *See also*
    Multicultural counselor preparation
    multicultural training in, 41–42, 103,
        105–107
Counselor Preparation, 1990–1992:
    Programs, Personnel, Trends (Hollis &
    Wantz), 41
Counselor role, 208, 209, 210–215
Counselors. *See* Multicultural counselors
Counselor self-awareness, 48
Covert racism, 169
Credibility, counselor, 172–173
Crisis intervenor role, 208, 215, 216
Cross-cultural communications
    role-play exercises in, 136–137, 157–158
    skill development training and, 134–137
    stereotyping and, 153
Cross-cultural counseling. *See* Multicultural
    counseling
Cross-Cultural Inventory, 224
Cross model of Black identity development,
    52–54, 74, 164
Cross-national sharing, 222, 228
Cubical models
    described, 46–47
    multicultural counseling variables and,
        177, 178
Cultural ambivalence, 169
Cultural assimilation, 24–25
Cultural assumptions and values summary,
    130–133, 146
"Cultural Awareness: Ethnicity and Identity"
    exercise, 145–146
"Cultural Awareness and Racism" exercise,
    169–171
Cultural baggage, 147
Cultural biases
    in counseling literature, 118–119,
        126–127

counselor awareness of, 231–233
in psychotherapy, 21–22, 118–119, 126–127
Cultural blind spot, 190
Cultural countertransference, 169
Cultural diversity
in Africa, 82–84
in Asia, 84–87
in Australia, 87–89
in Canada, 95–99
defined, 4
in Europe, 90–94
in Mexico, 99
in the Middle East, 94–95
in New Zealand, 89–90
race and ethnicity and, 5–6, 119
Cultural encapsulation, 26, 143
Cultural heritage, 144–147
Cultural novels, 121, 123–125, 238–239
Cultural pluralism, 4, 81–82
Cultural racism, 168
Cultural transference, 169
Culture
behavioral impact of, 8–18, 151
as context of human behavior, 18–21
defining, 4, 119
models for studying, 128–134
personality disorders and, 206
role of, in counseling, 6, 29–30, 119–120
Culture-bound syndromes, 206–207
Culture shock, 179, 211
"Culture—The Silent Partner Worksheet," 149–150, 151, 156, 189
Culturgrams, 146

Davis, Jesse B., 23
Decision-making processes, 16–17
Deficit emphasis/approach, 27, 109
Defining a nonracist white identity phase, 59–60
Demographics, multicultural, 34–35
Denial, 160–161
Developmental, defining, 225
Developmental counseling roles, 208–215, 216
Developmental facilitator role, 215, 216
Developmental model (multicultural counselor preparation). *See also specific stages of multicultural counselor preparation*
assumptions of, 109–111
goals of, 107–109
limitations of, 111–112
summary of (table), 104–105

Diagnostic and Statistical Manual of Mental Disorders (DSM-III- R/DSM-IV), 45, 206–207
Diagnostic intakes, 206–207
Diffuse subtype, 73, 194
Disintegration stage, 59–60
Diversity training, 4, 119
Dolls, ethnic, 67, 68
DSM-III-R/DSM-IV. See *Diagnostic and Statistical Manual of Mental Disorders*

Educational environment, multicultural counseling in, 215, 216
Education programs. *See also* Multicultural counselor preparation in multicultural counseling, 41–42, 103, 105–107
EEC (European Economic Community), 92
Ego identity. *See also* Racial and ethnic identity
adolescent development of, 70–71
Emic approach, 19, 44, 111
Encounter stage, 53
Encyclopedia of World Cultures, 146, 148
Engagement stage, 175
England. *See* United Kingdom
Environments for goal achievement (multiculturalcounselor preparation)
stage one, 118–137
stage two, 142–158
stage three, 162–179
stage four, 185–200
stage five, 205–217
Erikson's model of ethnic identity development, 70–71
Eskimo Americans. *See* Native Americans
Ethical guidelines, for multicultural counseling, 35, 37–39
Ethnic attitudes, 68–69
Ethnic awareness process
in children, 66–67
in counselor training programs, 144–147
Ethnic awareness stage, 56
Ethnic behaviors, 69
Ethnic culture, 5, 119
Ethnic groups. *See* Racial and ethnic groups
Ethnic heritage, 119, 144–147
Ethnic identity. *See* Racial and ethnic identity
Ethnic identity achievement stage, 199
Ethnic identity development models. *See* Racial and ethnic identity development models
Ethnic identity search/moratorium stage, 73, 74, 195–196

Ethnicity, defining, 119
Ethnic novels, 121, 123–125, 238–239
Ethnic self-identification process, 67–68, 77
Ethnocentricity, 28–29
Ethnocultural assessment model, 157, 190
Ethnocultural heritage, 144–147
Ethnocultural identification, 157, 190
Etic approach, 19, 44, 111
Etiology, client, 189, 204–205
Europe, multicultural counseling in, 90–94
European American, defined, 7
European Economic Community (EEC), 92
Evoking pseudotransference variable, 169
Existential approaches, 44, 45
Explanatory medical model, 156–157
Exposure stage, 61

Facilitator of indigenous healing systems role, 208, 209–210
Facilitator of indigenous support systems role, 208, 209
Family-definitions, 11, 16
Family heritage
expanding awareness of, 144–147
family history exercise, 145–146
Family therapy, 191, 213–214
Field dependency, 10
Field sensitivity, 10
Finland, multicultural counseling in, 90
First Nations People, 96, 98–99
Foreclosed identity status, 71
Foreclosed subtype, 73, 194
Forms
internship evaluation by student, 246–247
internship evaluation by supervisor, 244–245
practicum evaluation by student, 242–243
practicum evaluation by supervisor, 240–241
Fourth Force concept, 32–33, 219–220, 227
France, multicultural counseling in, 91
Friendship training program, 210–211

Gender issues, 32, 191, 226
Generational differences
culture and, 19
multicultural counselor training and, 121, 123
Germany, multicultural counseling in, 91–92
"Getting on the Right Track" program, 212

Gibbs' Model of Interpersonal Orientation, 48, 174–176, 184
"Give-up" person, 144
Goals (multicultural counselor preparation)
stage one, 107, 117–118
stage two, 107–108, 141–142
stage three, 108, 162
stage four, 184–185
stage five, 205
summary table, 234–235
Goals of counseling, 189–190
Great Society era, 27
Greece, multicultural counseling in, 92
Group facilitation training, 116, 161
Guidance. See Counseling

Handbook of Racial/Ethnic Minority Counseling Research (Ponterotto & Casas), 40, 223
Hardiman's model of White racial identity development, 59, 165, 169, 192
Healers, 82
Healing techniques
African, 82
indigenous, 209–210
Helms' model of White racial identity development, 59–60, 165, 192, 200
Helping services, 111, 147–148
Heritage, ethnocultural, 144–147
High-context cultures, 135
Hinduism, 12
Hispanic Journal of Behavioral Sciences, 31
Hispanics. See Latinos
"How Would You Paraphrase My English" (Zhang), 136–137

Identity: Youth and Crisis (Erikson), 70
Identity. See also Racial and ethnic identity
adolescent development of, 70–72
Identity diffusion status, 71
"I'll Fly Away" (TV series), 128
Immersion behavior, 160–161
Immersion/emersion stage, 53–54, 60, 199
Immigration, cultural assimilation and, 24–25
Incorporation stage, 57
India, multicultural counseling in, 84–85
Indians, American. See Native Americans
Indigenous healing systems, 208, 209–210
Indigenous models of therapy, 45–46
Indigenous support systems, 208, 209
Individualistic cultures, 19–20
Individual racism, 168
Information processor role, 215, 216

In-groups, 19–20
In-service staff consultant role, 215, 216
Institutional racism, 168
Instrumental skills, 176
Integration stage. See Redefinition and integration stage
Integrative awareness stage, 199
Intentional Interviewing and Counseling: Facilitating Client Development in a Multicultural Society (Ivey), 137
Intercultural communicator role, 215, 216
Intercultural Sourcebook (Hoopes & Ventura), 146
Internalization commitment stage, 54
Internalization stage, 54, 59
International Colleague Questionnaire, 237
International Journal for the Advancement of Counselling, 31, 81, 82
International multicultural counseling. See also Multicultural counseling
acceptance of, 79–81
in Africa, 82–84
in Asia, 84–87
in Australia and New Zealand, 87–90
in Canada, 95–99
in Europe, 90–94
in Mexico, 99
in the Middle East, 94–95
survey on, 81–82
International Round Table for the Advancement of Counseling (IRTAC), 80–81, 222
Internship experience. See also Counseling practicum
counselor roles and, 208–215, 216
goals for, 205
process guidelines for, 204–205
student characteristics and, 203–204
student's evaluation of (form), 246–247
supervision of, 205–208
supervisor's evaluation of (form), 244–245
support for student growth in, 215, 217
Interpersonal relationship skills, 174–176
Interpreter of the bureaucratic system role, 215, 216
Interpreters, multicultural, 207–208
Interracial, 166, 239
Intervention strategies, 232–233
Investigation stage, 174
Involvement stage, 174–175
Ireland, multicultural counseling in, 92
IRTAC. See International Roundtable for the Advancement of Counseling
Islam, 12

Israel, multicultural counseling in, 94–95
Ivey Taxonomy of the Effective Individual, 30

Jewish culture, ethnic literature on, 239
Johns Hopkins University School of Hygiene and Public Health Center for Communication Programs, The, 81
Journal of Black Psychology, The, 31
Journal of Counseling and Development, 31, 32, 38
Journal of Multicultural Counseling and Development, 31, 38, 142
Journal of Non-White-Concerns in Personnel and Guidance, 31
Journal of Psychotherapy and the Family, 213
Journal-writing, 117, 141, 187
Joy Luck Club, The (Tan), 19, 121
Judaism, 14
Just Therapy approach, 90

Killers of the Dream (Smith), 21, 128, 168
Kim model of Asian American racial identity development, 55–57, 74, 164–165
Kinesics, 135
Kleinman's explanatory medical model, 156–157, 189
Kluckhohn and Strodtbeck cultural model, 128–129

Lack of social consciousness stage, 59
Laender, 91
Language barriers, 207–208
Latinos. See also People of color
acculturation assessment of, 188
bicultural group training for, 211–212
cultural and ethnic literature on, 238–239
defined, 7
family therapy with, 214
racial and ethnic identity development model for, 57–58, 165
Learning experiences for goal achievement (multicultural counselor preparation)
stage one, 118–137
stage two, 142–158
stage three, 162–179
stage four, 185–200
stage five, 205–217
Literature, cultural and ethnic, 121, 123–124, 237–238
Lithuania, multicultural counseling in, 93
Locus of control/responsibility schema, 134, 143–144

People of color (*continued*). *See also specific racial or ethnic group by name*
  impact of ethnic heritage on, 144–147
  individual variations among, 153, 156–158
  racial identity development stages for, 193–200
  stereotyping of, 152–153
  value systems of, 148–152
Personality disorders, 206
Person/environment relationship, 227
Personnel and Guidance Journal, 30, 31
Philippines, multicultural counseling in, 85–86
Phinney's models of ethnic identity development, 72–75, 166, 225
Polytheism, 15
Ponterotto's White racial consciousness development model, 59–60, 166, 192
Power, racism and, 168
Practicum. *See* Counseling practicum
Pre-encounter stage, 52–53
Pre-exposure/pre-contact stage, 62, 114, 234
Pre-exposure stage, 61
Prejudice prevention, 111
Preventing Prejudice: A Guide for Counselors and Educators (Ponterotto & Pedersen), 169, 212–213
"Pride-in-identity" person, 143–144
Private self-disclosure exercise, 121, 122–123
Process guidelines (multicultural counselor preparation)
  stage one, 115–117
  stage two, 140–141
  stage three, 161–162
  stage four, 183–184
  stage five, 204–205
Pro-minority/antiracism stage, 62, 160, 235
Proverbs, cultural, 146
Proxemics, 135
Pseudo-independent stage, 60, 198
Psychological services, 80
Psychology of Personal Constructs (Kelly), 26
Psychotherapist role, 208, 215
Psychotherapy. *See also* Counseling
  cultural biases in, 21–22, 118–119, 126–127
  family therapy and, 191, 213–214
  psychological diagnoses and, 206–207
  racism and, 168–171
Psychotherapy, 31

Public self-disclosure exercise, 121, 122–123

Race, defining, 119
Race Awareness in Counselor Education (RACE) Committee, 94
Race is a Nice Thing to Have, A (Helms), 195, 213
Race Matters (West), 171
Racial and ethnic groups
  demographic reports on, 34–35, 36
  individual variations within, 153, 156–158
  nomenclature of, 5–6, 7–8
  sociopolitical history of, 147–148
  stereotyping, 152–153
  value systems of, 148–152
Racial and ethnic identity
  adolescent development of, 69–75, 166, 225
  adult development of, 75–78
  assessment of, 157, 188–189
  children's development of, 66–69
  cultural diversity and, 5–6, 119
  expanding awareness of, 144–147
  gender and, 32, 191, 226
  multicultural counselor training and, 114–115, 117
  self-esteem and, 74–75, 194–195
Racial and ethnic identity development models. *See also specific racial and ethnic identity development model by name*
  for adolescents, 69–75, 166, 225
  for African Americans, 52–55, 74, 164, 192
  applying information from, 191–193
  for Asian Americans, 55–57, 164–165
  for Latinos, 57–58, 165
  researching and developing, 225–226
  stages in, 193–200
  status inequality theory and, 76–78, 166–167
  for Whites, 58–62, 165–166, 192, 200
Racial/Cultural Identity Development Model (R/CID), 52, 225
Racial groups. *See* Racial and ethnic groups
Racial heritage, 119, 144–147
Racial identity. *See* Racial and ethnic identity
Racism (Miles), 171
Racism
  abandonment of racism phase and, 59–60

  pro-minority/antiracism stage and, 62, 160
  types of, 168
  understanding, 167–171
  white racial/ethnic development and, 197–198, 200
Rational-emotive therapy, 45
R/CID (Racial/Cultural Identity Development Model), 52, 225
Recovery of social self phase, 147
Redefinition and integration stage, 62, 182, 200, 235
Redefinition stage, 59
Redirection to Asian-American consciousness stage, 57
Reference groups, 76
Reintegration stage, 60, 198
Research
  on minority counseling, 40, 223–224
  on models of racial and ethnic identity development, 225–226
  on multicultural counselor training programs, 224–225
Resistance stage, 59
Resource people, classroom panels of, 149–152
Retreat into White culture stage, 62, 199, 235
RIAS-B (Black Racial Identity Attitude Scale), 54–55
Role-play exercises
  in cross-cultural communications, 136–137, 157–158
  racial and ethnic identity development models and, 167
Roles
  for counselors in educational settings, 215, 216
  for multicultural counselors, 208–215
"Roots paper" exercise, 146
Ruiz model of Chicano-Latino identity development, 57–58, 165

Sansei, 55, 57
Scientism, 15
Selective Client Variables, 177, 178
Selective Counseling Process Variables, 177, 178
Selective Counselor Variables, 177, 178
Selective permeability process, 76–77
Self-definitions, 16
Self-disclosure exercise, 121, 122–123
Self-esteem, 74–75, 194–195
Self-in-relation theory, 226

Whites (*continued*)
   minority group oppression by, 147–148
   racial and ethnic identity development
      models for, 58–62, 165–166,
      191–200
   recognition of oppression by, 124–125,
      128

status inequality and, 76–77
Women of color. *See also* People of color
   identity development issues for, 32, 191,
      226
*Women of Color: Integrating Ethnic and
   Gender Identities in Psychotherapy*
   (Comas-Diaz and Greene), 191

Workforce America (Loden & Rosener), 4
Working through stage, 58
World views concept, 30

Zealot-defensive stage, 61

TO THE OWNER OF THIS BOOK:

We hope that you have found *Pathways to Multicultural Counseling Competance: A Developmental Journey* useful. So that this book can be improved in a future edition, would you take the time to complete this sheet and return it? Thank you.

School and address: _____

Department: _____

Instructor's name: _____

1. What I like most about this book is: _____

_____

_____

2. What I like least about this book is: _____

_____

_____

3. My general reaction to this book is: _____

_____

4. The name of the course in which I used this book is: _____

_____

5. Were all of the chapters of the book assigned for you to read? _____

   If not, which ones weren't? _____

 6. In the space below, or on a separate sheet of paper, please write specific suggestions for improving this book and anything else you'd care to share about your experience in using the book.

_____

_____

_____

_____

_____

Optional:

Your name: _____ Date: _____

May Brooks/Cole quote you, either in promotion for *Pathways to Multicultural Counseling Competance: A Developmental Journey* or in future publishing ventures?

Yes: _____ No: _____

Sincerely,

Bea Wehrly

- FOLD HERE -

NO POSTAGE
NECESSARY
IF MAILED
IN THE
UNITED STATES

BUSINESS REPLY MAIL

FIRST CLASS   PERMIT NO. 358   PACIFIC GROVE, CA

POSTAGE WILL BE PAID BY ADDRESSEE

ATT: *Bea Wehrly* _____

Brooks/Cole Publishing Company
511 Forest Lodge Road
Pacific Grove, California 93950-9968

- -
FOLD HERE

Brooks/Cole is dedicated to publishing quality publications for education in the human services fields. If you are interested in learning more about our publications, please fill in your name and address and request our latest catalogue, using this prepaid mailer.

Name: _____

Street Address: _____

City, State, and Zip: _____

FOLD HERE

- -

BUSINESS REPLY MAIL		
FIRST CLASS	PERMIT NO. 358	PACIFIC GROVE, CA

POSTAGE WILL BE PAID BY ADDRESSEE

ATT: *Human Services Catalogue* _____

Brooks/Cole Publishing Company
511 Forest Lodge Road
Pacific Grove, California 93950-9968

NO POSTAGE
NECESSARY
IF MAILED
IN THE
UNITED STATES

FOLD HERE